GRE®

Graduate
Record
Examination

Prep

Course Book

ACKNOWLEDGMENTS

Special thanks to the team that made this book possible:

Arthur Ahn, Mikhail Alexeef, Gina Allison, Matthew Belinkie, Kim Bowers, Harry Broome, Brian Carlidge, Lauren Challman, Gerard Cortinez, Chris Cosci, Elisa Davis, Boris Dvorkin, Steve Ferges, Paula Fleming, Dan Frey, Joanna Graham, Adam Grey, Allison Harm, Craig Harman, Jack Hayes, Adam Hinz, Gar Hong, Rebecca Houck, Xandi Kagstrom, Sarah Krentz, Jennifer Land, Edwina Lui, Jenny Lynch, Keith Lubeley, Heather Maigur, Rachel Mason, Jennifer Moore, Jason Moss, Walt Niedner, Robert Reiss, S. Ross, Glen Stohr, Sascha Strelka, Gene Suhir, Ethan Weber, Lee A. Weiss, and many others who have contributed materials and advice over the years.

© 2018 Kaplan, Inc.

Published by Kaplan Publishing, a division of Kaplan, Inc.
750 Third Avenue
New York, NY 10017

ISBN: 978-1-5062-3505-9

10 9 8 7 6 5 4 3 2 1

TABLE OF CONTENTS

Getting the Most Out of Your Kaplan GRE Course

Welcome to Your Kaplan GRE Course

Congratulations. By starting this Kaplan GRE course, you've just taken a big step toward your goal of a higher GRE score. At Kaplan, we've been working with students in your position for the past 75 years, so we know it can be daunting to contemplate mastering such a high-stakes test as the GRE. Don't worry: we'll help you build GRE expertise throughout this course. To help you get started, we'd like to share some advice for structuring your study and reaching your score goals.

Schedule Your Test Day

The GRE is required for admission to graduate programs in everything from anthropology to zoology. All these programs have different admissions deadlines. Check out the websites of the schools you're interested in. Also, make sure you take the GRE at least three weeks before the deadline to ensure that schools receive your score on time.

While you can take the GRE multiple times (although no more than once every 21 days and no more than five times in a year), it's best to test once and to test confidently, so you want to give yourself enough time to get as much as possible out of your Kaplan course. We recommend that you take the GRE about two to four weeks after finishing your final class session (longer if you're enrolled in a course that meets more than once a week). Doing so gives you time to complete all of the required assignments, continue taking practice tests, and take full advantage of your Kaplan resources for personalized study. But don't wait so long that you lose momentum from the course. Three months of dedicated and consistent study works well for most test takers. As soon as you've given some thought to your goals and your available study time, schedule your GRE so that you have a clear target to work toward. Students who set their test date in advance tend to get the most out of the course.

Set Your Score Goals

As you begin your GRE preparation, spend some time setting your score goals. Base your score goals, above all, on the requirements of your target graduate programs. Some programs focus more on one section than another. Others require a minimum combined score before they'll even consider an applicant for admission or for scholarships. A good score is one that puts you in the 25th to 75th percentile of the students who attend your target program; many schools provide these data. An excellent score gives you a competitive advantage over other applicants to the programs you're considering. School websites or program-ranking sites can help you figure out a solid target score. You can also call programs that interest you and speak with someone from the admissions department.

Once you've completed the Kaplan Diagnostic Test, you'll have a good sense of your starting point. Where you end up will depend less on where you start than on how actively you practice and how willing you are to try the new techniques you'll learn to improve your score.

Establish a Baseline Score

The first step of the process is to log in to your account at **www.kaptest.com** and complete the Diagnostic Test (MST 1) before your first GRE class session. Plan on taking about 3 hours and 45 minutes to complete the test. Sit down with your computer in a quiet place with a stable Internet connection where you can concentrate without interruption. Just do the best you can.

Don't worry about your exact Diagnostic score. The Diagnostic is, as the name suggests, a diagnosis. It's *not* a prognosis for how much you can improve or how well you'll score on Test Day. The most important use of the Diagnostic is to focus your attention on the areas of the GRE that are your relative strengths and those in which you have opportunity for improvement. Knowing these areas will help you organize your preparation for the actual test. Review your Diagnostic Performance Summary to identify your strengths and areas of opportunity. Taking the Diagnostic will also trigger personal recommendations for you on the Resources page of your online courseware.

Structure Your GRE Preparation

The best time to create a study plan is at the beginning of your GRE course. First, write into your calendar the dates of your class sessions. Then, schedule your practice tests, which we call MSTs. (MST stands for *multi-stage test*, the test format of the GRE.) After you've attended two class sessions, begin taking and reviewing one Kaplan MST per week. Setting dates and times for your MSTs will better simulate Test Day and will help you fit all seven of them in. One week before Test Day, take your final MST (ideally *exactly* a week before: same time, same day). Then spend the rest of the week reviewing the explanations and reinforcing your strengths, as indicated by your most recent Performance Summary.

There is homework to complete between class sessions, too; do your best to block out short, frequent periods of study time throughout the week. The amount of time you spend studying each week will depend on your schedule and your test date, but your course is structured with the expectation that you'll study outside of class for 7–12 hours each week. Out-of-class work includes watching and reading preview and review assignments, taking and reviewing MSTs, reviewing the class sessions, and completing additional practice in the areas where you need extra work. If you have a longer time frame before Test Day, you can spread this study out. If you are taking the course under compressed conditions (more than one session per week) or are testing soon after your class is over, you might need more study time each week. At the very minimum, do the preview assignment before each class so as to get the most out of the coming session.

As you move through your GRE course, your study plan should be a living document that is molded each week based on your available study time and the results of your most recent MST. Your strengths and weaknesses are likely to change over the course of your class sessions and out-of-class practice. Keep checking Smart Reports to make sure you are addressing the areas that are most important to *your* score.

Raise Your Score

The big question everyone has when beginning a GRE course is how large a score increase to expect. It's difficult to make an exact score promise. We've seen consistently that the students who achieve the greatest success are the ones who participate actively in class, complete the required homework, and take practice tests at scheduled intervals. Our most successful students also make full use of the wide range of course materials, understand their areas of strength and opportunity, and check in with us with questions or to get advice.

Signing up for a GRE course is like joining a gym. Kaplan has great GRE gym equipment, and your teacher is like your personal trainer. But you'll see your GRE test-taking skills get into shape to the extent that you put in the effort. Merely signing up for a gym membership doesn't guarantee results, but it *can* give you the tools and motivation you need to succeed. Your Kaplan GRE course works the same way. Here are a few additional tips for success:

Participate actively in your class sessions. Whether your course is In Person, Live Online, or Self-Paced, active learning will pay off as you apply what you learn in class to the homework assignments.

Know that you're going to make mistakes as you practice inside and outside of class. It's normal. Consider this: every wrong answer you choose, *and then learn from*, reduces the chance that you'll get a similar question wrong on the one and only day when wrong answers matter. So make mistakes willingly and even happily now, while they don't count. Just resolve to learn from every one of them.

Have patience with your progress. As you take more practice tests, it's common to make progress in fits and starts and even to experience some dips along the way. Don't be alarmed—score improvements hardly ever follow a perfectly smooth upward trajectory. But if you're studying according to our recommendations, you can trust that you're moving in the right direction to get the score you want on Test Day.

Stick with the new methods you'll be learning. You will be learning and assimilating many new techniques and strategies throughout your Kaplan course. The more consistently you practice these, the more they will become second nature, thereby eliminating uncertainty and saving you valuable time on Test Day. When you are starting out, however, new techniques often take longer or feel more cumbersome than the way you might otherwise have approached the question. The best analogy may be learning to type. When you start out, you may be typing effectively with two or three fingers, keeping a decent pace. But once you start learning touch typing, what happens? You slow down, and errors increase—until you've mastered this faster, more efficient way. Then, you breeze along more expertly than ever. As you become the GRE equivalent of a 100-words-per-minute typist, resist the temptation to dwell on short-term trends between one practice test and the next; focus instead on practicing well. Aim for consistency and accuracy at first. Then emphasize pacing as you get closer to Test Day and grow more confident with applying the methods.

Make Time to Review

You lead a busy life in addition to preparing for the GRE, and it can often feel difficult to fit in much study time outside of class. It may be tempting to push ahead and cover new material as quickly as possible, but we recommend strongly that you schedule ample time for review.

This may seem counterintuitive—after all, your time is limited, so why spend it going over stuff you've already done? But the brain rarely remembers *anything* it sees or does only once. When you build a connection in the brain and then don't follow up on it, that knowledge may still be "in there" somewhere, but it is not accessible the way you need it to be on Test Day. When you carefully review notes you've taken or problems you've solved (and the explanations for them), the process of retrieving that information reopens and reinforces the connections you've built in your brain. This builds long-term retention and repeatable skill sets—exactly what you need to beat the GRE. Focus your review on the following areas:

Review the topics you've covered in class. Go session by session—read the notes you took, watch the Lesson on Demand for that session (via your online resources), remind yourself of what you did to answer questions successfully, and work through the review assignments to reinforce those skills.

Review your practice tests and quizzes by working through the answers and explanations and noticing trends in your performance. Review the questions you answered incorrectly *and* those you got right. Rework the questions you got wrong so you can be sure to know exactly what to do when you see a similar one in the future. For the questions you got correct, did you answer correctly for the right reasons, or did you follow a lucky hunch? Does the explanation offer an alternative, more efficient path to the right answer that you can add to your arsenal? Or maybe you aced the problem and should take note of your process so that you can repeat it on similar problems!

Come to Us for Help

Take this advice to heart as you embark on your GRE preparation with Kaplan. Reach out to your teacher or to our team of GRE experts at **KaplanGREFeedback@kaplan.com** with any questions you have about your Kaplan GRE course. We are here to support your efforts every step of the way, and we back up our promises with the Higher Score Guarantee. For more details and eligibility requirements, please see **www.kaptest.com/hsg**.

Thanks for choosing Kaplan. We wish you the best of luck on your journey to graduate school success.

PART ONE

Quantitative

CHAPTER 1

Quantitative Strategy

Lesson 1: **Introduction to the Quantitative Section**

You'll see two scored Quantitative sections, each with 20 questions in 35 minutes.

Recommended Test Day Timing

	Quantitative Comparison	**Problem Solving**	**Data Interpretation**
Number of Questions	Approx. 7–8	Approx. 9–10	Approx. 3
Time per Questions	1.5 minutes	1.5–2 minutes	2 minutes

Lesson 2: Problem Solving Questions and Picking Numbers

Problem Solving Variant 1

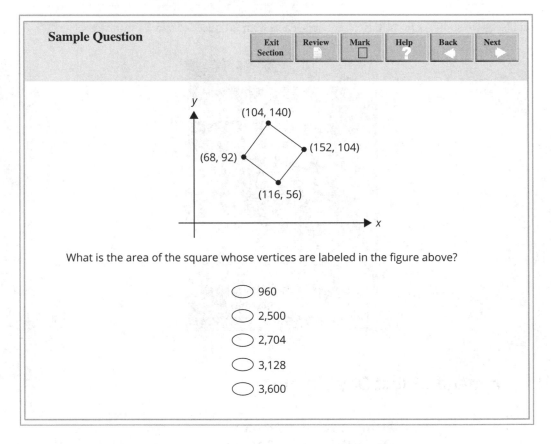

What is the area of the square whose vertices are labeled in the figure above?

- ○ 960
- ○ 2,500
- ○ 2,704
- ○ 3,128
- ○ 3,600

Problem Solving Variant 2

Sample Question

Exit Section | Review | Mark | Help ? | Back ◄ | Next ►

Integers x and y are factors of 60. The sum of x and y is greater than 18. Which of the following could be the values of x and y?

Indicate <u>all</u> such values.

☐ $x = 2$ and $y = 15$
☐ $x = 3$ and $y = 20$
☐ $x = 2$ and $y = 120$
☐ $x = 3$ and $y = 180$
☐ $x = 6$ and $y = 10$
☐ $x = 4$ and $y = 15$

Problem Solving Variant 3

Sample Question

Exit Section | Review | Mark | Help ? | Back ◄ | Next ►

How many five-digit numbers exist such that each digit after the first digit is greater than the digit to its immediate left?

THE KAPLAN METHOD

Problem Solving

STEP 1   What do they give you?

STEP 2   What do they want?

STEP 3   Choose a strategy.

    a.   Pick numbers

    b.   Backsolve

    c.   Do the traditional math

    d.   Take a strategic guess

STEP 4   Confirm your answer.

---

1.   Alistair's car payments were 5% lower in 2016 than in 2015. What was the ratio of Alistair's car payments in 2015 to his car payments in 2016?

    (A)   1:20

    (B)   1:5

    (C)   19:20

    (D)   20:19

    (E)   5:1

Picking numbers:

2. A flower shop sells flowers in a ratio of roses to carnations of 5:2. The ratio of carnations to tulips sold is 5:3. What is the ratio of roses to tulips?

    (A) 2:3

    (B) 3:2

    (C) 5:3

    (D) 25:6

    (E) 25:9

3. In company X, no employee is both a technician and an accountant. Also, in company X, $\frac{2}{5}$ of the employees are technicians, and $\frac{5}{16}$ of the remaining employees are accountants. What fraction of the total number of employees at company X are neither technicians nor accountants?

    (A) $\frac{23}{80}$

    (B) $\frac{33}{80}$

    (C) $\frac{3}{7}$

    (D) $\frac{47}{80}$

    (E) $\frac{57}{80}$

Permissible means:

Manageable means:

Pick Numbers when:

4.

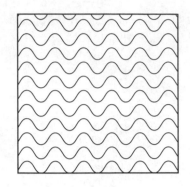

The figure shown represents a square garden. If each side is increased in length by 20%, by what percent is the area of the garden increased?

(A) 44%

(B) 50%

(C) 125%

(D) 144%

(E) 150%

5. The value of a certain stock rose by 40% from March to April, and then decreased by 30% from April to May. The stock's value in May was what percent of its value in March?

(A) 90%

(B) 98%

(C) 110%

(D) 130%

(E) 142%

6. If g and h are both odd integers, which of the following must also be odd?

    (A) $\dfrac{g}{h}$

    (B) $(g+h)^2$

    (C) $hg+h$

    (D) $(g-h)^2$

    (E) $(gh)^3$

Try These at Home

7. Kourtland and Caleb share an apartment. If each month Caleb pays c dollars and Kourtland pays k dollars, what percent of the total cost does Kourtland pay?

    (A) $\dfrac{k}{c}\%$

    (B) $\dfrac{c}{k}\%$

    (C) $\dfrac{k}{c+k}\%$

    (D) $\dfrac{100k}{c}\%$

    (E) $\dfrac{100k}{c+k}\%$

8. If $z > 0$, which of the following is equal to $\dfrac{z^3 + 2z^2 - 5z - 6}{z + 1}$?

   (A) $z^2 - 5z + 6$

   (B) $z^2 + 5z - 6$

   (C) $z^2 + z - 6$

   (D) $2z^2 - 5z + 5$

   (E) $2z^2 + z + 2$

Year	Change in Value
Year 1	+20%
Year 2	+5%
Year 3	−30%
Year 4	+20%

9. Leon invested some of his savings in a mutual fund at the beginning of Year 1, and Cecilia invested twice as much in the same investment at the same time. The annual increases or decreases in the value of the fund are shown in the table above. Cecilia withdrew 10% of the value of her fund at the end of each year, but Leon let his earnings or losses accumulate. To the nearest percent, the value of Cecilia's investment at the end of Year 4 was what percent of the value of Leon's investment?

   (A) 31%

   (B) 66%

   (C) 76%

   (D) 131%

   (E) 139%

Lesson 3: **Backsolving**

> **LEARNING OBJECTIVE**
>
> After this lesson, you will be able to:
> - Apply the Backsolving strategy to appropriate Problem Solving questions

On the GRE, numeric answer choices will always be in order from least to greatest or greatest to least.

When backsolving, start with (B) or (D).

- (A) 10
- (B) 20
- (C) 30
- (D) 40
- (E) 50

Backsolving:

10. The product of two consecutive positive integers is 156. What is the greater of the two integers?

- (A) 11
- (B) 12
- (C) 13
- (D) 14
- (E) 15

11. The surface area of a cube with side length $(x + 4)$ is 294. What is the value of x?

    (A) −10

    (B) −1

    (C) 3

    (D) 7

    (E) 19

12. Phillip has twice as many tropical fish as Jody. If Phillip gave Jody 10 of his tropical fish, he would have half as many as Jody. How many tropical fish do Phillip and Jody have together?

    (A) 10

    (B) 20

    (C) 30

    (D) 40

    (E) 60

Try These at Home

13. What is the value of a if $\dfrac{a+1}{a-3} - \dfrac{a+2}{a-4} = 0$?

    (A) −2

    (B) −1

    (C) 0

    (D) 1

    (E) 2

14. Of the 48 pencils in a school supply cabinet, 75% had black lead. An administrator added enough black lead pencils to the cabinet to bring the percentage with black lead up to 80%. How many total pencils were in the cabinet after the additional pencils were added?

   (A) 56
   (B) 60
   (C) 64
   (D) 68
   (E) 72

15. Which of the following is a possible value of k for which $-\dfrac{24}{\sqrt{k}}$ is an integer? Indicate all such values.

   [A] 9
   [B] 12
   [C] 16
   [D] 25
   [E] 64

Lesson 4: **Kaplan Quantitative Comparison Method**

LEARNING OBJECTIVE

After this lesson, you will be able to:

- Perform the steps of the Quantitative Comparison method

Quantitative Comparison Answer Choices

(A) Quantity A is greater.

(B) Quantity B is greater.

(C) The two quantities are equal.

(D) The relationship cannot be determined from the information given.

THE KAPLAN METHOD

Quantitative Comparison

STEP 1   Analyze the centered information and quantities.

STEP 2   Approach strategically.

16.

$$\frac{a}{b} = \frac{3}{7} = \frac{c}{d}$$

Quantity A	**Quantity B**
$a + d$	$b + c$

(A) Quantity A is greater.

(B) Quantity B is greater.

(C) The two quantities are equal.

(D) The relationship cannot be determined from the information given.

QC Strategy:

17.   In a three-digit number *n*, the hundreds digit is 3 times the units digit.

Quantity A	**Quantity B**
The units digit of *n*	4

Ⓐ Quantity A is greater.

Ⓑ Quantity B is greater.

Ⓒ The two quantities are equal.

Ⓓ The relationship cannot be determined from the information given.

18.

$$4 < x < 10$$
$$3 < y < 5$$

Quantity A	**Quantity B**
$x + y$	14

Ⓐ Quantity A is greater.

Ⓑ Quantity B is greater.

Ⓒ The two quantities are equal.

Ⓓ The relationship cannot be determined from the information given.

Try These at Home

19.

$$a + 2b = -8$$

Quantity A	**Quantity B**
a	*b*

Ⓐ Quantity A is greater.

Ⓑ Quantity B is greater.

Ⓒ The two quantities are equal.

Ⓓ The relationship cannot be determined from the information given.

20.   Rhonda is 5 times older than Frank is right now.

Quantity A	**Quantity B**
Rhonda's age in 13 years	Three times Frank's age in 13 years

- (A) Quantity A is greater.
- (B) Quantity B is greater.
- (C) The two quantities are equal.
- (D) The relationship cannot be determined from the information given.

21.

$$pt < 0$$
$$tq < 0$$
$$qr > 0$$

Quantity A	**Quantity B**
$\dfrac{r}{p}$	$\left(\dfrac{q}{t}\right)^3$

- (A) Quantity A is greater.
- (B) Quantity B is greater.
- (C) The two quantities are equal.
- (D) The relationship cannot be determined from the information given.

Lesson 5: **Quantitative Comparison Strategies**

LEARNING OBJECTIVE

After this lesson, you will be able to:

- Apply an appropriate strategy to a Quantitative Comparison question

22.
Data set $M = \{60, 9, 10, 20, 12, 7, 10, 8\}$

Quantity A	**Quantity B**
The mode of data set M	The mean of data set M

Ⓐ   Quantity A is greater.

Ⓑ   Quantity B is greater.

Ⓒ   The two quantities are equal.

Ⓓ   The relationship cannot be determined from the information given.

QC Strategy:

23.
A bag has 20 marbles that are either black or white.

Quantity A	**Quantity B**
The number of times one must randomly draw a marble from the bag, without replacing it, to ensure that at least 4 black marbles are selected	The number of times one must randomly draw a marble from the bag, without replacing it, to ensure that at least 4 white marbles are selected

Ⓐ   Quantity A is greater.

Ⓑ   Quantity B is greater.

Ⓒ   The two quantities are equal.

Ⓓ   The relationship cannot be determined from the information given.

QC Strategy:

24. $\sqrt{x^2 + 39} = 8$

Quantity A	Quantity B
x	4

    Ⓐ Quantity A is greater.

    Ⓑ Quantity B is greater.

    Ⓒ The two quantities are equal.

    Ⓓ The relationship cannot be determined from the information given.

QC Strategy:

25. $f(x) = x^2 - 6x + 8$

Quantity A	Quantity B
$f(-6)$	$f(6)$

    Ⓐ Quantity A is greater.

    Ⓑ Quantity B is greater.

    Ⓒ The two quantities are equal.

    Ⓓ The relationship cannot be determined from the information given.

QC Strategy:

26.

Quantity A	**Quantity B**
The sum of the integers from 19 to 31 inclusive	The sum of the integers from 22 to 32 inclusive

- Ⓐ Quantity A is greater.
- Ⓑ Quantity B is greater.
- Ⓒ The two quantities are equal.
- Ⓓ The relationship cannot be determined from the information given.

QC Strategy:

27.

$$g > 1$$

Quantity A	**Quantity B**
$\dfrac{g}{g+3} - 1$	$\dfrac{1}{g+3} - 1$

- Ⓐ Quantity A is greater.
- Ⓑ Quantity B is greater.
- Ⓒ The two quantities are equal.
- Ⓓ The relationship cannot be determined from the information given.

QC Strategy:

28. a is a positive integer.

Quantity A	**Quantity B**
$-3a + 15$	$-3(a + 5)$

(A) Quantity A is greater.

(B) Quantity B is greater.

(C) The two quantities are equal.

(D) The relationship cannot be determined from the information given.

QC Strategy:

Try These at Home

29. $x < 0 < y$

Quantity A	**Quantity B**
x^2y^2	$(xy)^3$

(A) Quantity A is greater.

(B) Quantity B is greater.

(C) The two quantities are equal.

(D) The relationship cannot be determined from the information given.

30. $xy < 0$

Quantity A	**Quantity B**
$x + y^2$	$\dfrac{y}{x}$

(A) Quantity A is greater.

(B) Quantity B is greater.

(C) The two quantities are equal.

(D) The relationship cannot be determined from the information given.

Lesson 6: **Kaplan Data Interpretation Method**

LEARNING OBJECTIVE

After this lesson, you will be able to:

● Apply the Data Interpretation Method

THE KAPLAN METHOD

Data Interpretation

STEP 1   Analyze the tables and graphs: examine the axes, scale, and legend.

STEP 2   Approach strategically.

Questions 31–33 are based on the following graph.

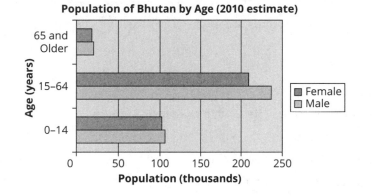

Population of Bhutan by Age (2010 estimate)

31.   Approximately what percent of Bhutan's total population was between the ages of 0 and 14 years in 2010?

  (A)   15%

  (B)   25%

  (C)   30%

  (D)   40%

  (E)   55%

32. What is the best estimate of the ratio of the female population age 65 and older to the female population age 0 to 14 years?

(A) 1:10

(B) 1:5

(C) 1:3

(D) 3:1

(E) 5:1

33. Which of the following ratios are greater than 1:2?

Indicate all such ratios.

A Males and females ages 0–14 to total population

B Males ages 0–14 to males and females ages 0–14

C Males ages 15–64 to total population

D Males and females ages 0–14 to males and females ages 15–64

E Males over 65 to males and females ages over 65

Try These at Home

Questions 34–36 refer to the following graphs.

New York and Wisconsin: Population by Official Census 1920–1980

Note: Drawn to scale.

**Density of Population by State
(per square mile, land area only)**

State	1920	1960	1970	1980
Arkansas	33.4	34.2	37.0	43.9
Illinois	115.7	180.4	199.4	205.3
New York	217.9	350.6	381.3	370.6
Texas	17.8	36.4	42.7	54.3
Wisconsin	47.6	72.6	81.1	86.5

34. What was the least densely populated of the listed states in 1960?

    (A) Arkansas
    (B) Illinois
    (C) New York
    (D) Texas
    (E) Wisconsin

35. In 1930, what was the approximate ratio of the number of people living in Wisconsin to the number of people living in New York?

   (A) 1:6
   (B) 1:5
   (C) 5:6
   (D) 6:5
   (E) 4:1

36. If, in 1830, the population density of New York was 44 people per square mile, and the area of New York has stayed relatively constant since then, approximately what was the population of New York in 1830, in millions?

   (A) 1.2
   (B) 2.0
   (C) 3.5
   (D) 4.0
   (E) 4.8

Quantitative Strategy Answer Key

1. **D**	10. **C**	19. **D**	28. **A**
2. **D**	11. **C**	20. **D**	29. **A**
3. **B**	12. **C**	21. **A**	30. **D**
4. **A**	13. **D**	22. **B**	31. **C**
5. **B**	14. **B**	23. **D**	32. **B**
6. **E**	15. **A, C, E**	24. **D**	33. **B, E**
7. **E**	16. **D**	25. **A**	34. **A**
8. **C**	17. **B**	26. **A**	35. **B**
9. **D**	18. **D**	27. **A**	36. **B**

Answers and Explanations

Quantitative Strategy Try These at Home Explanations

Lesson 2

7. E

Step 1. Notice that you are given variables to represent the dollar amounts that Caleb and Kourtland pay for the shared rent and expressions in those variables in the answer choices.

Step 2. Paraphrase the question: find the percent that a part (Kourtland's share) is of a whole (Kourtland and Caleb's total cost).

Step 3. Pick numbers for Caleb and Kourtland's share of the rent. This makes it simpler to find the percent of the cost Kourtland pays. Keep in mind that the numbers you choose do not need to be realistic, they simply need to be easy to work with. Make Kourtland's share $3 and Caleb's share $7. That means the percent of the cost that Kourtland pays is: $\dfrac{\$3}{(\$3+\$7)} = \dfrac{\$3}{\$10} = 30\%$

Plug the numbers into each choice to see which one equals 30% (be careful to correctly take into account the percent sign):

(A) $\dfrac{\$3}{\$7}\% = 0.43\%$. Eliminate (A).

(B) $\dfrac{\$7}{\$3}\% = 2.33\%$. Eliminate (B).

(C) $\dfrac{\$3}{(\$7+\$3)}\% = \dfrac{\$3}{\$10}\% = 0.30\%$. Eliminate (C).

(D) $\dfrac{100(\$3)}{\$7}\% = \dfrac{\$300}{\$7} = 42.9\%$. Eliminate (D).

(E) $\dfrac{100(\$3)}{\$3+\$7}\% = \dfrac{\$300}{\$10} = 30\%$.

Step 4. Recognize that plugging the numbers you picked into **(E)** and getting 30% confirms it is the correct answer.

8. C

Step 1. The question presents a complex one-variable polynomial expression and polynomials in the answer choices.

Step 2. You are asked which one of the choices (which are also polynomials) is equal to the given expression. It appears that using algebra to arrive at the answer would be complex and time-consuming.

Step 3. Pick numbers. Since exponents are involved, try a small integer such as $z=2$ and plug that value into the given expression:

$$\frac{z^3 + 2z^2 - 5z - 6}{z+1}$$
$$\frac{2^3 + 2(2^2) - 5(2) - 6}{2+1}$$
$$\frac{8 + 8 - 10 - 6}{3}$$
$$\frac{0}{3} = 0$$

Now plug $z=2$ into each of the answer choices to see which one(s) equal 0.

(A) $z^2 - 5z + 6 = 2^2 - 5(2) + 6 = 4 - 10 + 6 = 0$. This *could* be the correct choice, but when the choices are variables, you have to check all of them to be certain.

(B) $z^2 + 5z - 6 = 2^2 + 5(2) - 6 = 4 + 10 - 6 = 8$. Eliminate this choice.

(C) $z^2 + z - 6 = 2^2 + 2 - 6 = 4 + 2 - 6 = 0$. Along with (A), this *could* be correct.

(D) $2z^2 - 5z + 5$. You can eliminate this without actually having to do the calculations since it is an even number minus an even number plus an odd number, which must be odd. (For the record, this expression equals 3.)

(E) $2z^2 + z + 2$. Again, you don't have to calculate. All three terms are positive numbers, so their sum cannot be 0. Eliminate (E). (For the record, this expression equals 12.)

So the correct choice must be (A) or (C). Pick another value for z—try 3—and plug it into the original expression:

$$\frac{3^3 + 2(3^2) - 5(3) - 6}{3+1}$$

$$\frac{27 + 18 - 15 - 6}{4}$$

$$\frac{24}{4} = 6$$

For (A), $z^2 - 5z + 6 = 3^2 - 5(3) + 6 = 9 - 15 + 6 = 0$.
For (C), $z^2 + z - 6 = 3^2 + 3 - 6 = 9 + 3 - 6 = 6$. So **(C)** is correct.

Step 4. Double-check your calculations for the given expression and choice **(C)** to be certain they are equal.

9. D

Step 1. Two people invested in the same mutual fund at the same time, but Cecilia invested twice as much as Leon. The table shows the annual percentage gains or losses for the fund for 4 years. Both Leon and Cecilia allowed their gains or losses to accumulate, except that Cecilia withdrew 10% of the value of her fund at the end of each year.

Step 2. You need to determine what percent Cecilia's investment at the end of Year 4 is of Leon's investment.

Step 3. Since the amounts of the investments are not specified and the question deals with percentages, the best strategic approach is to pick $100 for Leon's investment, which makes Cecilia's initial investment $200. You may need a calculator to tackle this one.

First, calculate the ending value of Leon's investment. At the end of the first year, that is $100(1 + 0.20) = $100(1.20) = $120. At the end of the second year, it is $120(1.05) = $126. At the end of the third year, it is $126(1 - 0.3) = $126(0.70) = $88.20, and at the conclusion of year four, $88.20(1.20) = $105.84. Cecilia withdraws 10% of her holdings at the end of each year; that means that she leaves only 90% in. The value of her fund at the end of Year 4 is: $200(1.2)(0.9)(1.05)(0.9)(0.7)(0.9)(1.2)(0.9) = $138.88. Now compute Cecilia's amount as a percentage of Leon's: $\frac{138.88}{105.84} \times 100\% = 131\%$ (to the nearest percent). **(D)** is correct.

Step 4. Confirm that it is logical for Cecilia's Year 4 investment to be more than Leon's because of the larger initial investment and the positive net change in the investment over the four years.

Since there are numerous details in this question, there are trap answers. (A) is the percentage that the value of Cecilia's investment exceeded the value of Leon's; (B) would be correct if Cecilia had invested the same amount as Leon; and (C) was the value of Leon's fund as a percentage of Cecilia's.

Lesson 3

13. D

Applying Steps 1 and 2, the question presents a single-variable equation with two fractions with the goal of finding a. Since the algebra solution for this would be very complex, for Step 3, use the Backsolving strategy. Substitute the values in the answer choices into the equation. The one that gives you 0 must be correct.

$$(B): \frac{a+1}{a-3} - \frac{a+2}{a-4} = \frac{-1+1}{-1-3} - \frac{-1+2}{-1-4} = \frac{0}{-4} - \frac{1}{-5} \neq 0$$

Eliminate this answer choice.

Try another answer choice that is easy to work with.

$$(D): \frac{a+1}{a-3} - \frac{a+2}{a-4} = \frac{1+1}{1-3} - \frac{1+2}{1-4} = \frac{2}{-2} - \frac{3}{-3}$$
$$= -1 - (-1) = 0$$

Finally, in Step 4 confirm that because the equation is equal to 0, **(D)** is the answer.

14. B

The question analysis, Step 1, shows that there are 48 pencils, of which 75% have black lead, and that enough black lead pencils are added to bring the percentage of black lead pencils up to 80%. The task, Step 2, is to determine how many *total* pencils would be in the cabinet after the additional black pencils were added to the supply to reach that 80% level.

Choosing a strategy, Step 3, is facilitated by the fact that the answer choices are all numbers and arranged in ascending order, so this question is a good candidate for Backsolving. First, determine the original number of black lead pencils: $0.75 \times 48 = 36$. Now try (B) 60. To get to a total of 60 pencils, $60 - 48 = 12$ black lead pencils need to be added. This makes the total number of black lead pencils $36 + 12 = 48$. Thus, the percentage of pencils that would have black lead is $\frac{48}{60} \times 100\% = 80\%$, as stipulated in the question, so **(B)** is correct.

To confirm your choice, Step 4, be certain that you answered the question that was asked and that your calculations are correct. Since there is only one correct value and you used Backsolving, you do not need to calculate the values of any of the other choices.

15. A, C, E

The analysis in Steps 1 and 2 shows that there is a negative fractional expression with a square root in the denominator; the goal is to determine which choices result in an integer when plugged in for k. In deciding what strategy to use for Step 3, keep in mind that an integer is a whole number, which means that the square root of the number plugged in for k must also be a factor of 24 (keep in mind that integers can be positive, negative, or 0). All of the factors of 24 are integers as well, so (B) can be eliminated right away since the square root of 12 is not an integer (learning the perfect squares up to 100 is time well spent). Backsolving can be used to check the remaining choices:

$$(\textbf{A}): -\frac{24}{\sqrt{9}} = -\frac{24}{3} = -8$$

$$(\textbf{C}): -\frac{24}{\sqrt{16}} = -\frac{24}{4} = -6$$

$$(\textbf{D}): -\frac{24}{\sqrt{25}} = -\frac{24}{5} = -4.8$$

$$(\textbf{E}): -\frac{24}{\sqrt{64}} = -\frac{24}{8} = -3$$

In Step 4, confirm that **(A)**, **(C)**, and **(E)** are correct because they are the only choices that result in integers.

Lesson 4

19. D

Step 1. Analyze the centered information—in this case, an equation involving the variables a and b. Note that the sum of a and $2b$ is a negative number. This means that a and $2b$ cannot both be positive; at least one of them must be negative. Beyond that, nothing can be known for sure at this point.

Step 2. A good strategic approach would be to pick numbers to determine the relationship between a and b. You can pick a number for either a or b and then plug it into the equation in order to figure out the value of the other variable. It might be easier to pick a number for b because a is already in its simplest form and the algebra would be a bit simpler. Try $b = 2$, for example. Then $a + 2(2) = -8$. This simplifies to $a + 4 = -8$, or $a = -12$. In this case, since $2 > -12$, $b > a$. Now pick another number for b, and try to force a different relationship between a and b. Since you picked a positive number for b the first time, try a negative number this time—for example, $b = -4$. Then $a + 2(-4) = -8$. This simplifies to $a + (-8) = -8$, or $a = 0$. In this case, since $0 > -4$, $a > b$. The two cases produced different relationships between a and b, so the correct answer is **(D)**.

20. D

Step 1. The centered information describes the relationship between Rhonda's age and Frank's age at the present time. Keep in mind that this doesn't mean Rhonda was in the past or always will be in the future five times older than Frank. But the relationship between their current ages can be translated into algebra, using r for Rhonda's age right now and f for Frank's age right now: $r = 5f$.

Step 2. Note that both quantities refer to the future. Translated into algebra, Quantity A is $r + 13$ and Quantity B is $3(f + 13)$ or $3f + 39$. Since there is no way of knowing the current ages—that is, r and f—there is no way of calculating Quantity A or Quantity B. What you can do is pick different sets of numbers for r and f and see whether the relationship between Quantity A and Quantity B remains the same. Keep in mind that the numbers you pick must be permissible according to the centered information. So, for example, pick $f = 10$. That would mean

$r = 5(10) = 50$. With those numbers, Quantity A would be $r + 13 = 50 + 13 = 63$, and Quantity B would be $3f + 39 = 3(10) + 39 = 69$. In this case, Quantity B is greater. On the other hand, picking $f = 15$ would mean $r = 5(15) = 75$. Now Quantity A would be $r + 13 = 75 + 13 = 88$, while Quantity B would be $3(15) + 39 = 45 + 39 = 84$. In this case, Quantity A is greater. Since the two sets of numbers produce different relationships between Quantities A and B, the correct answer is (**D**).

21. A

Step 1. There are four separate variables that are all linked by inequalities. Quantity A is the product of two of the variables divided by one of the other variables. Quantity B is a fraction involving two of the variables cubed.

Step 2. Given all of the variables, a good strategic approach is to pick numbers. Since $pt < 0$, in one scenario p is positive and t is negative, so pick $p = 1$ and $t = -1$. If $t = -1$, then for $tq < 0$, q must be positive, so make $q = 2$. Finally, if $q = 2$, then given $qr > 0$, r must be positive, so make $r = 3$. Plugging those values into Quantity A results in:

$$\frac{r}{p} = \frac{3}{1} = 3$$

Plugging those values into Quantity B results in:

$$\left(\frac{q}{t}\right)^3 = \left(\frac{2}{-1}\right)^3 = (-2)^3 = -8$$

With the first set of numbers, Quantity A is greater. Next, try a set of numbers such that p is negative and t is positive. Pick $p = -1$ and $t = 1$. In order to keep $tq < 0$, q must be negative, so make $q = -2$. If $q = -2$, then for $qr > 0$, r must be negative, so make $r = -3$. Plugging those values into Quantity A results in: $\frac{r}{p} = \frac{-3}{-1} = 3$.

Plugging those same values into Quantity B results in:

$$\left(\frac{q}{t}\right)^3 = \left(\frac{-2}{1}\right)^3 = (-2)^3 = -8$$

Both sets of numbers result in Quantity A being greater, so (**A**) is the correct answer.

Lesson 5

29. A

Step 1. The centered information means that x is a negative number and y is a positive number, while the quantities compare squared terms and cubed terms.

Step 2. In Quantity A, both x^2 and y^2 are positive, and because the product of two positive numbers is positive, x^2y^2 in Quantity A is positive. The product of a negative number and a positive number is negative, so xy is negative. It follows that $(xy)^3$ in Quantity B is negative because a negative number raised to an odd exponent is negative. A positive number is always greater than a negative number, so Quantity A is greater, and (**A**) is correct.

30. D

Step 1. According to the centered information, either x is positive and y is negative, or x is negative and y is positive.

Step 2. Pick numbers for x and y to test the values of $x + y^2$ and $\frac{y}{x}$. If x is positive and y is negative, you might choose $x = 3$ and $y = -1$. In that case, $x + y^2 = 3 + (-1)^2 = 3 + 1 = 4$ and $\frac{y}{x} = \frac{-1}{3} = -\frac{1}{3}$, so Quantity A is greater. But what if x is negative and y is positive? Try $x = -3$ and $y = 1$. Then $x + y^2 = -3 + (1)^2 = -2$ and $\frac{y}{x} = \frac{1}{-3} = -\frac{1}{3}$, and Quantity B is greater. So the relationship cannot be determined from the given information, and (**D**) is correct.

Lesson 6

34. A

An analysis of the graph and table in Step 1 show that you need to use only the table to answer this question because the table provides the information on population density. In Step 2, look down the column for 1960 and find the state with the smallest density. It's Arkansas, with 34.2 people per square mile, and (**A**) is correct.

35. B

From Step 1 you know that the graph shows the population in Wisconsin in 1930 and the population in New York in 1930, but the different scales mean you can't estimate the ratios by comparing the respective heights of the two graphs—you need to find the actual figures. In Step 2, you can compare the thousands in Wisconsin to the thousands in New York. The ratio of Wisconsin's population in 1930 to that of New York's in the same year is approximately 2,600:13,000, which reduces to a ratio of 1:5, so **(B)** is correct.

36. B

From the analysis in Step 1, you will need information from both the graph and table to solve this question. The question gives the population density (ratio of the population to the amount of land) of New York for 1830. That means if the amount of land stays constant, then the density will increase at the same rate as the population. Now in Step 2, you could work with any of the four density figures given in the chart, but it's probably easiest to work with 1920's figure: New York's population in 1920 was approximately 10 million people, a nice round number to work with. In addition, the 1830 density was 44 people per square mile—very close to $\frac{1}{5}$ of the 1920 density, 217.9 people per square mile. That means the 1830 population must have been about one-fifth of the 1920 population. Based on the graph, the 1920 population was about 10 million, so the 1830 population must have been approximately $\frac{1}{5}$ of 10 million, or 2 million people, which means **(B)** is correct.

CHAPTER 2

Arithmetic and Number Properties

Lesson 1: **Order of Operations**

PEMDAS:

a.　$2 + 4 \div 3 =$

b.　$(2 + 4) \div 3 =$

1.　$5 \times \left(9 - 2^2\right) + 3 =$

　　Ⓐ　11

　　Ⓑ　28

　　Ⓒ　44

　　Ⓓ　46

　　Ⓔ　68

2. $\dfrac{4^2 + (2 - 3^2)}{5^2 - 3 \times 7} =$

    (A) $\dfrac{3}{4}$

    (B) 1

    (C) $\dfrac{8}{3}$

    (D) $\dfrac{9}{4}$

    (E) 2

Try These at Home

3.

Quantity A	**Quantity B**
$\dfrac{4^2 - 3 \times 2}{3^2}$	$\dfrac{2^4 - 2 \times 3}{2^3}$

    (A) Quantity A is greater.

    (B) Quantity B is greater.

    (C) The two quantities are equal.

    (D) The relationship cannot be determined from the information given.

4. $\dfrac{(6 + 2)x - \frac{1}{2}(5 + 3)}{\left(6 \times 3 - 4^2\right)^3 - (3 - 5)x} = 2$

What is the value of x?

    □

Lesson 2: **Fraction Operations**

To add or subtract fractions, you need a common denominator.

5. $\dfrac{x}{3} + \dfrac{x}{5}$

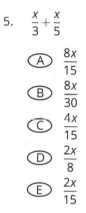

    Ⓐ $\dfrac{8x}{15}$

    Ⓑ $\dfrac{8x}{30}$

    Ⓒ $\dfrac{4x}{15}$

    Ⓓ $\dfrac{2x}{8}$

    Ⓔ $\dfrac{2x}{15}$

To divide fractions, multiply by the reciprocal.

6. Simplify the complex fraction: $\dfrac{\dfrac{7}{12} - \dfrac{1}{4}}{\dfrac{4}{9} + \dfrac{1}{3}}$.

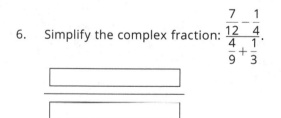

Try These at Home

7.

$$\frac{2}{y} = \frac{1}{x+4}$$

Quantity A	**Quantity B**
x	y

(A) Quantity A is greater.

(B) Quantity B is greater.

(C) The two quantities are equal.

(D) The relationship cannot be determined from the information given.

8. Four roommates pooled their funds to buy a television for their apartment. Janice contributed one-fourth of the total, Tanisha pitched in for one-sixth, and Leanne provided two-fifths. If the television cost $360, how much was the fourth roommate's share of the cost?

(A) $60

(B) $66

(C) $75

(D) $90

(E) $138

Lesson 3: **Exponent Rules**

To multiply numbers with the same base, add the exponents:

$$a^b \times a^c = a^{b+c}$$

a. $5^4 \times 5^3 =$

b. $3^{4x} \times 3^{(2x+4)} \times 3^{(x-2)} =$

To divide numbers with the same base, subtract the exponents:

$$\frac{a^b}{a^c} = a^{b-c}$$

c. $\dfrac{6^9}{6^8} =$

d. $\dfrac{4^{3x+2}}{4^{2x-1}} =$

To multiply numbers with different bases but the same exponent, multiply bases only:

$$a^c \times b^c = (ab)^c$$

e. $2^3 \times 3^3 =$

f. $(5x - 2)^4 \times (2x)^4 =$

To raise one exponent to another exponent, multiply the exponents:

$$(a^b)^c = a^{bc}$$

g. $(3^4)^3 =$

h. $\left(7^{2x}\right)^{4x} =$

Any number (except 0) raised to the 0 power is 1.

$$a^0 = 1$$

0^0 is undefined.

To simplify a negative exponent, change the number to 1 over the base to the positive exponent:

$$a^{-b} = \frac{1}{a^b}$$

i. $5^{-2} =$

j. $(3y)^{-4x} =$

9.   Evaluate $\dfrac{3^5 \times 9^2}{9^4}$.

  (A) 3^0

  (B) 3^1

  (C) 3^3

  (D) 9^1

  (E) 9^3

Drill answers from previous page: a. 5^7, b. $3^{(7x + 2)}$ c. 6^1, d. 4^{x+3}; e. 6^3, f. $(10x^2 - 4x)^4$ g. 3^{12}, h. $7^{(8x^2)}$

10.

Quantity A	**Quantity B**
$10^{-4} \times 10^{3}$	10^{-12}

Ⓐ Quantity A is greater.

Ⓑ Quantity B is greater.

Ⓒ The two quantities are equal.

Ⓓ The relationship cannot be determined from the information given.

11.

$$4^5 = \frac{4^{20}}{4^x}$$

Quantity A	**Quantity B**
x	4

Ⓐ Quantity A is greater.

Ⓑ Quantity B is greater.

Ⓒ The two quantities are equal.

Ⓓ The relationship cannot be determined from the information given.

Try These at Home

12.

$$ab \neq 0$$

Quantity A

$(a^{-2}b^{-2})^{-1}$

Quantity B

$(a^{-1}b^{-1})^{-2}$

    (A)   Quantity A is greater.

    (B)   Quantity B is greater.

    (C)   The two quantities are equal.

    (D)   The relationship cannot be determined from the information given.

13.

$$x \geq 0$$

Quantity A

5^{5x}

Quantity B

5^{x+5}

    (A)   Quantity A is greater.

    (B)   Quantity B is greater.

    (C)   The two quantities are equal.

    (D)   The relationship cannot be determined from the information given.

14.   If $x = (3^8)(81^5)$ and $y = (9^7)(27^{12})$, then $xy =$

    (A) 3^{48}

    (B) 3^{54}

    (C) 3^{61}

    (D) 3^{68}

    (E) 3^{78}

Drill answers from previous page: i. $\dfrac{1}{5^2}$, j. $\dfrac{1}{(3y)^{4x}}$

Lesson 4: **Radical Rules**

LEARNING OBJECTIVE

After this lesson, you will be able to:

- Apply radical rules

Square roots are always positive on the GRE.

$$x^2 = 9$$
$$x =$$
$$\sqrt{9} =$$

To multiply radicals, multiply the values outside the radical together, then multiply the values underneath the radical together:

$$a\sqrt{b} \times c\sqrt{d} = ab\sqrt{cd}$$

a. $3\sqrt{5} \times 4\sqrt{3} =$

b. $2x\sqrt{6y} + 3y\sqrt{x} =$

To divide radicals, divide the values outside the radical, then divide the values underneath the radicals:

$$\frac{a\sqrt{b}}{c\sqrt{d}} = \frac{a}{c}\sqrt{\frac{b}{d}}$$

c. $\dfrac{16\sqrt{90}}{8\sqrt{10}} =$

d. $\dfrac{8x^2\sqrt{25y}}{2x\sqrt{5y}} =$

When a value is raised to a fractional power, the numerator stays with the base and the denominator becomes the index:

$$a^{\frac{b}{c}} = \sqrt[c]{a^b}$$

e. $8^{\frac{1}{3}} =$

f. $(3x)^{\frac{2}{5}} =$

To add or subtract radicals, the values under the radical must be the same:

$$a\sqrt{b} + c\sqrt{b} = (a + c)\sqrt{b}$$
$$a\sqrt{b} - c\sqrt{b} = (a - c)\sqrt{b}$$

g. $4\sqrt{5} + 3\sqrt{2} - \sqrt{2} - 3\sqrt{5} =$

h. $7x\sqrt{3y} - 6t\sqrt{2r} + 4x\sqrt{3y} + 3t\sqrt{2r} =$

15. $\dfrac{\sqrt{5}\sqrt{60}}{\sqrt{3}}$

16.   What is the value of $\left(2\sqrt{2}\right)\left(\sqrt{6}\right) + 2\sqrt{3}$?

   (A)   18

   (B) $10\sqrt{3}$

   (C) $6\sqrt{6}$

   (D) $4\sqrt{2} + 2\sqrt{3}$

   (E) $6\sqrt{3}$

Drill answers from previous page: a. $12\sqrt{15}$, b. $6xy\sqrt{6xy}$, c. $2\sqrt{9} = 2 \times 3 = 6$, d. $4x\sqrt{5}$;
e. $\sqrt[3]{8} = 2$, f. $\sqrt[5]{(3x)^2}$

Try These at Home

17.

Quantity A	**Quantity B**
$\dfrac{2\sqrt{3}}{6}$	$\dfrac{1}{\sqrt{3}}$

- (A) Quantity A is greater.
- (B) Quantity B is greater.
- (C) The two quantities are equal.
- (D) The relationship cannot be determined from the information given.

18. $27^{\frac{2}{3}}$ is equal to which of the following?

- (A) 1
- (B) 3
- (C) 9
- (D) 18
- (E) 36

19. Which of the following expressions is equivalent to $\dfrac{\sqrt{7x}+3y}{\sqrt{7x}-\sqrt{3y}}$?

- (A) $1 - \dfrac{1}{\sqrt{7x}-\sqrt{3y}}$

- (B) $\dfrac{\sqrt{7x}+3y}{\sqrt{7x}-3y}$

- (C) $\dfrac{7x\sqrt{3y}+3y\sqrt{7x}}{7x-3y}$

- (D) $\dfrac{7x+\sqrt{3y}+3y+\sqrt{7x}}{7x-3y}$

- (E) $\dfrac{\left(\sqrt{7x}\right)\left(\sqrt{7x}+3y\right)+\left(\sqrt{3y}\right)\left(\sqrt{7x}+3y\right)}{7x-3y}$

Drill answers from previous page: g. $\sqrt{5}+2\sqrt{2}$, h. $11x\sqrt{3y}-3t\sqrt{2r}$

Lesson 5: **Positives and Negatives**

LEARNING OBJECTIVE

After this lesson, you will be able to:

- Manipulate expressions involving positive and negative numbers

To subtract a negative value, make the second value positive and add it to the first value:

$$a - (-b) = a + b$$

a. $7 - (-8) =$

b. $2x - (-4x) =$

To multiply or divide positive and negative numbers, follow these rules:

$$positive \times positive = \frac{positive}{positive} = positive$$

$$positive \times negative = \frac{positive}{negative} \text{ or } \frac{negative}{positive} = negative$$

$$negative \times negative = \frac{negative}{negative} = positive$$

c. $3 \times -4 =$

d. $\dfrac{(2y) \times (-3)}{(-4y) \times (-5y)} =$

20. $$ab < 0$$

Quantity A	**Quantity B**
$a - b$	$\dfrac{a}{b}$

- (A) Quantity A is greater.
- (B) Quantity B is greater.
- (C) The two quantities are equal.
- (D) The relationship cannot be determined from the information given.

Try These at Home

21. $$x > 3 \text{ and } y < -1$$

Quantity A	**Quantity B**
x^2y	xy^2

- (A) Quantity A is greater.
- (B) Quantity B is greater.
- (C) The two quantities are equal.
- (D) The relationship cannot be determined from the information given.

Drill answers from previous page: a. 15, b. $6x$, c. -12, d. $-\dfrac{3}{10y}$

22.

$$bc < 0$$
$$ab > 0$$
$$cd < 0$$

Quantity A	**Quantity B**
ac	bd

- (A) Quantity A is greater.
- (B) Quantity B is greater.
- (C) The two quantities are equal.
- (D) The relationship cannot be determined from the information given.

23. If, $x > y > 0$, which of the following expressions must be negative?

Indicate <u>all</u> such expressions.

- [A] $(x-y)^2(y-x)^2$
- [B] $(x-y)^3(y-x)^3$
- [C] $x^2 - y^3$
- [D] $2xy - x^2$
- [E] $-1(x-y)^2(y-x)$
- [F] $-5(x-y)(y-x)^2$

Lesson 6: **Odd and Even Integers**

LEARNING OBJECTIVE

After this lesson, you will be able to:

- Manipulate expressions involving odd and even integers

Odds/evens rules:	
odd ± odd =	odd × odd =
even ± even =	even × even =
odd ± even =	odd × even =

A negative number raised to an even integer must be _____.

A negative number raised to an odd integer must be _____.

24. The positive integer x is odd, and the positive integer y is even.

Quantity A	**Quantity B**
$(-1)^{2x+y}$	$\dfrac{1}{2}$

- (A) Quantity A is greater.
- (B) Quantity B is greater.
- (C) The two quantities are equal.
- (D) The relationship cannot be determined from the information given.

Try These at Home

25. If x and y are integers, and $x - y$ is an odd integer, then which of the following *must* be even?

(A) $xy + 3$

(B) $xy - x$

(C) $x^2 y^2$

(D) $(x - y)^2$

(E) $x^2 - y^2 + 2$

26.

x is an even integer

y is an odd integer

$-3 \leq x \leq 3$

$-1 \leq y \leq 1$

Quantity A	**Quantity B**
y^x	$y^{\frac{x}{y}}$

(A) Quantity A is greater.

(B) Quantity B is greater.

(C) The two quantities are equal.

(D) The relationship cannot be determined from the information given.

Lesson 7: **Prime Factorization**

> **LEARNING OBJECTIVE**
>
> After this lesson, you will be able to:
> - Determine the prime factors of an integer

A *factor* (or *divisor*) is an integer that divides evenly into another integer.

A *multiple* is the result of multiplying an integer by another integer.

Factors of 12:

Prime factorization of 12:

Multiples of 12:

27. What is the total number of unique prime factors of 450?

    (A) 2

    (B) 3

    (C) 4

    (D) 5

    (E) 6

28. 12^{34} is divisible by all of the following, except:

(A) 8

(B) 28

(C) 64

(D) 81

(E) 144

Try These at Home

29. Which of the following is the prime factorization of 550?

(A) 1×550

(B) $2 \times 5^2 \times 11$

(C) 10×55

(D) $2^2 \times 5 \times 11$

(E) $2^2 \times 5^2 \times 11$

30.

Quantity A	Quantity B
The greatest prime factor of 243	The smallest prime factor of 273

(A) Quantity A is greater.

(B) Quantity B is greater.

(C) The two quantities are equal.

(D) The relationship cannot be determined from the information given.

Arithmetic and Number Properties Answer Key

1. **B**
2. **D**
3. **B**
4. **5**
5. **A**
6. $\dfrac{3}{7}$
7. **D**

8. **B**
9. **B**
10. **A**
11. **A**
12. **C**
13. **D**
14. **E**
15. **10**

16. **E**
17. **C**
18. **C**
19. **E**
20. **D**
21. **B**
21. **B**
22. **B**

23. **B, F**
24. **A**
25. **C**
26. **C**
27. **B**
28. **A**
29. **B**
30. **C**

Answers and Explanations

Arithmetic and Number Properties
Try This At Home Explanations

Lesson 1

3. B

Both quantities have similar numbers, but PEMDAS needs to be applied to find the actual numeric values for each quantity. For Quantity A, applying the steps in order results in:

$$\frac{4^2 - 6}{3^2} = \frac{16 - 6}{9} = \frac{10}{9}$$

For Quantity B, applying the steps in order results in:

$$\frac{2^4 - 6}{2^3} = \frac{16 - 6}{8} = \frac{10}{8}$$

The numerators are the same, but Quantity B is larger because it has the smaller denominator. **(B)** is correct.

4. 5

The stem presents a complex equation containing the variable x and asks you to solve for the value of x. Use PEMDAS to simplify the equation, then manipulate the simplified version to determine x. Start by simplifying terms within parentheses:

$$\frac{8x - \frac{1}{2}(8)}{\left(18 - 4^2\right)^3 - (-2)x} = 2.$$ Next, work on the exponents:

$$\frac{8x - \frac{1}{2}(8)}{(18 - 16)^3 - (-2)x} = \frac{8x - \frac{1}{2}(8)}{(2)^3 - (-2)x} = \frac{8x - \frac{1}{2}(8)}{8 - (-2)x} = 2.$$

Next, attack the multiplication: $\frac{8x - 4}{8 + 2x} = 2$. Now that you've simplified the equation, multiply both sides by $8 + 2x$ to eliminate the fraction and get $8x - 4 = 16 + 4x$. This further simplifies to $4x = 20$, so $x = \mathbf{5}$.

Lesson 2

7. D

Clear the fractions in the equation by cross-multiplying:

$$(2)(x + 4) = (1)(y)$$
$$2x + 8 = y$$

If x is a positive number, such as 2, then $y = 2(4) + 8 = 16$, in which case y, or Quantity B, is greater. Next try a negative number for x, such as -2. Then, $y = 2(-2) + 8 = 4$. While y is still greater than x, the gap between x and y is narrowing, so try a number for x that is even more negative, perhaps -10. Now, $y = 2(-10) + 8 = -12$. Here x, or Quantity A, is greater. Since either quantity could be greater depending on the value of x, **(D)** is correct.

8. B

Total the known fractional contributions and subtract that fraction from one to determine the fractional part of the total that the fourth roommate kicked in. To add fractions, convert them to a common denominator. The least common denominator of $\frac{1}{4}$, $\frac{1}{6}$, and $\frac{2}{5}$ is 60. So:

$$\frac{1}{4} + \frac{1}{6} + \frac{2}{5} = \left(\frac{15}{15}\right)\frac{1}{4} + \left(\frac{10}{10}\right)\frac{1}{6} + \left(\frac{12}{12}\right)\frac{2}{5} \text{ and}$$

$\frac{15}{60} + \frac{10}{60} + \frac{24}{60} = \frac{49}{60}$. So the fourth roommate's portion was $1 - \frac{49}{60} = \frac{11}{60}$. Multiply this by the total cost to get $\frac{11}{60} \times 360 = 66$. This matches **(B)**.

Alternatively, you could approach the question like this: Janice gave $\frac{1}{4}$ of $360, or $90; Tanisha gave $\frac{1}{6}$ of $360, or $60; Leanne gave $\frac{2}{5}$ of $360, or $144. The first three roommates thus kicked in a total of $294. Subtract that from $360, and you get $66.

Lesson 3

12. C

When one exponent is raised to another, multiply the exponents. Simplifying Quantity A gives:

$$(a^{-2}b^{-2})^{-1} = a^2b^2$$

Simplifying Quantity B gives:

$$(a^{-1}b^{-1})^{-2} = a^2b^2$$

So the Quantities are equal, and the correct answer is (**C**).

13. D

One way of solving this problem is to use the strategy of Picking Numbers for the variable, x. Substitute values in for x to determine if Quantity A or B is greater. Be sure that in doing so, enough values of x are evaluated to present a wide range of possibilities. For example:

If $x = 0$:

Quantity A: $5^{5x} = 5^0 = 1$
Quantity B: $5^{x+5} = 5^5$, which is greater than 1.
So when $x = 0$, Quantity B would be greater.

If $x = 1$:

Quantity A: $5^{5x} = 5^5$
Quantity B: $5^{x+5} = 5^6$
So when $x = 1$, Quantity B would still be greater.

If $x = 2$:

Quantity A: $5^{5x} = 5^{10}$
Quantity B: $5^{x+5} = 5^7$
So when $x = 2$, Quantity A would be greater.

Since the relationship varies depending on the value of x, the correct answer is (**D**).

14. E

Problems involving multiple bases are typically best solved by first converting all the terms to the same base. Here, 3 can be conveniently used as the base for each term:

$$9 = 3 \times 3 = 3^2$$
$$27 = 3 \times 3 \times 3 = 3^3$$
$$81 = 3 \times 3 \times 3 \times 3 = 3^4$$

Substitute 3^2 for 9, 3^3 for 27, and 3^4 for 81 to yield the following:

$$x = (3^8)[(3^4)^5]$$
$$y = [(3^2)^7][(3^3)^{12}]$$

Use the laws of exponents $(b^a)^c = b^{ac}$ and $b^a b^c = b^{a+c}$ to simplify:

$$x = (3^8)(3^{4\times5}) = (3^8)(3^{20}) = 3^{8+20} = 3^{28}$$
$$y = (3^{2\times7})(3^{3\times12}) = (3^{14})(3^{36}) = 3^{14+36} = 3^{50}$$

Finally, multiply x times y:

$$xy = (3^{28})(3^{50}) = 3^{28+50} = 3^{78}$$

(**E**) is correct.

Lesson 4

17. C

Simplify Quantity A: $\dfrac{2\sqrt{3}}{6} = \dfrac{\sqrt{3}}{3}$

Get rid of the radical in the denominator of Quantity B by multiplying the numerator and denominator by $\sqrt{3}$:

$$\frac{1}{\sqrt{3}} = \frac{1}{\sqrt{3}} \times \frac{\sqrt{3}}{\sqrt{3}} = \frac{\sqrt{3}}{3}$$

So Quantity A is equal to Quantity B; the correct answer is (**C**).

18. C

Think of $27^{\frac{2}{3}}$ as $27^{2\times\frac{1}{3}}$. Because fractional exponents are roots, $x^{\frac{1}{3}} = \sqrt[3]{x}$. So $27^{\frac{2}{3}}$ means "take the cube root of 27 and square it." Since $3 \times 3 \times 3 = 27$, it follows that $\sqrt[3]{27} = 3$. Now square that cube root: $3^2 = 9$. (**C**) is correct.

19. E

The denominator, one square root minus another, is a pattern that you might encounter on the GRE. Since you want to get rid of radicals in a denominator, you can multiply the numerator and denominator by $\sqrt{7x} + \sqrt{3y}$. The expression then looks like this:

$$\frac{\left(\sqrt{7x} + \sqrt{3y}\right)\left(\sqrt{7x} + 3y\right)}{\left(\sqrt{7x} + \sqrt{3y}\right)\left(\sqrt{7x} - \sqrt{3y}\right)}$$

Notice that the denominator is a difference of perfect squares, $(a+b)(a-b) = \left(a^2 - b^2\right)$, so it becomes $\left(\sqrt{7x}\right)^2 - \left(\sqrt{3y}\right)^2 = 7x - 3y$. Now you have $\dfrac{\left(\sqrt{7x} + \sqrt{3y}\right)\left(\sqrt{7x} + 3y\right)}{7x - 3y}$. There's no answer choice that matches, so distribute the product of the two terms in the numerator: $\dfrac{\left(\sqrt{7x}\right)\left(\sqrt{7x} + 3y\right) + \left(\sqrt{3y}\right)\left(\sqrt{7x} + 3y\right)}{7x - 3y}$. This matches **(E)**.

Lesson 5

21. B

The centered information states that $x > 3$ and $y < -1$. Don't be concerned about the limits of the inequalities; the key is that x is positive and y is negative. As a result, Quantity A, $x^2 y$, is a positive number squared times a negative number, which is a positive number times a negative number, which must be negative. Quantity B, xy^2, is a positive number times a negative number squared. Since a negative number squared is a positive number, this product is positive. Positive numbers are greater than negative numbers, so **(B)** is correct.

22. B

Start by analyzing the centered information. None of the individual variables can be isolated in a way that establishes its sign definitively. However, as ab is positive, there are only two possibilities: a and b are either both positive or both negative.

If both a and b are positive, then c must be negative in order to make $bc < 0$, in which case d must be positive so that $cd < 0$. Given those signs, Quantity A, ac, must be negative, and Quantity B, bd, must be positive.

If both a and b are negative, then c must be positive so that $bc < 0$, in which case d must be negative so that $cd < 0$. In this case, Quantity A, ac, is still negative, and Quantity B, bd, is still positive. Thus, in both cases, Quantity B is greater, and the correct answer is **(B)**.

23. B, F

Given that x is greater than y and that both are positive, you are asked which of the choices *must* be negative. Since there is nothing to simplify, evaluate each choice individually.

(A) $(x - y)^2 (y - x)^2$ You don't need to evaluate the individual terms. Any number squared is positive. Thus, this expression is a positive number times a positive number, which must be positive. Eliminate (A).

(B) $(x - y)^3 (y - x)^3$ Since x is greater than y, $(x - y)$ is positive but $(y - x)$ is negative. A positive number raised to any power is positive, but a negative number raised to an odd power is negative. Therefore, this expression is a positive number times a negative number, which is negative. **(B)** is correct.

(C) $x^2 - y^3$ Both terms are positive, so this expression will be positive if x^2 is greater than y^3 and negative if y^3 is greater than x^2. Since you don't know the specific values of x and y, either case could be true. This expression could be negative but does not have to be, so eliminate (C). If you weren't certain of this conclusion, you could pick some numbers for x and y to verify that either case could be true. For example, if x were 3 and y were 2, the expression in (C) would be $9 - 8$, which is positive. But if x were 10 and y were 5, the expression would be $100 - 125$, which is negative.

(D) $2xy - x^2$ Again, both terms are positive. This expression is equivalent to $x(2y - x)$; x is positive, but $2y - x$ could be either positive or negative. Eliminate (D).

(E) $-1(x - y)^2 (y - x)$ You know that -1 is negative, $(x - y)^2$ is positive, and $y - x$ is negative, so the expression is made up of two negatives times a positive. Since there is an even number of negative terms, this expression is positive. Eliminate (E).

(F) $-5(x-y)(y-x)^2$ The -5 term is negative, $(x-y)$ is positive, and $(y-x)^2$ is positive. Thus, there is one negative number times two positive numbers, so the result must be a negative number. **(F)** is correct.

Lesson 6

25. C

The question states that $x-y$ is an odd integer. This means that one of the variables is odd while the other is even, but you can't tell which is which. (In other words, either x is even and y is odd, or x is odd and y is even.) Evaluate the answer choices to see which of them *must* be even. For (A), it doesn't matter which variable is even because the product of an even number and an odd number is even. So xy is even, which means that $xy+3$ is odd. (The sum of an even and an odd is odd.) Eliminate (A). Look at (B): xy is again even. So if x is odd, then $xy-x$ will be odd. However, if x is even, then $xy-x$ will also be even. The question asks for the choice that *must* be even, not for the one that merely *could* be even, so eliminate (B). Consider (C) x^2y^2. Since even numbers squared are even and odd numbers squared are odd, this is the product of an odd and an even, which must be even. **(C)** is correct.

For the record, (D) $(x-y)^2$ is the square of an odd number, so it must be odd, and (E) x^2-y^2+2 must be odd because x^2-y^2 is odd, and adding two keeps it odd.

26. C

The centered information stipulates that x is an even integer between -3 and 3, so the possible values for x are -2, 0, and 2. The y values need to be odd and between -1 and 1, so the possible y values are -1 and 1.

A good approach for Quantity A is to recognize that ±1 raised to an even power is 1. Since x must be even, the value of Quantity A is 1 for all allowable values of x. Then, to determine whether Quantity B can be something other than 1, test the different possibilities for the $\frac{x}{y}$ fraction in the exponent to see if any of them result in an odd number.

If $x=-2$ and $y=-1$ or $x=2$ and $y=1$, ±1 is raised to the second power, which means Quantity B is 1. If $x=-2$ and $y=1$ or $x=2$ and $y=-1$, ±1 is raised to the -2, which still means Quantity B is 1. Finally, if $x=0$ and $y=-1$ or $x=0$ and $y=1$, ±1 is raised to the 0, which also means Quantity B is 1. Since all possible scenarios make the two quantities equal, **(C)** is correct.

Lesson 7

29. B

Make a factor tree of 550, starting with the largest factors you can think of. The number 550 equals 10×55. However, this isn't the final answer because 10 and 55 are both not prime. So keep going: 55 equals 5×11, and 10 equals 2×5. Now you're done, since 2, 5, and 11 are all prime numbers. Putting it all together, the answer is $2\times5^2\times11$, which is **(B)**.

30. C

There is no centered information, so simplify the two quantities. Find Quantity A by listing the prime factors of 243, looking for the largest one. The number 243 equals 3×81, and 81 equals 9×9, or $3\times3\times3\times3$. *All* of the prime factors of 243 are 3, so the greatest prime factor of 243 is 3.

Quantity B is the smallest prime factor of 273. Work strategically by testing whether 273 is divisible by the smallest prime numbers. (Remember that 1 isn't considered prime.) The number 273 isn't divisible by 2, but it is divisible by 3: $273\div3=91$. Since you have already identified 3 as the smallest prime factor, you do not need to determine the rest of the prime factors.

Therefore, 3 is the smallest prime factor of 273 as well as the greatest prime factor of 243, and **(C)** is correct.

CHAPTER 3

Algebra, Ratios, and Formulas

Lesson 1: **Isolating a Variable**

LEARNING OBJECTIVE

After this lesson, you will be able to:

* Solve an equation in one variable

To isolate a variable, do the same thing to both sides of the equation:

a. $3x + 2 = 6x - 3$

b. $7y^2 + 6 = 4y^2 + 18$

1. $12x - 46 = -18 + 5x$

Quantity A	Quantity B
x	5

    Ⓐ   Quantity A is greater.

    Ⓑ   Quantity B is greater.

    Ⓒ   The two quantities are equal.

    Ⓓ   The relationship cannot be determined from the information given.

2.

Jacob has $0.65 in his pocket consisting of only *p* pennies and 9 nickels.

Quantity A	**Quantity B**
p	20

(A) Quantity A is greater.

(B) Quantity B is greater.

(C) The two quantities are equal.

(D) The relationship cannot be determined from the information given.

Try These at Home

3. In two years, J'Quan's age in years will be twice what it was four years ago. What is his age now?

(A) 4 years

(B) 7 years

(C) 10 years

(D) 12 years

(E) 14 years

4. If $2xy - 3 = 4x - 15$, what is the value of *x* when $y = 5$?

Drill answers from previous page: a. $x = \dfrac{5}{3}$, b. $y = \pm2$

Lesson 2: **Systems of Equations**

Solve for numeric values of *x* and *y*.

$$x + y = 5$$

$$x + 2y = 10$$

Substitution:

Combination:

5. If $a = 2b + \dfrac{1}{2}$ and $4b = 3$, what is the value of *a*?

　Ⓐ 1

　Ⓑ $1\dfrac{1}{2}$

　Ⓒ 2

　Ⓓ $2\dfrac{1}{2}$

　Ⓔ 3

6. If $3x + y = -1$ and $y - 2x = 4$, what is the value of $x + 2y$?

    Ⓐ −5

    Ⓑ −3

    Ⓒ 0

    Ⓓ 3

    Ⓔ 5

7. Full Force's annual dance recital was attended by 205 people, each of whom purchased a ticket. Children and youth tickets cost $3.50 and adult tickets cost $5.00. If Full Force collected $828.50 in ticket sales, how many adults attended?

    ☐ adults

Try These at Home

8.

$$5p + 6q = 74$$
$$q = 8$$

Quantity A	**Quantity B**
p	5

(A) Quantity A is greater.

(B) Quantity B is greater.

(C) The two quantities are equal.

(D) The relationship cannot be determined from the information given.

9.

$$\frac{k}{5} - \frac{j}{3} = \frac{7}{15}$$
$$2k + 3j = -8$$

Quantity A	**Quantity B**
j	k

(A) Quantity A is greater.

(B) Quantity B is greater.

(C) The two quantities are equal.

(D) The relationship cannot be determined from the information given.

Lesson 3: **Inequalities**

LEARNING OBJECTIVE

After this lesson, you will be able to:

- Solve inequalities for a range of values

When multiplying or dividing a negative number, remember to flip the inequality sign.

a. $-2x > 4$

b. $2x < -4$

10.   If $2x + 3 > 4x - 9$, which of the following could be the value of x?

Indicate <u>all</u> such values.

- A. -6
- B. 0
- C. 3
- D. 6
- E. 9

11.   If $\dfrac{3x}{-2} \geq -6$, which of the following could NOT be the value of x?

Indicate <u>all</u> such values.

- A. -13
- B. -3
- C. 0
- D. 4
- E. 5
- F. 8

Try These at Home

12.

$$\frac{3x+2}{4} > \frac{5+x}{2}$$

$$\frac{6y}{15} < \frac{10+y}{5}$$

Quantity A	**Quantity B**
$2x - 1$	$2y - 7$

(A) Quantity A is greater.

(B) Quantity B is greater.

(C) The two quantities are equal.

(D) The relationship cannot be determined from the information given.

Lesson 4: **Absolute Value**

> **LEARNING OBJECTIVE**
>
> After this lesson, you will be able to:
>
> - Solve equations that contain absolute value expressions

The absolute value of a number is its distance from zero on the number line.

a. $|x| = 2$

b. $|x + 3| = 10$

13.
$$|4x + 24| = 96$$
$$|4x| = 120$$

Quantity A	**Quantity B**
x	18

(A) Quantity A is greater.

(B) Quantity B is greater.

(C) The two quantities are equal.

(D) The relationship cannot be determined from the information given.

Drill answers from previous page: a. $x < -2$, b. $x < -2$

Try These at Home

14. If $|8x - 7| > 3x + 8$, then each of the following could be true <u>except</u>:

  Ⓐ $1 < x < 3$

  Ⓑ $-1 < x < 0$

  Ⓒ $2 < x < 4$

  Ⓓ $x = 3.5$

  Ⓔ $x = -1$

15.

$$2|-3y + 4| = 38$$
$$|-5y| = 25$$

Quantity A	**Quantity B**
y	5

  Ⓐ Quantity A is greater.

  Ⓑ Quantity B is greater.

  Ⓒ The two quantities are equal.

  Ⓓ The relationship cannot be determined from the information given.

Lesson 5: **Quadratics**

FOIL

$(x + 2)(x - 3)$

Reverse FOIL

$y^2 + 3y + 2$

Solving a Quadratic Equation

$x^2 - 2x = 15$

16. $x^2 + 5x + 6 = 0$

Quantity A	**Quantity B**
The square of the sum of the roots of the equation	25

  Ⓐ Quantity A is greater.

  Ⓑ Quantity B is greater.

  Ⓒ The two quantities are equal.

  Ⓓ The relationship cannot be determined from the information given.

17.
$$2x^2 + 4x - 30 = 0$$

Quantity A	**Quantity B**
The product of the roots of the equation	The sum of the roots of the equation

(A) Quantity A is greater.

(B) Quantity B is greater.

(C) The two quantities are equal.

(D) The relationship cannot be determined from the information given.

Try These at Home

18. If $x < -3$ and $x^2 + 5x + 12 = 8$, what is the value of $x + 2$?

(A) -4

(B) -2

(C) -1

(D) 0

(E) 3

19. Both *x* and *y* are integers. Which of the following expressions must be the square of an integer?

    Indicate __all__ such expressions.

    [A] $(x + y)(x - y) + 8xy + 17y^2$
    [B] $9x^4 - 12x^2y^2 + 4y^4$
    [C] $x^6 + 2x^3y^3 + y^6$

20.
$$3x^{\frac{2}{3}} + 2\sqrt[3]{x} - 8 = 0$$

Quantity A	Quantity B
x	$\dfrac{64}{25}$

(A) Quantity A is greater.

(B) Quantity B is greater.

(C) The two quantities are equal.

(D) The relationship cannot be determined from the information given.

Lesson 6: **Function Notation**

> **LEARNING OBJECTIVE**
>
> After this lesson, you will be able to:
> - Manipulate expressions and equations that use function notation

a. If $f(x) = x + 2$ then $f(5) =$

b. If $g(x) = x^2$ then $g(6) =$

21.

$$f(x) = 2x$$
$$g(x) = \frac{1}{2}x$$

Quantity A	**Quantity B**
$f(g(3))$	$g(f(3))$

- (A) Quantity A is greater.
- (B) Quantity B is greater.
- (C) The two quantities are equal.
- (D) The relationship cannot be determined from the information given.

22. Given that $f(x) = (x - 4)^2$ and $g(x) = x^2 - 5$, what is the value of $f(2) - g(2)$?

- (A) -1
- (B) 1
- (C) 3
- (D) 5
- (E) 9

Try These at Home

23. $f(x) = x^3 - 9x + 17$

Quantity A	**Quantity B**
$f(3)$	$f(-3)$

Ⓐ Quantity A is greater.

Ⓑ Quantity B is greater.

Ⓒ The two quantities are equal.

Ⓓ The relationship cannot be determined from the information given.

$$f(x) = \frac{x-1}{4}$$

24. If $\dfrac{w+1}{f(w)} = -2$, what is the value of w?

Ⓐ $-\dfrac{1}{4}$

Ⓑ $-\dfrac{1}{3}$

Ⓒ $\dfrac{1}{6}$

Ⓓ $\dfrac{1}{3}$

Ⓔ $\dfrac{2}{3}$

Drill answers from previous page: a. 7, b. 36

Lesson 7: **Symbolic Expressions**

LEARNING OBJECTIVE

After this lesson, you will be able to:

- Manipulate expressions and equations that include symbols

25.
$$\square n = 5n$$

Quantity A	**Quantity B**
$15 + \square 3$	$(\square 12) \div 2$

- (A) Quantity A is greater.
- (B) Quantity B is greater.
- (C) The two quantities are equal.
- (D) The relationship cannot be determined from the information given.

26.
$$\clubsuit j = j + 3 \text{ and } \blacktriangleleft j = \frac{j^2 + 2}{j}$$

Quantity A	**Quantity B**
$\blacktriangleleft(\clubsuit 2)$	$\clubsuit(\blacktriangleleft 2)$

- (A) Quantity A is greater.
- (B) Quantity B is greater.
- (C) The two quantities are equal.
- (D) The relationship cannot be determined from the information given.

27. If ♣$m = 3m$ and •$n = n + 7$, which of the following is the value of $[♣(•4) - 3(•2)]$?

(A) −9

(B) 1

(C) 6

(D) 13

(E) 20

Try These at Home

28. ♥x ♥ y ♥ $= (2x - y)^2$ and ☺a☺b☺ $= (a + 2b)^2$. If ☺ 5 ☺ $(n-1)$☺ $= 5n^2 + 4n$ and $n < 6$, then ♥ $2n$ ♥ 2 ♥ $=$

(A) 4

(B) 9

(C) 16

(D) 36

(E) 49

Lesson 8: **Ratios and Proportions**

LEARNING OBJECTIVES

After this lesson, you will be able to:

- Set up basic proportions
- Apply cross multiplication to proportion problems
- Apply the common multiplier principle to ratio problems

29. The ratio of green to blue marbles in a bag is 6:7. If there are 18 green marbles, how many total marbles are in the bag?

   (A) 18
   (B) 21
   (C) 27
   (D) 28
   (E) 39

30. If red, blue, and yellow gravels are to be mixed in the ratio 4:5:2 respectively, and 12 pounds of red gravel are available, how many pounds of the colored gravel mixture can be made? Assume there is enough blue and yellow gravel available to use all the red gravel.

   (A) 11
   (B) 22
   (C) 27
   (D) 33
   (E) 44

31. In a certain school, the ratio of boys to girls is 5:13. If there are 72 more girls than boys, how many boys are there?

    (A) 27
    (B) 36
    (C) 45
    (D) 72
    (E) 117

Try These at Home

32. The ratio of bluegills to minnows to sunfish to bass in a pond is 5:9:4:1. These are the only kinds of fish in the pond, and the total number of fish in the pond is between 100 and 200.

Quantity A	Quantity B
The smallest possible number of minnows in the pond	The largest possible number of bluegills in the pond

    (A) Quantity A is greater.
    (B) Quantity B is greater.
    (C) The two quantities are equal.
    (D) The relationship cannot be determined from the information given.

Lesson 9: **Percents**

a. $0.2 =$

b. $75\% =$

33.

Quantity A	**Quantity B**
40% of 0.75	$\dfrac{3}{5} \times \dfrac{3}{4}$

- (A)   Quantity A is greater.
- (B)   Quantity B is greater.
- (C)   The two quantities are equal.
- (D)   The relationship cannot be determined from the information given.

34.   If 12 is x% of 60, what is 30% of x?

- (A)   6
- (B)   15
- (C)   18
- (D)   24
- (E)   66

Try These at Home

35. The manager of a local grocery store earns an hourly wage of $21.00. The assistant manager earns 25% less than the manager. The stocker earns 60% less than the assistant manager. How much more does the manager make per hour than the stocker?

   (A) $6.30
   (B) $8.40
   (C) $9.45
   (D) $12.60
   (E) $14.70

36. Joe has a collection of 280 sports cards. If 30% of them are baseball cards, 25% of them are football cards, and the rest are basketball cards, how many basketball cards does Joe have?

   (A) 70
   (B) 84
   (C) 126
   (D) 154
   (E) 196

Drill answers from previous page: a. 20% or $\frac{1}{5}$, b. 0.75 or $\frac{3}{4}$

Lesson 10: **Percent Change**

LEARNING OBJECTIVE

After this lesson, you will be able to:

● Calculate percent change

$$Percent\ change = \frac{amount\ of\ change}{original\ whole} \times 100\%$$

a. Someone buys a stock for $400 and sells it for $600. What is the percent change?

b. Someone buys a stock for $600 and sells it for $400. What is the percent change?

Question 37 is based on the following graph.

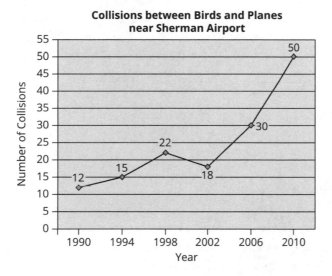

**Collisions between Birds and Planes
near Sherman Airport**

37. The number of collisions between birds and planes near Sherman Airport increased by approximately what percent between 1990 and 2010?

Ⓐ 3%

Ⓑ 37%

Ⓒ 193%

Ⓓ 245%

Ⓔ 317%

Question 38 is based on the following graph.

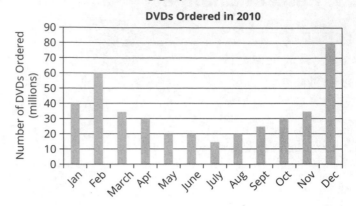

DVDs Ordered in 2010

38. There was a $41\frac{2}{3}$% change in the number of DVDs ordered between which two consecutive months in 2010?

   (A) February to March
   (B) April to May
   (C) May to June
   (D) August to September
   (E) November to December

Try These at Home

39. On Sundays only, the local organic farmers' market sells all fresh produce without the usual 8% sales tax and at a 20% discount. On Saturday, Brussels sprouts were $4.50/lb, tomatoes were $3/lb, and cucumbers were $2.50/lb. What is the approximate percent decrease in price between Saturday and Sunday if 3 lbs of Brussels sprouts, 2 lbs of cucumbers, and 5 lbs of tomatoes are purchased?

   (A) 7%
   (B) 20%
   (C) 26%
   (D) 33%
   (E) 52%

Drill answers from previous page: a. 50%, b. 33%

Lesson 11: **Rate and Average Speed Formulas**

LEARNING OBJECTIVES

After this lesson, you will be able to:

● Apply the 3-part speed and average speed formulas

Distance = Rate × Time

    a. You are driving 50 miles an hour for 2 hours. How far will you go?

    b. You travel 100 miles at 50 miles per hour. How long did you drive?

    c. It takes you 2 hours to travel 100 miles. How fast did you drive?

Speed for the entire journey $= \dfrac{total\ distance}{total\ time}$

    d. You travel 60 miles at 60 mph. Then there's very bad weather and you travel another 60 miles at only 30 mph. What is your average speed for the entire trip?

40. If Caroline drove 211 miles between 9:30 a.m. and 12:45 p.m. of the same day, what was her approximate average speed in miles per hour?

    (A) 50

    (B) 55

    (C) 60

    (D) 65

    (E) 70

41. Deonte travels 72 miles in 1 hour and 20 minutes and then 84 miles in 1 hour and 40 minutes. What is his average speed for the whole trip in miles per hour?

    (A) 50
    (B) 52
    (C) 54
    (D) 56
    (E) 58

Try These at Home

42. A flock of geese flies 10,920 kilometers without stopping, traveling at 70 kilometers per hour. How many days does this flight last?

    (A) 5.4
    (B) 6
    (C) 6.5
    (D) 156
    (E) 158

43. Haru, a truck driver, earns a bonus if she completes her route with an average speed of 56 miles per hour or more. She drives the first 108 miles of her route at a speed of 54 miles per hour, and the next 168 miles of her route at a speed of 56 miles per hour. At least how fast, in miles per hour, must Haru drive for the remaining 228 miles of her route to earn a bonus?

    [   ]

Drill answers from previous page: a. 100 miles, b. 2 hours, c. 50 mph, d. 40 mph

Lesson 12: **Combined Work Formula**

LEARNING OBJECTIVE

After this lesson, you will be able to:

● Solve combined work problems by applying the combined work formula

Combined Work Formula

$$\frac{AB}{(A+B)} = T$$

44. If Eugene can complete a project in 4 hours and Steve can complete the same project in 6 hours, how many hours will it take Eugene and Steve to complete the project if they work together?

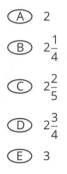

    Ⓐ 2

    Ⓑ $2\frac{1}{4}$

    Ⓒ $2\frac{2}{5}$

    Ⓓ $2\frac{3}{4}$

    Ⓔ 3

45. Pipe A can fill a tank in 3 hours. If pipe B can fill the same tank in 2 hours, how many minutes will it take both pipes to fill $\frac{2}{3}$ of the tank?

    (A) 30

    (B) 48

    (C) 54

    (D) 60

    (E) 72

46. Machine A can produce $\frac{1}{6}$ of a ton of paintbrushes in one hour. Machine B can produce $\frac{1}{14}$ of a ton of paintbrushes in one hour. Working together at their individual rates, how long would it take the two machines to produce 2 tons of paintbrushes?

    (A) 8 hours

    (B) 8 hours 24 minutes

    (C) 9 hours

    (D) 9 hours 46 minutes

    (E) 12 hours

Algebra, Ratios, and Formulas Answer Key

1. **B**	13. **B**	25. **C**	37. **E**
2. **C**	14. **A**	26. **B**	38. **A**
3. **C**	15. **B**	27. **C**	39. **C**
4. **−2**	16. **C**	28. **D**	40. **D**
5. **C**	17. **B**	29. **E**	41. **B**
6. **D**	18. **B**	30. **D**	42. **C**
7. **74**	19. **A, B, C**	31. **C**	43. **57**
8. **A**	20. **B**	32. **A**	44. **C**
9. **B**	21. **C**	33. **B**	45. **B**
10. **A, B, C**	22. **D**	34. **A**	46. **B**
11. **E, F**	23. **C**	35. **E**	
12. **A**	24. **B**	36. **C**	

Answers and Explanations

Algebra, Ratios, and Formulas
Try This At Home Explanations

Lesson 1

3. C

Translate the wording in the question stem to an equation. Set J equal to J'Quan's current age. In two years, he'll be $J + 2$; four years ago he was $J - 4$. So, $J + 2 = 2 \times (J - 4) = 2J - 8$. Add 8 to both sides of the equation to get $J + 10 = 2J$. Subtract J from both sides to see that $10 = J$, which is **(C)**.

4. −2

Since the value of y is provided, it will be more efficient to just plug that into the equation first and solve for x, rather than working with two variables to solve for x in terms of y and then substituting the value of y to get x. Restate the equation $2xy - 3 = 4x - 15$ as $2x(5) - 3 = 4x - 15$. This simplifies to $10x - 3 = 4x - 15$. Add 3 to both sides of the equation to get $10x = 4x - 12$. Now subtract $4x$ from both sides to see that $6x = -12$. Finally, divide by 6: $x = \mathbf{-2}$.

Lesson 2

8. A

The goal is to find p based on the two equations that are given, so use substitution to make the first equation in terms of only one variable. Substituting $q = 8$ into the first equation results in:

$$5p + 6(8) = 74$$
$$5p + 48 = 74$$
$$5p = 26$$
$$p = 5.2$$

Quantity A is 5.2, which is a little greater than 5, so **(A)** is correct.

9. B

For this question, combination is the best approach. Eliminate k by multiplying the top equation by 30 and the bottom equation by 3:

$$(30)\left(\frac{k}{5} - \frac{j}{3} = \frac{7}{15}\right)$$
$$(3)(2k + 3j = -8)$$
$$6k - 10j = 14$$
$$6k + 9j = -2$$

Subtract the second equation from the first to eliminate the variable k:

$$6k - 10j = 14$$
$$-(6k + 9j = -24)$$
$$\overline{-19j = 38}$$
$$j = -2$$

Now plug $j = -2$ into the second equation to solve for k:

$$2k + 3(-2) = -8$$
$$2k - 6 = -8$$
$$2k = -2$$
$$k = -1$$

Finally, plug in the values to solve for the quantities. Quantity B is greater, so **(B)** is correct.

Lesson 3

12. A

The centered information consists of two inequalities, one involving x and the other involving y. Simplify each of the inequalities. For the first one, multiply both sides by 4 to get $3x + 2 > 10 + 2x$. Subtract 2 and $2x$ from both sides to get $x > 8$. For the second inequality, multiply both sides by 15 to get $6y < 30 + 3y$. Subtract $3y$ from both sides to get $3y < 30$, and $y < 10$.

Quantity A deals with just x. Since $x > 8$, $2x - 1$ must be greater than $2(8) - 1$. Thus, Quantity A must be greater than 15. Quantity B deals with just y. Since $y < 10$, $2y - 7$ must be less than $2(10) - 7$. Therefore, Quantity B must be less than $20 - 7 = 13$. Since Quantity A must be greater than 15 and Quantity B must be less than 13, Quantity A is greater, so the answer is **(A)**.

Lesson 4

14. A

To solve an absolute value inequality (or equation), write out two possibilities: one in which the absolute value expression is positive, and one in which it's negative. Case 1 (positive): $(8x - 7) > 3x + 8$, so $5x > 15$, and $x > 3$.

Case 2 (negative): $-(8x - 7) > 3x + 8$, so $-8x + 7 > 3x + 8$, which means that $-1 > 11x$ and $x < -\frac{1}{11}$.

15. B

Both equations in the centered information must be true. The fact that the variable is preceded by a minus sign and that one of the equations multiplies the absolute value by 2 does not change how you approach the solution. To solve for y in order to compare its value with 5, start with the simpler equation, $|-5y| = 25$. Either $-5y = 25$ or $5y = -25$. So $y = \pm 5$. For the other equation, $2|-3y + 4| = 38$, simplify by dividing both sides by 2 to get $|-3y + 4| = 19$. If the quantity within the absolute value signs is positive, then $-3y + 4 = 19$, which means that $3y = -15$, and $y = -5$. Try the negative condition, $-3y + 4 = -19$. This simplifies to $3y = 23$. In this case, y does not equal either 5 or -5, so the only value of y that works for both equations is -5. Thus, Quantity B is greater and **(B)** is correct.

Lesson 5

18. B

The equation is quadratic, so all terms should be moved to one side and set equal to zero to solve for x. The equation $x^2 + 5x + 12 = 8$ becomes $x^2 + 5x + 4 = 0$. This can be factored to $(x + 4)(x + 1) = 0$, so either $x + 4 = 0$ or $x + 1 = 0$, and solving for x gives $x = -1$ or $x = -4$. The problem states that $x < -3$, so the only valid solution is $x = -4$. Once the value of x is specified, you can substitute in the value for x to solve: $x + 2 = -4 + 2 = -2$. Always make sure to confirm your answer, because (A) is the trap that represents the value of x; but, remember, you're looking for the value of $x + 2$. The answer is **(B)**.

19. A, B, C

First, evaluate (A): $(x + y)(x - y) + 8xy + 17y^2$.

Multiply the first two terms together:

$$(x + y)(x - y) = x^2 - y^2$$

Plug this into the initial equation and simplify:

$$x^2 - y^2 + 8xy + 17y^2 = x^2 + 8xy + 16y^2$$

Reverse FOIL the equation:

$$x^2 + 8xy + 16y^2 = (x + 4y)(x + 4y) = (x + 4y)^2$$

Since y is an integer, $4y$ is an integer. Since x and $4y$ are both integers, $x + 4y$ is an integer. So $(x + 4y)^2$ is the square of an integer, and it follows that expression (A) must be the square of an integer.

Next, consider expression (B): $9x^4 - 12x^2y^2 + 4y^4$.

Reverse FOIL the equation:

$9x^4 - 12x^2y^2 + 4y^4 - (3x^2 - 2y^2)(3x^2 - 2y^2) = (3x^2 - 2y^2)^2$

Since x is an integer, x^2 is an integer, as is $3x^2$. Since y is an integer, y^2 is an integer, as is $2y^2$. Since $3x^2$ and $2y^2$ are integers, $3x^2 - 2y^2$ is also an integer. Thus, $(3x^2 - 2y^2)^2$ is the square of an integer. Therefore, expression (B) must also be the square of an integer.

Lastly, evaluate expression (C): $x^6 + 2x^3y^3 + y^6$.

Reverse FOIL the equation:

$(x^3)^2 + 2(x^3)(y^3) + (y^3)^2 = (x^3 + y^3)(x^3 + y^3) = (x^3 + y^3)^2$

Since x is an integer, x^3 is an integer. Since y is an integer, y^3 is an integer. Since x^3 and y^3 are integers, $x^3 + y^3$ is an integer.

Thus, $(x^3 + y^3)^2$ is the square of an integer. So it turns out that expression (C) must also be the square of an integer.

Choices **(A)**, **(B)**, and **(C)** are all correct.

20. B

Strange-looking equations on the GRE are often quadratics in disguise. Note that $x^{\frac{2}{3}}$ is actually just $\sqrt[3]{x}$ squared. To make the equation look more manageable, try letting $\sqrt[3]{x} = m$. Then the equation becomes $3m^2 + 2m - 8 = 0$. Factoring this equation is made more challenging by the coefficient in front of the m^2 term. To factor an expression of the form $ax^2 + bx + c$, look for two numbers that multiply to ac and sum to b. In this case, the two numbers that multiply to $(3)(-8) = -24$ and sum to 2 are 6 and -4. Rewrite the equation, substituting $6m - 4m$ for $2m$. Then factor and solve for m:

$$3m^2 + 2m - 8 = 0$$
$$3m^2 + 6m - 4m - 8 = 0$$
$$3m(m + 2) - 4(m + 2) = 0$$
$$(3m - 4)(m + 2) = 0$$
$$m = \frac{4}{3} \text{ or } m = -2$$

At this point, substitute $\sqrt[3]{x}$ back in for m and cube each equation to find the possible values of x:

$$\sqrt[3]{x} = \frac{4}{3} \text{ or } \sqrt[3]{x} = -2$$
$$x = \left(\frac{4}{3}\right)^3 \text{ or } x = (-2)^3$$
$$x = \frac{64}{27} \text{ or } x = -8$$

Because Quantity B, $\frac{64}{25}$, is greater than both of the possible values of x, **(B)** is the correct answer.

Lesson 6

23. C

Since only one function is given, substitute the values of x in the two quantities and compare the results. Note that the constant value, 17, is identical in both quantities, so you can ignore that when making the comparison in order to simplify your calculations. For Quantity A, $x^3 - 9x = 3^3 - 9(3) = 27 - 27 = 0$. For Quantity B, $x^3 - 9x = (-3)^3 - 9(-3) = -27 - (-27) = 0$. The quantities are equal, so **(C)** is correct.

24. B

If $f(w) = \dfrac{w - 1}{4}$, then $\dfrac{w + 1}{f(w)} = \dfrac{w + 1}{\frac{w - 1}{4}}$. To divide by a fraction, invert the fraction and multiply, so $\dfrac{w + 1}{f(w)} = (w + 1)\left(\dfrac{4}{w - 1}\right)$. Set this equal to -2:

$\dfrac{4(w + 1)}{w - 1} = -2$. Multiply both sides by $(w - 1)$ to clear the fraction: $4(w + 1) = -2(w - 1)$. So $4w + 4 = -2w + 2$ and $6w = -2$. Thus, $w = -\dfrac{1}{3}$ and **(B)** is correct.

Lesson 7

28. D

Symbolism questions frighten a lot of students, but symbols are just odd-looking functions, and questions featuring them are typically best solved by substitution. Start by replacing the wacky shapes with simple function notation. Use an "h" for the hearts and an "s" for the smileys:

$$h(x, y) = (2x - y)^2$$
$$s(a, b) = (a + 2b)^2$$

Now the question becomes: given that $s(5, n - 1) = 5n^2 + 4n$ and $n < 6$, what is $h(2n, 2)$? Begin by plugging 5 and $n - 1$, respectively, into function s:

$$s(5, n - 1) = [5 + 2(n - 1)]^2 = (5 + 2n - 2)^2$$
$$= (2n + 3)^2 = 4n^2 + 12n + 9$$

The question says that this equals $5n^2 + 4n$, so set the quantities equal and solve the quadratic:

$$4n^2 + 12n + 9 = 5n^2 + 4n$$
$$n^2 - 8n - 9 = 0$$
$$(n - 9)(n + 1) = 0$$
$$n = 9 \text{ or } n = -1$$

The question states that $n < 6$, so n must equal -1. Now that you know that $n = -1$, you can find $h(2n, 2)$:

$$h(2n, 2) = h[(2)(-1), 2] = h(-2, 2)$$
$$h(-2, 2) = [2(-2) - 2]^2 = (-4 - 2)^2 = (-6)^2 = 36$$

The correct answer is **(D)**.

Lesson 8

32. A

The centered information shows the ratio of kinds of fish in the pond and provides a range for the total number of fish. In order to determine the smallest possible number of minnows and the largest possible number of bluegills, determine how many total fish could be in the pond.

Since the ratio of fish is 5:9:4:1, the total number of fish in the pond must be a multiple of $5 + 9 + 4 + 1 = 19$. The smallest multiple of 19 greater than 100 is $19 \times 6 = 114$, so 114 is the minimum possible number of fish. Since minnows make up 9 parts of the ratio, the number of minnows in this situation would be $9 \times 6 = 54$, which is the value of Quantity A.

The largest multiple of 19 smaller than 200 is $19 \times 10 = 190$, so this is the maximum possible number of fish. Bluegills make up 5 parts of the ratio, so the number of bluegills in this situation would be $5 \times 10 = 50$, which is the value of Quantity B. Therefore, **(A)** is correct.

Lesson 9

35. E

The manager of a grocery store makes $21.00 an hour. If the assistant manager makes 25% less than the manager, the assistant manager makes $21.00 \times 0.25 = 5.25 less, or $15.75. The stocker makes 60% less than the assistant manager, so he makes $15.75 \times 0.60 = 9.45 less, or $6.30. The question asks how much more the manager makes per hour than the stocker. Subtract the stocker's hourly wage from the manager's hourly wage: $21.00 - $6.30 = 14.70. The correct answer is **(E)**.

36. C

Joe has 280 sports cards in his collection. Of these, 30% are baseball cards and 25% are football cards. Therefore, 55% of the collection is baseball and football cards, and just a little less than half of the collection—45%—is basketball cards. Calculate 45% of the total: $280 \times 0.45 = 126$. The answer is **(C)**, 126 basketball cards.

Lesson 10

39. C

The goal is to find the percent decrease in the price. You can do this by finding the original price for the produce with tax as well as the price with the 20% discount (but also see below for a faster approach). The price for 3 lbs of Brussels sprouts, 2 lbs of cucumbers, and 5 lbs of tomatoes is:

$$\$4.50(3) + \$2.50(2) + \$3.00(5) = \$33.50$$

Factor in the 8% sales tax by multiplying the total by 1.08:

$$\$33.50 \times 1.08 = \$36.18$$

To find the 20% discount for Sundays, multiply the total (before sales tax) by $(1 - 0.2) = 0.8$:

$$\$33.50 \times 0.8 = \$26.80$$

Now plug the two prices into the percent decrease formula:

$$\frac{\$36.18 - \$26.80}{\$36.18} = \frac{\$9.38}{\$36.18} \approx 26\%$$

Alternatively, you can work with the percents in decimal form:

$$\frac{1.08 - 0.8}{1.08} = \frac{0.28}{1.08} \approx 26\%$$

Either strategy leads to **(C)** as the correct answer.

Lesson 11

43. C

Use the distance formula: $Distance = Rate \times Time$.
You know the distance the geese travel, as well as their
speed, so plug these values in to find the length of the
flight. (Just don't forget that the question asks for the
numbers of *days* the flight lasts, not the number of *hours*!)
$10,920 km = 70 kph \times hours$, so $156 = hours$. Then, divide
the hours by 24 to get the number of days: $156 \div 24 = 6.5$,
which is (**C**).

44. 57

$$\text{The average speed for an entire journey} = \frac{Total\ Distance}{Total\ Time}$$

You are given the average speed Haru must achieve to
earn a bonus, and her total distance is $108 + 168 + 228 =$
504 miles. If she drives 504 miles with an average speed
of 56 mph, then her total time is $504 \div 56 = 9$ hours. The
first 108 miles take her $108 \div 54 = 2$ hours, and the next
168 miles take her $168 \div 56 = 3$ hours. So, the final
228 miles must take her $9 - 2 - 3 = 4$ hours. You are
looking for her speed in miles per hour over the last
228 miles, so your answer is $228 \div 4 = \mathbf{57}$ miles per hour.

CHAPTER 4

Statistics, Probability, and Counting Methods

Lesson 1: **Average Formula**

$$Average = \frac{Sum\ of\ Terms}{Number\ of\ Terms}$$

49, 50, 61, x

Average $= 52$

$x =$

Balancing Approach

1. What is the sum of the five consecutive even numbers whose average (arithmetic mean) is 20?

    (A) 20
    (B) 95
    (C) 98
    (D) 100
    (E) 105

2. If Sierra's scores on her first three tests were 90, 93, and 98, what must she score on the fourth test to have 95 as her test average?

    (A) 95
    (B) 96
    (C) 97
    (D) 98
    (E) 99

3. The average (arithmetic mean) of a, b, and c is 70, and the average (arithmetic mean) of d and e is 120. What is the average (arithmetic mean) of a, b, c, d, and e?

    (A) 84

    (B) 90

    (C) 95

    (D) 96

    (E) 100

Try These at Home

4.   The numbers in a data set have a mean (arithmetic average) of 0.

Quantity A	**Quantity B**
Number of data elements below the mean	Number of data elements above the mean

(A) Quantity A is greater.

(B) Quantity B is greater.

(C) The two quantities are equal.

(D) The relationship cannot be determined from the information given.

Lesson 2: **Weighted Average**

LEARNING OBJECTIVES

After this lesson, you will be able to:

● Calculate weighted average

● Read a frequency distribution table

On Monday and Tuesday, an office worker drinks 1 cup of coffee a day. From Wednesday through Friday, the same office worker drinks 3 cups of coffee a day.

Day of Week	Cups per Day
Monday	1
Tuesday	1
Wednesday	3
Thursday	3
Friday	3

Average Formula:

Weighted Average

Cups	# of Days
1 cup	2
3 cups	3

Weighted Average as Percents

Cups	% of Days
1 cup	40%
3 cups	60%

5. If 20 students in one class had an average grade of 94% and 18 students from another class had an average grade of 92%, what is the average grade for all 38 students across both classes? Round to the nearest hundredth of a percent.

    (A) 91.50%

    (B) 92.75%

    (C) 93.00%

    (D) 93.05%

    (E) 93.95%

6. Rob has received scores of 96, 89, and 85 on 3 quizzes. If the exam is weighted twice as heavily as each of the three quizzes, what is the lowest score Rob can get on the exam to have a final average of at least 90?

    (A) 88

    (B) 89

    (C) 90

    (D) 91

    (E) 92

7. The average of John's test scores in his economics class is 80%. Only one test remains, and it is weighted at 25% of the final grade. If his final grade is based entirely on his test scores, what is the lowest percent John can receive on the final to earn an 85% in the class?

(A) 96%

(B) 97%

(C) 98%

(D) 99%

(E) 100%

Try These at Home

8. The following table gives the ages of students in a class at a high school. Find the mean.

Age	14	15	16	17	18
Number of students	4	8	7	1	2

(A) 14.5

(B) 14.8

(C) 15.0

(D) 15.2

(E) 15.5

Lesson 3: **Median, Mode, and Range**

2, 3, 4, 5, 5

Median:

2, 3, 4, 5, 5, 6

Median:

Mode:

Range:

9.   {−4, −3, 0, 2, 4, 6, 7, 9}

Quantity A	**Quantity B**
The average (arithmetic mean) of the set of numbers	The median of the set of numbers

   Ⓐ Quantity A is greater.

   Ⓑ Quantity B is greater.

   Ⓒ The two quantities are equal.

   Ⓓ The relationship cannot be determined from the information given.

Try These at Home

10. a, b, c, d, and e are positive integers.

$$(a + b)^2 = 25$$

$$c \times d \times e = 6$$

Quantity A	**Quantity B**
The range of a, b, c, d, and e.	4

   Ⓐ Quantity A is greater.

   Ⓑ Quantity B is greater.

   Ⓒ The two quantities are equal.

   Ⓓ The relationship cannot be determined from the information given.

Weight (kg)	Percent of sample
7	5%
8	10%
9	20%
10	10%
11	10%
12	5%
13	25%
14	10%
15	5%

11. A veterinarian is working with a dog breeders' association to analyze the weights of a sample of 240 healthy two-year-old purebred dachshunds. The veterinarian collects the above data.

Quantity A	**Quantity B**
median weight of the dogs in this sample	mean weight of the dogs in this sample

  Ⓐ Quantity A is greater.

  Ⓑ Quantity B is greater.

  Ⓒ The two quantities are equal.

  Ⓓ The relationship cannot be determined from the information given.

Lesson 4: **Probability Formula**

> **LEARNING OBJECTIVE**
>
> After this lesson, you will be able to:
>
> • Apply the basic probability formula

$$Probability = \frac{Desired\ outcomes}{Total\ possible\ outcomes}$$

12. One marble is randomly selected from a bag that contains only 4 black marbles, 3 red marbles, 5 yellow marbles, and 4 green marbles.

Quantity A	**Quantity B**
The probability of selecting either a black marble or a red marble	The probability of selecting either a yellow marble or a green marble

- Ⓐ Quantity A is greater.
- Ⓑ Quantity B is greater.
- Ⓒ The two quantities are equal.
- Ⓓ The relationship cannot be determined from the information given.

13. An integer x is selected at random from the set {17, 21, 23, 25, 27, 30, 33}.

Quantity A	**Quantity B**
The probability that the average (arithmetic mean) of 8, 16, and x is at least 17	$\frac{1}{2}$

- Ⓐ Quantity A is greater.
- Ⓑ Quantity B is greater.
- Ⓒ The two quantities are equal.
- Ⓓ The relationship cannot be determined from the information given.

Try These at Home

14. An aquarium keeps 72 fish in 4 different tanks. The second tank has 4 more fish than the first, the third tank has 4 more fish than the second, and the fourth tank has 4 more fish than the third. What is the probability that a given fish will be in the third tank?

   (A) $\dfrac{1}{8}$

   (B) $\dfrac{3}{16}$

   (C) $\dfrac{4}{18}$

   (D) $\dfrac{5}{18}$

   (E) $\dfrac{3}{10}$

15. A jar contains only pink, blue, and white gumballs. Of these, 15 are pink. The number of blue gumballs is three more than twice the number of white gumballs. The probability of pulling a pink or white gumball out of the jar is $\dfrac{2}{3}$. How many blue gumballs are in the jar?

   ┌─────────────────┐
   │   │
   └─────────────────┘

Lesson 5: **Multiple Dependent and Independent Events**

LEARNING OBJECTIVE

After this lesson, you will be able to:

- Calculate the probability of multiple independent or dependent events

Probability Keywords
or =
and =

A bag contains 5 marbles, 4 blue and 1 red.

Independent events

What is the probability of drawing 2 blue marbles in a row if you replace the first marble after taking it out of the bag?

Dependent events

What is the probability of drawing 2 blue marbles in a row if you don't replace the first marble after taking it out of the bag?

16. What is the probability of rolling a number greater than 2 twice in a row on a fair six-sided die, with each of the numbers 1–6 on each side?

    Ⓐ $\frac{1}{4}$

    Ⓑ $\frac{5}{18}$

    Ⓒ $\frac{4}{9}$

    Ⓓ $\frac{5}{9}$

    Ⓔ $\frac{2}{3}$

17. In a bag there are 6 red marbles, 7 blue marbles, and 3 black marbles. If two marbles are drawn without replacing the first, what is the probability of drawing a blue and then a red marble?

    Ⓐ $\frac{21}{128}$

    Ⓑ $\frac{7}{40}$

    Ⓒ $\frac{49}{256}$

    Ⓓ $\frac{3}{10}$

    Ⓔ $\frac{13}{16}$

18. If a fair six-sided die with faces numbered 1 through 6 is tossed 3 times, what is the probability of getting a 1 or a 2 on all three tosses?

Try These at Home

19. A pigeon is in an experiment with one round button and one square button. When the pigeon pecks the round button, there is a 75% chance that it gets a treat. When the pigeon pecks the square button, there is a 50% chance that it gets a treat. The pigeon is as likely to peck the round button as the square one.

Quantity A	Quantity B
The probability that the pigeon will get a treat after it pecks one of the buttons.	$\frac{5}{8}$

Ⓐ Quantity A is greater.

Ⓑ Quantity B is greater.

Ⓒ The two quantities are equal.

Ⓓ The relationship cannot be determined from the information given.

20. Sunjay writes each integer between -4 and 3, inclusive, on a different card. He places all of the cards into a hat. He then takes two cards out of the hat at random, one at a time and without replacement.

Quantity A	Quantity B
The probability that both cards Sunjay removes have an even number.	The probability that the first card Sunjay removes has an odd number and the second has an even number.

Ⓐ Quantity A is greater.

Ⓑ Quantity B is greater.

Ⓒ The two quantities are equal.

Ⓓ The relationship cannot be determined from the information given.

Lesson 6: **Multiplication Principle**

If there are 3 hats and 2 scarves, how many possible combinations of 1 hat and 1 scarf can be made?

Multiplication principle:

21. A quiz has 10 true/false questions. If each question is answered with "true" or "false" and none of them are left blank, in how many ways can the quiz be answered?

    Ⓐ 20

    Ⓑ 45

    Ⓒ 100

    Ⓓ 512

    Ⓔ 1,024

Try These at Home

22. Jerome is buying a new computer and has to decide which components to include in the computer. He is choosing among 3 different CPUs, 4 options for RAM, and 3 different capacity hard drives. If any of these components can be combined with any of the others, and Jerome must have one and only one of each type of component (CPU, RAM, and hard drive), how many different configurations can Jerome select from?

(A) 10
(B) 16
(C) 24
(D) 30
(E) 36

Lesson 7: **Slots Strategy for Permutations**

Factorials

How many ways can 5 books be arranged on a shelf?

Permutations: Slots Approach

How many ways can 3 books chosen from a group of 5 books be arranged on a shelf?

23. There are 10 finalists for the school spelling bee. A first, second, and third place trophy will be awarded and there can be no ties. In how many different ways can the judges award the three prizes?

(A) 6

(B) 27

(C) 120

(D) 720

(E) 1,000

24. Gloria has 7 shirts to display on 7 mannequins in her boutique. If she has already placed the first shirt on mannequin 1, how many different ways can she display the rest of the shirts?

  (A) 36
  (B) 49
  (C) 720
  (D) 840
  (E) 5,040

Try These at Home

25.

Quantity A	Quantity B
The number of ways to line up 4 objects chosen from 7 different objects	The number of ways to line up 3 objects chosen from 10 different objects

  (A) Quantity A is greater.
  (B) Quantity B is greater.
  (C) The two quantities are equal.
  (D) The relationship cannot be determined from the information given.

Lesson 8: **Combinations Formula**

Combinations Formula

$$_nC_k = \frac{n!}{k!(n-k)!}$$

26. If there are 5 books you want to buy at the bookstore, but you can only afford 3, how many ways are there to buy 3 of 5 books?

27. From a box of 12 candles, you are to remove 5. How many different sets of 5 candles could you remove?

   (A) 120
   (B) 300
   (C) 684
   (D) 792
   (E) 95,040

28. How many distinct combinations of 3 socks could be made by randomly selecting socks from a drawer containing 8 differently colored socks?

   (A) 56
   (B) 46
   (C) 28
   (D) 24
   (E) 19

Try These at Home

29. If 8 schools are all in the same conference, how many soccer games are played during the season if the teams all play each other exactly once?

   (A) 16
   (B) 28
   (C) 32
   (D) 46
   (E) 56

Statistics, Probability, and Counting Methods Answer Key

1. **D**
2. **E**
3. **B**
4. **D**
5. **D**
6. **C**
7. **E**
8. **E**
9. **B**
10. **D**
11. **B**
12. **B**
13. **B**
14. **D**
15. **9**
16. **C**
17. **B**
18. $\dfrac{1}{27}$
19. **C**
20. **B**
21. **E**
22. **E**
23. **D**
24. **C**
25. **A**
26. **10**
27. **D**
28. **A**
29. **B**

Answers and Explanations

Statistics, Probability, and Counting Methods
Try This At Home Explanations

Lesson 1

4. D

Be careful when the GRE poses a question like this without telling you the elements in the set. For example, the data set could be $\{-2, 0, 2\}$ or $\{-4, 0, 2, 2\}$. It could also be a set of many more elements. The correct answer is **(D)**.

Lesson 2

8. E

Rather than listing out all the individual values and adding them, calculate the weighted average, which is the mean. There are four 14s, eight 15s, seven 16s, one 17, and two 18s in the table, so:

$$4(14) + 8(15) + 7(16) + 1(17) + 2(18) = 341$$

There are $4 + 8 + 7 + 1 + 2 = 22$ numbers, so the mean is $\frac{341}{22}$, which equals 15.5.

The mean age is 15.5. **(E)** is correct.

Lesson 3

10. D

Quantity A will be greater if the largest and smallest values of a, b, c, d, and e are farther apart than 4, and smaller if they are closer together than 4. So consider what the minimum and maximum possible values of the given variables could be. Because $(a + b)^2 = 25$, $(a + b) = 5$. (Note that you need not consider -5, since all of the variables are positive integers.) It is either the case that one of a and b is 1 and the other is 4, or that one is 2 and the other is 3.

Since $c \times d \times e = 6$, it is possible that the variables are 1, 2, and 3. Combining this information with the "1 and 4" possibility from the previous equation, the range would be $4 - 1 = 3$, which is less than Quantity B. However, it is also possible that c, d, and e are 1, 1, and 6. In this case, the range would be $6 - 1 = 5$, which is greater than Quantity B. Multiple relationships between the quantities are possible, so **(D)** is correct.

11. B

The question presents data about the relative frequency of 240 dogs' weights.

Quantity A, the median weight of this sample, is the average weight of the 120th and 121st dogs when their weights are in order from least to greatest. The table is already in order from least to greatest, so add the percentages until you find where the midpoint of the sample, 50%, falls. That's $5 + 10 + 20 + 10 = 45\%$—not there yet. So keep going: $45 + 10 = 55\%$. That's over the midpoint, so the dogs whose weights you'd average to get the median weight are in the last category added, which is the 11 kg category. The median weight of dogs in this sample is 11 kg.

Calculating Quantity B, the mean weight, requires calculating a weighted average. Instead of working with the percentages of 240 dogs given, which would take a lot of time, remember that percentages represent ratios out of a whole of 100. Thus, $5\% = \frac{5}{100} = \frac{1}{20}$. Every 5% is 1 part out of 20, so represent 5% as 1, 10% as 2, 15% as 3, 20% as 4, and 25% as 5 parts. This approach maintains the proportionality of the categories while making the numbers easier to work with. In your weighted average formula, divide by the total of 20 parts.

$$\frac{1 \times 7 + 2 \times 8 + 4 \times 9 + 2 \times 10 + 2 \times 11 + 1 \times 12 + 5 \times 13 + 2 \times 14 + 1 \times 15}{20} =$$

$$\frac{7 + 16 + 36 + 20 + 22 + 12 + 65 + 28 + 15}{20} =$$

$$\frac{221}{20}$$

You can easily estimate that this fraction is slightly over 11 (since $\frac{220}{20} = 11$). Quantity A is exactly 11, so Quantity B is greater.

The correct answer is **(B)**.

Lesson 4

14. D

Probability is $\dfrac{Desired\ outcomes}{Possible\ outcomes}$; in this case, you are
looking for the number of fish in the third tank divided by the total number of fish. You know the total number of fish (72) but need to find the number in the third tank. If the first tank has x fish, then the second tank has $x + 4$ fish, the third tank has $x + 8$ fish, and the fourth tank has $x + 12$ fish. This means there are $(x) + (x + 4) + (x + 8) + (x + 12) = 4x + 24$ fish total. Set this equal to 72 to solve for x: $4x + 24 = 72$ so $4x = 48$ and x is 12. This means the third tank has $x + 8 = 12 + 8 = 20$ fish. Therefore, the probability of a given fish being in the third tank is $\dfrac{20}{72}$, which reduces to $\dfrac{5}{18}$, **(D)**.

15. 9

The probability formula is the number of desired outcomes divided by the number of total outcomes. In this case, the probability of pulling a pink or white gumball out of the jar is the number of pink and white gumballs added together, divided by the total number of gumballs. If you let w be the number of white gumballs, and b be the number of blue, then the probability of pulling a pink or white gumball is $\dfrac{15 + w}{15 + w + b} = \dfrac{2}{3}$. Since there are two variables, you'll need another equation to solve. You know that the *"number of blue gumballs is three more than twice the number of white gumballs,"* which can be expressed as $b = 2w + 3$. This allows you to substitute $(2w + 3)$ for b in the original equation: $\dfrac{15 + w}{15 + w + (2w + 3)} = \dfrac{2}{3}$. Simplify, and then cross-multiply to solve:

$$\frac{15 + w}{18 + 3w} = \frac{2}{3}$$

$$45 + 3w = 36 + 6w$$

So $9 = 3w$ and w is 3. You are looking for the number of blue gumballs, so plug the value for w back into one of your original equations to solve for the number of blue gumballs: $b = 2(3) + 3$, so $b =$ **9**.

Lesson 5

19. C

The centered information tells you the chance that the pigeon will get a treat from pecking either button. In Quantity A, the pigeon will either peck the round button *or* the square button. So to find the total probability that the pigeon will get a treat, add the probability that it will peck the round button and get a treat to the probability that it will peck the square button and get a treat. The chance that it will get a treat from the round button is $\dfrac{1}{2}$ (the probability of pecking the round button) times 75%, or $\dfrac{3}{4}$ (the probability that this will result in a treat). This gives a probability of $\dfrac{1}{2} \times \dfrac{3}{4} = \dfrac{3}{8}$ that it will peck the round button and get a treat. The probability that the pigeon will get a treat from the square button is $\dfrac{1}{2}$ (the probability of pecking the square button) times 50% (the probability that this will result in a treat), or $\dfrac{1}{2}$. This gives a probability of $\dfrac{1}{2} \times \dfrac{1}{2} = \dfrac{1}{4}$ that the pigeon will peck the square button and get a treat. Since the pigeon will peck the round button *or* the square button, *add* the two probabilities: $\dfrac{3}{8} + \dfrac{1}{4} = \dfrac{3}{8} + \dfrac{2}{8} = \dfrac{5}{8}$, so **(C)** is correct.

20. B

First, determine that there are eight integers (including 0) between -4 and 3, so the hat has eight cards. Then, note the phrase "without replacement," which indicates that the events are dependent.

For Quantity A, the probability that the first card drawn will be even is the number of even cards divided by the total number of cards. There are four even cards (-4, -2, 0, 2), yielding a $\dfrac{4}{8}$ probability of drawing an even card. At this point, one of the even cards has been removed from the hat, so the probability of drawing another even card is $\dfrac{3}{7}$. Thus, the probability of drawing two even cards in a row is $\dfrac{4}{8} \times \dfrac{3}{7}$. Hold off on simplifying this expression until you've found a value for Quantity B. (Waiting to simplify can sometimes make comparing the two quantities easier.)

For Quantity B, there are four odd cards, so the probability of drawing an odd first is $\dfrac{4}{8}$. At this point, one odd has been removed from the hat, so the probability of drawing an even is $\frac{4}{7}$. Thus, the probability of drawing an odd and then an even is $\frac{4}{8} \times \frac{4}{7}$. This is greater than $\frac{4}{8} \times \frac{3}{7}$ in Quantity A, so (**B**) is correct.

Lesson 6

22. E

The question describes the number of choices for each of three different components of a computer and asks for the total possible number of choices, given that any of the the choices can be combined with any of the others. Since Jerome chooses a CPU *and* RAM *and* a hard drive, the multiplication principle applies, and the total choices are $3 \times 4 \times 3 = 36$. (**E**) is correct.

Lesson 7

25. A

This is a straightforward permutations question because the objects are different and the quantities refer to "ways to line up," meaning that order matters. This can be solved using the slots method. For Quantity A, there are 4 slots and 7 choices, so there are a total of $7 \times 6 \times 5 \times 4 = 840$ ways to line up the 4 objects. For Quantity B, there are 3 slots and 10 objects, so there are a total of $10 \times 9 \times 8 = 720$ permutations. (**A**) is correct.

Lesson 8

29. B

n is the number of teams, so $n = 8$.

k is the number of teams at a time, so $k = 2$.

$$n^c k = \frac{n!}{(n-k)!k!}$$

$$8^c 2 = \frac{8!}{(8-2)!2!}$$

$$= \frac{8!}{6!2!}$$

$$= \frac{8 \times 7 \times 6!}{6!2!}$$

$$= \frac{8 \times 7}{2 \times 1}$$

$$= \frac{56}{2}$$

$$= 28, \text{ so (B) is correct.}$$

CHAPTER 5

Geometry

Lesson 1: **Supplementary, Vertical and Corresponding Angles**

LEARNING OBJECTIVES

After this lesson, you will be able to:

- Calculate the value of complementary and supplementary angles
- Calculate the value of vertical and corresponding angles

Complementary angles:

a°

b°

$a + b = 90$

Supplementary angles:

c° d°

$c + d = 180$

Vertical angles:

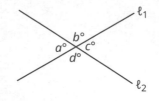

Corresponding angles:

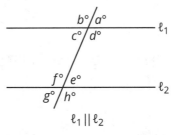

$$\ell_1 \parallel \ell_2$$

1. Find the measures, in degrees, of angles *GEF* and *DEG*.

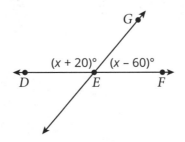

    (A) 30° and 150°

    (B) 50° and 110°

    (C) 50° and 130°

    (D) 90° and 170°

    (E) 110° and 130°

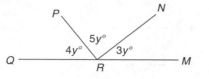

2. What is the degree measure of angle *PRM* shown?

[   ] degrees

3. Lines *m* and *n* are parallel lines cut by a transversal, *l*.

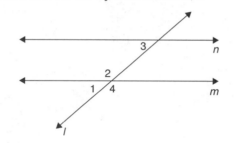

Quantity A	**Quantity B**
$\angle 1 + \angle 2$	$\angle 3 + \angle 4$

(A) Quantity A is greater.

(B) Quantity B is greater.

(C) The two quantities are equal.

(D) The relationship cannot be determined from the information given.

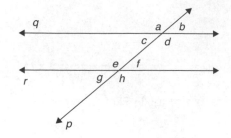

4. Lines *q* and *r* in the figure shown are parallel lines cut by transversal *p*. What is the sum of the measure of angles *a*, *d*, *f*, and *g* in degrees?

    ┌─────────────────┐ degrees
    └─────────────────┘

Try These at Home

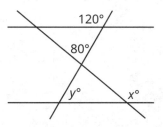

Lines *p* and *q* are parallel

5.
Quantity A	Quantity B
$x + y$	180

Ⓐ Quantity A is greater.

Ⓑ Quantity B is greater.

Ⓒ The two quantities are equal.

Ⓓ The relationship cannot be determined from the information given.

Lesson 2: **Interior Angles of a Triangle**

LEARNING OBJECTIVES

After this lesson, you will be able to:

- Given two interior angles of a triangle, calculate the third
- Recognize isosceles and equilateral triangles

Sum of the Interior Angles of a Triangle:

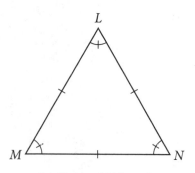

Equilateral Triangle

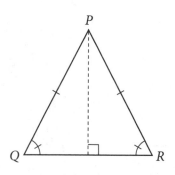

Isosceles Triangle

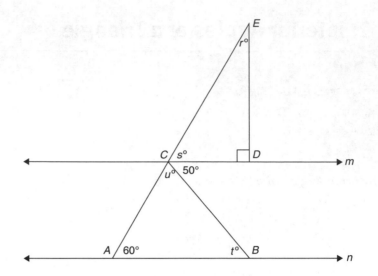

6.   In the figure shown, line *m* is parallel to line *n*. What is the value of *s* − 2*r*?

[   ]

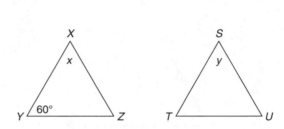

7.   In the triangles above, *XY* = *XZ* and *ST* = *TU* = *SU*.

Quantity A	**Quantity B**
x	*y*

   (A) Quantity A is greater.

   (B) Quantity B is greater.

   (C) The two quantities are equal.

   (D) The relationship cannot be determined from the information given.

Try These at Home

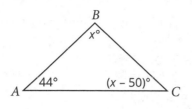

8.

Quantity A	**Quantity B**
The length of side *AB*	The length of side *BC*

Ⓐ Quantity A is greater.

Ⓑ Quantity B is greater.

Ⓒ The two quantities are equal.

Ⓓ The relationship cannot be determined from the information given.

9. In triangle *ABC*, angle *A* measures seven degrees less than half the measure of angle *B*. If angle *C* measures 49°, then what is the measure of angle *A* in degrees?

Lesson 3: **Area and Perimeter of a Triangle**

LEARNING OBJECTIVES

After this lesson, you will be able to:

- Calculate the area of a triangle
- Calculate the perimeter of a polygon

Area of a triangle: $A = \frac{1}{2}bh$

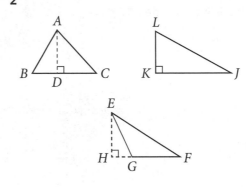

Perimeter of a Polygon = sum of its sides

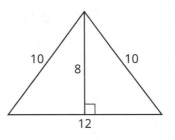

Area:

Perimeter:

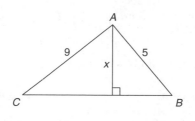

10. The area of triangle *ABC* is 6*x*. What is the perimeter of triangle *ABC*?

(A) 12

(B) 17

(C) 20

(D) 25

(E) 26

Try These at Home

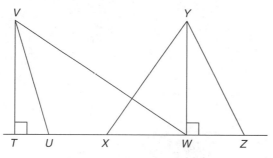

11. The area of triangle *UVW* is greater than the area of triangle *XYZ*.

$$UX = WZ$$

Quantity A	**Quantity B**
TV	*YW*

(A) Quantity A is greater.

(B) Quantity B is greater.

(C) The two quantities are equal.

(D) The relationship cannot be determined from the information given.

12. An equilateral triangle has three equal sides and three equal interior angles. The height of an equilateral triangle is $\frac{\sqrt{3}}{2}s$, where s is the length of a side. The length of each side of equilateral triangle ABC is $4\sqrt{3}$.

Quantity A	**Quantity B**
The perimeter of $\triangle ABC$ in cm	The area of $\triangle ABC$ in cm^2

(A) Quantity A is greater.

(B) Quantity B is greater.

(C) The two quantities are equal.

(D) The relationship cannot be determined from the information given.

Lesson 4: **Triangle Inequality Theorem**

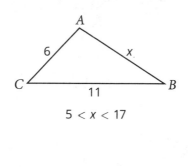

$$5 < x < 17$$

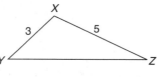

13. In the figure shown, which of the following could be the length of *YZ*?

    Indicate <u>all</u> such lengths.

    A 2
    B 3
    C 5
    D 8
    E 9

14. The length of one side of a triangle is 12. The length of another side is 18. Which of the following could be the perimeter of the triangle?

Indicate <u>all</u> such perimeters.

- [A] 30
- [B] 36
- [C] 44
- [D] 48
- [E] 60

Try These at Home

15. Two sides of a triangle are 17 cm and 8 cm in length. Which of the following CANNOT be the length of the third side?

- (A) 9 cm
- (B) 12 cm
- (C) 17 cm
- (D) 20 cm
- (E) 24 cm

Lesson 5: **Pythagorean Theorem**

Pythagorean Theorem: $a^2 + b^2 = c^2$

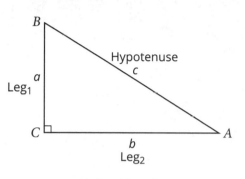

Right Triangle

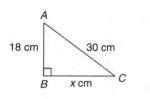

16. What is the area of triangle *ABC* in square centimeters?

[_____] square centimeters

17. What is the value of *x* in the triangle shown?

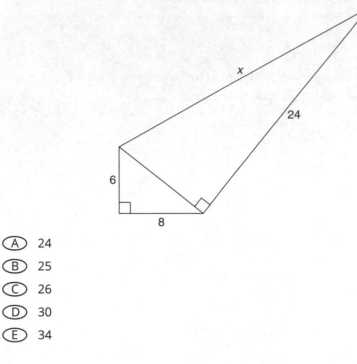

(A) 24

(B) 25

(C) 26

(D) 30

(E) 34

Try These at Home

18.

Quantity A	**Quantity B**
The hypotenuse of a right triangle with leg lengths 7 and 24	25

(A) Quantity A is greater.

(B) Quantity B is greater.

(C) The two quantities are equal.

(D) The relationship cannot be determined from the information given.

19. An isosceles triangle has sides of *r*, *r*, and 1.2*r*. What is the area of the triangle?

(A) $0.36r^2$

(B) $0.4r^2$

(C) $0.48r^2$

(D) $0.6r^2$

(E) $0.64r^2$

Lesson 6: **45–45–90 and 30–60–90 Triangles**

LEARNING OBJECTIVE

After this lesson, you will be able to:

- Given the length of one side of a 45-45-90 or 30-60-90 triangle, calculate the lengths of the other two sides

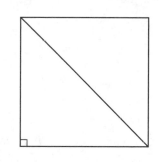

Square divided into 45-45-90 Right Triangles

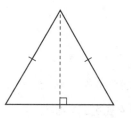

Equilateral Triangle divided into 30-60-90 Right Triangles

20. The perimeter of a square is 48 inches. The length, in inches, of its diagonal is

 (A) $6\sqrt{2}$

 (B) $8\sqrt{2}$

 (C) $12\sqrt{2}$

 (D) $24\sqrt{2}$

 (E) $48\sqrt{2}$

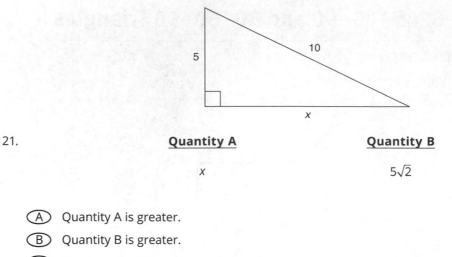

21.

Quantity A	Quantity B
x	$5\sqrt{2}$

   (A) Quantity A is greater.

   (B) Quantity B is greater.

   (C) The two quantities are equal.

   (D) The relationship cannot be determined from the information given.

Try These at Home

22.

Quantity A	Quantity B
The area of a triangle with sides 6, 8, and 10	The area of an equilateral triangle with side 8

   (A) Quantity A is greater.

   (B) Quantity B is greater.

   (C) The two quantities are equal.

   (D) The relationship cannot be determined from the information given.

23. Jessica and Earl are creating decorations for a party by cutting triangles out of $8\frac{1}{2}$ inch by 11 inch sheets of construction paper. Jessica is cutting out equilateral triangles and Earl is cutting out 45-45-90 isosceles triangles. Both persons create the largest possible triangles they can given the limitations of their shapes.

To the nearest square inch, how much greater is the area of each triangle that Earl is making than the one that Jessica is making?

(A) The areas are equal

(B) 2 in²

(C) 4 in²

(D) 5 in²

(E) 8 in²

Lesson 7: **Area of a Parallelogram**

LEARNING OBJECTIVE

After this lesson, you will be able to:

• Calculate the area of a parallelogram

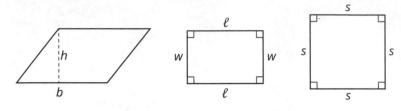

Parallelogram, Rectangle, Square

Area of a Parallelogram: $A = bh$

Area of a Rectangle: $A = lw$

Area of a Square: $A = s^2$

24. The following figure shows three squares and a triangle. What is the area of square A?

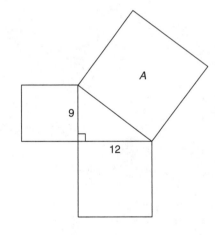

- (A) 108
- (B) 169
- (C) 225
- (D) 450
- (E) 504

25. What is the area of the rectangle shown?

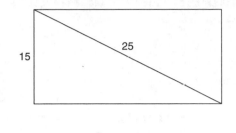

    (A) 150

    (B) 300

    (C) 375

    (D) 400

    (E) 625

Try These at Home

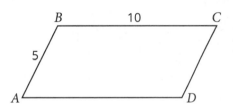

Parallelogram ABCD is not a rectangle

26.

Quantity A	**Quantity B**
Area of the parallelogram	50

    (A) Quantity A is greater.

    (B) Quantity B is greater.

    (C) The two quantities are equal.

    (D) The relationship cannot be determined from the information given.

Lesson 8: **Sum of the Interior Angles of a Polygon**

Formula for the sum of the interior angles of a polygon: $(n - 2)(180)$

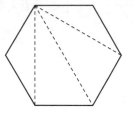

27. The sum of the interior angles of a regular polygon is less than 540°. Which could be the polygon?

Indicate all such polygons.

A triangle

B quadrilateral

C pentagon

D hexagon

Try These at Home

polygon *P* has *n* sides

polygon *Q* has 2 fewer sides than polygon *P*

$n \geq 5$

28.

Quantity A	Quantity B
The average measure of an interior angle in polygon *Q*	$\dfrac{180n}{n-2} - \dfrac{700}{n-2}$

(A) Quantity A is greater.

(B) Quantity B is greater.

(C) The two quantities are equal.

(D) The relationship cannot be determined from the information given.

Lesson 9: **Area and Circumference of a Circle**

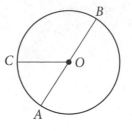

Area of a Circle: $A = \pi r^2$

Circumference of a Circle: $C = 2\pi r$

29. The area of a circle is 36π square meters. What is the circumference of the circle?

  (A) 36 m

  (B) 12π m

  (C) 48 m

  (D) 36π m

  (E) 144 m

30. The diameter of a circle is 12 feet. What is the area of the circle?

  (A) 6π ft^2

  (B) 36 ft^2

  (C) 12π ft^2

  (D) 144 ft^2

  (E) 36π ft^2

31.

Quantity A	Quantity B
The number of square units in the area of a circle with a radius of 4	The number of units in the circumference of a circle with a radius of 8

(A) Quantity A is greater.

(B) Quantity B is greater.

(C) The two quantities are equal.

(D) The relationship cannot be determined from the information given.

Try These at Home

32. Circle A has an area of 9π. Circle B has an area of 49π. If the circles intersect at exactly one point, which of the following could be the distance from the center of circle A to the center of circle B?

(A) 6

(B) 10

(C) 21

(D) 29

(E) 58

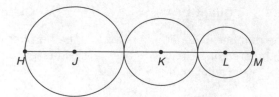

33. In the figure shown, *J*, *K*, and *L* are the centers of the three circles. The radius of the circle with center *J* is four times the radius of the circle with center *L*, and the radius of the circle with center *J* is two times the radius of the circle with center *K*. If the sum of the areas of the three circles is 525π square units, what is the measure, in units, of *JL*?

- (A) 35
- (B) 45
- (C) 50
- (D) 65
- (E) 70

Lesson 10: **Multiple Figures**

34. In the figure shown, the hypotenuse of the triangle coincides with the diameter of the semicircle. What is the circumference of the semicircle?

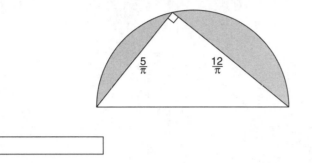

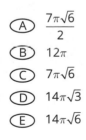

35. What is the circumference of the semicircle in the figure shown?

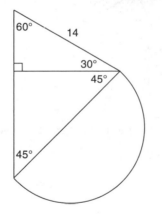

(A) $\dfrac{7\pi\sqrt{6}}{2}$

(B) 12π

(C) $7\pi\sqrt{6}$

(D) $14\pi\sqrt{3}$

(E) $14\pi\sqrt{6}$

36. A square is inscribed inside a shaded circle, as shown. The circumference of the circle is $6\pi\sqrt{2}$. What is the area of the shaded region?

Ⓐ $12\pi - 6\sqrt{2}$

Ⓑ $12\pi - 18$

Ⓒ $18\pi - 6$

Ⓓ $18\pi - 36$

Ⓔ $36\pi - 18$

Try These at Home

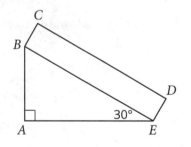

37. Quadrilateral *BCDE* is a rectangle. The length of *DE* is *z* and the length of *AB* is $z\sqrt{3}$.

Quantity A	Quantity B
The area of triangle *ABE*	The area of rectangle *BCDE*

Ⓐ Quantity A is greater.

Ⓑ Quantity B is greater.

Ⓒ The two quantities are equal.

Ⓓ The relationship cannot be determined from the information given.

38. Triangle *ABC* is an equilateral triangle inscribed in a circle. The length of each minor arc between vertices of the triangle is 4π. What is the area of $\triangle ABC$?

   (A) $12\sqrt{3}$
   (B) $12\sqrt{6}$
   (C) 36
   (D) $27\sqrt{3}$
   (E) 48

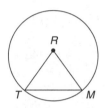

39. Equilateral triangle *RMT* has one vertex at the center of a circle. Its other vertices lie on the circle. The radius of the circle is 10. What is the ratio of the length of minor arc *TM* to the length of segment *TM*?

   (A) $3:\pi$
   (B) $10\pi:3$
   (C) $10:3\pi$
   (D) $\pi:3$
   (E) $10:3$

Lesson 11: **Uniform Solids**

LEARNING OBJECTIVES

After this lesson, you will be able to:

● Calculate the surface area of uniform solids
● Calculate the volume of uniform solids

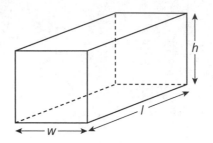

Rectangular Solid

Surface area of a rectangular solid: $SA = 2(wl + hl + hw)$

Volume of a rectangular solid: $V = lwh$

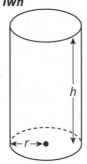

Cylinder

Surface Area of a Cylinder: $SA = 2\pi rh + 2\pi r^2$

Volume of a Cylinder: $V = \pi r^2 h$

40. A cylinder has a surface area of 22π. If the cylinder has a height of 10, what is its radius?

    (A) $\frac{1}{2}$

    (B) 1

    (C) 2.2

    (D) π

    (E) 4

41. The cylinders in the figure shown have the same volume. What is *h*?

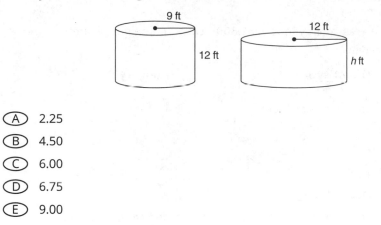

- Ⓐ 2.25
- Ⓑ 4.50
- Ⓒ 6.00
- Ⓓ 6.75
- Ⓔ 9.00

42. The surface area of a cube is 96 square units.

Quantity A	**Quantity B**
The volume of the cube	256

- Ⓐ Quantity A is greater.
- Ⓑ Quantity B is greater.
- Ⓒ The two quantities are equal.
- Ⓓ The relationship cannot be determined from the information given.

Try These at Home

43. The total surface area of a cylinder is $1,800\pi$ cm^2. The height of the cylinder is three times its radius.

Quantity A	**Quantity B**
The volume of the cylinder	4×10^4 cm^3

   Ⓐ Quantity A is greater.

   Ⓑ Quantity B is greater.

   Ⓒ The two quantities are equal.

   Ⓓ The relationship cannot be determined from the information given.

44. A cube has edges 10 cm long. What is the distance from any corner on the bottom of the cube to the center of the top face of the cube?

   Ⓐ $5\sqrt{3}$

   Ⓑ $5\sqrt{6}$

   Ⓒ $6\sqrt{5}$

   Ⓓ $10\sqrt{2}$

   Ⓔ 20

Lesson 12: Coordinate Geometry

Slope Formula: $m = \dfrac{(y_2 - y_1)}{(x_2 - x_1)}$

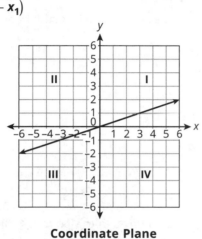

Coordinate Plane

45. What is the slope of the line that passes through the points (4, 8) and (−1, −2)?

46. What is the slope of the line represented by the equation $y = 8x + 3$?

47. Line *m* on a coordinate plane can be defined by the equation $-2x + 3y = 6$.

<table>
<tr><td>**Quantity A**</td><td>**Quantity B**</td></tr>
<tr><td>The slope of a line parallel to line *m*</td><td>The slope of a line perpendicular to line *m*</td></tr>
</table>

- (A) Quantity A is greater.
- (B) Quantity B is greater.
- (C) The two quantities are equal.
- (D) The relationship cannot be determined from the information given.

48. A line whose slope is $-\frac{1}{4}$ passes through the points (4, 3) and (*x*, 1). What is the value of *x*?

- (A) −12
- (B) −4
- (C) 0
- (D) 8
- (E) 12

49. A line is represented by the equation $4x + 3y = 12$.

<table>
<tr><th>Quantity A</th><th>Quantity B</th></tr>
<tr><td>The value of the x-intercept of the line</td><td>The value of the y-intercept of the line</td></tr>
</table>

   Ⓐ Quantity A is greater.

   Ⓑ Quantity B is greater.

   Ⓒ The two quantities are equal.

   Ⓓ The relationship cannot be determined from the information given.

Try These at Home

50. If $x = \left(y^2 - 1\right)\left(y^2 - 5y + 6\right)$, then which of the following is NOT a y-intercept of the graph of this equation?

   Ⓐ −1

   Ⓑ 0

   Ⓒ 1

   Ⓓ 2

   Ⓔ 3

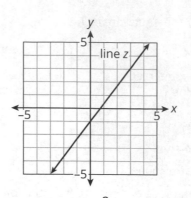

51. In the figure above, line z has a slope of $\frac{3}{2}$. Line a is perpendicular to line z and passes through the point (3, 2).

Quantity A	**Quantity B**
The x-intercept of line a	The y-intercept of line a

   Ⓐ Quantity A is greater.

   Ⓑ Quantity B is greater.

   Ⓒ The two quantities are equal.

   Ⓓ The relationship cannot be determined from the information given.

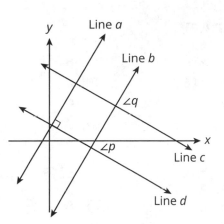

52. Line *a* is defined by $2y = x + 4$; line *b* is defined by $x = 2y + 4$; and line *c* is defined by $y = 12 - \dfrac{11}{5}x$.

Quantity A	Quantity B
The measure of $\angle p$	The measure of $\angle q$

Ⓐ Quantity A is greater.

Ⓑ Quantity B is greater.

Ⓒ The two quantities are equal.

Ⓓ The relationship cannot be determined from the information given.

Geometry Answer Key

1. **C**	15. **A**	29. **B**	42. **B**
2. **120**	16. **216**	30. **E**	43. **B**
3. **C**	17. **C**	31. **C**	44. **B**
4. **360**	18. **C**	32. **B**	45. **2**
5. **A**	19. **C**	33. **B**	46. **8**
6. **0**	20. **C**	34. $\frac{13}{2}$	47. **A**
7. **C**	21. **A**	35. **A**	48. **E**
8. **B**	22. **B**	36. **D**	49. **B**
9. **39**	23. **D**	37. **B**	50. **B**
10. **E**	24. **C**	38. **D**	51. **A**
11. **A**	25. **B**	39. **D**	52. **B**
12. **C**	26. **B**	40. **B**	
13. **B, C**	27. **A, B**	41. **D**	
14. **C, D**	28. **B**		

Answers and Explanations

Geometry Try This At Home Explanations

Lesson 1

5.   A

By the rules of parallel lines, y is supplementary to $120°$ because it's equal to the corresponding angle that is supplementary to $120°$, so $y = 180 - 120 = 60$. By the rules of vertical angles, the top angle of the triangle that has y in it is 80. Thus, the final angle of that triangle—which is supplementary to x—is $180 - 80 - 60 = 40$. This means that $x = 180 - 40 = 140$, and $x + y = 140 + 60 = 200$. Because $200 > 180$, **(A)** is correct.

Lesson 2

8.   B

The sum of the measures of the interior angles of a triangle is $180°$, so $x + (x - 50) + 44 = 180$. Combine like terms to get $2x - 6 = 180$. So, $2x = 186$ and $x = 93$. This means that the angle at vertex C measures $93° - 50° = 43°$, making it the smallest of the three interior angles. The side opposite the smallest angle in a triangle is the shortest. The side that is opposite vertex C is AB, so that is the shortest side. The length of side BC is greater than the length of side AB, and **(B)** is correct.

9.   39

Let x be the measure of angle B. Then angle A measures $(0.5)x - 7$. Given that angle C measures $49°$ and that the angles of a triangle always add to $180°$, the following is true:

$$x + [(0.5)x - 7] + 49 = 180°$$

$$1.5x + 42 = 180°$$

$$1.5x = 138°$$

$$x = 92°$$

Note that x is the measure of angle B, but the question asks for the measure of angle A. Take half of x and subtract 7:

$$A = (0.5)x - 7 = (0.5)(92) - 7 = 46 - 7 = \mathbf{39}$$

Lesson 3

11.   A

You are given that the area of triangle UVW is greater than the area of triangle XYZ. Make note of the other information conveyed by the diagram. The height of each triangle is indicated by the right angle box in each triangle, but no other information is given about the heights. Notice that the bases of the triangles are overlapping in the diagram; they have segment XW in common. Segment UW is the base of triangle UVW, and segment XZ is the base of triangle XYZ.

It may be helpful to draw the triangles separately to keep the information given about triangle UVW and triangle XYZ organized as you apply the area formula to each one.

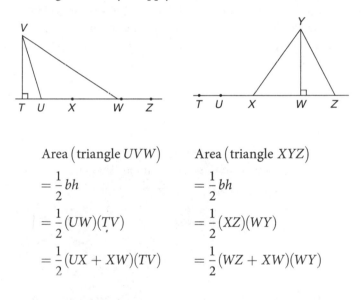

Area (triangle UVW)

$$= \frac{1}{2} bh$$

$$= \frac{1}{2}(UW)(TV)$$

$$= \frac{1}{2}(UX + XW)(TV)$$

Area (triangle XYZ)

$$= \frac{1}{2} bh$$

$$= \frac{1}{2}(XZ)(WY)$$

$$= \frac{1}{2}(WZ + XW)(WY)$$

The key to making the correct comparison is recognizing that the bases of the triangles are the same length. You are given that $UX = WZ$ and certainly $XW = XW$. If the area of triangle UVW is greater, as the question states, it is because its height is greater. Therefore, $TV > YW$ and the answer is **(A)**.

12. C

Quantity A, the perimeter of $\triangle ABC$, is the sum of the side lengths, which is $4\sqrt{3} + 4\sqrt{3} + 4\sqrt{3} = 12\sqrt{3}$ cm. Quantity B, the area of $\triangle ABC$, can be calculated using the formula $A = \frac{1}{2}bh$. The height of this triangle is $\frac{\sqrt{3}}{2}s = \frac{\sqrt{3}}{2}\left(4\sqrt{3}\right) = \frac{4(3)}{2} = 6$. Thus, the area of $\triangle ABC$ is $\frac{1}{2}\left(4\sqrt{3}\right)(6) = 12\sqrt{3}$ cm^2. The two quantities are equal, so **(C)** is correct.

Lesson 4

15. A

The triangle inequality theorem states that the length of each side of a triangle must be less than the sum of the lengths of the other two sides and greater than the difference in the lengths of the other two sides. Therefore, the length of the unknown side in this question must be less than $17 + 8$, which is 25, and greater than $17 - 8$, which is 9. All of the choices are less than 25, but (A) is not greater than 9, so **(A)** is correct.

Lesson 5

18. C

You can use the Pythagorean theorem, $a^2 + b^2 = c^2$, to find the hypotenuse of the right triangle. The letters a and b represent the legs, so $7^2 + 24^2 = c^2$.

$$49 + 576 = c^2$$
$$625 = c^2$$
$$25 = c$$

Solving the equation for c, you get $c = 25$. So Quantity A and Quantity B are equal. The answer is **(C)**.

19. C

The height of the isosceles triangle splits the triangle into two right triangles with a base of $\frac{1}{2}(1.2r) = 0.6r$ and a hypotenuse of r. Solve for h using the Pythagorean theorem: $(0.6r)^2 + h^2 = r^2$. So, $h^2 = r^2 - 0.36r^2 = 0.64r^2$. Thus, $h = \sqrt{0.64r^2} = 0.8r$. (You might have noticed that this is a 3:4:5 triangle with a multiplier of 0.2, which makes the ratio (0.6):(0.8):(1.0).) Remember that you calculated the height using a base of $0.6r$. The base of the full triangle is $1.2r$, so the area, $\frac{1}{2}bh$, is $\frac{1}{2}(1.2r)(0.8r) = 0.48r^2$.

Lesson 6

22. B

A 6:8:10 triangle is a multiple of a 3:4:5 special right triangle. Because this is a right triangle with legs of 6 and 8, the base and height of the triangle are 6 and 8, and you can plug these into the area formula: $A = \frac{1}{2}(6)(8) = 24$.

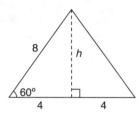

An equilateral triangle has three equal angles of 60°. Hence, when you drop the height as shown in the figure, you bisect the angle at the top, creating two 30-60-90 triangles. The ratios of a 30-60-90 triangle are $1 : \sqrt{3} : 2$, so the height, h, of the equilateral triangle is $4\sqrt{3}$. The area is $A = \frac{1}{2}(8)\left(4\sqrt{3}\right) = 16\sqrt{3}$. You can divide both quantities by 8 so that Quantity A is equal to 3 and Quantity B is equal to $2\sqrt{3}$. If you square both sides to make them look more alike, then Quantity A is 3^2, which equals 9. Quantity B is 4×3, which equals 12. Quantity B is larger, so the correct answer is **(B)**.

23. D

Determine the area of the largest triangle each person can make and subtract the area of Jessica's triangle from the area of Earl's. The question specifies that each person makes the largest possible triangle, so check various possible orientations of the triangles.

Start with Jessica's equilateral triangles. Check to see if using the 11 inch dimension as a side of an equilateral triangle will work. The height of such a triangle can be determined by splitting it into two 30-60-90 triangles. The long leg of these will be the height of the equilateral triangle. Using the side ratios of this pattern triangle, $1:\sqrt{3}:2$, multiplied by half the side length of the equilateral triangle, the height would be $\frac{11}{2}\sqrt{3} \approx 9.5$. (If you didn't recall the side ratios, you could have used the Pythagorean theorem.) Since the paper is only $8\frac{1}{2}$ inches wide, Jessica cannot cut this triangle from the given paper; she'll make $8\frac{1}{2}$ inch equilateral triangles instead. The height of these triangles will be $\frac{8.5}{2}\sqrt{3} \approx 7.361$ and the area will be $\frac{1}{2}(8.5)(7.361) \approx 31.284$ square inches.

If Earl uses the 11 inch side for the hypotenuse of his isosceles triangle, the height will divide it into two smaller 45-45-90 triangles, so the height and half the hypotenuse will be equal legs of $\frac{11}{2} = 5.5$ inches. If he uses the 8.5 inch side and 8.5 inches of the 11 inch side as legs, that will be a larger triangle with an area of $\frac{1}{2}(8.5)(8.5) = 36.125$. Therefore, Earl's triangles will be approximately $36.125 - 31.284 = 4.841$ square inches greater in area than Jessica's. This rounds to 5, which is (**D**).

Lesson 7

26. B

The formula for the area of a parallelogram is *base × height*, where the height is perpendicular to the base, and, since the parallelogram is not a rectangle, the height needs to be drawn in. Draw in a perpendicular line from the base of the parallelogram to form a right triangle:

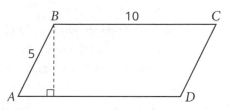

Parallelogram *ABCD* is not a rectangle

If 5 is the hypotenuse of the right triangle formed by the height, then the height must be less than 5 (the hypotenuse is always the longest side of a triangle). If the height is less than 5, then the area of the parallelogram must be less than 50, and (**B**) is correct.

Lesson 8

28. B

The sum of the interior angles of a polygon is $(x - 2)(180)$, where x is the polygon's number of sides. Polygon Q has $n - 2$ sides, so the sum of the interior angles of polygon Q is found as follows:

$$[(n - 2) - 2](180)$$

$$= (n - 4)(180)$$

$$= 180n - 720$$

Recall that *Average = Sum ÷ Number*. Quantity A therefore equals $\frac{180n - 720}{n - 2} = \frac{180n}{n - 2} - \frac{720}{n - 2}$. This is identical to Quantity B, except that Quantity B has 700 instead of 720. Because a smaller number is subtracted in Quantity B than in Quantity A, Quantity B is greater and (**B**) is correct.

Lesson 9

32. B

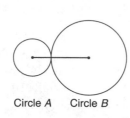

Circle A   Circle B

Draw a figure similar to the one shown to help visualize the information given. Recall that the area of a circle is πr^2. The area of circle A is 9π. So, $9 = r^2$, and $r = 3$. So the radius of circle A is 3. The area of circle B is 49π. So, $49 = r^2$, and $r = 7$. So the radius of circle B is 7. If the circles intersect at exactly one point, this means that the two circles are next to each other just touching each other (i.e., they are tangent to each other). To find the distance from the center of circle A to the center of circle B, simply add their radii: $3 + 7 = 10$. The correct answer is (**B**).

33. B

To solve this problem, use the formula for the area of a circle, $A = \pi r^2$, where r is the radius. Before you find the length of JL, you have to find the length of the radius of each circle. Since the radii of circles J and K are four and two times the radius of circle L, respectively, you can set up the equation, where r represents the radius of circle L:

$$\pi(4r)^2 + \pi(2r)^2 + \pi(r)^2 = 525\pi$$
$$16r^2\pi + 4r^2\pi + r^2\pi = 525\pi$$
$$21r^2\pi = 525\pi$$
$$r^2 = 25$$
$$r = 5$$

If the radius of circle L is 5 units, the radius of circle K is 10 units, and the radius of circle J is 20 units. So the length of line segment JL is composed of the radius of circle L, the diameter of circle K, and the radius of circle J. This equals $20 + 10 + 10 + 5$ or 45 units. The correct choice is (**B**).

Lesson 10

37. B

The key to determining the areas of the two polygons is calculating the length of the common side, BE. Since ABE is a 30-60-90 right triangle, the side ratios of which are $1:\sqrt{3}:2$, the length of BE is twice the length of AB, or $2z\sqrt{3}$, and the length of AE is $z\sqrt{3}(\sqrt{3}) = 3z$. The formula for the area of a triangle is $\frac{1}{2}bh$, so the area of ABE is $\left(\frac{1}{2}\right)(z\sqrt{3})(3z) = 1\frac{1}{2}z^2\sqrt{3}$. The area of a rectangle is length times width, so the area of rectangle BCDE, which is Quantity B, is $2z\sqrt{3} \times z = 2z^2\sqrt{3}$. Therefore, (**B**) is correct.

38. D

Use the information given to determine the dimensions and angles you need to find the area of $\triangle ABC$. Since the interior angles of an equilateral triangle are $60°$, apply the central angle theorem to determine that the central angle of the each arc is $2 \times 60° = 120°$. Find the circumference of the circle: $\frac{120°}{360°} = \frac{4\pi}{C}$, so the circumference is 12π. Since $C = 2\pi r$, the radius is 6. Alternatively, you could have reasoned that there are 3 equal arcs of 4π, so the circumference is $3 \times 4\pi = 12\pi$.

Draw a sketch and add some lines to help subdivide the figure into smaller components to utilize the limited information given.

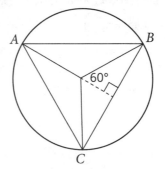

Draw radii from the center of the circle to points A, B, and C to create three smaller congruent triangles. Draw a perpendicular from the center of the circle to side BC. This bisects the central angle ($120°$), so it creates two 30-60-90 triangles with the radius as their hypotenuses. Since the side ratio of such a triangle is $1:\sqrt{3}:2$ and the radius is 6, the sides of the triangles are $3:3\sqrt{3}:6$. The area of one of these small triangles is $\frac{1}{2}bh = \frac{1}{2}(3)(3\sqrt{3})$. The inscribed equilateral triangle is composed of 6 such triangles, so its area is $(6)\frac{1}{2}(3)\left(3\sqrt{3}\right) = 27\sqrt{3}$, which is **(D)**.

39. D

Because the triangle is equilateral, it has three 60° angles, and all sides have length 10. The length of minor arc *TM* is $\frac{60}{360}$ the length of the entire circle. So, arc *TM* has length $\frac{60}{360} \times 2\pi r = \frac{1}{6} \times 2\pi(10) = \frac{10\pi}{3}$. The length of segment *TM* is 10. The ratio of the length of arc *TM* to the length of segment *TM* is $\frac{3}{10} = \frac{10\pi}{3} \times \frac{1}{10} = \frac{\pi}{3}$.

Lesson 11

43. B

The surface area of a cylinder is $2\pi r^2 + 2(\pi rh)$. Since the height is 3 times the radius, substitute $3r$ for h and set the formula equal to the given surface area: $1800\pi = 2\pi r^2 + 2\pi r(3r)$. Divide both sides by the common factor of 2π and combine the terms on the right side to get $900 = 4r^2$. So $r^2 = 225$ and $r = 15$. Since $h = 3r$, the height of the cylinder is 45.

The formula for the volume of a cylinder is $\pi r^2 h$. Plug in the values of r and h to yield $\pi(15)^2(45) = 10{,}125\pi$, which is the value of Quantity A. The value of Quantity B converts to 40,000. Since π is a bit more than 3, 40,000 is greater than $10{,}125\pi$. **(B)** is correct.

44. B

Draw a sketch to help visualize this situation.

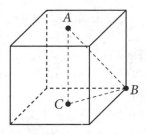

When solving three-dimensional problems such as this, subdivide the information you need into two-dimensional components. The point *C* at the center of the bottom of the cube will be directly below point *A* at the center of the top as shown by line *AC* in the sketch. Line *AB*, meanwhile, connects point *A* to point *B* at the bottom right corner of the cube. (Any corner will do since cubes are symmetrical.) The length of line *AB* is the dimension that the question asks you to find. Line *BC* connects the bottom corner to the center of the bottom of the cube. These three lines form a right triangle in a plane. Line *AC* is the length of a side of the cube, 10, but you'll need to calculate the length of line *BC*.

Since point *C* is at the center of the bottom side of the cube, *BC* is half the diagonal of the bottom of the cube. Since that diagonal creates a 45-45-90 right triangle, which has the side ratio of $1:1:\sqrt{2}$, the length of the diagonal is $10\sqrt{2}$. Therefore, the length of *BC* is $5\sqrt{2}$. So, line *AB* is the hypotenuse of a right triangle with legs of 10 and $5\sqrt{2}$. Solve for *AB* using the Pythagorean theorem: $AB^2 = 10^2 + \left(5\sqrt{2}\right)^2 = 100 + 50$. So $AB^2 = 150$, and $AB = \sqrt{150} = \sqrt{25 \times 6} = 5\sqrt{6}$. **(B)** is correct.

Lesson 12

50. B

Since y-intercepts occur at points where $x = 0$, don't attempt to restate this equation; just find the points where $x = 0$. Factor the right side using reverse FOIL to get $x = \left[(y+1)(y-1)\right]\left[(y-2)(y-3)\right]$. If any one of the terms on the right side equals 0, then $x = 0$. The first term is 0 when $y = -1$, the second when $y = 1$, the third when $y = 2$, and the fourth when $y = 3$. The only choice that is not one of these is (**B**).

Alternatively, you could have backsolved by plugging in the choices as the value of y to see if $x = 0$. Only $y = 0$, which is $x = (-1)(6)$, does not result in $x = 0$.

51. A

Define line z in standard $y = mx + b$ format. The question provides the slope, $\frac{3}{2}$, and you can read the y-intercept, -1, from the figure. So, the equation for line z is $y = \frac{3}{2}x - 1$. The slope of any line perpendicular to this line is the negative reciprocal of the slope of line z, or $-\frac{2}{3}$. Since line a passes through the point $(3,2)$, plug those values into the slope-intercept equation and solve for b, which is the y-intercept: $2 = \left(-\frac{2}{3}\right)(3) + b$

$$2 = -2 + b$$
$$4 = b$$

So the y-intercept of line a, which is Quantity B, is 4. To get the x-intercept, set y to 0 and solve for x: $0 = -\frac{2}{3}x + 4$

$$\frac{2x}{3} = 4$$
$$2x = 12$$
$$x = 6$$

The x-intercept, which is Quantity A, is 6. (**A**) is correct.

52. B

Convert all the equations for the lines to $y = mx + b$ format. Line a is $2y = x + 4$, so $y = \frac{x}{2} + 2$. Convert the equation for line b so that y is a function of x: if $x = 2y + 4$, then $2y = x - 4$ and $y = \frac{x}{2} - 2$. Finally, rearrange the terms for line c: $y = 12 - \frac{11}{5}x = -\frac{11}{5}x + 12$. Lines a and b appear parallel in the figure. Parallel lines have identical slopes. Since both of these lines have a slope of $\frac{1}{2}$, they are indeed parallel. From the diagram, you can ascertain that line d is a transversal that intersects lines a and b at right angles. Therefore $\angle p$ (Quantity A) is $90°$. In order to compare this to $\angle q$ (Quantity B), you need to know the angles formed by the intersection of lines b and c.

The slope of both lines a and b is $\frac{1}{2}$. Since the slopes of perpendicular lines are negative reciprocals, the slope of line d is $-\left| \frac{1}{\frac{1}{2}} \right| = -2$. The slope of line c is $-\frac{11}{5} = -2\frac{1}{5}$. This is steeper than the slope of line d, so $\angle q$ is greater than $\angle p$.

(**B**) is correct.

PART TWO

Verbal

CHAPTER 6

Short Verbal

Lesson 1: Introduction to the Verbal Section

You'll see two scored Verbal sections, each with 20 questions in 30 minutes.

Recommended Test Day Timing

	Text Completion	Sentence Equivalence	Reading Comprehension
Number of Questions	Approx. 6	Approx. 4	Approx. 10
Time Per Question	1–1.5 minutes	1 minute	1–3 minutes, depending on length, to read the passage and 1 minute to answer each question

Text Completion and Sentence Equivalence questions constitute the Short Verbal question types. You can think of the Verbal section as half Short Verbal and half Reading Comprehension.

Lesson 2: **Kaplan Short Verbal Method: Text Completion**

LEARNING OBJECTIVE

After this lesson, you will be able to:

- Apply the steps of the Short Verbal Method to Text Completion questions

---

THE KAPLAN METHOD

Short Verbal

STEP 1   Read the sentence, looking for clues.

STEP 2   Predict an answer.

STEP 3   Select the best match(es) from among the choices.

STEP 4   Confirm your answer by reading it into the sentence.

---

1.   The diffident toddler was so uncomfortable at the birthday party that he constantly _____ his mother's side.

    (A) strayed from

    (B) fled

    (C) abjured

    (D) cleaved to

    (E) avoided

2.   Having test-driven this car in a variety of realistic conditions and found its performance lackluster at best, I have to say that the maker's sanguine claims are _____.

    (A) understated

    (B) impeccable

    (C) unfounded

    (D) plausible

    (E) mediocre

Lesson 3: **Structural Clues**

Straight-ahead Road Signs	Detour Road Signs
And	But
Since	Despite
Also	Yet
Thus	However
Because	Unless
: (colon)	Rather
Likewise	Although
Moreover	While
Similarly	On the other hand
In addition	Unfortunately
Consequently	Nonetheless
Therefore	Conversely

3. In the world of professional team sports, individual prowess has its place, but ultimately the players are valued chiefly for their _____ qualities.

   (A) ethical
   (B) inspirational
   (C) dispersive
   (D) singular
   (E) collaborative

4. After a destructive, summer-long drought, during which the crops _____ Midwestern farmers did not know whether to welcome or curse the heavy, late-August rains that finally swept through the region, washing away critical topsoil.

Ⓐ acclimated

Ⓑ persevered

Ⓒ languished

Ⓓ plundered

Ⓔ retracted

5. Now that the message of the underground, counterculture youth movement is being (i) _____ by the mass media, many of the movement's followers, once loyal to the cause, have (ii) _____.

Blank (i)		Blank (ii)	
A	reported on	D	defected
B	contradicted	E	retaliated
C	promulgated	F	acquiesced

6. Although he founded an entire magazine about the art of the interview, Warhol was himself a (i) _____ interview subject, revealing little about his life and work and often supplying (ii) _____ answers to straightforward questions.

Blank (i)		Blank (ii)	
A	definitive	D	ominous
B	callow	E	meticulous
C	laconic	F	enigmatic

7. A dictionary that provides the (i) _____ of words—that is, the origin and development of their meanings—offers proof of a (ii) _____ language. Over time, words not only change but sometimes even (iii) _____ their meanings. "Nice," for example, is an instance of such a word. Today it means "agreeable" or "pleasant," whereas in Middle English it meant "stupid" or "ignorant."

Blank (i)		Blank (ii)		Blank (iii)	
A	toxicology	D	nascent	G	reverse
B	etymology	E	living	H	amend
C	taxonomy	F	faltering	I	exchange

Try These at Home

8. Despite the widespread popularity of soy products among American consumers, discussion about the effects of soy on human health remains _____.

    Ⓐ conclusive
    Ⓑ contentious
    Ⓒ preposterous
    Ⓓ enlightening
    Ⓔ fraudulent

9. Although the chairman's new policies cut costs at the time, his strategy was ultimately revealed to be _____, and his lack of foresight crippled the department in the long run.

    Ⓐ vacuous
    Ⓑ myopic
    Ⓒ prescient
    Ⓓ ingenuous
    Ⓔ ingenious

10. In the United Kingdom, a "stately home" is usually a large and impressive (i) _____, often centuries old, composed of many magnificent rooms worthy of noble occupation. Their surroundings match their interiors: such houses are generally set in (ii) _____, well-tended grounds and are likely to look out over (iii) _____ of breathtaking beauty. Luckily, as a by-product of an ever-changing economy, stately homes are now often open to the public.

Blank (i)		Blank (ii)		Blank (iii)	
A	edifice	D	confined	G	veneers
B	architecture	E	mown	H	vignettes
C	apartment	F	expansive	I	vistas

11. In the writer's view, now and then in the (i) _____ of politics, a person of observable integrity and moral strength appears in a way that draws public attention to the central rather than the (ii) _____ matters that affect our lives. Such a person is vital for a number of reasons: he or she cuts through the natural (iii) _____ of competing interests, focuses on key issues, posits realistic solutions, and brings together opponents who might otherwise never agree.

Blank (i)		Blank (ii)		Blank (iii)	
A	existence	D	weaker	G	usefulness
B	hurly-burly	E	confidential	H	distractions
C	practice	F	peripheral	I	succession

12. The development of drama over the centuries has been (i) _____ journey, from the open-air stylized performances of Greek and Roman tragedies and comedies to the more recent "three-walled" room of indoor theater. Yet, much has remained unchanged—actors in costume still (ii) _____ the stage before audiences who willingly suspend their (iii) _____ in order to enter into the "reality" of events created for them.

Blank (i)		Blank (ii)		Blank (iii)	
A	a remarkable	D	strut	G	interest
B	a modest	E	stalk	H	concern
C	an implacable	F	straddle	I	disbelief

Lesson 4: **Advanced Text Completion**

LEARNING OBJECTIVES

After this lesson, you will be able to:

- Make accurate predictions for missing words with subtle structural or context clues
- Apply elimination strategies with tough vocabulary

13. The (i) _____ genius of the late Glenn Gould is (ii) _____ in his imaginative (iii) _____ for piano of Wagner's *Siegfried Idyll*, which the composer originally scored for full orchestra and presented to his wife Cosima on her birthday.

Blank (i)		Blank (ii)		Blank (iii)	
A	unexceptional	D	apparent	G	diminution
B	overrated	E	ineluctable	H	homage
C	unmistakable	F	incommensurate	I	adaptation

14. Although the European Economic Community was established to (i) _____ the economic growth of all its member nations (ii) _____, some express (iii) _____ at what they claim is their unfair burden in maintaining the organization.

Blank (i)		Blank (ii)		Blank (iii)	
A	retard	D	inequitably	G	enthusiasm
B	promote	E	vigorously	H	ennui
C	measure	F	equally	I	resentment

15. Pedagogical studies tend to overlook students' motivation and focus instead on differences in learning styles. However, a teacher's ability to (i) _____ students' passion for a subject is paramount to students' learning. The well-intentioned efforts by (ii) _____ scholars with little teaching experience who design intricate strategies intended to (iii) _____ students' specific struggles are woefully insufficient: they cannot instill enthusiasm.

Blank (i)		Blank (ii)		Blank (iii)	
A	aggrandize	D	saprophytic	G	mitigate
B	foster	E	gregarious	H	exacerbate
C	enervate	F	unseasoned	I	aggravate

16. The ongoing salmon crisis is the result of (i) _____ of problems, among them pollution, introduction of nonnative species, and pesticide use. Such issues speak to decades of (ii) _____ management at the political level. At this point, (iii) _____ solution will require both an understanding of history and foresight of future challenges.

Blank (i)		Blank (ii)		Blank (iii)	
A	a reclamation	D	methodical	G	a sustainable
B	a multitude	E	adequate	H	an exigent
C	an exhibition	F	paltry	I	a conspicuous

17. Such a (i) _____ manuscript must be approached with (ii) _____. Only the most seasoned editor should be considered for the job.

Blank (i)		Blank (ii)	
A	poignant	D	circumspection
B	frivolous	E	creativity
C	labyrinthine	F	fecundity

18. The Perito Moreno Glacier, located inside Glaciers National Park in Patagonia, houses the so-called Curve of the Sighs. This (i) _____ is earned due to the (ii) _____ view of snow-tipped mountains above and icy, slate-hued waters and the foot of the glacier below.

Blank (i)		Blank (ii)	
A	appellation	D	bucolic
B	aphorism	E	calorific
C	benediction	F	panoramic

Try These at Home

19. In the workplace, it is important that employees (i) _____ the (ii) _____ of the company rather than the other way around.

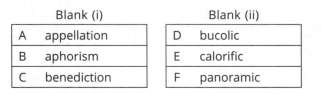

Blank (i)		Blank (ii)	
A	object to	D	standards
B	conform to	E	idiosyncrasies
C	balk at	F	peccadilloes

20. It is hard to believe that the highly (i) _____ game of soccer began many centuries ago as a rowdy (ii) _____ without rules, fought cross-country by entire villages determined to get possession of an inflated pig's bladder.

Blank (i)		Blank (ii)	
A	structured	D	séance
B	pell-mell	E	massacre
C	helter-skelter	F	brawl

21. Ambition is a useful (i) _____ that leads people to great achievement, but it can also be (ii) _____ force, as Shakespeare showed in his tragedy *Macbeth*.

Blank (i)		Blank (ii)	
A	tenet	D	an ersatz
B	indicator	E	a pulsating
C	motivator	F	a destructive

22. The (i) _____ young children were a top priority for their mother and commanded most of her attention. They had such (ii) _____ level of volatile energy that ordinary activities were not enough to keep them occupied for an extended period of time. She devoted herself to channeling their energy into (iii) _____ pursuits.

Blank (i)		Blank (ii)		Blank (iii)	
A	earthy	D	an eclectic	G	salutary
B	froward	E	a pedestrian	H	provocative
C	limpid	F	a robust	I	dour

23. Jurisprudence requires a dispassionate approach on the part of the judge or arbiter. Law and custom require that a definite (i) _____ be made in every case, regardless of how strong the winning argument seems. Therefore, a judge is forced to behave as if a verdict is (ii) _____. This is true even when, in fact, the evidence may not be (iii) _____.

Blank (i)		Blank (ii)		Blank (iii)	
A	deadlock	D	negotiable	G	conclusive
B	dispute	E	irrelevant	H	accessible
C	determination	F	self-evident	I	substantiated

24. As a general rule, feuds between individuals or groups tend to arise in societies that (i) _____ centralized government, because public justice, such as the kind meted out by a strong, centralized authority or sophisticated judicial system, is difficult to (ii) _____. In such societies, it is therefore not surprising that private recourse is more (iii) _____.

Blank (i)	Blank (ii)	Blank (iii)
A espouse	D identify	G objectionable
B lack	E enforce	H prevalent
C affirm	F recognize	I brutal

Lesson 5: **Using Vocabulary Resources**

LEARNING OBJECTIVE

After this lesson, you will be able to:

- Use vocabulary resources effectively

Word Roots

CRED: to believe, to trust

credentials, credible, incredible, incredulous

GEN: birth, creation

carcinogenic, genesis, progeny, regenerate

VOC/VOK: call, word

advocate, avow, vocation, vociferous

Words in Context

Inchoate: not fully formed; disorganized; just coming into being

The ideas expressed in Nietzsche's mature work also appear in an *inchoate* form in his earliest writing.

Words with similar meanings: amorphous, unorganized, incoherent, incomplete, incipient

Word Groups

Criticize/criticism: castigate, diatribe, pillory, revile, tirade

Difficult to understand: abstruse, arcane, obscure, perplexing

Vocabulary-Building Resources

- GRE Pocket Reference
- GRE Flash Cards and App
- GRE Channel: How to Build Your Vocabulary
- Vocabulary notebook

Lesson 6: **Kaplan Short Verbal Method:**
Sentence Equivalence

LEARNING OBJECTIVE

After this lesson, you will be able to:

● Apply the Short Verbal Method to Sentence Equivalence questions

THE KAPLAN METHOD

Short Verbal

STEP 1   Read the sentence, looking for clues.

STEP 2   Predict an answer.

STEP 3   Select the best match(es) from among the choices.

STEP 4   Confirm your answer by reading it into the sentence.

25. Although the report indicated a disturbing rise in obesity, many people, by choosing junk food over nutrition, continue to _____ the problem.

   A   exacerbate

   B   extort

   C   abhor

   D   compound

   E   attenuate

   F   mitigate

26. A notoriously private figure, the actor remained _____ when the paparazzi confronted him about recent rumors that his longtime marriage was on the brink of collapse.

   A   ambivalent

   B   reticent

   C   gregarious

   D   taciturn

   E   pompous

   F   imperious

27. Although the band received a glowing reception during its exhaustive world tour, the much-anticipated debut album met with uniformly _____ reviews.

   A   deprecating

   B   deferential

   C   obsequious

   D   unorthodox

   E   eloquent

   F   disparaging

28. Despite the senator's blatant lies about her role in the scandal, many voters showed their _____ when it came time for reelection.

   A   resilience

   B   fortitude

   C   ignominy

   D   constancy

   E   ambivalence

   F   allegiance

29. Despite being known by the moniker "the accidental president," Gerald Ford was _____ posthumously for actions he took to address both the Vietnam War and the Watergate scandal.

   - [A] emancipated
   - [B] extolled
   - [C] indemnified
   - [D] lauded
   - [E] denigrated
   - [F] belittled

Try These at Home

30. When the patron requested books by an amusing author to help lift her spirits, the librarian suggested Wodehouse, claiming him likely to induce _____ in most readers.

   - [A] lugubriousness
   - [B] mirth
   - [C] poignancy
   - [D] gravity
   - [E] merriment
   - [F] solemnity

31. Because historical reenactors at Renaissance Fairs must maintain high standards of
_____, they eschew any anachronisms, such as watches and cell phones.

    A virtuosity

    B dictation

    C controversy

    D naiveté

    E verisimilitude

    F authenticity

32. The elevated names of hybrid tea roses, which are created by cross-breeding
two types of roses, belie their typically more _____ surroundings: few would
expect to encounter "Madame Caroline Testout" or "Souvenir de Claudius Denoyel"
growing alongside humble daffodils.

    A unexceptional

    B hortatory

    C pedestrian

    D lofty

    E preeminent

    F abstruse

Short Verbal Timed Practice

33. Despite much informed (i) _____ and a great deal of scientific interest and money invested in research on the subject, the precise nature of the relationship between sunspot cycles and the weather on Earth remains (ii) _____.

Blank (i)		Blank (ii)	
A	confusion	D	decisive
B	conjecture	E	elusive
C	evidence	F	clear

34. (i) _____ in crimes committed by juveniles has been noted in recent years. This trend has occurred despite the fact that, over the same period of time, increased attention has been (ii) _____ juvenile delinquency by law enforcement.

Blank (i)		Blank (ii)	
A	A decrease	D	given to
B	An escalation	E	withdrawn from
C	A decline	F	requested for

35. The Strait of Bab-el-Mandeb has earned itself the _____ "Gates of Tears" for the large number of fatal disasters that have befallen those attempting its navigation.

- (A) sobriquet
- (B) veneration
- (C) machination
- (D) syncopation
- (E) condemnation

36. Although intended as only a white lie to avoid conflict, the _____, when discovered, stirred the same resentment the original falsehood sought to avoid.

   (A) euphemism
   (B) guile
   (C) candor
   (D) sophism
   (E) mendacity

37. When the vitamin and supplement company issued the report, even the company's most (i) _____ customers questioned it, calling it (ii) _____ used to lure buyers. Within three months, the company (iii) _____ as much in a public announcement, confirming the suspicion.

Blank (i)		Blank (ii)		Blank (iii)	
A	devout	D	a sanction	G	conceded
B	incredulous	E	an artifice	H	retaliated
C	obtuse	F	an enigma	I	recuperated

38. While (i) _____ the public outcry for a new approach, the panel encouraged consumers to (ii) _____ current measures to stabilize the problem. These measures, the panel emphasized, had (iii) _____ unemployment in the past.

Blank (i)		Blank (ii)		Blank (iii)	
A	dismissing	D	steadfastly support	G	curtailed
B	acknowledging	E	vehemently oppose	H	confirmed
C	explicating	F	carefully question	I	imparted

39. She was _____ spender, as evidenced by her life of luxury, which included a collection of fine wines and jewelry from around the world.

   A   an exorbitant

   B   an expedient

   C   an erratic

   D   a lavish

   E   a penitent

   F   a desultory

40. Although the candidate was warned repeatedly by his campaign staff that he had a congenial public image to uphold, he continued to release _____ campaign ads.

   A   polemical

   B   hackneyed

   C   amiable

   D   riveting

   E   gripping

   F   contentious

41. American consumers responded to a surge in the economy with an increase in spending, countering last year's trend toward _____.

   - A   ambiguity
   - B   parsimony
   - C   benevolence
   - D   opulence
   - E   abundance
   - F   frugality

42. The defendant, charged with conspiring to defraud investors, steered clear of the public eye; nonetheless, the press _____ each day outside the courthouse, hoping to stop him for an interview.

   - A   skulked
   - B   disseminated
   - C   amassed
   - D   languished
   - E   convened
   - F   dispersed

Lesson 7: **Advanced Sentence Equivalence**

LEARNING OBJECTIVES

After this lesson, you will be able to:

- Make accurate predictions for missing words in sentences with subtle clues
- Apply elimination strategies to questions featuring tough vocabulary

43. One of the most _____ events of the transition from Late Antiquity to the Early Middle Ages was the diaspora of Germanic tribes into lands that were once held securely by the Roman Empire, giving the time period the name "Migration Era."

   A seminal
   B abstract
   C momentous
   D gratuitous
   E diluvial
   F trifling

44. Mozart manifested the signs of _____ genius when he began composing music at the precocious age of five.

   A refined
   B incipient
   C staggering
   D nascent
   E fathomless
   F piddling

45. Without more robust funding, the charity's goals will go unfulfilled; furthermore, thousands of _____ children will want for basic necessities.

- A prodigal
- B malnourished
- C vagrant
- D impecunious
- E indigent
- F overindulged

46. The fashion designer's silk scarf wasn't popular initially; the public found it gaudy until a model discovered the accessory and _____ it.

- A vilipended
- B disavowed
- C engendered
- D indulged
- E championed
- F espoused

47. One of the most commonly perpetuated myths about Einstein is that he failed math; on the contrary, he excelled at the subject, developing _____ it at a young age.

- A a predilection for
- B an enmity toward
- C an acquiescence to
- D an antipathy toward
- E a penchant for
- F a reminiscence about

48. The pundits agreed that the speech was both deeply profound and _____ in its delivery, and it was well received by audiences.

   A   pellucid

   B   affable

   C   militant

   D   asinine

   E   perspicuous

   F   magisterial

49. The two boxers battled toe-to-toe until the final round, when the longtime champion of the ring was finally _____ by his young opponent's stamina.

   A   exiled

   B   thwarted

   C   decimated

   D   galvanized

   E   annihilated

   F   stymied

Try These at Home

50. Not wanting to be caught _____, the graduate student spent hours frantically preparing for every possible question that the faculty committee might pose during her thesis defense.

    A unaware

    B easily

    C quickly

    D unrehearsed

    E early

    F red-handed

51. Only in response to the _____ of the ambassador did the magistrate relent and agree to drop the charges against the tourist.

    A approbation

    B behest

    C ingenuousness

    D delight

    E circumlocution

    F urging

52. Nigel was usually a model of equanimity, so his _____ demeanor during the attorney's cross-examination left many surprised.

    [A] staid

    [B] equanimous

    [C] testy

    [D] placid

    [E] discomposed

    [F] jubilant

53. After repeated attempts to resolve grievances, 500 sanitation workers went on strike; consequently, city leaders _____ measures to address the issue.

    [A] flouted

    [B] concerted

    [C] contrived

    [D] consecrated

    [E] spurned

    [F] levied

54. By the fifth sequel, the director had become _____ in his delivery; even the most die-hard fans of the series lost interest.

    [A] convoluted

    [B] cautious

    [C] remedial

    [D] perfunctory

    [E] unpleasant

    [F] mundane

55. Within a few short years, the young city council member was able to rise in the political ranks due to her _____ supporters, savvy and skillful team, and incandescent wit.

   [A] intelligent

   [B] ardent

   [C] lenient

   [D] intrepid

   [E] zealous

   [F] recalcitrant

56. In any economy, the success of a business is dependent on two things: the degree to which it can _____ borrowed money and its ability to withstand fluctuations in the market.

   [A] invert

   [B] capitalize

   [C] expound

   [D] conjure

   [E] repudiate

   [F] leverage

Short Verbal Answer Key

1. **D**	15. **B, F, G**	29. **B, D**	43. **A, C**
2. **C**	16. **B, F, G**	30. **B, E**	44. **B, D**
3. **E**	17. **C, D**	31. **E, F**	45. **D, E**
4. **C**	18. **A, F**	32. **A, C**	46. **E, F**
5. **C, D**	19. **B, D**	33. **B, E**	47. **A, E**
6. **C, F**	20. **A, F**	34. **B, D**	48. **A, E**
7. **B, E, G**	21. **C, F**	35. **A**	49. **B, F**
8. **B**	22. **B, F, G**	36. **E**	50. **A, D**
9. **B**	23. **C, F, G**	37. **A, E, G**	51. **B, F**
10. **A, F, I**	24. **B, E, H**	38. **B, D, G**	52. **C, E**
11. **B, F, H**	25. **A, D**	39. **A, D**	53. **B, C**
12. **A, D, I**	26. **B, D**	40. **A, F**	54. **D, F**
13. **C, D, I**	27. **A, F**	41. **B, F**	55. **B, E**
14. **B, F, I**	28. **D, F**	42. **C, E**	56. **B, F**

Answers and Explanations

Short Verbal Try These At Home Explanations

Lesson 3

8. B

"Despite" is a detour road sign that directs you to look for a contrast. If the popularity of soy is widespread, that means many people like to consume it. Because of the detour road sign, you can surmise that the effects of soy on health may be an issue people do not agree on. The correct answer is **(B)** *contentious*, which means "likely to cause disagreement." That choice is perfect for the context of describing a "discussion." Go ahead and rule out (A) *conclusive* and (D) *enlightening*, since they both suggest agreement. (C) *preposterous* and (E) *fraudulent* are too extreme for the context.

9. B

The detour road sign "although" will help you with this sentence. You are told that the policies were initially effective at cutting costs, but that "his lack of foresight crippled the department in the long run." The straight-ahead road sign "and" connects this "lack of foresight" with the blank, so you can predict an answer meaning "shortsighted." **(B)** *myopic* means "shortsighted," and it is the right answer. (A) *vacuous* would mean the plans lacked intelligence or importance. While you know the plans did not turn out well eventually, they did accomplish some good (they cut costs), so to describe them as "vacuous" does not correctly identify the problem. (C) *prescient* means "farsighted," the opposite of what you are looking for. (D) *ingenuous* means "sincere" or "guileless," and (E) *ingenious* means "brilliant." Neither of these fits the sentence.

10. A, F, I

In these sentences, key words lead to the correct choices. The term "stately home" suggests that a word meaning "building" would fit best in the first blank. **(A)** *edifice* is another word for "building" and has the connotation of size or importance. It is the correct choice here. (B) *architecture* is a profession or a style of construction, and (C) *apartment* is a portion of a building.

The buildings' interiors have "many magnificent rooms," and since their surroundings match, they are likely to be of great extent, which eliminates (D) *confined*. With its meaning of "abundant" or "sizeable," **(F)** *expansive* is the

logical choice for the second blank. The grounds may or may not be (E) *mown*, but this choice does not fit the clue of matching "many magnificent rooms."

Such a great house would likely "look out over" scenic "views," which is the meaning of **(I)** *vistas*, the correct choice. (G) *veneers* are thin coverings, and (H) *vignettes* are short, descriptive pieces of literature. Neither makes sense in this context.

11. B, F, H

Use the key words in these sentences as clues to the blanks. The first choice here requires a word that contrasts with a good person who brings order and direction to a situation that lacks them. Only **(B)** *hurly-burly*, meaning "commotion" or "disorder," matches the sense of the sentence. The words (A) *existence* and (C) *practice* are too general, and neither implies a chaotic situation.

The detour road sign "rather than" indicates that the adjective in the blank describing the "matters that affect our lives" is the opposite of "central." (D) *weaker* and (E) *confidential* do not contrast with "central." **(F)** *peripheral*, which means "at the edge of," is the opposite of "central" and is correct.

The second sentence lists achievements of the good politician, so the "competing interests" that "he or she cuts through" would not have the characteristic of (G) *usefulness*. As the word "focuses" suggests, it is the **(H)** *distractions* of competing interests that prevent political progress, making this the correct choice for the third blank. There might be a (I) *succession* of competing interests, but "cutting through" it doesn't make sense.

12. A, D, I

Key words are important in evaluating the answer choices in this passage. The first sentence suggests that the "journey" of drama over the centuries has been substantial. The word **(A)** *remarkable*, meaning "extraordinary" or "very noteworthy," is true to the nature of the journey and is the correct choice. (B) *modest* is the opposite of what's needed for the blank. The meaning of (C) *implacable*, "incapable of being appeased or changed," makes no sense in this context.

In the second blank, the word must describe the common movements of actors on the stage. To **(D)** *strut*, to "walk proudly or pompously," is the best choice because it is more general and suggests the natural confidence of a performer. Actors may occasionally **(E)** *stalk* around the stage, but the word is too limited to fit the meaning here. The word **(F)** *straddle* has the specific meaning of standing with legs wide apart, which does not fit this situation.

The choice for the third blank is dictated by the phrase "in order to enter into the 'reality' of events created for them." Members of any audience know that a stage performance is not "real," but they put aside that knowledge in order to enjoy the play. **(I)** *disbelief* is therefore correct; people often use the phrase "willing suspension of disbelief" to describe an audience's acceptance of the events in a play. Audiences do not put aside their **(G)** *interest*, which rules out that choice. The word **(H)** *concern*, which can also mean "interest" or "sense of unease," is also illogical in this context.

Lesson 4

19. B, D

Reading this question through, you can see that it hinges on the relationship between the company and its employees. Employees must follow the rules of their employers, so for the first blank, you can reasonably predict that it will require a word with a meaning similar to "obey." Looking at the options, **(B)** *conform to* makes sense. **(A)** *object to* and **(C)** *balk at* are wrong, as it is important that employees not do those things. For the second blank, you have already predicted that employees must obey rules, so predict "rules" for this blank. **(D)** *standards* are practices to which companies would want their employees to conform, and it is the correct answer. **(E)** *idiosyncrasies* means "quirks," and **(F)** *peccadilloes* means "minor faults," neither of which employees would be expected to imitate.

20. A, F

This question has a detour road sign that's a bit longer than usual. The phrase "It is hard to believe" indicates that the answer choices will contrast with one another. The second blank is a term described as "rowdy," so you can safely predict that the first blank will have the meaning of "calm" or "orderly" to describe early soccer.

The second blank is easier. With the context clue of "rowdy," **(F)** *brawl* works well. You can eliminate **(D)** *séance* because this is a ritual to speak with the dead. A séance would never be described as "rowdy," nor would it describe a contest over an inflated pig's bladder. **(E)** *massacre* does not fit because it is too extreme: while people fought over the pig's bladder, nothing indicates that they fought until they had killed each other in large numbers.

You can now answer the first blank with certainty. **(A)** *structured* fits the prediction and contrasts with the rowdy brawl described in the second part of the sentence. Both **(B)** *pell-mell* and **(C)** *helter-skelter* describe unstructured situations, so they cannot be correct.

21. C, F

The conjunction "but" is a detour road sign, signaling a change in direction between the two blanks. For the first blank, ambition is described as being useful in leading people to achievement. A good prediction is *inducement*. Looking at the options, **(C)** *motivator* fits perfectly; ambition motivates people to great achievement. **(B)** *indicator* is a passive word, not an agent that effects action. **(A)** *tenet*, a component of a philosophy, does not work in this context because it does not "induce" action—it works more as a guide than as an impetus.

The second blank must contrast with "useful" and "achievement" and therefore has a negative charge. **(F)** *destructive* fits perfectly; it's strongly negative, and "destructive force" contrasts perfectly with "useful motivator" as a description of ambition. **(D)** *ersatz*, which means "artificial," is too neutral to contrast with "motivator." **(E)** *pulsating*, meaning "throbbing," makes no sense in this context.

22. B, F, G

It's difficult to predict for the first blank, as all you're told is that the children were time-consuming for their mother. You need more contextual clues, so move on to the second blank. Here, you're looking for something to describe the children's energy level. Their energy is characterized as "volatile" ("explosive"), so they must have an *intense* level of energy. Make that your prediction. **(F)** *robust* ("vigorous") fits perfectly. **(D)** *eclectic* ("varied") and **(E)** *pedestrian* ("ordinary") don't make sense. Now that you know the children are high-energy, you can predict something like "unruly" for the first blank, since that blank describes the children. Looking at the answer choices, **(B)** *froward*, meaning "not easily controlled," works perfectly. (A) *earthy* means "crude," so that is wrong, and (C) *limpid*, which means "calm or untroubled," is the opposite of what you need. For the final blank, remember that the mother is trying to direct the children's energy towards something "constructive" so that they will make productive use of their time. This is close to choice **(G)** *salutary*, which means "beneficial" or "useful," so that's your answer. (H) *provocative* ("provoking to anger or desire") and (I) *dour* ("gloomy") do not make sense in this context, as they do not describe pursuits that parents would encourage for their children.

23. C, F, G

Here, "law and custom" require that something definite be made in a courtroom—predict *verdict* for the first blank. If a verdict must be reached, predict that the judge may have to assume that a verdict is *always possible* when, in fact, the evidence might not be *compelling*. For the first blank, (A) *deadlock* might have sounded tempting, since you often hear about "deadlocked juries," but this is the opposite of what you need. A *dispute*, (B), is what is settled in a courtroom, not what is reached there. The best choice here is **(C)** *determination*. For the second blank, you can rule out (E) *irrelevant* immediately, since the verdict is the most relevant thing in a courtroom. You might have initially liked (D) *negotiable* because sometimes the outcomes of trials are negotiated, but once a verdict is reached, it might be appealed but it cannot be negotiated. **(F)** *self-evident* is the best choice for the second blank. For the third blank, while it's not an exact match to your prediction, the most logical choice is **(G)** *conclusive*. It's illogical to say that the evidence may not be *accessible*, choice (H), or *substantiated*, (I); without at least some evidence, there generally wouldn't even be a trial. "[Because] law and custom require that a definite *determination* be made . . . a judge is forced to behave as if a verdict is *self-evident* . . . when in fact, the evidence may not be *conclusive*."

24. B, E, H

The word "because" is a straight-ahead road sign that indicates a close connection between the first two clauses. The first clause tells you that feuds tend to arise in societies that have a certain relationship with centralized government. In the second clause, you learn more about these societies—there is something difficult about public

justice in them. The second sentence, in turn, tells you that this difficulty has an effect on the concept of "private recourse." These must be societies that *don't have* strong, centralized governments—because "public justice is difficult to *obtain*," private recourse becomes "more *common*." For the first blank, **(B)** *lack* matches your prediction. Societies that *espouse*, (A), or *affirm*, (C), central governments are the opposite of what you're looking for. For the second blank, the best fit is **(E)** *enforce*. It doesn't make sense to say that "public justice is difficult to *identify*," (D), or *recognize*, (F). For the third blank, *prevalent*, **(H)**, matches the prediction and is correct. (G) *objectionable* is the opposite of what you need here: you may find the concept of "private recourse" objectionable, but those in the societies referred to in the sentence would not. (I) *brutal* is not supported by the information in the sentence.

Lesson 6

30. B, E

The sentence opens with the word "When," which functions as a straight-ahead road sign. The missing word will be in accord with the key words in the first half of the sentence. The patron wants an "amusing" and uplifting author. Predict something like "laughter" or "joy." **(B)** *mirth* and **(E)** *merriment* both mean "gladness" or "hilarity," and are the correct answers. (A) *lugubriousness* and (C) *poignancy* both mean "sadness," and are the opposite of what you're looking for. Finally, (D) *gravity* and (F) *solemnity* both mean "dignity" or "seriousness," and are likewise the opposite of what you want.

31. E, F

This sentence features the straight-ahead road sign "because," so the second half of the sentence will follow from the first part. These reenactors "eschew any anachronisms," a phrase that features challenging vocabulary. Use the context to work out the meaning. Since the examples of modern technology don't fit the historical setting, the reenactors don't use them. (Indeed, "eschew any anachronisms" means "avoid anything that is from a different time.") Turn that into a prediction: the reenactors are trying to achieve "realism." **(E)** *verisimilitude* and **(F)** *authenticity* both mean "true or real," so they match the prediction and are the correct answers. Verisimilitude offers a good opportunity to use root words: it's from the Latin roots *verus* ("true") and *similis* ("like"). (A) *virtuosity* means "great skill," which might work in the sentence but doesn't have a match among the choices. None of (B) *dictation* ("saying words"), (C) *controversy* ("disagreement"), or (D) *naiveté* ("lack of experience") matches the context of the sentence.

32. A, C

This sentence sets up a contrast between the "elevated names" of fancy roses and their "more typical surroundings." Predict "humble" (which appears later in the sentence) or "unassuming." (A) *unexceptional* and (C) *pedestrian* both match. Keep an eye out for words like *pedestrian*, which have multiple meanings when used as different parts of speech. The noun *pedestrian* means "a walking person," while the adjective means "drab." (B) *hortatory*, "trying to encourage someone to act," is unrelated, although it sounds similar to horticulture ("the act of gardening"). (D) *lofty* and (E) *preeminent* both match the adjective "elevated" from early in the sentence. Because of the contrast word "belie," though, they are the opposite of what's needed. (F) *abstruse* means "puzzling," which is unrelated to the sentence.

Lesson 7

50. A, D

This question contains a subtle detour road sign, "not." The student spent hours preparing, so you're looking for something similar in meaning to "unprepared." (A) *unaware* is pretty close, so hold on to that one. (D) *unrehearsed* works perfectly, since it would imply she hadn't prepared properly. (B) *easily*, (C) *quickly*, and (E) *early* all give the sentence the same meaning. None of these words captures the idea that the student wants to be prepared "for every possible question." Preparing just a little would prevent her from being caught in an error right away. Eliminate these. (F) *red-handed* is a trap answer. The subject is a graduate student, not a thief, so "caught red-handed" doesn't work in this context.

51. B, F

You're told that the magistrate "relented" (gave in) as a result of some action that the ambassador took. It's unclear whether the ambassador used power or persuasion, so consider words such as "insistence" or "plea." Both are good predictions. Both correct choices will mean one or the other.

(B) *behest,* "a strongly worded request," works very well; a strongly worded request could induce someone to relent. (F) *urging* creates a sentence similar to the one created by (B) *behest.* Those two are the correct answers. (A) *approbation* means "approval," which doesn't make sense given that the ambassador seems to disapprove of the charges. (C) *ingenuousness* means "frankness" or "naïveté" and does not fit the context of the sentence. (D) *delight* also does not make sense in this context. (E) *circumlocution* means "roundabout speech," which is not typically very persuasive.

52. C, E

The key to this question is the context key word "surprised." Since Nigel is typically a model of "equanimity" (calm), the correct answer choices, describing surprising behavior on his part, must mean something like "unsettled." (C) *testy,* "irritable," and (E) *discomposed*, "out of sorts," create sentences that indicate that Nigel lost his cool and failed to remain calm. These are the correct answers. You can eliminate (A) *staid*, (B) *equanimous,* and (D) *placid,* as those are all synonyms for "calm," from which the sentence detours. (F) *jubilant,* "overjoyed," can also be rejected; although excessive joy does depart from "calm," no other word in the answer choices would create an equivalent sentence.

53. B, C

The word "consequently" means "as a result." Considering the tone of the sentence, think about how city leaders might have responded. (A) *flouted* means "disregarded." It's unlikely that city leaders disregarded the issues after such extreme measures by the workers. Look for a word that suggests a more proactive response. (B) *concerted* and (C) *contrived* mean "devised or planned" and fit the context of the sentence. Although these are likely the correct answers, check the remaining choices just to be sure. (D) *consecrated* means "declared sacred," which doesn't make sense and can be eliminated. (E) *spurned* has a meaning similar to *flouted*. Like *flouted*, this is opposite to the response that is likely to have occurred. You may be familiar with (F) *levied* from historical contexts, as in "a tax was levied." The word *levied* means "collected" and doesn't make sense in context. Stick with options (B) and (C); they are synonyms and create sentences with similar meanings.

54. D, F

Use the key phrase "lost interest" to determine the tone of the word in the blank. The semicolon separating the two clauses acts as a straight-ahead road sign. You need a negative word to describe the director's work, which has become rote or boring. (A) *convoluted* means "intricate." Depending on the type of story, an "intricate" film might be boring or very interesting. There's not enough context to make this choice a logical certainty. (B) *cautious* is another choice that could go either way. A "cautious" delivery might make for a better or worse fifth film. (C) *remedial* contains the word *remedy*, which means "cure." This does not fit the context of the sentence. **(D)** *perfunctory* and **(F)** *mundane* are synonyms meaning "in a routine manner." They fit the tone of the sentence. You can also rule out choice (E) *unpleasant*. Even though the film may be unpleasant, the phrase "by the fifth sequel" suggests fatigue or boredom on the part of the director. **(D)** and **(F)** are correct.

55. B, E

Ask yourself what kind of supporters a young politician would need in order to move up quickly in local government. (A) *intelligent* fits in the sentence, so hold on to it for now. (B) *ardent* means "eager, full of passion." This word is more precise in context than (A), so see if you can find a synonym for it. (C) *lenient* is not the best fit for the context. *Lenient* is similar to "tolerant," but it has a negative connotation, implying that a lenient person may allow people to do things they are not supposed to. *Intrepid*, (D), means "fearless." This choice is possible as well, so we'll keep it under consideration as we move on to the final choices. Somebody who is (F) *recalcitrant* is stubborn and resists authority, which doesn't apply here. **(E)** *zealous* is a synonym for **(B)** *ardent*. Since both *ardent* and *zealous* fit the sentence and are synonyms, you can get rid of *intelligent* and *intrepid*. Even though they would fit, no other word matches either to create a sentence with the same meaning.

56. B, F

The straightforward road sign "and" means that the verb for the blank matches "ability" in the accompanying phrase. You're looking for a word that means "use" and that fits with "borrowed money." (A) *invert* means "to put upside down or inside out," which doesn't make sense, so eliminate it. (B) *capitalize* means "to take advantage of." This describes a business strategy and fits in context. (C) *expound* is "to explain." A business will most likely not have to explain its borrowed money as a business strategy—unless it gets into trouble! (D) *conjure* means "to imagine or make up." This doesn't work in context. (E) *repudiate* means "to reject." Move on to the last choice, **(F)** *leverage,* which is the synonym you needed; like *capitalize,* it means "to take advantage of." **(B)** and **(F)** are the correct answers. This is a good example of a situation where the answers are not quite synonyms, but the words affect the meaning of the sentence similarly.

CHAPTER 7

Reading Comprehension and Reasoning

Lesson 1: **Structural Reading**

LEARNING OBJECTIVES

After this lesson, you will be able to:

- Summarize the key points in each paragraph
- State the author's purpose

Question 1 is based on the following passage.

The barely edible rarity known as *casu marzu* is a cheese so dangerous that it has been illegal to sell, serve, or in some cases even possess in its native Italy. And yet, it is one of the most sought-after dishes for weddings there. What starts out as a firm hunk of cheese made from sheep's milk is soaked in brine, smoked, and left in a cellar to age. The step that infringes European food and hygiene laws comes next, when holes are drilled into the cheese so that cheese flies and fly larvae can be inserted into the center of the cheese. The flies are then free to spawn thousands upon thousands of maggots that consume, digest, and expel a fermented cheese by-product. The result is an extremely runny and flowing substance that, live maggots and all, is spread over dry bread or crackers and consumed. In fact, the Italians who produce and eat the cheese today, and do so with the same delight and confidence that their ancestors did hundreds of years ago, insist that the maggots must be alive within the cheese. If they are not, they warn, the cheese has clearly ripened too much and become too toxic for consumption.

This makes the maggots a considerable factor in preparing the cheese. The agile and nimble creatures are said to jump as high as six inches from the cheese with considerable precision, often targeting a potential new host's eyes. They are also quite hardy and, if not thoroughly masticated during eating, might survive passage through the stomach and live on as an internal parasite. As if the danger of fly larvae taking up residence in one's intestines isn't troublesome enough, the liquid excretions from the cheese are capable of burning the skin, eyes, and tongue. Even the cheese itself, properly formed, can cause a burning, itching skin irritation that can last for a week after eating.

All of these gastronomic hazards, some of which can be lethal, belie the fact that the cheese is still a considerable black market item, consumed in sizable amounts in the Sardinia region of Italy, but very little by even the most curious outsiders who must ask why people, particularly people in celebration, would subject themselves to such a concoction. The answer for this, as with many other seemingly unpalatable foods such as raw fish, eggs, and ground cockroach eaten in other parts of the world, is that the dish has traditionally been seen as an aphrodisiac, thus making it sought after not just for the aforementioned weddings, but also for the bachelor parties that precede them.

1.   Based on the passage, with which of the following statements would the author most likely agree?

   (A) Despite the process *casu marzu* goes through in order to be formed, the end product must taste delicious, or else people would not make it.

   (B) Some people are willing to eat foods with potential health risks based on traditional claims about those foods.

   (C) The popularity of *casu marzu* in Sardinia suggests that the laws regarding food and hygiene making the food illegal are not enforced there.

   (D) Long-standing traditions, such as *casu marzu*, should, based on their cultural importance, be given some degree of exemption from legal regulation.

   (E) *Casu marzu*'s continued popularity as a wedding food probably means that claims regarding its effects have a basis in fact.

Question 2 is based on the following passage.

The Stone of Scone, originally a Scottish coronation stone, had been held in Westminster Abbey in London from 1296 until Christmas Day 1950, when a quartet of Scottish university students and nationalists liberated the stone. After first hiding it in England, they smuggled it past English roadblocks and brought the stone back to Scotland. The British government initiated a hunt but was unable to locate the stone until its presence at a Scottish Abbey was made known over a year later. The stone was promptly taken back to London, but Scottish protests eventually triumphed, and in 1996 the stone was moved to Scotland. However, despite its position as a national treasure of Scotland, the English consider it to be on loan and expect the Scots to return it when needed for English coronations.

2. Based on the passage, what is the author's opinion of the ownership of the Stone of Scone?

   (A) It is the rightful property of England.

   (B) It is the rightful property of Scotland.

   (C) Both countries are part of the British Empire, and therefore it belongs to both.

   (D) Both countries have used it for coronations, and therefore it belongs to both.

   (E) Both countries have legitimate claims, and therefore it is unclear.

Lesson 2: **Reading Comprehension Method**

LEARNING OBJECTIVE

After this lesson, you will be able to:

- Perform the steps of the Reading Comprehension Method

THE KAPLAN METHOD

Reading Comprehension

STEP 1   Read the passage strategically.

STEP 2   Analyze the question stem.

STEP 3   Research the relevant text.

STEP 4   Make a prediction.

STEP 5   Evaluate the answer choices.

Questions 3 and 4 are based on the following passage.

Decompression sickness, colloquially known as "the bends," occurs when inert gas bubbles are formed and expelled from organic tissue during rapid ascent following an extended period of prolonged intensive atmospheric pressure. This is most commonly experienced during deepwater dives. Surface divers capable of descending to sufficient depth, or scuba divers using air tanks, supersaturate their lungs with air, which diffuses throughout the body. When a diver remains at high pressure for a sufficiently long time, nitrogen, a gas present in the air and breathed into the body, is driven into the muscle tissue in elevated amounts and subsequently released again as pressure subsides. When pressure on the body decreases as the diver nears the surface, the diver must take care to rise gradually and expel excess gas through the mouth, nose, and ears. Without these pressure balances, the gas bubbles that form in the tissue can disrupt the joints and organs. In mild cases, the diver suffers from painful sensations in the knees, elbows, hips, and shoulders. In extreme cases, the bubbles can impede or rupture blood vessels in the brain or spine, which can lead to paralysis or even death.

3.   Select the sentence that identifies the preventative process for circumventing decompression sickness during the conclusion of a deepwater dive.

4.   Consider each of the choices separately and select all that apply.

Which of the following must have occurred in order to initiate a case of decompression sickness in a diver according to the passage?

[A]   The person suffering decompression sickness must have experienced a decrease in atmospheric pressure.

[B]   A supply of nitrogen sufficient to form high levels of gas bubbles must be present in the muscle tissue of the person suffering decompression sickness.

[C]   The person suffering decompression sickness must have used a breathing apparatus, such as a scuba tank that supplies air to a diver.

Questions 5 and 6 are based on the following passage.

British Naval Officer Robert Scott (1868–1912) made his intent to discover the South Pole public, but that did not stop Norwegian explorer Roald Amundsen (1872–1928) from trying to beat him to it. In 1910, Amundsen raced to Antarctica and headed for the pole with 4 crewmen and 52 sled dogs. Scott's party left base camp ten days later with 17 men, 2 motorized sleds, 10 ponies, and 34 dogs. Scott's motor sleds broke down, the ponies had to be shot, and Scott sent all but four men back to base camp. The remaining crewmen hauled the sleds the rest of the way. Amundsen planted the Norwegian flag on the South Pole on December 14, 1911. A demoralized Scott raised the British flag on January 17, 1912. Amundsen and crew skied back to camp in good health. Scott's team, however, walked in temperatures that reached –30°F, losing two men along the way. A blizzard trapped the remaining three in a tent, which became their grave on March 29, 1912. A search party, discovering the tent, built a cairn, or monument of stones, marking the spot with a cross made of skis. When news of Scott's death reached civilization, England fell into mourning. The cross and cairn honoring Robert Scott still stand today.

5. Which conclusion about the competition between the two explorers does the passage steer the reader toward?

    (A) Scott would not have died if Amundsen had not forced him to compete.

    (B) Scott never should have tried for the South Pole because he was not a good explorer.

    (C) Amundsen was destined to win the historic conquest of the South Pole.

    (D) The English public followed the race to the South Pole with more interest than the Norwegian public did.

    (E) Despite losing the race to the South Pole, Scott's efforts were heroic.

6. With which of the following statements is the author most likely to agree?

    (A) Amundsen's conquest seems anticlimactic compared to Scott's disastrous defeat.

    (B) Scott wanted to conquer the South Pole more than Amundsen did.

    (C) Amundsen was better prepared to discover the South Pole by using common-sense skills suited to Antarctica.

    (D) Amundsen exploited Scott's preparations and ruined his expedition; Scott's defeat was Amundsen's fault.

    (E) Amundsen and Scott both viewed the discovery of the South Pole in part as a competitive race.

Questions 7–9 are based on the following passage.

Painting is a process that is ordinarily associated with a brush and a palette, but as an artist who was far from ordinary, Jackson Pollock used neither when creating some of his most famous works. Pollock (1912–1956) is one of the most influential figures in American painting. His unique style of painting and artistic point of view made him stand out from his contemporaries. Pollock painted in an entirely abstract manner. Instead of using an easel, he placed his canvases on the floor or against a wall. Employing a "drip and splash" method, Pollock poured and dripped his paint from the can onto the canvas. Instead of brushes, he manipulated the paint with sticks and knives. Pollock's works created a new, "all-over" style of painting in which there is no focal point and no differentiation is made among areas of the painted surface. His scattered painting style may be a reflection of his unstable mental state, as he was known to battle depression and alcoholism. While his volatile personality may have contributed to his legacy, Pollock will primarily be remembered for his tremendous contributions to the art world.

7.   The primary purpose of this passage is to address which of the following issues related to Pollock as an artist?

(A) How he developed his unique style

(B) How his methods influenced future artists

(C) Whether his personal life affected his work

(D) How his influential style represented a significant departure from more conventional art

(E) Whether he should be revered for his work

8.   The passage states each of the following EXCEPT:

   (A) Pollock's work was similar to that of his peers.

   (B) The all-over painting method placed no importance on any particular piece of the painting.

   (C) Pollock suffered from mental health issues.

   (D) Pollock's "drip and splash" method created art without the use of conventional painting tools.

   (E) Pollock's legacy will reflect his artistic ability.

9.   Based on the information in the passage, which word best describes Pollock as an artist?

   (A) Plain

   (B) Gloomy

   (C) Inventive

   (D) Literal

   (E) Traditional

Questions 10–13 are based on the following passage.

Cinematic renditions of historic pieces of literature provide an informative glimpse into the cultural and social context in which the films were made. Shakespeare's *Henry V* is a prime example, as it has been in circulation within the English-speaking world for over 400 years and has been reinterpreted in a number of different milieus. Since the source material has not changed, the way in which different artists and directors treat the play indicates not only the predispositions of the interpreter, but also the prevailing social and political views of the audience. This is acutely noticeable in a play like *Henry V*, which is highly charged with nationalistic concerns.

The play was written during the reign of Elizabeth I, when English national identity (and the modern English language) had begun to crystallize and the language and culture we know today approached their present form. It is a historical biography of King Henry V of England, who waged a bloody campaign during The Hundred Years' War with the aim of conquering France. The introduction of the play features an adviser to the King explaining, in a confusing and nearly incomprehensible fashion, the justification for Henry's claim to the French throne. The text of the play itself has been interpreted as being ambiguous in its treatment of Henry's character. Henry has a number of rousing, heroic speeches, but he is also shown to be coldly unmerciful, as in the case of his refusal to pardon petty thieves.

Shakespeare's play has been adapted in two famous film versions. The first, directed by Laurence Olivier, was made during the Second World War, immediately before the invasion of Normandy was launched in 1944. Critics of the film have emphasized the pageantry, bravado, and nationalistic undertones of this version. The battle scenes in the film are understated and tame, with little of the carnage that would be expected of a medieval melee. They are shot in beautiful weather, and the actors are clad in radiant colors. The scene with Henry's harsh justice is omitted. The film was funded, in part, by the British government and is widely understood to have been intended as a propaganda film, made in anticipation of D-day. The second version, directed by Kenneth Branagh, was made in 1989, only a few years after the Falklands War, and was much harsher in tone. The battle scenes are gory and are shot in gray, dismal weather. The actors wear muddy, blood-smeared costumes reflective of the period. The scene with Henry's harsh justice is included.

10. The primary purpose of this passage is to

    Ⓐ   describe Shakespeare's Henry V.

    Ⓑ   denounce the intrusion of government involvement with the arts.

    Ⓒ   describe cinematic interpretation of literature.

    Ⓓ   teach the reader about cinematic versions of theater.

    Ⓔ   explain the effect of contemporary situations upon interpretation of literature.

11. Consider each of the choices separately and select all that apply.

    The author would most likely agree with which of the following?

    A Original works of art are more reflective of their societal contexts than are cinematic adaptations of such works.

    B Contemporary events influence the adaptation of historical source material.

    C War is likely to produce good cinema.

12. Which of the following most accurately describes the relationship between the highlighted sentences?

    A The first is an example of an argument; the second is a counterexample.

    B The first is a synthesis of disparate ideas; the second is one of the components of that synthesis.

    C The first is the topic of the passage; the second is an argument in support of it.

    D The first presents an assertion; the second provides an example to support that assertion.

    E The first is a thesis; the second is the antithesis.

13. It can be inferred that the author

    A regards texts as being open to interpretation.

    B prefers the Olivier version.

    C dislikes Henry.

    D prefers Branagh's version.

    E believes directors should remain as faithful to the original as possible.

Try These at Home

Questions 14–16 are based on the following passage.

The reversal of the Chicago River in 1900 is considered one of the greatest engineering feats of all time. The project involved building a deep channel through miles of solid bedrock in an effort to make the waters of the Chicago River—and its associated untreated sewage—flow out of Chicago and away from Lake Michigan, which was the source of the city's water supply. The project seemed impossible at the time, but it was deemed necessary after a flood in 1885 caused the Chicago River to foul the city's water supply and subsequently killed almost 12 percent of the population as a result of exposure to cholera and other water-borne diseases. In 1889, engineers started construction on the 28-mile channel that would connect Lake Michigan at Chicago with the Des Plaines River at Lockport, Illinois. This complex task gave workers the ability to isolate and reverse the flow of the Chicago River. At the end of the yearlong project, the city's water supply became safer and the river's new mouth at Lake Michigan became a major port that served thousands of cargo ships each year.

14. Which one of the following statements reflects the main idea of the passage?

    (A) Sewage disposal was a serious problem in Chicago during the late 1800s.

    (B) Water-borne diseases can spread easily and kill large populations.

    (C) The reversal of the Chicago River is a tremendous accomplishment in the field of engineering.

    (D) The reversal of the Chicago River opened the river's mouth to Lake Michigan.

    (E) Connecting Lake Michigan to the Des Plaines River was a key component of plans to reverse the flow of the Chicago River.

15. Consider each of the choices separately and select all that apply.

Based on the passage, what can one infer about the reversal of the Chicago River and its status as a great engineering feat?

A The logistics of drilling through 28 miles of bedrock and connecting rivers was extremely difficult.

B The river-reversal project in Chicago was successful, whereas similar projects were unsuccessful in several other cities.

C The project proved that strong engineering can make things that seem impossible possible.

16. Which one of the following was NOT a benefit of reversing the Chicago River?

(A) Engineers created a cure for water-borne illnesses.

(B) The project's engineers gained recognition for their achievement.

(C) Citizens received safer drinking water.

(D) The city became a major port for industry.

(E) Lake Michigan became a cleaner body of water.

Question 17 is based on the following passage.

The Hague Convention for the Protection of Cultural Property in the Event of Armed Conflict (1954) was an international response to the destruction of cultural artifacts during World War II. Overseen by the United Nations Educational, Scientific, and Cultural Organization (UNESCO), the parties that participated in the convention (numbering over 100) pledged to safeguard locations and items of cultural significance during armed conflict, as well as preempt possible threats to the preservation of culture during times of peace. The Hague Convention is significant in that it formally established in its preamble that "damage to cultural property belonging to any people whatsoever means damage to the cultural heritage of all mankind, since each people makes its contribution to the culture of the world." However, it is difficult to enforce, particularly in the case of pieces of cultural heritage that are claimed by multiple States. An example of this is the possession of some of the Dead Sea Scrolls in the aftermath of the Six Day War (1967), a hotly debated topic between Jordan and Israel today. Both countries are signatories to the convention, but both claim their efforts to hold the scrolls amount to rightful possession, rather than theft as forbidden in the convention.

17. Which of the following statements about the Hague Convention of 1954 is NOT supported by the passage?

(A) It was a reaction to despoliation and destruction of cultural heritage during World War II.

(B) It asserted the international significance of all cultural heritage.

(C) It is the focus of controversy in some cases even to this day.

(D) It is overseen by a division of the United Nations.

(E) It included strong and effective measures for enforcement.

Questions 18 and 19 are based on the following passage.

Few today would argue that including women in modern productions of Shakespeare's plays, a practice almost universally forbidden in Shakespeare's time, detracts from the presentation as a whole. However, in realizing gender equality through the assignment of women to female roles, a layer of both added humor and dramatic challenge is removed from several of the Bard's works, including a light comedy (*Twelfth Night*), a dark comedy (*The Merchant of Venice*), and a romance (*As You Like It*). In each, a female character, whom Shakespeare would have imagined played by a man, disguises herself as a man. A male actor of Shakespeare's age would have had to move beyond instilling feminine qualities in his character and into sustaining a feminine undercurrent beneath a superficial masculine pretension within an obviously masculine form. To the historic audience of *As You Like It*, the spectacle of a young man pretending to be young Rosalind pretending to be an old man brought additional "fourth wall" humor to the event. That humorous presentation may be lost on today's audiences, for whom assigning one gender to play another within a gender-mixed cast might come across more as a surprising distraction than as an added laugh.

18. Consider each of the choices separately and select all that apply.

    Which of the following options would reflect a modern return to the same gender humor the author describes in the passage?

    A Changing a male character to a female character and having the role played by a woman

    B Casting a male actor to play the part of Rosalind in *As You Like It*

    C Casting a female actor in the role of a male servant in *The Taming of the Shrew*, who disguises himself as a woman

19. Select the sentence in the passage that expresses the author's overall thesis.

Lesson 3: **Advanced Reading Comprehension**

LEARNING OBJECTIVE

After this lesson, you will be able to:

● Apply structural reading to dense, detailed passages

Questions 20–22 are based on the following passage.

A pioneering figure in modern sociology, French social theorist Emile Durkheim examined the effect of societal cohesion on emotional well-being. Believing that scientific methods should be applied to the study of society, Durkheim studied the levels of integration in various social formations and the impact that such cohesion had on individuals within the group. He postulated that social groups with high levels of integration serve to buffer their members from frustrations and tragedies that could otherwise lead to desperation and self-destruction. Integration, in Durkheim's view, generally arises through shared activities and values. Durkheim distinguished between *mechanical solidarity* and organic solidarity in classifying integrated groups. Mechanical solidarity dominates in groups in which individual differences are minimized and group devotion to a common goal is high. Durkheim identified mechanical solidarity among groups with little division of labor and high degrees of cultural similarity, such as among more traditional and geographically isolated groups. *Organic solidarity*, in contrast, prevails in groups with high levels of individual differences, such as those with a highly specialized division of labor. In such groups, individual differences are a powerful source of connection rather than of division. Because people engage in highly differentiated ways of life, they are by necessity interdependent. In these societies, there is greater freedom from some external controls, but such freedom occurs in concert with the interdependence of individuals, not in conflict with it. Durkheim realized that societies may take many forms and, consequently, that group allegiance can manifest itself in a variety of ways. In both types of societies outlined previously, however, Durkheim stressed that adherence to a common set of assumptions about the world was a necessary prerequisite for maintaining group integrity and avoiding social decay.

20. Which of the following is NOT a feature of an organic societal formation, according to Emile Durkheim?

    Ⓐ Members are buffered from individual frustration that would lead the individual to cease being a productive member of society.

    Ⓑ Citizens operate independently in their daily lives, but toward a common overall goal.

    Ⓒ Each person must come to accept a series of assumptions that form a collective worldview shared by the formation.

    Ⓓ Workers have an even division of labor and share the work of common tasks.

    Ⓔ Individual differences are celebrated, and have a strengthening effect on the society.

21. Consider each of the choices separately and select all that apply.

    Which of the following might be examples of a mechanical solidarity societal formation as explained by the passage?

    A A religious order living in a monastery with an evenly distributed division of labor

    B A company comprising a group of architects, carpenters, plumbers, and construction workers who can design and complete all facets of a building project from start to finish

    C A xenophobic tribe living in an isolated fishing village amid an uncolonized set of islands

22. Select the sentence in the passage that explains why a society displaying organic solidarity tends more toward social codependence than does a mechanical societal formation.

Questions 23 and 24 are based on the following passage.

It is possible for a product to become a victim of its own success. When a product is so new, so innovative, or so well marketed that it dominates the marketplace and the mindset of the consumer, it can be easy to associate the product's brand name with the product itself. When a type of product is nearly universally known or referred to by the brand name of one version of the product, the brand name becomes a victim of "genericism." Aspirin (acetylsalicylic acid), the escalator (moving stair), and the pogo stick (hopping toy) are all former brand names whose success and popularity led to such general and widespread use of the name that the inventors or parent companies were unable to maintain their trademark protections and even lost their competitive advantage against similar products described with the term that had once been a definitive brand name. All it takes is one court ruling for a term that has shifted away from its identity as a trusted brand name to become forever identified as a generic product. When this happens, a company is likely to lose a profitable beachhead within the consumer consciousness. Therefore, companies are highly motivated to use lawsuits and advertisements to dissuade others from making product identifications, such as a permutation of the original brand name, that even passingly resemble their trademarks.

The loss of revenue due to a shift to genericism is compounded by the large amounts of money companies may spend in an attempt to keep it from happening. Despite spending millions of dollars in legal and public relations campaigns, the company Kimberly-Clark has been fighting an uphill battle to keep people from referring to all forms of tissues as *Kleenex*. Google has laid heavy pressure on dictionary publishers that include the term *googled* to define the word as a Web search using the Google search engine instead of any Web search. The risk for a company facing a genericized trademark is not only the loss of a profitable brand's trademark but also the sense of superiority that comes with that brand name. Once, people seeking to keep their coffee hot or milk cold for hours would only depend on a Thermos brand vacuum flask. Unfortunately, the product was so successful and in such high demand that the other companies' vacuum flasks became colloquially known as Thermoses as well. The term became so general that any such product is usually identified as a *thermos*, and the Thermos company lost U.S. protections for the trademark. Now, instead of spending to protect its brand name, the company that first created the product, Thermos, LLC, spends its marketing dollars to make sure that, when people "Google" the term *thermos*, pages for their company's stores and products are the first to appear.

23. According to the above passage, which of these statements is NOT true?

    (A) Only one company can refer to its product as "aspirin."

    (B) Kimberly-Clark would prefer that people refer to its product as "Kleenex brand tissues."

    (C) Companies that lose U.S. protection of their trademarks also stand to lose money on the brands associated with those trademarks.

    (D) Genericism is a by-product of a company's successful positioning of a product so that it assumes a place of dominance with the general public.

    (E) Americans' awareness of the distinction between a product and its brand name is key to preventing a trademark from becoming genericized.

24. Select the sentence in the passage that identifies what ultimately is required for a trademark to become fully "genericized."

Try These at Home

Questions 25 and 26 are based on the following passage.

To poets of the Modern era, 1910–1940, the Romantic verses of previous generations failed to express the chaos of industrialism and devastation of World War I. Modern poets found new influences when "The International Exhibition of Modern Art" opened at New York's Armory building in February 1913. The Armory Show, as it came to be known, exposed Americans to Modern European artists like Kandinsky, Picasso, and Munch. The show also shattered traditional notions of art and introduced techniques such as abstract cubism, in which objects are fragmented and reassembled. The public was shocked, and the press criticized the show, ridiculing one abstract painting in particular, "Nude Descending a Staircase," by Marcel Duchamp, in which a single figure is captured taking successive steps. Most Modern poets, however, loved the show. William Carlos Williams reportedly burst into laughter when he viewed Duchamp's controversial painting. Williams observed motion in an art form previously limited to still-life. He understood that words no longer had to be static. He began infusing movement into his imagery. New poetic styles sprang to life as other poets applied the techniques of visual art to poetry.

25. The main point of the passage is best stated in which of the following sentences?

   (A) Marcel Duchamp gave Modern American poets a way to express the effects of industrialism and war.

   (B) The general public and the press hated the Armory Show because the pieces did not follow conventional, traditional artistic techniques.

   (C) Using words instead of paint, Modern American poets applied the abstract and cubist techniques of Modern European visual art to poetry.

   (D) One form of art can easily influence and shape another.

   (E) William Carlos Williams was influenced by Marcel Duchamp to apply cubist techniques to his poetry.

26. Consider each of the choices separately and select all that apply.

   Which of the following conclusions is supported by the passage?

   [A] Cubism was too abstract for anyone except other artists to understand.

   [B] Traditional forms of artistic expression were rejected by artists in 1913.

   [C] Artistic forms of expression are shaped by world events, social and political.

Lesson 4: **Reasoning Questions**

> **LEARNING OBJECTIVE**
>
> After this lesson, you will be able to:
> • Formulate statements to strengthen or weaken the conclusion of an argument

Question 27 is based on the following passage.

For the past year, a network television talk-show host has been making fun of the name of a particular brand of chainsaw, the Tree Toppler. The ridicule is obviously taking its toll: in the past 12 months, sales of the Tree Toppler have declined by 15 percent, while the sales of other chainsaws have increased.

27. Which of the following, if true, casts the most serious doubt on the conclusion drawn above?

(A) The talk-show host who is ridiculing the Tree Toppler name actually owns a Tree Toppler.

(B) The number of product complaints from owners of the Tree Toppler has not increased in the past year.

(C) The average price of all chainsaws has increased by 10 percent in the past year.

(D) The number of stores that sell the Tree Toppler has remained steady for the past year.

(E) A year ago, a leading consumer magazine rated the Tree Toppler as "intolerably unsafe."

Question 28 is based on the following passage.

Archaeologists found the ruins of a Mayan city they named X near the site of another Mayan city that is known to have been destroyed by a major earthquake in 950 c.e. The archaeologists hypothesized that the same earthquake destroyed both cities.

28. All of the following, if true, would strengthen the archaeologists' hypothesis EXCEPT:

   (A) The Mayans built all of their cities primarily of masonry, which provides little stability in case of earth tremors.

   (B) Records of another society that came to control the region in approximately 1000 c.e. contain no records of either city.

   (C) City X does not lie on a fault line, as the neighboring city does.

   (D) Archaeologists found no inscriptions written after 950 c.e. in city X, but many written before that date.

   (E) The pattern of collapsed buildings in city X is consistent with earthquake damage in other cities destroyed by earthquake.

Question 29 is based on the following passage.

In the results of a long-term medical study, babies exposed to Mozart's music from the age of four weeks developed into young adults who were, on average, not only better performing scholastically, but also physically more adept than young adults who had not been exposed to Mozart's music from an early age. Therefore, parents who wish to improve the strength and scholastic performance of their children should expose their infants to classical music from the age of four weeks.

29. Which of the following, if true, best supports the argument above?

(A) Children who were exposed to Mozart starting at the age of eight weeks also exhibited better scholastic performance as young adults.

(B) High-school students who study music tend to be better at math than those students who do not.

(C) Long-term medical studies are difficult to undertake and require large amounts of outside funding.

(D) When infants listen to Mozart's music, it stimulates their brains and increases the rate of brain cell growth.

(E) Babies who listen to classical music from composers other than Mozart also tend to develop into young adults with greater strength and better scholastic performance than other young adults.

Question 30 is based on the following passage.

A social worker surveyed 200 women, each of whom had recently given birth to her first child. Half of the women surveyed had chosen to give birth in a hospital or obstetrics clinic; the other half had chosen to give birth at home under the care of certified midwives. Of the 100 births that occurred at home, only 5 presented substantial complications, whereas 17 of the hospital births presented substantial complications. The social worker concluded from the survey that the home is actually a safer environment in which to give birth than a hospital or clinic.

30. Which of the following, if true, most seriously calls the social worker's conclusion into question?

(A) Women who give birth in hospitals and clinics often have shorter periods of labor than do women who give birth at home.

(B) Many obstetricians discourage patients from giving birth at home.

(C) All of the women in the study who had been diagnosed as having a high possibility of delivery complications elected to give birth in a hospital.

(D) Women who give birth at home tend to experience less stress during labor than women who deliver in hospitals.

(E) Pregnant doctors prefer giving birth in a hospital.

Try These at Home

Question 31 is based on the following passage.

According to a recent study, advertisements in medical journals often contain misleading information about the effectiveness and safety of new prescription drugs. The medical researchers who wrote the study concluded that the advertisements could result in doctors prescribing inappropriate drugs to their patients.

31. The researchers' conclusion would be most strengthened if which of the following were true?

(A) Advertisements for new prescription drugs are an important source of revenue for medical journals.

(B) Editors of medical journals are often unable to evaluate the claims made in advertisements for new prescription drugs.

(C) Doctors rely on the advertisements as a source of information about new prescription drugs.

(D) Advertisements for new prescription drugs are typically less accurate than medical journal articles evaluating those same drugs.

(E) The Food and Drug Administration, the government agency responsible for drug regulation, reviews advertisements for new drugs only after the ads have already been printed.

Question 32 is based on the following passage.

A study of children's television-watching habits by the federal Department of Education found that children aged 7–10 who watched more than 25 hours of television per week performed worse in school than children of the same age who watched fewer than 25 hours of television per week. Therefore, parents of children aged 7–10 should prohibit their children from watching more than 25 hours of television per week.

32. Which of the following, if true, would best strengthen the argument above?

   (A) A separate study, by a renowned graduate school of education, found that when parents prohibited their children from watching any television, the children's reading scores increased rapidly and significantly, and stayed high indefinitely.

   (B) Children who watched more than 25 hours of television per week also performed worse on measures of physical fitness than children who watched fewer than 25 hours per week.

   (C) The television shows that children aged 7–10 are most likely to watch are saturated with advertisements for products, such as toys and candy, of little educational value.

   (D) The Department of Education study gave appropriate weight to children of backgrounds representative of children nationwide.

   (E) Children who develop a habit of extensive television watching are more likely than others to maintain that habit as an adult.

Reading Comprehension and Reasoning Answer Key

1. **B**
2. **B**
3. *"When pressure on the body decreases as the diver nears the surface, the diver must take care to rise gradually and expel excess gas through the mouth, nose, and ears."*
4. **A, B**
5. **E**
6. **E**
7. **D**
8. **A**
9. **C**
10. **E**
11. **B**
12. **D**
13. **A**
14. **C**
15. **A, C**
16. **A**
17. **E**
18. **B, C**
19. *"However, in realizing gender equality through the assignment of women to female roles, a layer of both added humor and dramatic challenge are removed from several of the Bard's works, including a light comedy* (Twelfth Night), *a dark comedy* (The Merchant of Venice), *and a romance* (As You Like It)."
20. **D**
21. **A, C**
22. *"Because people engage in highly differentiated ways of life, they are by necessity interdependent."*
23. **A**
24. *"All it takes is one court ruling for a term that has shifted away from its identity as a trusted brand name to become forever identified as a generic product."*
25. **C**
26. **C**
27. **E**
28. **C**
29. **E**
30. **C**
31. **C**
32. **D**

Answers and Explanations

Reading Comprehension and Reasoning
Try This At Home Explanations

Lesson 2

14. C

This Global question asks you to identify the main point of the passage. The author's thesis statement in the first sentence should guide you to the correct answer. While (A) refers to one of the reasons for the reversal of the Chicago River, it is not the main point of the passage because it does not address the topic of the passage, which is the Chicago River itself. (B) also does not reference the Chicago River. Choices (C), (D), and (E) each reference the Chicago River, but only (C) mentions it in the context of a major engineering feat, making **(C)** the best choice. (D) and (E) reference only minor features in the passage (specific details of the project).

15. A, C

Examine the statements one by one. **(A)** can be inferred because the passage uses words such as "solid" to describe the bedrock and "complex" to describe the process of connecting the rivers. These words suggest that the job was difficult. Moreover, the second sentence in the passage serves as support for the author's statement that reversing the Chicago River was "one of the greatest engineering feats of all time." If drilling through all that bedrock had not been difficult, the author would have little basis to make that claim. (B) cannot be inferred because the passage does not compare the Chicago River project to any others. **(C)** can be inferred because the statement references a section of the passage that states that the project seemed impossible but was ultimately successful.

16. A

This is an Detail Except question that rewards you for identifying the statement that is *not* stated in the passage. Each of the four wrong choices will be stated in the text. (E) follows from the section of the passage that states that untreated sewage no longer flowed into Lake Michigan after the river was reversed. (D) is stated in the last sentence. (C) also paraphrases the final sentence, which states directly that the city's water became "safer." (B) follows from the passage's first sentence: the Chicago project

"is considered one of the greatest engineering feats." **(A)** distorts the passage. Engineers didn't "cure" the diseases mentioned in the passage; they made it possible to prevent them by improving the quality of Chicago's drinking water.

17. E

This is an Inference Except question. The four incorrect choices will follow logically from the passage; the correct answer will not. (A) is easily eliminated because it directly paraphrases the statement in the first sentence of the paragraph about the reason the Hague Convention was adopted. Likewise for (B), which is confirmed by the quote taken from the convention's preamble, stating that "each people makes its contribution to the culture of the world." (C) refers to the example of the dispute over ownership of the Dead Sea Scrolls following the Six Day War. (D) follows from the second sentence of the passage. The Hague Convention is overseen by UNESCO, which, as the name implies, is a division of the United Nations. **(E)**, however, directly contradicts the latter portion of the passage, which states that the Hague Convention is difficult to enforce. Therefore, this is the correct answer.

18. B, C

The aspect of gender humor specified in the text by the author involves an actor of one gender playing the role of the other gender who is then disguised in the form of the actor's original gender. Modern versions of this can be accomplished by a man playing a woman's role disguised as a man, or a woman playing a man's role disguised as a woman. These versions are the ones contained in choices **(B)** and **(C)**. Simply changing the part from its original gender, as in (A), is insufficient.

19. *"However, in realizing gender equality through the assignment of women to female roles, a layer of both added humor and dramatic challenge are removed from several of the Bard's works, including a light comedy* (Twelfth Night)*, a dark comedy* (The Merchant of Venice)*, and a romance* (As You Like It)*."*

The task here is the most fundamental in all of Reading Comprehension: find the topic sentence. That sentence, initially identified by the transition "however" clearly outlines the premise of the paragraph: modern productions, which tend to assign roles to actors who are the same gender as their characters, have removed an aspect of humor that was intended in Shakespeare's time. Keep in mind that the author does not argue that such a loss is negative or positive, only that it exists. This is why the passage's initial, evaluative sentence is not correct.

Lesson 3

25. C

In this question, you are asked to identify the statement that expresses the main point of the passage. The author begins with large concepts and narrows the information to a single specific event and the influence it had on one person. The claim in (A) is lopsided. The author suggests that poets found new influences in art, not only that of Marcel Duchamp and not only on the subjects of war and industry. The statement in (B) is supported by the passage, but the reason why the general public reacted negatively to the show is an aside intended to provide context for Williams's response. **(C)** best states the connection made in the paragraph and is the correct response. You can disregard (D) as too vague and too broad; nothing implies that influence across genres of art is "easy." (E) merely states the specific example given to support the main point.

26. C

This question asks you to evaluate the veracity of the general statements by making inferences using evidence from the passage. The claim in (A) cannot be supported as there is no proof that all viewers other than artists disliked cubism or that cubism was disliked because it was misunderstood. There is also no evidence to suggest that (B) is correct. Because artists invented new styles that "shattered traditional notions" does not necessarily mean the artists rejected old styles. **(C)** is supported, as the author of the paragraph directly correlates world events with new forms of artistic expression.

Lesson 4

31. C

This question stem asks you to find an answer choice that would strengthen the researchers' conclusion outlined in the second sentence of the stimulus: the researchers believe that misleading drug advertisements in medical journals might lead doctors to prescribe the wrong drugs. Any answer choice that makes this more likely will be correct; therefore, look for a choice that further suggests doctors will end up prescribing inappropriate drugs based on misleading ads.

(C) does this perfectly. By asserting that doctors actually depend on the advertisements for information, it strengthens the bond between the researchers' evidence and their conclusion and therefore strengthens their argument. (A) is irrelevant to this issue—the journals' revenues have no direct connection to the prescribing of drugs. (B) critiques the wrong party—even if *editors of medical journals* can't discern true claims from false, maybe doctors still can. Neither (D) nor (E) tells you anything new. Both support the notion that advertisements are inaccurate or misleading, but the falsehood of the ads is already established in the passage, so neither (D) nor (E) will further strengthen the researchers' argument regarding actual prescriptions.

32. D

Strengthen the argument by finding an answer choice that supports the conclusion: children aged 7–10 shouldn't watch more than 25 hours of TV per week. Since the author uses a study as evidence, the most likely way this argument will be strengthened is by bolstering the legitimacy of this evidence. Strive to quickly eliminate answers that are irrelevant to the issue.

(A) might sound very official, but it errs on two crucial details: first, the cited study in (A) is about children who are *prohibited* from watching television, not just kept down to 25 hours. It also only mentions "children" as its subjects rather than the age range given by the stimulus. While this choice does suggest that "less TV equals better grades," it does not strengthen the argument's specific conclusion and doesn't consider the original argument's evidence at all. (B) is irrelevant because it ventures into measures of physical fitness rather than performance in school. (C) is likewise irrelevant; it offers a possible *explanation* for why TV doesn't educate children but avoids strengthening this author's conclusion that children's television time should be limited.

(D) is correct. If the Department of Education study—the one cited in the stimulus —was appropriately weighted and the sample was representative, then it legitimizes the author's evidence and strengthens the argument.

The adults in (E) are irrelevant to the argument, which is confined to children's television time and scholastic achievement.

CHAPTER 8

Analytical Writing Measure

Lesson 1: Analytical Writing Introduction and Kaplan Method

Every GRE includes two essays:

- Analyze an Issue
- Analyze an Argument

These essays do not contribute to your overall 130–170 Verbal score. Each essay receives a score of 0–6 from both a human grader and a computer grader. The scores for each essay type are averaged, and the results are then averaged to yield an overall Analytical Writing score of 0–6.

THE KAPLAN METHOD

Analytical Writing

STEP 1   Take the issue/argument apart.

STEP 2   Select the points you will make.

STEP 3   Organize, using Kaplan's essay templates.

STEP 4   Type your essay.

STEP 5   Proofread your work.

Lesson 2: **Issue Essay**

Issue Essay Directions

Directions: You will be given a brief quotation that states or implies a topic of general interest, along with explicit instructions on how to respond to that topic. Your response will be evaluated according to how well you:

- respond to the specific directions the task gives you.
- reflect on the complexities of the issue.
- organize and develop your thoughts.
- support your reasoning with relevant examples.
- express yourself in standard written English.

Example Issue Essay tasks

Write your own response to the recommendation in which you discuss why you either agree or disagree with it. Support your response with evidence and/or examples. Use a hypothetical set of circumstances to illustrate the consequences of accepting or rejecting the recommendation, and explain how this informs your thinking.

Develop a response to the claim in which you discuss whether or not you agree with it. Focus specifically on the most powerful or compelling examples that could be used to refute your position.

Step 1: Take the issue apart.

Agree (support one position)

-
-
-
-

Disagree (support the opposite position)

-
-
-
-

Step 2: Select the points you will make.

Step 3: Organize, using Kaplan's Issue Essay template.

- **Paragraph 1:** Paraphrase the issue and state your position.
- **Paragraph 2:** State and elaborate on the strongest point in support of your position.
- **Paragraph 3:** State and elaborate on another point.
- **(Additional paragraphs):** Add more points, as time permits.
- **Second to last paragraph:** Address any specific task in the directions. Some prompts will require you to address an opposing viewpoint and refute it.
- **Final paragraph:** Summarize your position in a way that addresses the specific instructions.

Step 4: Type your essay.

Step 5: Proofread your work.

1. People who work in the arts and humanities should earn less than those who work in the sciences and economics because the benefit of the arts and humanities to the population is less important than that of scientific or economic endeavors.

   Write your own response to the recommendation in which you discuss why you either agree or disagree with it. Support your response with evidence and/or examples. Use a hypothetical set of circumstances to illustrate the consequences of accepting or rejecting the recommendation, and explain how this informs your thinking.

2. Educational institutions have a responsibility to dissuade students from pursuing fields of study in which they are unlikely to succeed.

   Develop a response to the claim in which you discuss whether or not you agree with it. Focus specifically on the most powerful or compelling examples that could be used to refute your position.

3. The main reason we should study history is to ensure that we do not repeat the mistakes of the past.

    Write a response in which you examine your own position on the statement. Explore the extent to which you either agree or disagree with it, and support your reasoning with evidence and/or examples. Be sure to reflect on ways in which the statement might or might not be true, and how this informs your thinking on the subject.

4. Claim: It is in the best interest of the U.S. government to cease funding the National Aeronautics and Space Administration (NASA).

    Reason: The cost of a federal agency like NASA is gargantuan, and the returns on the investment are limited. Funding could be better allocated to dealing with pressing social problems, such as homelessness and poverty.

    Develop a response to the claim in which you discuss whether or not you agree with it. Focus specifically on the most powerful or compelling examples that could be used to refute your position.

Lesson 3: **Breaking Down Arguments**

Argument Essay Directions

Directions: You will be presented with a short passage that asserts an argument or position, along with explicit instructions on how to respond to the passage. Your task is to evaluate the logical soundness of the author's argument. You are NOT being asked to present your views on the subject. Your response will be evaluated according to how well you:

- respond to the specific directions the task gives you.
- analyze and interpret important elements of the passage.
- organize and develop your analysis.
- support your reasoning with relevant examples.
- express yourself in standard written English.

Breaking Down Arguments

Conclusion:

Evidence:

Assumption:

Scope Shifts

Poison is dangerous. Therefore, chemical X is dangerous.

Conclusion:

Evidence:

Assumption:

Socrates is human. Therefore, Socrates is mortal.

Conclusion:

Evidence:

Assumption:

Overlooked Possibilities

Robert's car has a dented fender again. Clearly, Robert is a terrible driver.

Conclusion:

Evidence:

Assumption:

My TA gave me a bad grade on my last paper. It's obvious that my TA doesn't like me.

Conclusion:

Evidence:

Assumption:

Lesson 4: **Argument Essay**

Step 1: Take the argument apart.

Conclusion:

Evidence:

Assumptions:

Step 2: Select the points you will make. Which assumptions are most central? Which can you write the most about?

Step 3: Organize, using Kaplan's Argument Essay template.

- **Paragraph 1:** Paraphrase the conclusion and evidence. Summarize the goal of your essay, according to the specific instructions.
- **Paragraph 2:** State and evaluate the most important assumption.
- **Paragraph 3:** State and evaluate another assumption.
- **Additional paragraphs, as time permits:** State and evaluate another assumption. Be sure you have responded to the task. For instance, some essay tasks require a discussion of how the argument might be strengthened. Another option is to address a specific task in each body paragraph, instead of devoting a paragraph to this.
- **Final paragraph:** Conclude by summarizing your main points.

Step 4: Type your essay.

Use strong transitions to connect your paragraphs and ideas.

-
-
-

Step 5: Proofread your work.

5. The following appeared in a memo from an advertisement by Pest Protection, Inc.:

    "Gardens along the coast are already being infested by the mill bug, a slimy purple pest that can decimate a vegetable garden in seconds flat. If you live within 100 miles of the coast, you need the Pest Protection cure today. Thousands of satisfied customers who have used our chemical-free treatments have never had mill bug problems. One treatment per year will ensure that you never have to lose your valuable crops to this pest."

    Write a response in which you examine the underlying assumptions of the argument. Be sure to explain how the argument hinges on these assumptions and what the implications are for the argument if the assumptions prove unfounded.

6. The following memorandum is from the production manager of SingSong radio:

    "This year, in deference to our many listeners who do not celebrate any of the winter holidays, we will not play holiday music related to any religion on our station. According to an online survey of our listeners, fewer than 20 percent indicated that they enjoy listening to religious songs. Eighty percent noted in the survey that if SingSong began broadcasting religious music (of any faith or denomination), they would 'dramatically' reduce their listening hours.

    "Therefore, to retain our listeners during the holidays, we will respectfully decline any requests for holiday music this year."

    Write a response in which you discuss what questions would need to be answered to decide how likely the stated recommendation is to yield the predicted result. Be sure to explain how the answers to these questions would help to evaluate the recommendation.

7. The following is a letter to the editor of a psychology journal:

"The data collected from a variety of studies now suggest a relationship between the medicine Hypathia and heightened risk of anxiety in patients afflicted with bipolar disorder. In 1950, before Hypathia was widely used to treat bipolar disorder, relatively few patients were diagnosed as anxious or had symptoms that suggested anxiety. However, in five studies published between 2005 and 2010, more than 60 percent of the subjects with bipolar disorder who took Hypathia demonstrated symptoms of anxiety or reported having episodes of heightened anxiety."

Write a response in which you discuss one or more viable alternatives to the proposed explanation. Justify, with support, why your explanation could rival the proposed explanation and explain how your explanation(s) can plausibly account for the facts presented in the argument.

8. A recently issued five-year study on the common cold investigated the possible therapeutic effect of a raw food diet. Raw foods contain antioxidants that boost the immune system. While many foods are naturally rich in antioxidants, food-processing companies also sell isolated antioxidants. The five-year study found a strong correlation between a raw food diet and a steep decline in the average number of colds reported by study participants. A control group that increased their antioxidant intake using supplements did not have a decrease in the number of colds. Based on these study results, some health experts recommend a raw food diet over the use of packaged antioxidants.

Write a response in which you discuss what questions would need to be answered in order to assess the reasonableness of both the recommendation and the argument upon which it is based. Be sure to explain how the answers to these questions would help to evaluate the recommendation.

PART THREE

Additional Practice

CHAPTER 9

Additional Quantitative Practice

Arithmetic and Number Properties

Number Operations Practice Set

> **Directions:** Solve the following questions and select the best answer from those given. Each question has one correct answer unless otherwise noted.

1.

Quantity A	**Quantity B**
$\dfrac{1}{2} - \dfrac{1}{3} + \dfrac{1}{4} - \dfrac{1}{5}$	$\dfrac{2}{3} - \dfrac{1}{2} + \dfrac{2}{5} - \dfrac{1}{4}$

- Ⓐ Quantity A is greater.
- Ⓑ Quantity B is greater.
- Ⓒ The two quantities are equal.
- Ⓓ The relationship cannot be determined from the information given.

2.

$$y \neq -4$$
$$y \neq 0$$

Quantity A	**Quantity B**
$\dfrac{x}{4+y}$	$\dfrac{x}{4} + \dfrac{x}{y}$

- Ⓐ Quantity A is greater.
- Ⓑ Quantity B is greater.
- Ⓒ The two quantities are equal.
- Ⓓ The relationship cannot be determined from the information given.

 229

3.

$$k < m < 0$$

Quantity A

$$\dfrac{k-m}{k+m}$$

Quantity B

$$\dfrac{m-k}{k+m}$$

Ⓐ Quantity A is greater.

Ⓑ Quantity B is greater.

Ⓒ The two quantities are equal.

Ⓓ The relationship cannot be determined from the information given.

4.

$$a > b > c > 2$$

Quantity A

$$\dfrac{3a+2b}{b-c} - \dfrac{b-2a}{1+c}$$

Quantity B

$$\dfrac{2(c+a)}{a+1} + \dfrac{3(b+a-c)}{c-b}$$

Ⓐ Quantity A is greater.

Ⓑ Quantity B is greater.

Ⓒ The two quantities are equal.

Ⓓ The relationship cannot be determined from the information given.

5. $3.44 =$

Ⓐ $\dfrac{14}{25}$

Ⓑ $\dfrac{33}{25}$

Ⓒ $3\dfrac{11}{50}$

Ⓓ $3\dfrac{11}{25}$

Ⓔ $3\dfrac{22}{25}$

6. $\dfrac{(0.020)(0.0003)}{0.002} =$

   - (A) 0.3
   - (B) 0.03
   - (C) 0.003
   - (D) 0.0003
   - (E) 0.00003

7. $\dfrac{\frac{1}{6} + \frac{1}{3} + 2}{\frac{3}{4} + \frac{5}{4} + 3} =$

   - (A) $\dfrac{1}{3}$
   - (B) $\dfrac{1}{2}$
   - (C) $\dfrac{5}{8}$
   - (D) $\dfrac{2}{3}$
   - (E) 1

8. For which of the following expressions would the value be greater if 160 were replaced by 120?

   Select all such expressions.

   - [A] $1{,}000 - 160$
   - [B] $\dfrac{160}{1} + 160$
   - [C] $\dfrac{1}{1 - \frac{1}{160}}$
   - [D] $160^{-2} + 160^{2}$

$$\frac{5}{9}, \frac{5}{12}, \frac{23}{48}, \frac{11}{24}, \frac{3}{7}$$

9. What is the positive difference between the largest and smallest of the fractions above?

(A) $\frac{1}{12}$

(B) $\frac{5}{36}$

(C) $\frac{1}{4}$

(D) $\frac{1}{3}$

(E) $\frac{7}{18}$

10. If x, y, and z are all positive and $0.04x = 5y = 2z$, then which of the following is true?

(A) $x < y < z$

(B) $x < z < y$

(C) $y < x < z$

(D) $y < z < x$

(E) $z < y < x$

Exponents and Radicals Practice Set

Directions: Solve the following questions and select the best answer from those given. Each question has one correct answer unless otherwise noted.

1. $x \neq 0$

Quantity A	Quantity B
$\sqrt{x^2 + 9}$	$x + 3$

(A) Quantity A is greater.

(B) Quantity B is greater.

(C) The two quantities are equal.

(D) The relationship cannot be determined from the information given.

2. $0 < x < y < 1$

Quantity A	**Quantity B**

$$\frac{\left(xy^{-2}\right)^{-3}}{x^{-8}}$$

- (A) Quantity A is greater.
- (B) Quantity B is greater.
- (C) The two quantities are equal.
- (D) The relationship cannot be determined from the information given.

3.   Which of the following is NOT equal to 0.0675?

- (A) 67.5×10^{-3}
- (B) 6.75×10^{-2}
- (C) 0.675×10^{-1}
- (D) 0.00675×10^{2}
- (E) 0.0000675×10^{3}

4.   If $x > 0$, then $(4^x)(8^x) =$

- (A) 2^{9x}
- (B) 2^{8x}
- (C) 2^{6x}
- (D) 2^{5x}
- (E) 2^{4x}

5.   What positive number, when squared, is equal to the cube of the positive square root of 16?

- (A) 64
- (B) 56
- (C) 32
- (D) 8
- (E) 2

6.   Which of the following expressions is equal to 8^5?

Select all such expressions.

- [A] $2^5 \cdot 4^5$
- [B] 2^{15}
- [C] $2^5 \cdot 2^{10}$

7. If $27^n = 9^4$, then $n =$

    (A) $\dfrac{4}{3}$

    (B) 2

    (C) $\dfrac{8}{3}$

    (D) 3

    (E) 8

8. If $xyz \neq 0$, then $\dfrac{x^3 yz^4}{xy^{-2}z^3} =$

    (A) $x^2 y^3 z$

    (B) $x^4 y^{-1} z^7$

    (C) $x^2 y^{-1} z$

    (D) $x^2 y^3 z^2$

    (E) $x^4 yz$

9. If $x^a \cdot x^b = 1$ and $x \neq \pm 1$, then $a + b =$

    (A) x

    (B) -1

    (C) 0

    (D) 1

    (E) It cannot be determined from the information given.

10. If $n \neq 4$, which of the following is equivalent to $\dfrac{n - 4\sqrt{n} + 4}{\sqrt{n} - 2}$?

    (A) $\sqrt{n}$

    (B) $2\sqrt{n}$

    (C) $\sqrt{n} + 2$

    (D) $\sqrt{n} - 2$

    (E) $n + \sqrt{n}$

Number Properties Practice Set

Directions: Solve the following questions and select the best answer from those given. Each question has one correct answer unless otherwise noted.

1.
$$x = 165$$
$$y = 2$$
$$z = 41$$

Quantity A	**Quantity B**
$\dfrac{x^x}{5}$	$55(x)^{y^2 z}$

- (A) Quantity A is greater.
- (B) Quantity B is greater.
- (C) The two quantities are equal.
- (D) The relationship cannot be determined from the information given.

2. Which of the following is <u>not</u> a factor of 168?

- (A) 21
- (B) 24
- (C) 28
- (D) 32
- (E) 42

3. What is the smallest positive integer that is evenly divisible by both 21 and 9?

- (A) 189
- (B) 126
- (C) 63
- (D) 42
- (E) 21

4. If n is an odd number, which of the following must be even?

- (A) $\dfrac{n-1}{2}$
- (B) $\dfrac{n+1}{2}$
- (C) $n^2 + 2n$
- (D) $2n + 2$
- (E) $3n^2 - 2n$

5. If the integer P leaves a remainder of 4 when divided by 9, all of the following must be true except:

- (A) The number that is 4 less than P is a multiple of 9.
- (B) The number that is 5 more than P is a multiple of 9.
- (C) The number that is 2 more than P is a multiple of 3.
- (D) When divided by 3, P will leave a remainder of 1.
- (E) When divided by 2, P will leave a remainder of 1.

6. If the product of two integers is an even number and the sum of the same two integers is an odd number, which of the following must be true?

- (A) The two integers are both odd.
- (B) The two integers are both even.
- (C) One of the two integers is odd and the other is even.
- (D) One of the integers is 1.
- (E) The two integers are consecutive.

7. If both the product and sum of four integers are even, which of the following could be the number of even integers in the group?

Select all that apply.

- [A] 0
- [B] 2
- [C] 4

8. A wire is cut into three equal parts. The resulting segments are then cut into 4, 6 and 8 equal parts respectively. If each of the resulting segments has an integer length, what is the minimum length of the wire?

- (A) 24
- (B) 36
- (C) 48
- (D) 54
- (E) 72

9. How many positive integers less than 60 are equal to the product of a positive multiple of 5 and an even number?

   (A) 4
   (B) 5
   (C) 9
   (D) 10
   (E) 11

10. A vault holds only 8-ounce tablets of gold and 5-ounce tablets of silver. If there are 130 ounces of gold and silver total, what is the greatest amount of gold that can be in the vault, in ounces?

   (A) 40
   (B) 80
   (C) 120
   (D) 128
   (E) 130

Equations and Inequalities Practice Set

Directions: Solve the following questions and select the best answer from those given. Each question has one correct answer unless otherwise noted.

1.
$$a^2 + a - b = 10$$
$$a^2 + 5a + 3b = 30$$

Quantity A	**Quantity B**
$a + b$	6

   (A) Quantity A is greater.
   (B) Quantity B is greater.
   (C) The two quantities are equal.
   (D) The relationship cannot be determined from the information given.

2.

$$t = 5r - \frac{12}{s}$$
$$-3 \leq r \leq 3$$
$$2 \leq s \leq 6$$

Quantity A	**Quantity B**
The maximum value of t less the minimum value of t	33

- (A) Quantity A is greater.
- (B) Quantity B is greater.
- (C) The two quantities are equal.
- (D) The relationship cannot be determined from the information given.

3.

$$xy - 5x = -16$$
$$y = x - 3$$

Quantity A	**Quantity B**
x	4

- (A) Quantity A is greater.
- (B) Quantity B is greater.
- (C) The two quantities are equal.
- (D) The relationship cannot be determined from the information given.

4.

$$a < y < b$$
$$c < z < d$$
$$z > y$$

Quantity A	**Quantity B**
b	c

- (A) Quantity A is greater.
- (B) Quantity B is greater.
- (C) The two quantities are equal.
- (D) The relationship cannot be determined from the information given.

5. What is the value of a if $ab + ac = 21$ and $b + c = 7$?

    (A) -3
    (B) -1
    (C) 0
    (D) 3
    (E) 7

6. If $\dfrac{x+3}{2} + x + 3 = 3$, then $x =$

    (A) -3
    (B) $-\dfrac{3}{2}$
    (C) -1
    (D) 0
    (E) 1

7. In the equation $mx + 5 = y$, m is a constant. If $x = 2$ when $y = 1$, what is the value of x when $y = -1$?

    (A) -1
    (B) 0
    (C) 1
    (D) 2
    (E) 3

8. If $a > b > c$, then all of the following could be true except:

    (A) $b + c < a$
    (B) $2a > b + c$
    (C) $2c > a + b$
    (D) $ab > bc$
    (E) $a + b > 2b + c$

9. If $4 < -\dfrac{1}{3}z$, which of the following could be the value of z?

    (A) -15
    (B) -12
    (C) 0
    (D) 12
    (E) 18

10. Line A passes through the point $(-3, -2)$ and has a slope of 0.8. Line B is defined by the equation $x = 11.2 - 2y$. Which of the following are the coordinates of the intersection of lines A and B?

(A) $(-6.0, -4.0)$

(B) $(2.0, 5.6)$

(C) $(4.0, 2.6)$

(D) $(4.0, 3.6)$

(E) $(5.6, 4.0)$

Quadratics Practice Set

Directions: Solve the following questions and select the best answer from those given. Each question has one correct answer unless otherwise noted.

1.
$$x^2 - 9x + 32 = 12$$

Quantity A	Quantity B
x	3

(A) Quantity A is greater.

(B) Quantity B is greater.

(C) The two quantities are equal.

(D) The relationship cannot be determined from the information given.

2.
$$a^2 - 6 = 3$$
$$b^2 + 9b + 20 = 0$$

Quantity A	Quantity B
The minimum value of a	The maximum value of b

(A) Quantity A is greater.

(B) Quantity B is greater.

(C) The two quantities are equal.

(D) The relationship cannot be determined from the information given.

3.
$$4x^3 - 4x^2 - 8x - y^2 - 7y + 12 = 0$$

Quantity A	**Quantity B**
x	y

A) Quantity A is greater.

B) Quantity B is greater.

C) The two quantities are equal.

D) The relationship cannot be determined from the information given.

4.
$$y = -5$$
$$x^2 - 4x - 10 = 11$$

Quantity A	**Quantity B**
The maximum value of xy	35

A) Quantity A is greater.

B) Quantity B is greater.

C) The two quantities are equal.

D) The relationship cannot be determined from the information given.

5. If $\dfrac{p}{p+2} = \dfrac{p-3}{4}$, the value of p could be

A) −6

B) −4

C) 1

D) 3

E) 6

6. If $2w^2 - 2w - 12 = 0$ and $z^2 - 4z = 5$, what is the range of the maximum and minimum values of wz?

7. If $2x^2 - 5xy - 3y^2 = 0$ and $x > 3$, which of the following could be the value of y?

Select <u>all</u> such values.

- [A] -8
- [B] -4
- [C] -2
- [D] 0
- [E] 1
- [F] 2

8. If $3x^2 + 5xy - 12y^2 = 0$ and $y = 3$, which of the following could be the value of x?

- (A) -9
- (B) -4
- (C) 0
- (D) 3
- (E) 9

9. If $x - 2\sqrt{5x} + 5 = 0$, what is the value of x?

- (A) -5
- (B) $-\sqrt{5}$
- (C) $\sqrt{5}$
- (D) 5
- (E) 25

10. If $3x^2 - 7x + 3 = 0$, which of the following could be the value of x?

- (A) $\dfrac{-7 + \sqrt{13}}{6}$
- (B) $\dfrac{-3 + \sqrt{85}}{6}$
- (C) $\dfrac{3 + \sqrt{13}}{6}$
- (D) $\dfrac{7 + \sqrt{13}}{6}$
- (E) $\dfrac{7 - \sqrt{85}}{6}$

Functions and Symbolism Practice Set

> **Directions:** Solve the following questions and select the best answer from those given. Each question has one correct answer unless otherwise noted.

1.
$$f(x) = x^2 - 6x - 3$$

Quantity A	**Quantity B**
$f(2)$	$f(4)$

- (A) Quantity A is greater.
- (B) Quantity B is greater.
- (C) The two quantities are equal.
- (D) The relationship cannot be determined from the information given.

2.
$$a \heartsuit b = a^2 - ab - b^2$$
$$x < y < 0$$

Quantity A	**Quantity B**
$x \heartsuit y$	$(x + y)^2$

- (A) Quantity A is greater.
- (B) Quantity B is greater.
- (C) The two quantities are equal.
- (D) The relationship cannot be determined from the information given.

3.
$$m \clubsuit n = \frac{m + n}{m} - 6$$
$$10 \clubsuit x = 34$$

Quantity A	**Quantity B**
x^2	160,000

- (A) Quantity A is greater.
- (B) Quantity B is greater.
- (C) The two quantities are equal.
- (D) The relationship cannot be determined from the information given.

4. $f(x) = x + 2$ and $g(x) = \sqrt{x} + 3$

Quantity A	**Quantity B**
$g(f(2))$	4

(A) Quantity A is greater.

(B) Quantity B is greater.

(C) The two quantities are equal.

(D) The relationship cannot be determined from the information given.

5.   If $g(y) = \dfrac{y^3 + 15}{7}$, $m = 5$, and $n = 3$, then $g(m) - g(n) =$

(A) -14

(B) $-\dfrac{16}{7}$

(C) $\dfrac{16}{7}$

(D) 14

(E) 20

6.   If $\spadesuit z = \dfrac{z + 2}{z - 2}$ and $w = 4$, the value of $\spadesuit w - \spadesuit(-w)$ is

(A) $-3\dfrac{1}{3}$

(B) 0

(C) $\dfrac{1}{3}$

(D) $2\dfrac{2}{3}$

(E) $3\dfrac{1}{3}$

7.   Given $f(x) = -(x + 4)^2 - 3$, which of the following must be true?

(A) $f(x)$ is minimized when $x = 4$

(B) $f(x)$ is maximized when $x = 4$

(C) $f(x)$ is minimized when $x = -4$

(D) $f(x)$ is maximized when $x = -4$

(E) $f(x)$ has no maximum

8.   If p ## $q = (p - 5)(q + 3)$ and 2 ## $x = -30$, what is the value of x?

[   ]

9. If $f(x) = -x^2 + 2x + 5$, for which of the following values of x is $f(x) > 0$?

   Select all such values.

   A −4
   B −2
   C 0
   D 2
   E 4
   F 6

10. If z is the sum of two consecutive integers and $a \updownarrow b = \dfrac{a^3 - b}{b}$, then which of the following statements could be false?

   Select all such statements.

   A $z \updownarrow 2$ is odd
   B $z \updownarrow 2$ is even
   C $2 \updownarrow z$ is odd
   D $2 \updownarrow z$ is even
   E $z \updownarrow 2$ is not an integer
   F $2 \updownarrow z$ is not an integer

Ratios and Proportions Practice Set

Directions: Solve the following questions and select the best answer from those given. Each question has one correct answer unless otherwise noted.

1.
$$\frac{a}{b} = \frac{c}{d}$$

Quantity A	**Quantity B**
$\dfrac{a}{d}$	$\dfrac{bc}{d^2}$

   (A) Quantity A is greater.
   (B) Quantity B is greater.
   (C) The two quantities are equal.
   (D) The relationship cannot be determined from the information given.

2.

$$\frac{a}{b} = \frac{1}{3}$$
$$\frac{a+3}{b} = \frac{1}{2}$$

Quantity A	**Quantity B**
b	21

- (A) Quantity A is greater.
- (B) Quantity B is greater.
- (C) The two quantities are equal.
- (D) The relationship cannot be determined from the information given.

3. The ratio of donuts to muffins at a certain coffee shop is 5:4, and the ratio of muffins to croissants is 7:3.

Quantity A	**Quantity B**
The ratio of donuts to croissants	3:1

- (A) Quantity A is greater.
- (B) Quantity B is greater.
- (C) The two quantities are equal.
- (D) The relationship cannot be determined from the information given.

4.

$$abcd \neq 0$$
$$ad > bc$$
$$bd > 0$$

Quantity A	**Quantity B**
$\dfrac{a}{b}$	$\dfrac{c}{d}$

- (A) Quantity A is greater.
- (B) Quantity B is greater.
- (C) The two quantities are equal.
- (D) The relationship cannot be determined from the information given.

5. In a certain class, 3 out of 24 students are in student organizations. What is the ratio of students in student organizations to students not in student organizations?

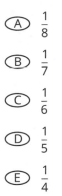

  (A) $\dfrac{1}{8}$

  (B) $\dfrac{1}{7}$

  (C) $\dfrac{1}{6}$

  (D) $\dfrac{1}{5}$

  (E) $\dfrac{1}{4}$

6. On a scaled map, a distance of 10 centimeters represents 5 kilometers. If a street is 750 meters long, what is its length on the map, in centimeters? (1 kilometer = 1,000 meters)

  (A) 0.015

  (B) 0.15

  (C) 1.5

  (D) 15

  (E) 150

7. If the ratio of tics to tacs is 1:3, and the ratio of tacs to tocs is 2:5, what is the ratio of tics to tocs?

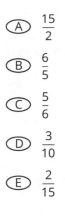

  (A) $\dfrac{15}{2}$

  (B) $\dfrac{6}{5}$

  (C) $\dfrac{5}{6}$

  (D) $\dfrac{3}{10}$

  (E) $\dfrac{2}{15}$

8. At a certain high school, $\dfrac{2}{3}$ of the students play on sports teams. Of the students who play sports, $\dfrac{1}{4}$ play on the football team. If there are a total of 240 students in the high school, how many students play on the football team?

  (A) 180

  (B) 160

  (C) 80

  (D) 60

  (E) 40

9. Jane knits 72 stitches to the line and uses $\frac{1}{4}$ inch of yarn in each of the stitches. How many lines can she knit with 10 yards of yarn? (1 yard = 3 feet; 1 foot = 12 inches)

  (A) 10
  (B) 20
  (C) 30
  (D) 40
  (E) 50

10. John buys R pounds of cheese to feed N people at a party. If $N + P$ people come to the party, how many more pounds of cheese must John buy in order to feed everyone at the original rate?

  (A) $\dfrac{NP}{R}$

  (B) $\dfrac{N}{RP}$

  (C) $\dfrac{N+P}{R}$

  (D) $\dfrac{P}{NR}$

  (E) $\dfrac{PR}{N}$

Percents Practice Set

Directions: Solve the following questions and select the best answer from those given. Each question has one correct answer unless otherwise noted.

1.

Quantity A	Quantity B
0.0125% of 1000	1.25

  (A) Quantity A is greater.
  (B) Quantity B is greater.
  (C) The two quantities are equal.
  (D) The relationship cannot be determined from the information given.

2. The price of an item that originally sold for $150 was reduced by 20%. The new price was then further reduced by x% to a final price of $102.

Quantity A	Quantity B
x	12

- (A) Quantity A is greater.
- (B) Quantity B is greater.
- (C) The two quantities are equal.
- (D) The relationship cannot be determined from the information given.

3. Janine wants to increase the percent profit on her cookie sales. Her percent profit when the cookies are priced at $5 a box is 20%, so she decides to increase the price of her cookies by $1 per box. Her new percent profit is p.

Quantity A	Quantity B
p	25%

- (A) Quantity A is greater.
- (B) Quantity B is greater.
- (C) The two quantities are equal.
- (D) The relationship cannot be determined from the information given.

4. Two weeks ago, Roshni considered buying a television that cost $1,500. The manager offered her a 25% discount, but she declined. A week later she joined the store's rewards club and decided to buy the television during the upcoming clearance sale. The day before the clearance sale began, television prices were marked up by 35%. During the clearance sale, everything in the store was half off and rewards club members received an additional 15% discount.

Quantity A	Quantity B
The difference between the price Roshni would have paid for the television two weeks ago and the price she paid during the clearance sale	$275

- (A) Quantity A is greater.
- (B) Quantity B is greater.
- (C) The two quantities are equal.
- (D) The relationship cannot be determined from the information given.

5.   A store sells a watch for a profit of 25% of the cost. What percent of the selling price is the profit?

   (A)   5%

   (B) $16\frac{2}{3}$%

   (C)   20%

   (D) $33\frac{1}{3}$%

   (E)   45%

6.   A factory cut its labor force by 16%, then increased it by 25% of the new number. What was the net percent change in the size of the workforce?

   (A)   a 5% decrease

   (B)   no net change

   (C)   a 5% increase

   (D)   a 9% increase

   (E)   a 10% increase

7.   If a dealer had sold a stereo for $600, he would have made a 20% profit. Instead, the dealer sold it for a 40% loss. At what price was the stereo sold?

   (A) $300

   (B) $315

   (C) $372

   (D) $400

   (E) $440

8.   A store offers a variety of discounts that range from 10–25%, inclusive. If a book is discounted to a price of $2.40, what was its greatest possible price originally?

   (A) $2.67

   (B) $3.00

   (C) $3.20

   (D) $10.80

   (E) $24.00

Rates, Average Speed, and Combined Work Practice Set

Directions: Solve the following questions and select the best answer from those given. Each question has one correct answer unless otherwise noted.

1. Annalise and Claire run laps around a $\frac{1}{4}$ mile track. They run in the same direction, start at the same time and place, and run for 36 minutes. Annalise runs at a constant speed of 8 miles per hour, and Claire maintains a constant rate of 6 miles per hour.

Quantity A	**Quantity B**
The number of times Annalise passes Claire	4

    Ⓐ Quantity A is greater.
    Ⓑ Quantity B is greater.
    Ⓒ The two quantities are equal.
    Ⓓ The relationship cannot be determined from the information given.

2.

Quantity A	**Quantity B**
A $1,000 investment compounded quarterly 20 times at 1% quarterly interest	A $1,000 investment compounded annually for 5 years at 4% annual interest

    Ⓐ Quantity A is greater.
    Ⓑ Quantity B is greater.
    Ⓒ The two quantities are equal.
    Ⓓ The relationship cannot be determined from the information given.

3. Working together, machines P and Q can complete a task in $2\frac{1}{2}$ hours. Machine P can complete the task in 4 hours working alone.

Quantity A	**Quantity B**
The time it would take Machine Q to complete the task working alone	9 hours

    Ⓐ Quantity A is greater.
    Ⓑ Quantity B is greater.
    Ⓒ The two quantities are equal.
    Ⓓ The relationship cannot be determined from the information given.

4. Two cars travel away from each other in opposite directions at 24 miles per hour and 40 miles per hour, respectively. If the first car travels for 20 minutes and the second car for 45 minutes, how many miles apart will they be at the end of their trips?

    (A) 22

    (B) 24

    (C) 30

    (D) 38

    (E) 42

5. A certain mule travels at $\frac{2}{3}$ the speed of a certain horse. If it takes the horse 6 hours to travel 20 miles, how many hours will the trip take the mule?

    (A) 4

    (B) 8

    (C) 9

    (D) 10

    (E) 30

6. A car travels 60 kilometers in one hour before a piston breaks, then travels at 30 kilometers per hour for the remaining 60 kilometers to its destination. What is the car's average speed in kilometers per hour for the entire trip?

    (A) 20

    (B) 40

    (C) 45

    (D) 50

    (E) 60

7. Working alone, Allen can paint a room in 12 hours. Working alone, Charles can paint the same room in 6 hours. How many hours would it take Allen and Charles to paint the room if they work together?

    (A) 2

    (B) 3

    (C) $3\frac{3}{7}$

    (D) 4

    (E) $4\frac{1}{2}$

8. If a driver travels m miles per hour for 4 hours and then travels $\frac{3}{4}m$ miles per hour every hour thereafter, how many miles will she drive in 10 hours?

  (A) $\frac{15}{2}m$

  (B) $8m$

  (C) $\frac{17}{2}m$

  (D) $10m$

  (E) $\frac{21}{2}m$

9. A motorist travels 90 miles at rate of 20 miles per hour. If she returns the same distance at a rate of 40 miles per hour, what is the average speed for the entire trip, in miles per hour?

  (A) 20

  (B) $\frac{65}{3}$

  (C) $\frac{80}{3}$

  (D) 30

  (E) $\frac{130}{3}$

10. Phil is making a 40-kilometer canoe trip. If he travels at 30 kilometers per hour for the first 10 kilometers and at 15 kilometers per hour for the rest of the trip, how many minutes longer will it take him than if he makes the entire trip at 20 kilometers per hour?

  (A) 15

  (B) 20

  (C) 35

  (D) 45

  (E) 50

11. If snow falls at a rate of x centimeters per minute, how many hours would it take for y centimeters to fall?

  (A) $\frac{x}{60y}$

  (B) $\frac{y}{60x}$

  (C) $\frac{60x}{y}$

  (D) $\frac{60y}{x}$

  (E) $60xy$

Averages Practice Set

Directions: Solve the following questions and select the best answer from those given. Each question has one correct answer unless otherwise noted.

1.

$$\text{Set } S = \{-4, 1, 3, 5, x\}$$

Quantity A	**Quantity B**
The average of set S	x

A) Quantity A is greater.
B) Quantity B is greater.
C) The two quantities are equal.
D) The relationship cannot be determined from the information given.

2. The number of cars observed passing a point on a road each hour for 6 consecutive hours was 12, 13, 9, 8, 9, and 15.

Quantity A	**Quantity B**
The increase in the average if the next observation is 12.	$\dfrac{1}{6}$

A) Quantity A is greater.
B) Quantity B is greater.
C) The two quantities are equal.
D) The relationship cannot be determined from the information given.

3.

Quantity A	**Quantity B**
The average of 2^2, 3^2, and 4^2	9

A) Quantity A is greater.
B) Quantity B is greater.
C) The two quantities are equal.
D) The relationship cannot be determined from the information given.

4. Ms. Solis administered a four-question quiz to her class. Ten students had a perfect score, four got 3 questions right, another four scored 2, and three only answered 1 question correctly. The weighted average of the class scores was 3.0.

Quantity A	**Quantity B**
The number of students who scored 0	1

  - (A) Quantity A is greater.
  - (B) Quantity B is greater.
  - (C) The two quantities are equal.
  - (D) The relationship cannot be determined from the information given.

5. A student averages 72 on 5 tests. If the lowest score is dropped, the average rises to 84. What is the lowest score?

  - (A) 18
  - (B) 24
  - (C) 32
  - (D) 43
  - (E) 48

6. The average (arithmetic mean) of two numbers is $3n - 4$. If one of the numbers is n, then the other number is

  - (A) $2n - 4$
  - (B) $3n - 4$
  - (C) $5n - 8$
  - (D) $5n + 8$
  - (E) $6n - 8$

7. Fifteen movie theaters average 600 customers per theater per day. If 6 of the theaters close down but the total theater attendance stays the same, what is the average daily attendance per theater among the remaining theaters?

  - (A) 500
  - (B) 750
  - (C) 1,000
  - (D) 1,200
  - (E) 1,500

8. If the average (arithmetic mean) of 18 consecutive odd integers is 534, then the least of these integers is

(A) 517

(B) 518

(C) 519

(D) 521

(E) 525

9. The average (arithmetic mean) of 6 positive numbers is 5. If the average of the least and greatest of these numbers is 7, what is the average of the other 4 numbers?

(A) 3

(B) 4

(C) 5

(D) 6

(E) 7

10. If the average (arithmetic mean) of a, b, and 7 is 13, what is the average of $a + 3$, $b - 5$, and 6?

(A) 7

(B) 9

(C) 10

(D) 12

(E) 16

11. In a group of 60 workers, the average salary is $160 a day per worker. If some of the workers earn $150 a day and all the rest earn $200 a day, how many workers earn $150 a day?

(A) 12

(B) 24

(C) 36

(D) 48

(E) 54

Statistics Practice Set

> **Directions:** Solve the following questions and select the best answer from those given. Each question has one correct answer unless otherwise noted.

1.

Quantity A	**Quantity B**
The median of the six smallest positive even integers	6

- Ⓐ Quantity A is greater.
- Ⓑ Quantity B is greater.
- Ⓒ The two quantities are equal.
- Ⓓ The relationship cannot be determined from the information given.

2.

Value	Number of Occurrences
0	3
1	4
2	3
3	2
4	1
5	1
6	0
7	1

Quantity A	**Quantity B**
The mean of the values in the table	The median of the values in the table

- Ⓐ Quantity A is greater.
- Ⓑ Quantity B is greater.
- Ⓒ The two quantities are equal.
- Ⓓ The relationship cannot be determined from the information given.

3.

$$x = -2, y = 2, \text{ and } z = 1$$

Quantity A   **Quantity B**

The range of x^2, y^2 and z^2 The range of $x, y,$ and z

   (A) Quantity A is greater.

   (B) Quantity B is greater.

   (C) The two quantities are equal.

   (D) The relationship cannot be determined from the information given.

4.   The average of a set of 5 numbers is 6. An additional element, a, is added to the set so that the average increases to 7.

Quantity A   **Quantity B**

The value of a 12

   (A) Quantity A is greater.

   (B) Quantity B is greater.

   (C) The two quantities are equal.

   (D) The relationship cannot be determined from the information given.

5.   The mean of the numbers $\{-1, 0, 1, 2, 3, 4, 5, \text{ and } x\}$ is 2. What is the mode of these numbers?

   (A) 1

   (B) 2

   (C) 3

   (D) 4

   (E) 5

Value	# of Observations
1	1
2	3
3	2
4	2
5	z
6	2
7	4
8	2
9	3
10	2
11	1

6. The table above lists the numbers of observations for each of 11 values, with one unknown number of observations, z. If the weighted average of the values is 6, the value of z is

    (A) 1
    (B) 2
    (C) 3
    (D) 4
    (E) 5

7. The variables a, b, c, d, and e are all different positive integers. Which of the following has the least standard deviation?

    (A) $\{a, b, c, d, e\}$

    (B) $\left\{\dfrac{a}{2}, \dfrac{b}{2}, \dfrac{c}{2}, \dfrac{d}{2}, \dfrac{e}{2}\right\}$

    (C) $\{0.7a, 0.7b, 0.7c, 0.7d, 0.7e\}$

    (D) $\{2a, 2b, 2c, 2d, 2e\}$

    (E) $\{a + 2, b + 2, c + 2, d + 2, e + 2\}$

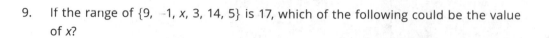
8. In a set of numbers, the mean is 12, and 17 is 1.25 standard deviations from the mean. What is the standard deviation?

   [   ]

9. If the range of {9, −1, x, 3, 14, 5} is 17, which of the following could be the value of x?

   Select all such values.

   A   −17
   B   −14
   C   −3
   D   8
   E   16
   F   17

10. There are 30 teachers in the mathematics and science departments at a certain school. Of these teachers, 20 are certified math teachers and 14 are certified science teachers. Not all teachers in the math and science departments are necessarily certified in either subject matter. Which of the following could be the number of teachers certified in both math and science?

    Select all such numbers.

    A   0
    B   5
    C   7
    D   10
    E   14
    F   16

Counting Methods and Probability Practice Set

> **Directions:** Solve the following questions and select the best answer from those given. Each question has one correct answer unless otherwise noted.

1. Loquanda is playing a beanbag tossing game. Her probability of scoring a point on any given attempt is 50%.

Quantity A	**Quantity B**
The probability that Loquanda will score exactly 1 point on 2 tosses	The probability that Loquanda will score exactly 2 points on 4 tosses

    (A) Quantity A is greater.

    (B) Quantity B is greater.

    (C) The two quantities are equal.

    (D) The relationship cannot be determined from the information given.

2. Raghu rolls two fair six-sided dice numbered 1 through 6.

Quantity A	**Quantity B**
The probability that Raghu rolls at least one number lower than a 5.	The probability that Raghu does not roll the same number twice.

    (A) Quantity A is greater.

    (B) Quantity B is greater.

    (C) The two quantities are equal.

    (D) The relationship cannot be determined from the information given.

3.

Quantity A	**Quantity B**
The number of permutations of 3 objects selected from a group of 6	The number of combinations of 4 objects selected from a group of 9

    (A) Quantity A is greater.

    (B) Quantity B is greater.

    (C) The two quantities are equal.

    (D) The relationship cannot be determined from the information given.

4. Vlada's board game collection consists of 3 bidding games, 5 worker placement games, and 7 area control games. There is no overlap among the categories.

Quantity A	Quantity B
The number of ways to select 3 board games such that no two of them belong to the same category	The number of ways to select 4 board games such that exactly 2 are bidding games

(A) Quantity A is greater.

(B) Quantity B is greater.

(C) The two quantities are equal.

(D) The relationship cannot be determined from the information given.

5. When Percy plays darts, the probability of his getting a bullseye increases by 40% with each subsequent throw. If the likelihood of Percy getting a bullseye on his first throw is 1 in 5, what is the probability that Percy throws 3 bullseyes in a row? (Round to the nearest tenth.)

(A) 87.2%

(B) 22.2%

(C) 8.7%

(D) 2.2%

(E) 0.9%

6. In how many different ways can the letters A, B, C, D, E, and F be arranged if A and B must be next to each other and E and F must be next to each other?

[   ]

7. Of the five people in a room, three wear glasses and three have beards. Which of the following events CANNOT have a probability greater than 50%?

Select all such events.

A One person selected at random wears glasses and has a beard

B One person selected at random neither wears glasses nor has a beard

C One person selected at random wears glasses but does not have a beard

D Two people selected at random have at least one beard and one pair of glasses between them

E Three people selected at random each have either a pair of glasses or a beard or both

8. A youth club with 12 children is taking a field trip to an arboretum. A counselor divides the children into 3 groups of 4 and appoints a leader for each group. When the children line up in single file to enter the arboretum, they must stay in their groups, and the leader of each group must be at the front of each group. How many different ways can the children line up?

   Ⓐ 648

   Ⓑ 1,296

   Ⓒ 7,776

   Ⓓ 41,472

   Ⓔ 82,944

9. There are 495 possible combinations of x objects selected from a group of 12 distinct objects. What is the value of x?

   Ⓐ 2

   Ⓑ 3

   Ⓒ 4

   Ⓓ 5

   Ⓔ 6

10. Hubert wants to arrange 7 distinct plush horse dolls in a single row on his shelf. Three of the dolls are purple, 3 are burgundy, and 1 is mauve. If no two adjacent dolls can have the same color and the purple dolls can't go on the ends, then in how many different ways can Hubert arrange the dolls?

    Ⓐ 4

    Ⓑ 27

    Ⓒ 144

    Ⓓ 2,520

    Ⓔ 5,040

Lines and Angles Practice Set

Directions: Solve the following questions and select the best answer from those given. Each question has one correct answer unless otherwise noted.

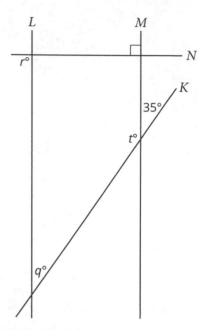

Line *L* is parallel to Line *M*

1.

Quantity A	**Quantity B**
$2q$	$t - r$

Ⓐ Quantity A is greater.

Ⓑ Quantity B is greater.

Ⓒ The two quantities are equal.

Ⓓ The relationship cannot be determined from the information given.

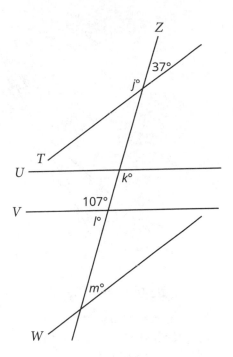

Line $T \parallel$ Line W, and Line $U \parallel$ Line V

2.

Quantity A	**Quantity B**
360°	$k + j + l + m$

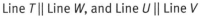

- Ⓐ Quantity A is greater.
- Ⓑ Quantity B is greater.
- Ⓒ The two quantities are equal.
- Ⓓ The relationship cannot be determined from the information given.

Line segment HJ = 13
Line segment GI = 9
Each line segment has an integer value

3.

Quantity A	**Quantity B**
$GJ - x$	15

- Ⓐ Quantity A is greater.
- Ⓑ Quantity B is greater.
- Ⓒ The two quantities are equal.
- Ⓓ The relationship cannot be determined from the information given.

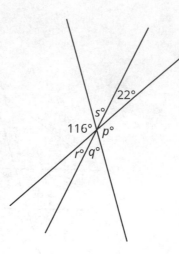

4.

	Quantity A	**Quantity B**
	The measure of one of the angles formed when angle p is bisected	The measure of the angle that complements angle q

(A) Quantity A is greater.

(B) Quantity B is greater.

(C) The two quantities are equal.

(D) The relationship cannot be determined from the information given.

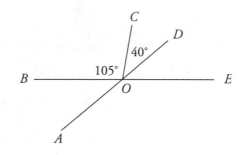

5. In the figure above, what is the measure of $\angle AOE$?

(A) 35°

(B) 45°

(C) 75°

(D) 105°

(E) 145°

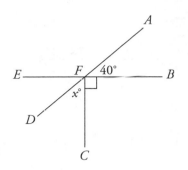

6. In the figure above, *EB* is perpendicular to *FC*, and *AD* and *EB* intersect at point *F*. What is the value of *x*?

    (A) 30
    (B) 40
    (C) 50
    (D) 60
    (E) 130

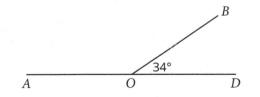

7. In the figure above, *v* = 2*w*, *w* = 2*x*, and $x = \dfrac{y}{3}$. What is the value of *y*?

    (A) 18
    (B) 36
    (C) 45
    (D) 54
    (E) 60

Line segment CO is the angle bisector of ∠AOB

8. What is the degree measure of ∠COD?

    [   ]

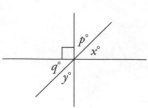

9. According to the figure above, which of the following statements MUST be true?

Select <u>all</u> such statements.

A $p = x$ and $q = y$

B $x + y = 90$

C $x = y = 45$

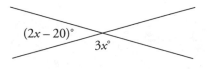

10. In the figure above, $x =$

   A   40

   B   60

   C   80

   D   100

   E   120

Triangles Practice Set

Directions: Solve the following questions and select the best answer from those given. Each question has one correct answer unless otherwise noted.

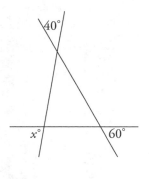

1. In the figure above, $x =$

    (A) 60

    (B) 80

    (C) 85

    (D) 90

    (E) 100

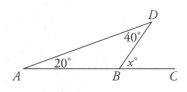

2. In the figure above, what is the value of x?

    (A) 120

    (B) 110

    (C) 90

    (D) 70

    (E) 60

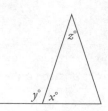

3. In the figure above, $x = 2z$ and $y = 3z$. What is the value of z?

    (A) 24
    (B) 30
    (C) 36
    (D) 54
    (E) 60

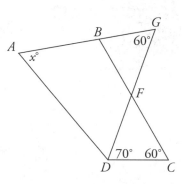

4. In the figure above, if $AD \parallel BC$, then $x =$

    (A) 20
    (B) 30
    (C) 50
    (D) 60
    (E) 70

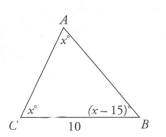

5. In △*ABC* above, which of the following statements must be true?

   Select <u>all</u> such statements.

   A $x > 50$

   B $AC < 10$

   C $AB > 10$

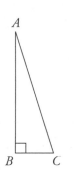

6. In the figure above, the area of △*ABC* is 6. If *BC* is $\frac{1}{3}$ the length of *AB*, then *AC* =

   Ⓐ $\sqrt{2}$

   Ⓑ 2

   Ⓒ 4

   Ⓓ 6

   Ⓔ $2\sqrt{10}$

7. What is the length of the hypotenuse of an isosceles right triangle of area 32?

   Ⓐ 4

   Ⓑ $4\sqrt{2}$

   Ⓒ 8

   Ⓓ $8\sqrt{2}$

   Ⓔ $8\sqrt{3}$

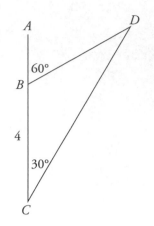

8. In the figure above, if ∠DBA has a measure of 60°, ∠DCB has a measure of 30°, and BC = 4, what is the length of BD?

    Ⓐ √2

    Ⓑ 4

    Ⓒ 4√2

    Ⓓ 4√3

    Ⓔ 8

9. The lengths of two sides of a right triangle are $\frac{d}{3}$ and $\frac{d}{4}$, where $d > 0$. If one of these sides is the hypotenuse, what is the length of the third side of the triangle?

    Ⓐ $\frac{5d}{12}$

    Ⓑ $\frac{d}{\sqrt{7}}$

    Ⓒ $\frac{d}{5}$

    Ⓓ $\frac{d}{12}$

    Ⓔ $\frac{d\sqrt{7}}{12}$

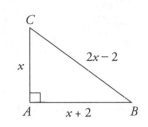

10. In right triangle *ABC* above, $x =$

   (A) 6

   (B) 8

   (C) $6\sqrt{2}$

   (D) 10

   (E) 13

Polygons Practice Set

Directions: Solve the following questions and select the best answer from those given. Each question has one correct answer unless otherwise noted.

1.

Quantity A	**Quantity B**
The measure of the greatest interior angle of a pentagon	105°

   (A) Quantity A is greater.

   (B) Quantity B is greater.

   (C) The two quantities are equal.

   (D) The relationship cannot be determined from the information given.

2. A circular garden with a diameter of 40 feet is encircled by a walkway that is 10 feet wide.

Quantity A	**Quantity B**
The area of the garden	The area of the walkway

   (A) Quantity A is greater.

   (B) Quantity B is greater.

   (C) The two quantities are equal.

   (D) The relationship cannot be determined from the information given.

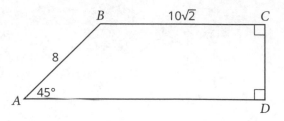

3.

Quantity A	Quantity B
The area of quadrilateral *ABCD*	96

- (A) Quantity A is greater.
- (B) Quantity B is greater.
- (C) The two quantities are equal.
- (D) The relationship cannot be determined from the information given.

4.

Quantity A	Quantity B
The area of a regular hexagon with a side length of *s*	$2s^2\sqrt{3}$

- (A) Quantity A is greater.
- (B) Quantity B is greater.
- (C) The two quantities are equal.
- (D) The relationship cannot be determined from the information given.

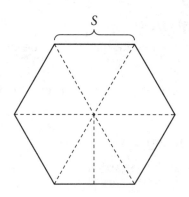

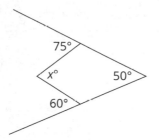

5. In the figure above, $x =$

    Ⓐ 85
    Ⓑ 90
    Ⓒ 95
    Ⓓ 120
    Ⓔ 140

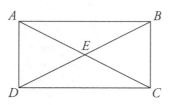

6. In the figure above, *ABCD* is a rectangle. If the area of $\triangle AEB$ is 8, what is the area of $\triangle ACD$?

    Ⓐ 8
    Ⓑ 12
    Ⓒ 16
    Ⓓ 24
    Ⓔ 32

7. The perimeter of a rectangle is $6w$. If one side has length $\frac{w}{2}$, what is the area of the rectangle?

    Ⓐ $\frac{w^2}{4}$

    Ⓑ $\frac{5w^2}{4}$

    Ⓒ $\frac{5w^2}{2}$

    Ⓓ $\frac{11w^2}{4}$

    Ⓔ $\frac{11w^2}{2}$

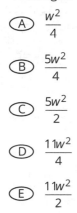

8. The length of each side of square A is increased by 100% to make square B. If the length of the side of square B is increased by 50% to make square C, by what percent is the area of square C greater than the sum of the areas of squares A and B?

   (A) 75%

   (B) 80%

   (C) 100%

   (D) 150%

   (E) 180%

9. A rectangle with integer side lengths has perimeter 10. What is the greatest number of these rectangles that can be cut from a piece of paper with width 24 and length 60?

   (A) 144

   (B) 180

   (C) 240

   (D) 360

   (E) 480

10. The perimeter of a rectangle is 24 and its width is greater than or equal to 2. Which of the following could be the area of the rectangle?

    Select all that apply.

    A 12

    B 24

    C 30

    D 36

    E 40

    F 48

Circles Practice Set

Directions: Solve the following questions and select the best answer from those given. Each question has one correct answer unless otherwise noted.

1. If the area of a circle is 64π, then the circumference of the circle is

   (A) 8π

   (B) 16π

   (C) 32π

   (D) 64π

   (E) 128π

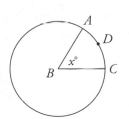

2. In the figure above, the ratio of the circumference of circle *B* to the length of arc *ADC* is 8:1. What is the value of *x*?

    (A) 30
    (B) 45
    (C) 60
    (D) 75
    (E) 90

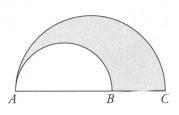

3. The figure above displays two semicircles, one with diameter *AB* and one with diameter *AC*. If *AB* has a length of 4 and *AC* has a length of 6, what fraction of the area of the larger semicircle does the area of the shaded region represent?

    (A) $\dfrac{1}{3}$

    (B) $\dfrac{4}{9}$

    (C) $\dfrac{1}{2}$

    (D) $\dfrac{5}{9}$

    (E) $\dfrac{2}{3}$

4. A line segment joining two points on the circumference of a circle is 1 inch from the center of the circle at its closest point. If the circle has a 2-inch radius, what is the length of the line segment?

   (A) 1
   (B) $\sqrt{2}$
   (C) 2
   (D) $2\sqrt{2}$
   (E) $2\sqrt{3}$

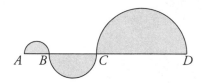

5. Each of the three shaded regions above is a semicircle. If $AB = 4$, $CD = 2BC$, and $BC = 2AB$, then the area of the entire shaded figure is

   (A) 28π
   (B) 42π
   (C) 84π
   (D) 96π
   (E) 168π

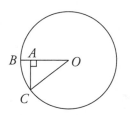

6. In the figure above, if the area of the circle with center O is 100π and CA has a length of 6, what is the length of AB?

   (A) 2
   (B) 3
   (C) 4
   (D) 5
   (E) 6

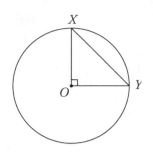

7. In the figure above, O is the center of the circle. If the area of triangle XOY is 25, what is the area of the circle?

    Ⓐ 25π

    Ⓑ $25\pi\sqrt{2}$

    Ⓒ 50π

    Ⓓ $50\pi\sqrt{3}$

    Ⓔ 625π

8. If the diameter of a circle increases by 50%, by what percent will the area of the circle increase?

    Ⓐ 25%

    Ⓑ 50%

    Ⓒ 100%

    Ⓓ 125%

    Ⓔ 225%

9. If an arc with a length of 12π is $\frac{3}{4}$ of the circumference of a circle, what is the shortest distance between the endpoints of the arc?

    Ⓐ 4

    Ⓑ $4\sqrt{2}$

    Ⓒ 8

    Ⓓ $8\sqrt{2}$

    Ⓔ 16

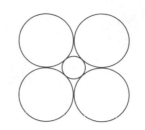

10. The total area of the four equal circles in the figure above is 36π, and the circles are all tangent to one another. What is the diameter of the smaller circle?

(A) $6\sqrt{2}$

(B) $6 + \sqrt{2}$

(C) $3\sqrt{2} - 3$

(D) $6\sqrt{2} - 6$

(E) $6\sqrt{2} + 6$

Multiple Figures Practice Set

Directions: Solve the following questions and select the best answer from those given. Each question has one correct answer unless otherwise noted.

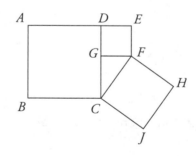

1. In the figure above, square *ABCD* has area 49 and square *DEFG* has area 9. What is the area of square *FCJH*?

(A) 25

(B) 32

(C) 40

(D) 48

(E) 69

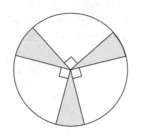

2. In the circle above, three right angles have vertices at the center of the circle. If the radius of the circle is 8, what is the combined area of the shaded regions?

    (A) 8π

    (B) 9π

    (C) 12π

    (D) 13π

    (E) 16π

3. If a square of side x and a circle of radius r have equal areas, what is the ratio $\frac{x}{r}$?

    (A) $\frac{2}{\pi}$

    (B) $\sqrt{\pi}$

    (C) $\frac{\pi}{2}$

    (D) π

    (E) π^2

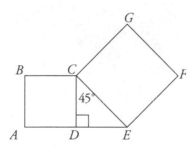

4. In the figure above, *ABCD* and *CEFG* are squares. If the area of *CEFG* is 36, what is the area of *ABCD*?

    (A) 6

    (B) $6\sqrt{2}$

    (C) 9

    (D) 18

    (E) 24

5. A triangle and a circle have equal areas. If the base of the triangle and the diameter of the circle each have length 5, what is the height of the triangle?

(A) $\frac{5}{2}$

(B) $\frac{5}{2}\pi$

(C) 5π

(D) 10π

(E) It cannot be determined from the information given.

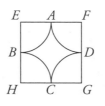

6. In the figure above, if *EFGH* is a square and the arcs are all quarter-circles of length π, what is the perimeter of *EFGH*?

(A) 1

(B) 2

(C) 4

(D) 8

(E) 16

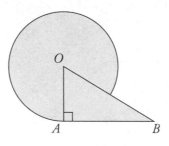

7. In the figure above, if radius *OA* is 8 and the area of right triangle *OAB* is 32, what is the area of the shaded region?

(A) $64\pi + 32$

(B) $60\pi + 32$

(C) $56\pi + 32$

(D) $32\pi + 32$

(E) $16\pi + 32$

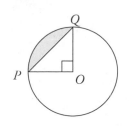

8. In circle O above, if ΔPOQ is a right triangle and radius OP is 2, what is the area of the shaded region?

   Ⓐ $4\pi - 2$

   Ⓑ $4\pi - 4$

   Ⓒ $2\pi - 2$

   Ⓓ $2\pi - 4$

   Ⓔ $\pi - 2$

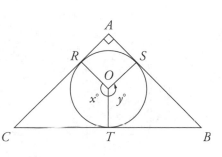

9. In the figure above, right triangle ABC is circumscribed about a circle O. If R, S, and T are the three points at which the triangle is tangent to the circle, then what is the value of $x + y$?

   Ⓐ 180

   Ⓑ 210

   Ⓒ 240

   Ⓓ 270

   Ⓔ It cannot be determined from the information given.

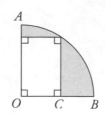

10. In the figure above, *AB* is an arc of a circle with center *O*. If the length of arc *AB* is 5π and the length of *CB* is 4, what is the sum of the areas of the shaded regions?

   (A) 25π − 60
   (B) 25π − 48
   (C) 25π − 36
   (D) 100π − 48
   (E) 100π − 36

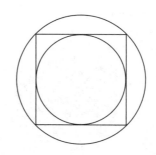

11. In the figure above, the smaller circle is inscribed in the square and the square is inscribed in the larger circle. If the length of each side of the square is *s*, what is the ratio of the area of the larger circle to the area of the smaller circle?

   (A) 2√2 : 1
   (B) 2 : 1
   (C) √2 : 1
   (D) 2*s* : 1
   (E) *s*√2 : 1

Uniform Solids Practice Set

> **Directions:** Solve the following questions and select the best answer from those given. Each question has one correct answer unless otherwise noted.

1. A plumber wants to wrap a 3-foot long section of pipe that has an outer diameter of 1 inch with insulation.

Quantity A	**Quantity B**
The area of insulation needed	108 in^2

    (A) Quantity A is greater.
    (B) Quantity B is greater.
    (C) The two quantities are equal.
    (D) The relationship cannot be determined from the information given.

2. Uniform solids A and B have equal volumes. Solid A is $10\sqrt{3}$ inches high and its base is an equilateral triangle with 4-inch sides. The base of rectangular solid B is 3 inches by 4 inches.

Quantity A	**Quantity B**
The height of Solid B	12 inches

    (A) Quantity A is greater.
    (B) Quantity B is greater.
    (C) The two quantities are equal.
    (D) The relationship cannot be determined from the information given.

3. What is the ratio of the volume of a cylinder with radius r and height h to the volume of a cylinder with radius h and height r?

    (A) $\dfrac{r}{h}$

    (B) $\dfrac{h}{r}$

    (C) $\dfrac{1}{1}$

    (D) $\dfrac{\pi r}{h}$

    (E) $\dfrac{h}{\pi r}$

4. A cube and a rectangular solid are equal in volume. If the lengths of the edges of the rectangular solid are 4, 8, and 16, what is the length of an edge of the cube?

(A) 4

(B) 8

(C) 12

(D) 16

(E) 64

5. When 16 cubic meters of water are poured into an empty cubic container, it fills the container to 25% of its capacity. What is the length of one edge of the container, in meters?

(A) $2\sqrt{2}$

(B) 4

(C) $4\sqrt{2}$

(D) 8

(E) 16

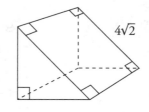

6. If the solid above is half of a cube, then the volume of the solid is

(A) 16

(B) 32

(C) 42

(D) 64

(E) $64\sqrt{2}$

7. Milk is poured from a full rectangular container with dimensions 4 inches by 9 inches by 10 inches into a cylindrical container with a diameter of 6 inches. Assuming the milk does not overflow the container, how many inches high will the milk reach?

   (A) $\dfrac{60}{\pi}$

   (B) 24

   (C) $\dfrac{40}{\pi}$

   (D) 10

   (E) 3π

8. What is the radius of the largest sphere that can be placed inside a cube of volume 64?

   (A) $6\sqrt{2}$

   (B) 8

   (C) 4

   (D) $2\sqrt{2}$

   (E) 2

9. Each dimension of a certain rectangular solid is an integer less than 10. If the volume of the rectangular solid is 24 and one edge has length 4, which one of the following could be the total surface area of the solid?

   (A) 48

   (B) 52

   (C) 56

   (D) 60

   (E) 96

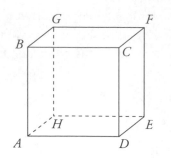

10. Which of the following statements about the cube above must be true?

Select all such statements.

A FD is parallel to GA.

B △GCF and △AHD have the same area.

C AF = GD

Coordinate Geometry Practice Set

Directions: Solve the following questions and select the best answer from those given. Each question has one correct answer unless otherwise noted.

1. A triangle's vertices lie at the following 3 points in the coordinate plane: A(−5, −2); B(3, −2); and C(3, 2).

Quantity A	Quantity B
The area of triangle ABC	15

(A) Quantity A is greater.

(B) Quantity B is greater.

(C) The two quantities are equal.

(D) The relationship cannot be determined from the information given.

2. Line R is defined by the equation $y = \dfrac{x}{2} + 3$ and line S is defined by the equation $x = 9 - y$.

Quantity A	Quantity B
The x coordinate of the intersection of lines R and S	The y coordinate of the intersection of lines R and S

Ⓐ Quantity A is greater.

Ⓑ Quantity B is greater.

Ⓒ The two quantities are equal.

Ⓓ The relationship cannot be determined from the information given.

3. Line Z is perpendicular to the line defined by $y = 3x - 9$ and crosses that line at a point whose x-coordinate is 4.

Quantity A	Quantity B
The y-intercept of line Z	4

Ⓐ Quantity A is greater.

Ⓑ Quantity B is greater.

Ⓒ The two quantities are equal.

Ⓓ The relationship cannot be determined from the information given.

4. The coordinates of point P are (a, b). Point P', with coordinates (c, d), is the reflection of point P over the x-axis.

Quantity A	Quantity B
b	$-d$

Ⓐ Quantity A is greater.

Ⓑ Quantity B is greater.

Ⓒ The two quantities are equal.

Ⓓ The relationship cannot be determined from the information given.

5. Which of the following is a point on the graph of $3x - 2y = 4$?

Ⓐ $(0, 2)$

Ⓑ $(1, 4)$

Ⓒ $(2, 0)$

Ⓓ $(2, 1)$

Ⓔ $(2, 4)$

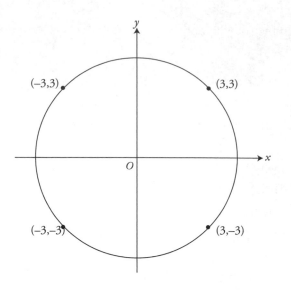

6. What is the area of the circle above with its center at the origin?

(A) 9

(B) 18

(C) 9π

(D) 18π

(E) 36π

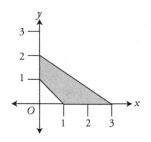

7. In the figure above, what is the area of the shaded region?

(A) $\dfrac{3}{2}$

(B) 2

(C) $\dfrac{5}{2}$

(D) $\dfrac{7}{2}$

(E) 5

8.   What is the shortest distance between the point with (x, y) coordinates $(2, 7)$ and the line with the equation $y = -1$?

   (A) 8

   (B) 6

   (C) 5

   (D) 3

   (E) 1

9.   What value of d is required so that the line $y = 7x + d$ passes through the point $(-3, 4)$?

   (A) 1

   (B) 4

   (C) 7

   (D) 17

   (E) 25

10.   What is the equation of the line that passes through the points $(2, -7)$ and $(6, -1)$?

   (A) $y = -\dfrac{2}{3}x + 3$

   (B) $y = \dfrac{2}{3}x - \dfrac{25}{3}$

   (C) $y = x - 5$

   (D) $y = \dfrac{3}{2}x + 10$

   (E) $y = \dfrac{3}{2}x - 10$

Number Operations Answer Key

1. **B**	4. **A**	7. **B**	9. **B**
2. **D**	5. **D**	8. **A, C**	10. **D**
3. **A**	6. **C**		

Exponents and Radicals Answer Key

1. **D**	4. **D**	7. **C**	9. **C**
2. **B**	5. **D**	8. **A**	10. **D**
3. **D**	6. **A, B, C**		

Number Properties Answer Key

1. **B**	4. **D**	7. **B, C**	9. **B**
2. **D**	5. **E**	8. **E**	10. **C**
3. **C**	6. **C**		

Equations and Inequalities Answer Key

1. **B**	4. **D**	7. **E**	9. **A**
2. **A**	5. **D**	8. **C**	10. **D**
3. **C**	6. **C**		

Quadratics Answer Key

1. **A**	4. **B**	7. **A, F**	9. **D**
2. **A**	5. **E**	8. **A**	10. **D**
3. **B**	6. **25**		

Functions and Symbolism Answer Key

1. **C**	4. **A**	7. **D**	9. **C, D**
2. **B**	5. **D**	8. **7**	10. **A, B, C, D, F**
3. **B**	6. **D**		

Ratios and Proportions Answer Key

1. **C**	4. **A**	7. **E**	9. **B**
2. **B**	5. **B**	8. **E**	10. **E**
3. **B**	6. **C**		

Percents Answer Key

1. **B**	3. **A**	5. **C**	7. **A**
2. **A**	4. **B**	6. **C**	8. **C**

Rates, Average Speed, and Combined Work Answer Key

1. **C**	4. **D**	7. **D**	10. **B**
2. **A**	5. **C**	8. **C**	11. **B**
3. **B**	6. **B**	9. **C**	

Averages Answer Key

1. **D**	4. **B**	7. **C**	10. **D**
2. **B**	5. **B**	8. **A**	11. **D**
3. **A**	6. **C**	9. **B**	

Statistics Answer Key

1. **A**	4. **C**	7. **B**	9. **C, E**
2. **A**	5. **B**	8. **4**	10. **B, C, D, E**
3. **B**	6. **C**		

Counting Methods and Probability Answer Key

1. **A**	4. **B**	7. **B, C**	9. **C**
2. **A**	5. **D**	8. **B**	10. **C**
3. **B**	6. **96**		

Lines and Angles Answer Key

1. **A**	4. **A**	7. **D**	9. **B**
2. **C**	5. **E**	8. **107**	10. **A**
3. **D**	6. **C**		

Triangles Answer Key

1. **B**	4. **E**	7. **D**	9. **E**
2. **E**	5. **A, B**	8. **B**	10. **A**
3. **C**	6. **E**		

Polygons Answer Key

1. **A**	4. **B**	7. **B**	9. **D**
2. **B**	5. **A**	8. **B**	10. **B, C, D**
3. **C**	6. **C**		

Circles Answer Key

1. **B**	4. **E**	7. **C**	9. **D**
2. **B**	5. **B**	8. **D**	10. **D**
3. **D**	6. **A**		

Multiple Figures Answer Key

1. **A**	4. **D**	7. **C**	9. **D**
2. **E**	5. **B**	8. **E**	10. **B**
3. **B**	6. **E**		

Uniform Solids Answer Key

1. **A**	4. **B**	7. **C**	9. **B**
2. **B**	5. **B**	8. **E**	10. **A, B, C**
3. **A**	6. **B**		

Coordinate Geometry Answer Key

1. **A**	4. **C**	7. **C**	9. **E**
2. **B**	5. **D**	8. **A**	10. **E**
3. **A**	6. **D**		

Answers and Explanations

Number Operations Explanations

1. B

The first half of Quantity A, $\dfrac{1}{2} - \dfrac{1}{3} = \dfrac{3}{6} - \dfrac{2}{6} = \dfrac{1}{6}$, has the same value as the first half of Quantity B,

$\dfrac{2}{3} - \dfrac{1}{2} = \dfrac{4}{6} - \dfrac{3}{6} = \dfrac{1}{6}$, so ignore it. The second half of Quantity A, $\dfrac{1}{4} - \dfrac{1}{5} = \dfrac{5}{20} - \dfrac{4}{20} = \dfrac{1}{20}$, is smaller than the second half of Quantity B, $\dfrac{2}{5} - \dfrac{1}{4} = \dfrac{8}{20} - \dfrac{5}{20} = \dfrac{3}{20}$, so **(B)** is correct.

2. D

Pick some numbers. If $x = 0$, then both quantities equal 0. Eliminate (A) and (B). However, if x is pretty much anything other than 0, then the two quantities are not the same. For example, if $x = y = 4$, then Quantity A is $4 \div 8 = 0.5$ while Quantity B is $1 + 1 = 2$. The answer is **(D)**.

3. A

Compare piece by piece. In Quantity A, $k - m$ is negative (if you have a hard time picturing this, pick numbers—for example, $-2 - (-1) = -2 + 1 = -1$) and $k + m$ is negative, too (negative + negative = negative). So, Quantity A is negative $\div$ negative = positive.

In Quantity B, $m - k$ is positive (again, pick numbers if you aren't sure—for example, $-1 - (-2) = -1 + 2 = 1$) while $k + m$ is still negative. So, Quantity B is positive $\div$ negative = negative.

Any positive number is greater than any negative number, so Quantity A is greater than Quantity B, and **(A)** is correct.

4. A

Hacking out the fraction arithmetic or picking numbers would take forever, so there has to be a shortcut. Compare the quantities piece by piece.

The first fraction in Quantity A is greater than its counterpart in Quantity B. Its numerator is bigger ($3a > 2a$ and $2b > 2c$) and its denominator is smaller ($a + 1$ is greater than a, whereas $b - c$ is less than a). A bigger number divided by a smaller number will always be bigger.

The second fraction in Quantity A is negative. Its numerator is negative because $a > b$, while its denominator is positive because $c > 2$. However, this negative fraction is subtracted, which is equivalent to adding a positive. The second fraction in Quantity B is also negative, since its numerator is positive while its denominator is negative ($b > c$, so subtracting b from c will yield a number less than 0). Unlike in Quantity A, this negative fraction is added, which is equivalent to subtracting a positive.

In summary, then, Quantity A is "bigger number + positive," while Quantity B is "smaller number − positive." Quantity A must be greater, and **(A)** is correct.

5. D

You are asked to find the fractional equivalent of 3.44. Since there are two digits to the right of the decimal point, the denominator of the fractional part is 100.

$$3.44 = 3\frac{44}{100} = 3\frac{11}{25}$$

6. C

Cancel a factor of 0.002 from numerator and denominator. Since 0.02 is simply 10 times 0.002, you can simply rewrite the problem as 10 times 0.0003. Multiplying a decimal by 10 is the same as moving the decimal point 1 place to the right. So the result is 0.003. Look for ways to avoid extensive calculation and save yourself from calculator keystroke errors.

7. B

Approach I:

$$\frac{\dfrac{1}{6} + \dfrac{1}{3} + 2}{\dfrac{3}{4} + \dfrac{5}{4} + 3} = \frac{\dfrac{1}{2} + 2}{\dfrac{8}{4} + 3}$$

$$= \frac{2\dfrac{1}{2}}{5} = \frac{5}{2} \div 5 = \frac{5}{2} \cdot \frac{1}{5} = \frac{1}{2}$$

Approach II:

Multiply numerator and denominator by the least common multiple of all the denominators. Here, the LCM is 12:

$$\frac{12\left(\frac{1}{6}+\frac{1}{3}+2\right)}{12\left(\frac{3}{4}+\frac{5}{4}+3\right)}$$

$$\frac{2+4+24}{9+15+36}=\frac{30}{60}=\frac{1}{2}$$

8. A, C

In the first expression, if you were to subtract a smaller number from 1,000, the result would be a larger number. So if you substituted 120 for 160 in this expression, your result would be greater. This choice is correct.

The second expression is equivalent to $160 + 160 = 320$. If you were to replace each 160 with 120, the result would be $120 + 120$, which is 240. Eliminate this choice.

The third expression is toughest to evaluate. The overall fraction will be a larger value if the denominator is smaller. So focus on the denominator and assess whether replacing 160 with 120 in the denominator makes the denominator smaller or larger. $1 - \frac{1}{120}$ is smaller than $1 - \frac{1}{160}$ since a larger value fraction (due to the smaller denominator) is being subtracted from 1. So by replacing 160 with 120, you get a smaller value in the denominator of the expression and, therefore, a larger value for the entire expression. This choice is correct.

In the fourth expression, the second term will have a significantly smaller value if 160 is replaced by 120. The first term is a small positive fraction. Changing 160 to 120 in the first term does not change its value very much. Overall, the expression will be smaller if 160 is replaced by 120. Eliminate this choice.

(A) and **(C)** are the correct answers.

9. B

Start by picking out the largest and smallest fractions. As the only fraction greater than $\frac{1}{2}$, $\frac{5}{9}$ is the greatest. The other four are close together, but it's easy to find a common denominator for $\frac{5}{12}$, $\frac{11}{24}$, and $\frac{23}{48}$. Convert everything to 48ths:

$$\frac{5}{12}=\frac{20}{48} \text{ and } \frac{11}{24}=\frac{22}{48},$$

$$\text{so } \frac{5}{12}<\frac{11}{24}<\frac{23}{48}.$$

$$\text{Is } \frac{5}{12}<\frac{3}{7}?$$

Using cross-multiplication, $7 \times 5 = 35$, and $12 \times 3 = 36$, so $\frac{5}{12}<\frac{3}{7}$.

To find the difference between $\frac{5}{9}$ and $\frac{5}{12}$ use the least common denominator, 36.

$$\frac{5}{9}\cdot\frac{4}{4}=\frac{20}{36}, \frac{5}{12}\cdot\frac{3}{3}=\frac{15}{36}$$

$$\frac{20}{36}-\frac{15}{36}=\frac{5}{36}$$

10. D

Change the decimal to a fraction:

$$0.04=\frac{4}{100} \text{ or } \frac{1}{25}$$

Therefore, $\frac{1}{25}x = 5y = 2z$. Multiply all the terms by 25 to eliminate the fraction in front of the x.

$$x = 125y = 50z$$

Since all the terms are positive, you know that x has the greatest value and that it takes more y's than z's to equal one x. So x has the greatest value, and y has the least value.

Exponents and Radicals Explanations

1. D

Test a positive and a negative number. If $x = -3$, then Quantity B is 0 and Quantity A $= \sqrt{(-3)^2 + 9} = \sqrt{9+9} = \sqrt{18}$. Eliminate (B) and (C). If $x = 3$, then Quantity A is the same as before, which is just a little over 4. Meanwhile, Quantity B $= 3 + 3 = 6$. Eliminate (A). The correct answer is **(D)**.

2. B

Simplify each quantity using exponent properties:

Quantity A $= \dfrac{\left(xy^{-2}\right)^{-3}}{x^{-8}} = \dfrac{x^{-3}y^6}{x^{-8}} = x^5y^6$

Quantity B $= \left(\dfrac{y}{x^2y^3}\right)^{-2} = \dfrac{y^{-2}}{x^{-4}y^{-6}} = x^4y^4$

Now think strategically. According to the centered information, x and y are both fractions between 0 and 1. This means that the higher the power to which they are raised, the smaller they get. (For example, $(0.5)^2 = 0.25$, $(0.5)^3 = 0.125$, and so on.) Because Quantity A has larger exponents for both x and y, it must be smaller. Choice **(B)** is correct.

3. D

To multiply or divide a number by a power of 10, move the decimal point to the right or left, respectively, the same number of places as the number of zeros in the power of 10. Multiplying by a negative power of 10 is the same as dividing by a positive power. For instance: $3 \times 10^{-2} = \dfrac{3}{10^2}$

Keeping this in mind, assess the choices one by one. Remember: you are looking for the choice that is NOT equal to 0.0675.

$67.5 \times 10^{-3} = 0.0675$; eliminate.

$6.75 \times 10^{-2} = 0.0675$; eliminate.

$0.675 \times 10^{-1} = 0.0675$; eliminate.

$0.00675 \times 10^2 = 0.675$

(D) is the correct answer.

4. D

Note that the answer choices all have base 2, so start by expressing 4 and 8 as powers of 2.

$(4^x)(8^x) = (2^2)^x \cdot (2^3)^x$

To raise a power to an exponent, multiply the exponents:

$(2^2)^x = 2^{2x}$

$(2^3)^x = 2^{3x}$

To multiply powers with the same base, add the exponents:

$2^{2x} \cdot 2^{3x} = 2^{(2x+3x)} = 2^{5x}$

5. D

The positive square root of 16 equals 4.

The cube of 4 is $4 \times 4 \times 4$, or 64.

Now you need a positive number whose square is 64. That's 8, so **(D)** is correct.

6. A, B, C

This question is a good review of the laws of exponents. In order to make the comparison easier, try to transform 8^5 and each of the three options so that they have a common base. Since 2 is the smallest base among the expressions to be compared, use it for the common base. Since $8^5 = (2^3)^5 = 2^{3 \cdot 5} = 2^{15}$, look for options equivalent to 2^{15}.

(A) $2^5 \cdot 4^5 = 2^5 \cdot (2^2)^5 = 2^5 \cdot 2^{2 \times 5} = 2^5 \cdot 2^{10} = 2^{5+10} = 2^{15}$

(B) 2^{15}

(C) $2^5 \cdot 2^{10} = 2^{5+10} = 2^{15}$

It turns out that all three are equivalent to 2^{15} or 8^5. Note that for choice (A), you could also simply multiply the bases together, since the exponent is the same, to see that $2^5 \cdot 4^5 = 8^5$.

7. C

Express both 9 and 27 as an exponent with a common base. Use 3 as the base since $3^2 = 9$ and $3^3 = 27$. The equation then becomes:

$$\begin{aligned} 27^n &= 9^4 \\ \left(3^3\right)^n &= \left(3^2\right)^4 \\ 3^{3 \times n} &= 3^{2 \times 4} \\ 3^{3n} &= 3^8 \end{aligned}$$

If two powers with the same base are equal, the exponents must be equal.

$$\begin{aligned} 3n &= 8 \\ n &= \frac{8}{3} \end{aligned}$$

8.   A

First, break up the expression to separate the variables, transforming the fraction into a product of three simpler fractions:

$$\frac{x^3yz^4}{xy^{-2}z^3} = \left(\frac{x^3}{x}\right)\left(\frac{y}{y^{-2}}\right)\left(\frac{z^4}{z^3}\right)$$

Now carry out each division by keeping the base and subtracting the exponents.

$$\frac{x^3}{x} = x^{3-1} = x^2$$

$$\frac{y}{y^{-2}} = y^{1-(-2)} = y^{1+2} = y^3$$

$$\frac{z^4}{z^3} = z^{4-3} = z^1 = z$$

The answer is the product of these three expressions, or x^2y^3z.

9.   C

You are told that $x^a \cdot x^b = 1$. Since $x^a \cdot x^b = x^{a+b}$, you know that $x^{a+b} = 1$. If a power is equal to 1, either the base is 1 or -1, or the exponent is zero. Since you are told that $x \neq 1$ and $x \neq -1$, the exponent must be zero; therefore, $a + b = 0$.

10.   D

Try to get rid of the denominator by factoring it out of the numerator. $n - 4\sqrt{n} + 4$ is a difficult expression to work with. It may be easier if you let $t = \sqrt{n}$. Keep in mind then that $t^2 = (\sqrt{n})(\sqrt{n}) = n$.

Then $n - 4\sqrt{n} + 4 = t^2 - 4t + 4$.

Using FOIL in reverse:

$$t^2 - 4t + 4 = (t-2)(t-2) = (\sqrt{n}-2)(\sqrt{n}-2)$$

So $\dfrac{n - 4\sqrt{n} + 4}{\sqrt{n}-2} = \dfrac{(\sqrt{n}-2)(\sqrt{n}-2)}{(\sqrt{n}-2)}$

$$= \sqrt{n} - 2$$

Alternatively, you could pick a number for n and try each answer choice to see which one gives the same result as the expression in the question.

Number Properties Explanations

1.   B

When the numbers in a problem are intractably big, break them down into their prime factors.

$165 = 3 \times 5 \times 11$

This means that $x^x = 3^{165} \times 5^{165} \times 11^{165}$. For Quantity A, this is then divided by 5. So:

Quantity A $= 3^{165} \times 5^{164} \times 11^{165}$

In Quantity B, note that $y^2z = 2^2(41) = 164$ and $55 = 11 \times 5$. Again, break all the numbers into their prime factors:

Quantity B $= 5 \times 11 \times (3 \times 5 \times 11)^{164} = 5 \times 11 \times 3^{164} \times 5^{164} \times 11^{164} = 3^{164} \times 5^{165} \times 11^{165}$

In the end, the two quantities are very similar, except that Quantity A has an extra 3, whereas Quantity B has an extra 5. Consequently, Quantity B is greater, and the answer is **(B)**.

2.   D

One way to do this problem is to find the prime factorization of 168:

$$168 = 2 \times 84$$
$$= 2 \times 2 \times 42$$
$$= 2 \times 2 \times 6 \times 7$$
$$= 2 \times 2 \times 2 \times 3 \times 7$$

Now, go through the answer choices. You've already seen that 42 is a factor of 168, and 21 is a factor of 42, so 21 is also a factor of 168. This eliminates (A) and (E). (B) 24 is 8×3 or $2 \times 2 \times 2 \times 3$, so it's also a factor of 168. (C) 28 is 4×7 or $2 \times 2 \times 7$, so 28 is a factor of 168. That leaves only **(D)**. Indeed, 32 has five factors of 2, which is more factors of 2 than 168 has.

3.   C

In this question, you need to find the smallest integer divisible by both 9 and 21. The fastest method is to start with the smallest answer choice and test each one for divisibility. (E) is clearly divisible by 21, but not by 9. Similarly, (D) is just 2×21, but it is not divisible by 9. **(C)**, 63, is divisible by both 21 ($21 \times 3 = 63$) and 9 ($9 \times 7 = 63$).

Another approach is to find the prime factors of 9 and 21, and by eliminating shared factors, find the least common multiple. Breaking each into prime factors:

$$21 = 3 \times 7$$

$$9 = 3 \times 3$$

You can drop one factor of 3 from the 9, since it is already present in the factors of 21. The least common multiple is $3 \times 3 \times 7$, or 63.

4.   D

Pick a sample odd value for n, such as 3. If you plug 3 into an expression and get an odd result, then you know that answer choice cannot be correct. (You want the one that is even for **any** odd value.)

$\dfrac{n-1}{2} = \dfrac{3-1}{2} = \dfrac{2}{2} = 1$. Not even.

$\dfrac{n+1}{2} = \dfrac{3+1}{2} = \dfrac{4}{2} = 2$. Even. Try another value, such as 1.

$\dfrac{1+1}{2} = \dfrac{2}{2} = 1$. So this doesn't have to be even.

$n^2 + 2n = (3)^2 + 2(3) = 9 + 6 = 15$. No.

$2n + 2 = 2(3) + 2 = 6 + 2 = 8$. Even.

You could try some more values for n here or just use logic: if you double an odd number you get an even result, and if you then add 2, you still have an even number. So **(D)** will always be even and is the correct answer.

Just for practice:

$$3n^2 - 2n = 3(3)^2 - 2(3) = 21. \text{ No.}$$

5.   E

You need to find the one choice that isn't **always** true. To find it, test each choice. (A) is always true: since $P \div 9$ has a remainder of 4, P is 4 greater than some multiple of 9. And if $P - 4$ is a multiple of 9, then the next multiple of 9 would be $(P - 4) + 9$, or $P + 5$; thus (B) is also true. With (C), since $P - 4$ is a multiple of 9, it is also a multiple of 3. By adding 3s, you will see that $(P - 4) + 3$, or $P - 1$, and $(P - 4) + 3 + 3$, or $P + 2$, are also multiples of 3. (C) must be true. Next, since $P - 1$ is a multiple of 3, when P is divided by 3, it will have a remainder of 1, and (D) is always true.

This only leaves (E). In simpler terms, (E) states that P is always odd. Since multiples of 9 are alternately odd and even (9, 18, 27, 36 . . .), $P - 4$ could either be even or odd, so P also could be either even or odd. **(E)** is not always true, so it is the correct answer choice.

6.   C

If two numbers have an even product, at least one of the numbers is even, so eliminate (A). If both numbers were even, their sum would be even, but you know the sum of these numbers is odd, so eliminate (B). If one number is odd and the other is even, their product is even and their sum is odd, so **(C)** is correct. (D) and (E) both can be true, but they're not necessarily true.

7.   B, C

Since these four integers have an even product, at least one of them must be even, so (A) is impossible. Is it possible for exactly 2 of the 4 to be even? If there are 2 odds and 2 evens, the sum is even, since odd + odd = even and even + even = even. Also, if there's at least 1 even among the integers, the product is even, making **(B)** possible. Similarly, **(C)** gives an even product and an even sum, so the correct answers are **(B)** and **(C)**.

8.   E

The wire can be divided into three equal parts, each with integral length, so the minimum length must be a multiple of 3. Unfortunately, all of the answer choices are multiples of 3. One of those 3 pieces is cut into 8 pieces, again all with integer lengths, so the length of the wire must be at least 3×8 or 24. Another of those three segments is cut into 6 pieces. The remaining segment is cut into 4 equal pieces; however, since 4 is a factor of 8, you only need to find the least common multiple of 6 and 8. In other words, the thirds have an integer length evenly divisible by both 6 and 8. The smallest common multiple of 6 and 8 is 24, so the minimum length of the wire is 3×24 or 72.

9.   B

You need to determine how many integers between 1 and 59 are even multiples of 5. All even multiples of 5 must be multiples of 10. The multiples of 10 between 0 and 60 are 10, 20, 30, 40, and 50. That's 5 altogether.

10. C

The vault has 130 ounces total of gold and silver. Each tablet of gold weighs 8 ounces, and each tablet of silver 5 ounces. Not all of the 130 ounces can be gold, since 130 is not a multiple of 8. There must be some silver in the vault as well. The largest multiple of 8 less than 130 is 16×8 or 128, but this can't be the amount of gold either, since it leaves only $130 - 128$ or 2 leftover ounces for the silver, and each silver tablet weighs 5 ounces. So, look at the multiples of 8 less than 128 until you find one that leaves a multiple of 5 when subtracted from 130. In fact, the next smallest multiple of 8, 15×8 or 120, leaves $130 - 120$ or 10 ounces of silver, and since $2 \times 5 = 10$, this amount works. That's 15 tablets of gold for a total of 120 ounces, and 2 tablets of silver, for a total of 10 ounces. So 120 ounces is the greatest possible amount of gold.

Equations and Inequalities Explanations

1. B

For questions that require the value of some combination of variables, you may not have to solve for the values of the individual variables. In this case, you can subtract the first equation from the second:

$$a^2 + 5a + 3b = 30$$
$$\underline{-(a^2 + a - b = 10)}$$
$$4a + 4b = 20$$

Because what you need to know is the value of $a + b$, merely divide this result by 4 to get $a + b = 5$. Since this is less than 6, **(B)** is correct.

2. A

The maximum value of t occurs when the $5r$ term is greatest and the $\frac{12}{s}$ term is smallest; the minimum value of t occurs when the $5r$ term is smallest and the $\frac{12}{s}$ term is greatest. To find the maximum for t, plug in 3 for r and 6 for s: $5(3) - \frac{12}{6} = 15 - 2 = 13$. To get the minimum, plug in -3 for r and 2 for s. This is $5(-3) - \frac{12}{2} = -15 - 6 = -21$. Thus, the difference between the maximum and minimum values of t is $13 - (-21) = 34$, which is greater than 33. **(A)** is correct.

3. C

The centered information provides two equations with two variables, so use substitution to solve for x: $xy - 5x = -16$ becomes $x(x - 3) - 5x = x^2 - 3x - 5x = -16$. This simplifies to $x^2 - 8x + 16 = 0$ in standard quadratic form, which factors to $(x - 4)^2 = 0$. Therefore, $x = 4$ and the two quantities are equal.

4. D

Although z is greater than y, that doesn't provide information about the two given ranges. Pick $y = 2$ and $z = 5$, for instance: $a < 2 < b$ and $c < 5 < d$. Then b could be 3 and c could be 4, and c would be greater than b. However, b could also be something like 10 and c could be still be 4, in which case b would be greater. **(D)** is correct.

5. D

Factor the first equation:

$$ab + ac = 21$$
$$a(b + c) = 21$$

You're told that $b + c = 7$, so substitute 7 for $b + c$ in the first equation:

$$a(b + c) = 21$$
$$a(7) = 21$$

Now solve for a:

$$a = \frac{21}{7} = 3$$

6. C

Start with the equation given:

$$\frac{x + 3}{2} + x + 3 = 3$$

Multiply both sides of the equation by 2 to get rid of the 2 in the denominator of the fraction on the left side.

$$\frac{2(x + 3)}{2} + 2(x + 3) = 2(3)$$
$$(x + 3) + 2(x + 3) = 6$$

Next, multiply out the parentheses and combine like terms. The equation becomes:

$$x + 3 + 2x + 6 = 6$$
$$3x + 9 = 6$$

Now, isolate the variable on one side of the equation:

$$3x + 9 - 9 = 6 - 9$$
$$3x = -3$$

Finally, divide both sides by the coefficient of the variable.

$$\frac{3x}{3} = \frac{-3}{3}$$
$$x = -1$$

7.   E

First, find the value of m by substituting $x = 2$ and $y = 1$ into $mx + 5 = y$, and solve for m.

$$
\begin{aligned}
mx + 5 &= y \\
m(2) + 5 &= 1 \\
2m + 5 &= 1 \\
2m + 5 - 5 &= 1 - 5 \\
2m &= -4 \\
m &= \frac{-4}{2} \\
m &= -2
\end{aligned}
$$

Since you're told m is a constant, m must be -2 regardless of the values of x and y. You can rewrite $mx + 5 = y$ as $-2x + 5 = y$, or $5 - 2x = y$.

Now, if $y = -1$, then $5 - 2x = -1$.

Solve for x:

$$
\begin{aligned}
5 - 2x - 5 &= -1 - 5 \\
-2x &= -6 \\
x &= \frac{-6}{-2} \\
x &= 3
\end{aligned}
$$

8.   C

You are told $a > b > c$, and asked which of the answer choices **cannot** be true. If you can find just one permissible set of values for a, b, and c that satisfies an answer choice, then that answer choice is eliminated.

$b + c < a$. This inequality can be true if a is sufficiently large relative to b and c. For example, if $a = 10$, $b = 3$, and $c = 2$, $a > b > c$ still holds, and $b + c < a$. No good.

$2a > b + c$. This is always true because a is greater than either b or c. So $a + a = 2a$ must be greater than $b + c$. For instance, $2(4) > 3 + 2$.

$2c > a + b$. This inequality can never be true. The sum of two smaller numbers (c's) can never be greater than the sum of two larger numbers (a and b). This is the correct answer.

$ab > bc$. This will be true when the numbers are all positive. Try $a = 4$, $b = 3$, and $c = 2$.

$a + b > 2b + c$. Again, this can be true if a is large relative to b and c. Try $a = 10$, $b = 2$, and $c = 1$.

9.   A

Solve the inequality for z by multiplying both sides by -3. Remember to flip the inequality when multiplying or dividing by a negative number. So, $-12 > z$; only (**A**) conforms to this. Alternatively, you could have chosen to backsolve to find the answer.

10. D

Begin by expressing the equations for both lines in the format, $y = mx + b$. The slope of line A is 0.8, so that equation is $y = 0.8x + b$. Since that line passes through the point $(-3, -2)$, plug those values into the equation to get $-2 = 0.8(-3) + b = -2.4 + b$. So $b = 0.4$ and the equation for line A is $y = 0.8x + 0.4$. Convert the equation for line B, $x = 11.2 - 2y$, to the same format: $2y = 11.2 - x$. Thus, $y = 5.6 - \frac{x}{2}$. In order to find the point where the two lines intersect, set the two equations for y equal to each other: $0.8x + 0.4 = 5.6 - \frac{x}{2}$. Add $\frac{x}{2}$ to and subtract 0.4 from both sides to get $1.3x = 5.2$, so $x = 4.0$ at the point where the two lines intersect. Plug that value for x into either equation to get $y = 3.6$. (**D**) is correct.

Quadratics Explanations

1. A

Restate the given equation in standard quadratic form by subtracting 12 from both sides to get $x^2 - 9x + 20 = 0$. You might be tempted to select (D) since most quadratic equations have two solutions. To be safe, however, factor the quadratic to get $(x - 5)(x - 4) = 0$. So x is either 4 or 5, either of which is greater than 3. Therefore, Quantity A is greater, so **(A)** is the correct answer.

2. A

Notice that $a^2 - 6 = 3$ becomes $a^2 - 9 = 0$ when 3 is subtracted from both sides. This factors readily into $(a + 3)(a - 3) = 0$, so a = ±3. Factor $b^2 + 9b + 20 = 0$ to get $(b + 4)(b + 5) = 0$, which means that b can be −4 or −5. Both of these values are less than the minimum value of a, which is −3. **(A)** is correct.

3. B

Notice that the expressions for x and for y are both equal to zero, so they can be solved separately. Starting with $4x^3 - 4x^2 - 8x = 0$, all terms contain the factor $4x$, so this equates to $4x(x^2 - x - 2) = 0$, which can be further factored to $4x(x - 2)(x + 1) = 0$. So x can be 0, 2, or −1. Factor $y^2 - 7y + 12 = 0$ into $(y - 3)(y - 4) = 0$. Thus, y can be either 3 or 4. Since both of these values are greater than any of the three possible values of x, **(B)** is correct.

4. B

Convert $x^2 - 4x - 10 = 11$ to the standard quadratic format, $x^2 - 4x - 21 = 0$. Factor this to $(x - 7)(x + 3) = 0$, so the possible values of x are 7 and −3. Watch the signs carefully. Since $y = -5$, the *maximum* value for xy will be $(-5)(-3) = 15$. This is less than 35, so **(B)** is correct.

5. E

Cross multiply $\dfrac{p}{p+2} = \dfrac{p-3}{4}$ to get the quadratic equation $4p = p^2 - p - 6$. Subtract $4p$ from each side: $p^2 - 5p - 6 = 0$. Factor this to get $(p - 6)(p + 1) = 0$. Therefore, p can be 6 or −1. The only choice that matches either of these is **(E)**.

6. 25

Make the first equation easier to factor by dividing all terms by 2 to get $w^2 - w - 6 = 0$. This factors to $(w - 3)(w + 2) = 0$, so w can be either 3 or −2. Restate the second equation in standard quadratic form, $z^2 - 4z - 5 = 0$. This is $(z - 5)(z + 1) = 0$, so z is either 5 or −1. The least value for wz is $(5)(-2) = -10$, and the greatest value is $(5)(3) = 15$. Therefore, the range is $15 - (-10) = $ **25**.

7. A, F

First, solve for x in terms of y. The equation $2x^2 - 5xy - 3y^2 = 0$ can be factored to $(2x + y)(x - 3y) = 0$. So, either $x = -\dfrac{y}{2}$ or $x = 3y$. Plug in each answer choice for y and evaluate both equations for x to see if x is greater than 3.

(A) If $y = -8$, then $-\dfrac{y}{2} = -\dfrac{-8}{2} = 4$, so **(A)** is a correct choice and there is no need to evaluate the other possibility.

(B) If $y = -4$, then $-\dfrac{y}{2} = -\dfrac{-4}{2} = 2$ and $3y = 3(-4) = -12$. Neither value is greater than 3, so eliminate (B).

(C) If $y = -2$, then $-\dfrac{y}{2} = -\dfrac{-2}{2} = 1$ and $3y = 3(-2) = -6$. Neither value is greater than 3, so eliminate (C).

(D) If $y = 0$, then $x = 0$; eliminate (D).

(E) If $y = 1$, then $-\dfrac{y}{2} = -\dfrac{1}{2}$ and $3y = 3(1) = 3$. However, the question stipulates $x > 3$, so eliminate (E) as well.

(F) If $y = 2$, then $3y = 6$, so **(F)** is a correct choice.

8. A

Plug in 3 for y in the given quadratic expression to get $3x^2 + 5x(3) - 12(3^2) = 3x^2 + 15x - 108$. All the coefficients are divisible by 3, so the equation further simplifies to $x^2 + 5x - 36 = 0$. This factors to $(x + 9)(x - 4) = 0$. So x could be either −9 or 4. Only choice **(A)** matches.

9. D

At first, this might not appear to be a quadratic because there are no squared terms, but the second term, $-2\sqrt{5}x$, is a hint that the first term, x, is $\left(\sqrt{x}\right)^2$ and the last term, 5, is $\left(\sqrt{5}\right)^2$. So the equation can be written as $\left(\sqrt{x}\right)^2 - 2\left(\sqrt{5}\right)\left(\sqrt{x}\right) + \left(\sqrt{5}\right)^2 = 0$, which factors to $\left(\sqrt{x} - \sqrt{5}\right)^2$. Thus, $\sqrt{x} = \sqrt{5}$ and $x = 5$. **(D)** is correct.

10. D

Some quick examination determines that there are no readily identifiable integer factors for this quadratic equation. Therefore, use the quadratic formula, $\dfrac{-b \pm \sqrt{b^2 - 4ac}}{2a}$, to find the solutions. Plugging the coefficients into the formula results in $\dfrac{-(-7) \pm \sqrt{(-7)^2 - 4(3)(3)}}{2(3)}$. This simplifies to $\dfrac{7 \pm \sqrt{49 - 36}}{6} = \dfrac{7 \pm \sqrt{13}}{6}$. Thus the two solutions are $\dfrac{7 + \sqrt{13}}{6}$ and $\dfrac{7 - \sqrt{13}}{6}$. You can quickly eliminate (A), (B), and (C) by looking at the first term in the numerator. Both (D) and (E) have the correct first term, but the $\sqrt{85}$ in the numerator eliminates (E), leaving **(D)** as the correct answer.

Functions and Symbolism Explanations

1. C

Evaluate $f(x)$ for $x = 2$ (Quantity A) and $x = 4$ (Quantity B) and compare the results. Quantity A is $2^2 - 6(2) - 3 = 4 - 12 - 3 = -11$. Quantity B is $4^2 - 6(4) - 3 = 16 - 24 - 3 = -11$. Therefore, the quantities are equal.

2. B

Simplify both quantities, then compare piece by piece.

In Quantity A, substituting x for a and y for b gives:

$$x^2 - xy - y^2$$

In Quantity B, expanding with FOIL gives:

$$(x + y)(x + y) = x^2 + xy + xy + y^2 = x^2 + 2xy + y^2$$

Now compare piece by piece. Both quantities have x^2, so that can be ignored. Because x and y are both negative, xy is positive (negative × negative = positive). Thus, $2xy$ in Quantity B (which is positive) is greater than $-xy$ in Quantity A (which is negative). Similarly, because a negative number squared will always be positive, y^2 in Quantity B is greater than $-y^2$ in Quantity A. As a result, each piece of Quantity B is equal to or greater than the corresponding piece of Quantity A, so Quantity B is greater.

3. B

Substitute 10 for m and x for n, then use algebra to solve for x:

$$10 \clubsuit x = \frac{10 + x}{10} - 6 = 34$$

$$\frac{10 + x}{10} = 40$$

$$10 + x = 400$$

$$x = 390$$

Now compare strategically. If x were 400, then x^2 (Quantity A) would equal 160,000 (Quantity B). However, x is a little less than 400, so x^2 must be a little less than 160,000, so Quantity B is greater.

4. A

To solve for $g(f(x))$, work from the inside out. That is, solve for $f(x)$, then plug that value in for x in $g(x)$. When $x = 2$, $f(x) = 2 + 2 = 4$. So $g(f(2)) = g(4) = \sqrt{4} + 3 = 2 + 3 = 5$. Therefore, Quantity A is greater.

5. D

Find $g(m)$:

$$g(m) = g(5) = \frac{5^3 + 15}{7} = \frac{125 + 15}{7} = \frac{140}{7} = 20$$

Find $g(n)$:

$$g(n) = g(3) = \frac{3^3 + 15}{7} = \frac{27 + 15}{7} = \frac{42}{7} = 6$$

Subtract to solve:

$$g(m) - g(n) = 20 - 6 = 14$$

6. D

Symbolism questions are merely function questions in disguise, so just plug in the value of w. Thus, $\spadesuit w = \dfrac{w + 2}{w - 2}$, and $\spadesuit w - \spadesuit(-w) = \dfrac{4 + 2}{4 - 2} - \dfrac{-4 + 2}{-4 - 2} = \dfrac{6}{2} - \dfrac{-2}{-6}$. This simplifies to $3 - \dfrac{1}{3} = 2\dfrac{2}{3}$.

7. D

A squared quantity cannot be negative; thus, $(x + 4)^2$ is either 0 or positive. This implies that $-(x + 4)^2$ is either 0 or negative, so the greatest that $-(x + 4)^2$ can possibly be is 0. This occurs when $x + 4 = 0$, or $x = -4$. Choice **(D)** is correct. Note that $f(x)$ has no minimum: the further x gets from -4, whether positive or negative, the more negative $f(x)$ gets. Note, too, that while the -3 affects the value of the maximum, it does not affect which x-value achieves that maximum.

8. 7

Plug the known values from 2 ## $x = -30$ into the original symbolism function: 2 ## $x = (2 - 5)(x + 3) = -30$. So, $-3(x + 3) = -30$. Thus, $x + 3 = 10$, and $x = 7$.

9. C, D

In order to determine which choices result in $f(x)$ being greater than zero, substitute each choice for x in the equation for $f(x)$. Starting with (A), $f(-4) = -(-4)^2 + 2(-4) + 5 = -16 - 8 + 5 = -19$. Eliminate (A). For (B), $f(-2) = -(-2)^2 + 2(-2) + 5 = -4 - 4 + 5 = -3$, so you can eliminate (B) also. Since $f(0)$ can be easily evaluated as 5, **(C)** is a correct choice. Check (D): $f(2) = -(2)^2 + 2(2) + 5 = -4 + 4 + 5 = 5$. So **(D)** is also correct. For (E), $f(4) = -(4)^2 + 2(4) + 5 = -16 + 8 + 5 = -3$. Eliminate (E). There is no need to fully calculate (F) since the $-x^2$ term will dominate when $x = 6$.

10. A, B, C, D, F

Any two consecutive integers will include one odd integer and one even integer. Thus, z is odd (odd + even = odd).

Each answer choice has either $z \updownarrow 2$ or $2 \updownarrow z$, so consider those two possibilities:

$$z \updownarrow 2 = \frac{\text{odd}^3 - 2}{2} = \frac{\text{odd} - 2}{2} = \frac{\text{odd}}{2}$$

An odd number divided by 2 is never an integer, so (A) and (B) must both be false while (E) must be true. Select **(A)** and **(B)** and eliminate (E). (Recall that only integers can be even or odd.)

$$2 \updownarrow z = \frac{2^3 - \text{odd}}{\text{odd}} = \frac{8 - \text{odd}}{\text{odd}} = \frac{\text{odd}}{\text{odd}}$$

An odd number divided by another odd number can be odd ($7 \div 1 = 7$) or a non-integer ($3 \div 5 = 0.6$). Thus, **(C)**

and **(F)** could be true or false, while **(D)** must be false. All five of the choices are therefore correct.

Ratios and Proportions Explanations

1. C

Picking Numbers could be your first thought because there are only variables in the question (and it is a valid approach), but manipulating the proportion in the centered information to make the quantities look alike is more efficient. Convert the left side of the proportion to $\frac{a}{d}$ by multiplying both sides of the equation by $\frac{b}{d}$. Thus, $\frac{b}{d}\left(\frac{a}{b}\right) = \frac{b}{d}\left(\frac{c}{d}\right)$, which simplifies to $\frac{a}{d} = \frac{bc}{d^2}$. The two quantities are equal.

2. B

This question provides a system of two variables with two equations given in the form of ratios. Cross multiply $\frac{a}{b} = \frac{1}{3}$ to get $3a = b$. Substitute $3a$ for b in the second proportion: $\frac{a + 3}{3a} = \frac{1}{2}$. Cross multiply: $2a + 6 = 3a$, so $a = 6$. Since $b = 3a$, $b = 3(6) = 18$. This is less than 21, so **(B)** is correct.

3. B

Since muffins are the common item in both ratios, manipulate the ratios so that the muffin term is the same in each. Because the coefficient is 4 in one ratio and 7 in the other, use $4 \times 7 = 28$. That means there are $\frac{5}{4} \times 28 = 35$ donuts and $\frac{3}{7} \times 28 = 12$ croissants. Therefore, the ratio of donuts to muffins to croissants is 35:28:12, and Quantity A is 35:12. Since 3:1 is equivalent to 36:12, Quantity B is greater.

4. A

That $abcd \neq 0$ means that none of the variables is zero. Manipulate and evaluate the two inequalities to compare $\frac{a}{b}$ to $\frac{c}{d}$. Since bd is positive, you can divide both sides of the inequality $ad > bc$ by bd and maintain the inequality. Thus $\frac{ad}{bd} > \frac{bc}{bd}$. Cancelling out like terms results in $\frac{a}{b} > \frac{c}{d}$. Therefore, **(A)** is correct.

5. B

Since 3 out of 24 students are in student organizations, the remaining $24 - 3$ or 21 students are not in student organizations. Therefore, the ratio of students in organizations to students not in organizations is

$$\frac{\text{\# in organizations}}{\text{\# not in organizations}} = \frac{3}{21} = \frac{1}{7}.$$

6. C

Start by converting kilometers to meters. Since a meter is smaller than a kilometer, multiply 5 kilometers times 1000 meters/kilometer. So a length of 10 centimeters on the map represents 5,000 meters; therefore, 1 centimeter must represent $\frac{1}{10}$ as much, or 500 meters. To determine how many centimeters would represent 750 meters you could set up a proportion here, but it's quicker to use common sense. You have a distance $\frac{3}{2}$ as great as 500 meters $\left(750 = \frac{3}{2} \times 500\right)$, so you need a map distance $\frac{3}{2}$ as great as 1 centimeter, or $\frac{3}{2} = 1.5$ centimeters.

7. E

Get both tics and tocs in terms of the same number of tacs. Since you are given the value of tics in terms of 3 tacs, and tocs in terms of 2 tacs, use the LCM of 2 and 3, or 6. If 1 tic equals 3 tacs, then 2 tics equal 6 tacs. If 2 tacs equal 5 tocs, then 6 tacs equal 3×5 or 15 tocs. Therefore, 2 tics = 6 tacs = 15 tocs, and the ratio of tics:tacs:tocs is 2:6:15. You don't care about tacs anymore, just tics and tocs. The ratio of tics:tocs is 2:15.

8. E

Find the number of students who play on any sports team, then multiply by $\frac{1}{4}$ to find the number of students who play football. $\frac{2}{3}$ of the 240 students play some sport, or $\frac{2}{3} \times 240$ or 160 students. $\frac{1}{4}$ of these play football; that equals $\frac{1}{4} \times 160$ or 40 students. Therefore, 40 students play football.

9. B

If Jane knits 72 stitches to the line and uses $\frac{1}{4}$ inch of yarn per stitch, that means she uses

$$72 \frac{\text{stitches}}{\text{line}} \times \frac{1 \text{ inch}}{4 \text{ stitch}} = 18 \text{ inches of yarn per line.}$$

But you need to find out how many lines she can knit with 10 **yards** of yarn. Since there are three feet in a yard and twelve inches in a foot, there must be

$$3 \frac{\text{feet}}{\text{yard}} \times 12 \frac{\text{inches}}{\text{feet}} = 36 \text{ inches in a yard. So 18 inches is}$$

$\frac{18}{36}$ or $\frac{1}{2}$ yard. Each line requires $\frac{1}{2}$ yard of yarn to knit; each yard of yarn is enough for 2 lines. Therefore, 10 yards of yarn is enough for 10×2 or 20 lines.

10. E

If John buys R pounds for N people, he is planning on feeding his guests cheese at a rate of

$$\frac{R \text{ pounds}}{N \text{ people}} = \frac{R}{N} \text{ pounds per person.}$$

You need to know how much additional cheese John must buy for the extra P people. If John is buying $\frac{R}{N}$ pounds of cheese for each person, then he will need $P \times \frac{R}{N}$ or $\frac{PR}{N}$ pounds for the extra P people. Check your answer by seeing if the units cancel out:

$$P \text{ people} \times \frac{R \text{ pounds}}{N \text{ people}} = \frac{PR}{N} \text{ pounds.}$$

Another approach would be to pick numbers. Say John buys 10 pounds of cheese for 5 people (that is, $R = 10$ and $N = 5$). Then everyone gets 2 pounds of cheese. Also, say 7 people come, 2 more than expected (that is, $P = 2$). Then he needs 14 pounds to have enough for everybody to consume 2 pounds of cheese. Since he already bought 10 pounds, he must buy an additional 4 pounds. Therefore, any answer choice that equals 4 when you substitute 10 for R, 5 for N, and 2 for P is possibly correct:

$$\frac{(5)(2)}{10} \neq 4. \quad \text{Discard}$$

$$\frac{5}{(10)(2)} \neq 4. \quad \text{Discard}$$

$$\frac{5+2}{10} \neq 4. \quad \text{Discard}$$

$$\frac{2}{(5)(10)} \neq 4. \quad \text{Discard}$$

$$\frac{(2)(10)}{5} = 4. \quad \text{Correct}$$

Since only the fifth choice, (E), gives 4, that must be the correct choice.

Percents Explanations

1. B

Recall that "% of" means "divide by 100, then multiply." To divide by 100, move the decimal point two places to the left to get 0.000125. To multiply by 1000, move the decimal point three places to the right to get 0.125. Thus, Quantity B is greater than Quantity A.

2. A

The first price reduction was 20% of $150, which is $30. So the item was priced at $150 − $30 = $120 at that point. This means that the second price reduction was $120 − $102 = $18. To determine the value of x, use the formula for percent decrease, $\dfrac{\text{amount of change}}{\text{original amount}} \times 100\%$. This is $\dfrac{18}{120} \times 100\% = 15\%$, so Quantity A is greater than Quantity B.

3. A

Using the percent change formula is the key to solving this question, but before you can solve for p it is a good idea to find the cost to bake a box of cookies. Plug the $5 price for a box of cookies, the 20% profit, and b as the cost to bake a box of cookies into the percent change formula. The result is:

$$\frac{\$5 - b}{\$5} = 0.2$$
$$\$5 - b = \$1$$
$$\$4 = b$$

After finding $b = \$4$, plug the new price, $\$5 + \$1 = \$6$, into the percent change formula again in order to find the new percent profit:

$$\frac{\$6 - \$4}{\$6} = p$$
$$\frac{\$2}{\$6} = p$$
$$33\tfrac{1}{3}\% = p$$

The new percent profit is greater than 25%, so (A) is correct.

4. B

The best approach for this question is to work through the individual percent increases/decreases in each scenario to determine what the final prices for the television will be. This is also a good time to use the percent increase/decrease multiplication rules to reduce the number of calculations:

1. Change the percents into decimals.
2. Percent increase: Multiply by [1 + (increase as a decimal)]
3. Percent decrease: Multiply by [1 − (decrease as decimal)]

The price two weeks ago with the manager's discount was $1,500 × (1 − 0.25) = $1,500 × (0.75) = $1,125.

The price during the clearance sale is a bit more complicated. First, calculate the 35% markup before the sale begins: $1,500 × (1 + 0.35) = $1,500 × (1.35) = $2,025. Then, take half off of that price because of the clearance sale: $\dfrac{\$2,025}{2} = \$1,012.50$. Finally, calculate the 15% rewards club discount: $1,012.50 × (1 − 0.15) = $1,012.50 × (0.85) = $860.63.

Quantity A is the difference between the two final prices: $1,125 − $860.63 = $264.37. Since Quantity A is a little bit less than Quantity B, (B) is correct.

5. C

The easiest approach here is to pick a number for the cost of the watch, and from that work out the profit and selling price. As is often true with percent problems, the best number to pick is 100. If the watch costs the store $100, then the profit will be 25% of $100, or $25. The selling price equals the cost to the store plus the profit: $100 + $25, or $125. The profit represents $\dfrac{25}{125}$ or $\dfrac{1}{5}$ of the selling price. The percent equivalent of $\dfrac{1}{5}$ is 20%.

6. C

Choose a sample value that is easy to work with; see what happens with 100 jobs. If the factory cuts its labor force by 16%, it eliminates 16% of 100 jobs, or 16 jobs, leaving a work force of 100 − 16, or 84 people. The factory then increases this work force by 25%. 25% of 84 is $\frac{1}{4}$ of 84, or 21. The factory adds 21 jobs to the 84 it had, for a total of 105 jobs. Since the factory started with 100 jobs and finished with 105, it gained 5 jobs overall. This represents $\frac{5}{100}$ or 5% of the total it started with. There was a 5% increase.

7. A

Find the cost of the stereo to the dealer, then subtract 40% of the cost to find the price it was sold for. The selling price equals the dealer's cost plus the profit. The dealer would have made a 20% profit if he had sold the stereo for $600; therefore, letting x represent the cost to the dealer:

$$600 = x + 20\% \text{ of } x$$
$$600 = 120\% \text{ of } x$$
$$600 = \frac{6}{5}x$$
$$x = \frac{5}{6} \cdot 600 = 500$$

Instead, the dealer sold the stereo at a loss of 40%. Since 40% or $\frac{2}{5}$ of 500 is 200, he sold the stereo for $500 − $200 = $300.

8. C

You want to find the greatest possible original price of the item. Since you are given the price after the discount, the greatest original price will correspond to the greatest discount.

So to have the greatest original price, $2.40 must be the cost after a 25 percent discount. Then $2.40 is 100% − 25% = 75% of the original price. If the original price is p, then:

$$\$2.40 = 0.75p$$
$$\frac{2.40}{0.75} = p$$
$$p = \$3.20$$

Rates, Average Speed, and Combined Work Explanations

1. C

Since Annalise runs 8 − 6 = 2 miles per hour faster than Claire and there are 4 laps per mile, she runs 2 × 4 = 8 laps per hour faster. Convert the 36 minutes to hours: $\dfrac{36 \text{ min}}{60 \frac{\text{min}}{\text{hr}}} = 0.6$ hr. So, in 0.6 hours, Annalise will run 8 × 0.6 = 4.8 laps more than Claire. In order to do that, she has to pass Claire 4 times.

2. A

At first glance this comparison may seem formidable, but think about what the quantities represent. Think of Quantity A as depositing $1,000 in an account that pays 4% annual interest compounded quarterly for 5 years. Hence, the interest rate per quarter is one-fourth of the annual rate, or 1%. The number of times that the compounding occurs is 4 × 5 = 20. Quantity B has the same 4% annual interest, but the compounding occurs annually. The two quantities both represent the final amount of an initial $1,000 invested for 5 years at a 4% interest rate. However, Quantity A is compounded more frequently, thus resulting in a greater end value.

If you didn't recognize this relationship, you could have made the quantities look alike by using exponent rules to restate Quantity A, which is equal to $\$1{,}000(1.01)^{20}$, as $\$1{,}000(1.01^4)^5$. Compare that to Quantity B, which is $\$1{,}000(1.04)^5$. Because 1.01^4 is slightly greater than 1.04, Quantity A is greater than Quantity B.

3. B

When a Quantitative Comparison question compares a numerical value to an unknown quantity, you may be able to use Backsolving. Plug 9 hours into the simplified combined work formula, $T = \dfrac{AB}{A + B}$, and compare the resulting time to $2\frac{1}{2}$ hours. So $T = \dfrac{4 \times 9}{4 + 9} = \dfrac{36}{13} = 2\dfrac{10}{13}$. This is greater than $2\frac{1}{2}$ hours, so 9 hours is slower than Q's actual speed and **(B)** is correct.

4. D

Since the cars are traveling in opposite directions, the distance between the two cars equals the sum of the distances each car travels. The first car travels 20 minutes or a third of an hour, so it goes only $\frac{1}{3}$ the distance it would travel in an hour, or $\frac{1}{3}$ of 24 miles, or 8 miles. The second car travels 45 minutes or $\frac{3}{4}$ of an hour. It goes $\frac{3}{4}$ of the distance it would go in an hour, or $\frac{3}{4}$ of 40, or 30 miles. The two cars are then $8 + 30$, or 38 miles apart.

5. C

Find the mule's rate by taking two-thirds of the horse's rate. The horse travels 20 miles in 6 hours; therefore, the horse's speed is $\frac{20 \text{ miles}}{6 \text{ hours}}$. The mule travels at $\frac{2}{3}$ this speed:

$$\frac{2}{3} \times \frac{20 \text{ miles}}{6 \text{ hours}} = \frac{20 \text{ miles}}{9 \text{ hours}}$$

Now you can use this rate to determine how long it takes the mule to make the trip. The mule needs 9 hours to travel 20 miles.

6. B

The average speed equals the total distance the car travels divided by the total time. You're told the car goes 60 kilometers in an hour before its piston breaks, then travels another 60 kilometers at 30 kilometers an hour. The second part of the trip must have taken 2 hours (if you go 30 miles in one hour, then you'll go twice as far, 60 miles, in 2 hours). So the car travels a total of $60 + 60$, or 120 miles, and covers this distance in $1 + 2$, or 3 hours. Its average speed equals 120 miles divided by 3 hours, or 40 miles per hour.

Notice that the average speed over the entire trip is *not* simply the average of the two speeds traveled over the trip. (That would be the average of 60 and 30, which is 45.) This is because the car spent different amounts of time traveling at these two different rates. Be wary of problems that ask for an average rate over a trip that encompassed different rates.

7. D

Solve using the combined work formula:

$$\frac{ab}{a+b} = \frac{(12)(6)}{12+6} = \frac{72}{18} = 4$$

8. C

Apply the distance formula, Distance = Rate × Time, to the two segments of the trip. In the first 4 hours, the driver travels $4m$ miles. In the next 6 hours (10 total − 4 driven = 6 remaining), she drives $6 \times \frac{3}{4}m = \frac{9}{2}m$ miles. The total number of miles she drives is then $\left(4m + \frac{9}{2}m\right)$ miles, or $\frac{17}{2}m$ miles.

9. C

$$\text{Average miles per hour} = \frac{\text{Total miles}}{\text{Total hours}}$$

The total miles is easy: she travels 90 miles there and 90 miles back, for a total of 180 miles. You can calculate the time for each part of the trip, and then add them for the total time.

Going there: she travels 90 miles at 20 miles per hour. Since distance = rate × time, time = $\frac{\text{distance}}{\text{rate}}$. So it takes him $\frac{90 \text{ miles}}{20 \text{ miles/hour}} = \frac{9}{2}$ hours to travel there.

Coming back: she travels 90 miles at 40 miles per hour, so it takes her $\frac{90}{40} = \frac{9}{4}$ hours to return home.

$$\text{The total time} = \frac{9}{2} + \frac{9}{4} = \frac{18}{4} + \frac{9}{4} = \frac{27}{4} \text{ hours.}$$

Therefore, the average speed is:

$$\frac{\text{Total miles}}{\text{Total hours}} = 180 \div \frac{27}{4} = 180 \cdot \frac{4}{27} = \frac{80}{3}$$

(Note that the average speed is *not* just the average of the two speeds; since the motorist spends more time going there than coming back, the average is closer to the speed going there. You could eliminate all but the second and third choices using this logic.)

10. B

First find how long the trip takes him at the two different rates, using the formula:

$$\text{time} = \frac{\text{distance}}{\text{rate}}$$

He travels the first 10 km at 30 km per hour, so he takes $\frac{10}{30} = \frac{1}{3}$ hour for this portion of the journey.

He travels the remaining 30 km at 15 km per hour, so he takes $\frac{30}{15} = 2$ hours for this portion of the journey.

So the whole journey takes him $2 + \frac{1}{3} = 2\frac{1}{3}$ hours. Compare this to the amount of time it would take to make the same trip at a constant rate of 20 km per hour. If he traveled the whole 40 km at 20 km per hour, it would take $\frac{40}{20} = 2$ hours. This is $\frac{1}{3}$ hour, or 20 minutes, shorter.

11. B

Approach I:

First figure out how many minutes it would take for y centimeters of snow to fall. The snow is falling at a constant rate of x centimeters per minute; set up a proportion to find how long it takes for y centimeters. The ratio of minutes passed to centimeters fallen is a constant.

$$\frac{1 \text{ minute}}{x \text{ centimeters}} = \frac{m \text{ minutes}}{y \text{ centimeters}}$$

Solve for m:

$$m \text{ minutes} = y \text{ centimeters} \cdot \frac{1 \text{ minute}}{x \text{ centimeters}}$$

$$m \text{ minutes} = \frac{y}{x} \text{ minutes}$$

Now convert from $\frac{y}{x}$ minutes to hours:

$$\frac{y}{x} \text{ minutes} \times \frac{1 \text{ hour}}{60 \text{ minutes}} = \frac{y}{60x} \text{ hours}$$

Always be sure to keep track of your units; set them up to cancel out when doing conversions.

Approach II:

First find out how long it takes for 1 centimeter of snow to fall. You will eventually have to convert from minutes to hours, so you might as well do it now. If x centimeters of snow fall every minute, then 60 times as much, or $60x$ centimeters, will fall in an hour. Then 1 centimeter of snow will fall in the reciprocal of $60x$, or $\frac{1}{60x}$ hours. 1 centimeter falls in $\frac{1}{60x}$ hours, so y centimeters will fall in y times as many hours, or $\frac{y}{60x}$ hours.

Averages Explanations

1. D

There are two ways to approach this question. You could pick numbers to attempt to "force" different results. Although x appears at the end of the set, there are no limitations on the value of x. Try a negative number for x such as -1. The average would then be $\frac{-4+1+3+5+(-1)}{5} = \frac{4}{5}$. So, for $x = -1$, the average is greater than x. Try a relatively large positive number such as 10. Now the average is $\frac{-4+1+3+5+10}{5} = \frac{15}{5} = 3$. For $x = 10$, the average is less than x, so the relationship cannot be determined.

Alternatively, you could use algebra. The average is $\frac{-4+1+3+5+x}{5} = \frac{5+x}{5}$, which you are comparing to x. Multiply both quantities by 5 so that you are comparing $5 + x$ to $5x$. Without actually calculating, you can see that for $x = 0$, the quantity $5 + x$ is greater than x, but, for large values of x, the quantity $5x$ will be greater.

2. B

The average without the additional observation was $\frac{12+13+9+8+9+15}{6} = \frac{66}{6} = 11$. When the additional observation is added, the total becomes $66 + 12 = 78$, but there are now 7 observations, so the average is $\frac{78}{7} = 11\frac{1}{7}$.

Thus, the increase in the average is $\frac{1}{7}$, which is less than $\frac{1}{6}$.

3. A

Although the average of 2, 3, and 4 is the middle value, 3, the average of 2^2, 3^2, and 4^2 is $\dfrac{4+9+16}{3} = \dfrac{29}{3} = 9\dfrac{2}{3}$. Therefore, Quantity A is greater.

4. B

This is a weighted average question. Set x equal to the number of students who scored 0. There were 21 students not including those with a 0. So,

$3.0 = \dfrac{10(4)+4(3)+4(2)+3(1)+x(0)}{21+x} = \dfrac{40+12+8+3}{21+x}$

$= \dfrac{63}{21+x}$. Since $\dfrac{63}{21} = 3$, x must be 0. **(B)** is correct.

5. B

Think in terms of sums. The difference between the sum of all the scores and the sum of the 4 highest scores will be the lowest score.

The average of all 5 tests is 72, so the sum of all the scores is $5 \times 72 = 360$.

The average of the 4 highest scores is 84, so the sum of the 4 highest scores is $4 \times 84 = 336$.

The difference between the sum of all the scores and the sum of the 4 highest scores will be the lowest score; that is, $360 - 336 = 24$.

6. C

Use the average formula and label the other number x:

$$\frac{n+x}{2} = 3n - 4$$
$$n+x = 2(3n-4)$$
$$n+x = 6n - 8$$
$$x = 6n - 8 - n$$
$$x = 5n - 8$$

7. C

The key to this problem is that the total theater attendance stays the same after six theaters close. No matter how many theaters there are:

Total attendance = (Number of theaters) × (Average attendance)

We know that originally there are 15 theaters, and they average 600 customers per day. Plug these values into the formula above to find the total theater attendance:

Total attendance $= (15)(600) = 9,000$

Even after the 6 theaters close, the total attendance remains the same. Now, though, the number of theaters is only 9:

$$\text{New average attendance} = \frac{\text{Total attendance}}{\text{New number of theaters}}$$
$$= \frac{9,000}{9}$$
$$= 1,000$$

8. A

The average of a group of evenly spaced numbers is equal to the middle number. Here there is an even number of terms (18), so the average is between the two middle numbers, the 9th and 10th terms. This means that the 9th consecutive odd integer here will be the first odd integer less than 534, which is 533. Once you have the 9th term, you can count backward to find the first.

10th	Average	9th	8th	7th
535	534	533	531	529

6th	5th	4th	3rd	2nd	1st
527	525	523	521	519	517

9. B

You can't find individual values for any of these 6 numbers. However, with the given information you can find the sum of the 6 numbers, and the sum of just the largest and smallest. Subtracting the sum of the smallest and largest from the sum of all 6 will leave the sum of the four others, from which you can find their average.

The sum of all 6 numbers is (average of all 6 numbers) × (number of values) = 5 × 6, or 30.

The sum of the greatest and smallest can be found in the same way: 2 × average = 2 × 7 = 14.

The sum of the other 4 numbers is (the sum of all six) − (the sum of the greatest and smallest) = (30 − 14) = 16.

The sum of the other 4 numbers is 16. Their average is $\dfrac{16}{4}$ or 4.

10. D

To find the average of $a + 3$, $b - 5$, and 6, determine their sum, then divide this sum by 3. Even without knowing a and b, you can determine their sum. Since the average of a, b, and 7 is provided, find the sum of these 3 values by multiplying the average by the number of terms: $13 \times 3 = 39$. From that, determine the sum of a and b. If $a + b + 7 = 39$, then $a + b = 39 - 7$, or 32. Now, remember you're asked for the average of $a + 3$, $b - 5$, and 6. The sum of these expressions can be rewritten as $a + b + 3 - 5 + 6$, or, as $a + b + 4$. If $a + b = 32$, then $a + b + 4 = 32 + 4$, or 36. Therefore, the sum is 36 and the number of terms is 3, so the average is $\frac{36}{3}$, or 12.

11. D

If the average salary of the 60 workers is $160, the total amount received by the workers is $60 \times \$160$ or $9,600. This equals the total income from the $150 workers plus the total income from the $200 workers. Let x represent the number of $150 workers.

Since there are 60 workers altogether, and everyone earns either $150 or $200, then $60 - x$ workers must earn $200. Set up an equation for the total amount received by the workers by multiplying the rate times the number of workers receiving that rate and adding:

$$150x + 200(60 - x) = 9,600$$

Solve this equation to find x, the number of workers earning $150:

$$
\begin{aligned}
150x + 12,000 - 200x &= 9,600 \\
-50x &= -2,400 \\
50x &= 2,400 \\
x &= 48
\end{aligned}
$$

There are 48 workers earning $150.

Statistics Explanations

1. A

The 6 smallest positive even integers are 2, 4, 6, 8, 10, and 12. Since there are an even number of values in this group, the median is the average of the third and fourth greatest values, which are 6 and 8. The average of these two values is 7, so Quantity A is greater.

2. A

There are 15 values in the table, so the median is the eighth greatest value. Since there are 3 zeroes and 4 ones, the eighth, ninth, and tenth values are all 2, so that is the median. The mean of the data is the same as the weighted average. This can be calculated by multiplying each value times its number of occurrences, adding all these products, and dividing by the number of values: $\frac{3(0) + 4(1) + 3(2) + 2(3) + 1(4) + 1(5) + 0(6) + 1(7)}{15}$. This is $\frac{32}{15}$, which is greater than 2, so **(A)** is correct.

3. B

Plug the given values for the variables into the two quantities. For Quantity A, $x^2 = 4$, $y^2 = 4$, and $z^2 = 1$, so the range is $4 - 1 = 3$. For Quantity B, the range is $2 - (-2) = 4$, so the correct choice is **(B)**.

4. C

Since average $= \dfrac{\text{sum of the values}}{\text{number of values}}$, the original sum of the values $=$ (average) $\times$ (the number of values), which is $6 \times 5 = 30$. Adding a to the set increases the average to 7 and the number of values to 6, so the new sum of the values is $7 \times 6 = 42$. This means that $30 + a = 42$, and $a = 12$. **(C)** is correct.

5. B

Rearrange the formula for mean (average) to sum of values $=$ average $\times$ number of values. The number of values, including x, is 8 and the mean is 2, so the sum of the values is $2 \times 8 = 16$. The sum of the values other than x is 14, so x must be $16 - 14 = 2$. Therefore, 2, choice **(B)**, must be the mode because it's the only number that appears twice.

6.   C

To calculate a weighted average, take the sum of the products of each value times the number of occurrences of that value and divide that sum by the total number of occurrences. The total number of occurrences is $1 + 3 + 2 + 2 + z + 2 + 4 + 2 + 3 + 2 + 1 = 22 + z$. So

$$6 = \frac{1(1) + 2(3) + 3(2) + 4(2) + 5(z) + 6(2) + 7(4) + 8(2) + 9(3) + 10(2) + 11(1)}{22 + z}.$$

This equates to $6(22 + z) = 1 + 6 + 6 + 8 + 5z + 12 + 28 + 16 + 27 + 20 + 11$. Add up the products to get $132 + 6z = 135 + 5z$. Thus, $z = 3$.

7.   B

The answer choices are compared to each other rather than calculated. Start with (A) as the "base" case. Since standard deviation is a measure of dispersion, the values in (B) will be half as far apart as those in (A), so the standard deviation of (B) will be less than that of (A). The values in (C) are less dispersed than those in (A) but farther apart than those in (B). Eliminate (C). For (D), since each value is multiplied by 2, the dispersion will be greater and you can eliminate this choice. Finally, (E) merely adds 2 to each of the values. This increases the mean but doesn't change the dispersion of the values. **(B)** is correct.

8.   4

The difference between 17 and the mean of 12 is 5. So $1.25 \times$ the standard deviation $= 5$, which means that the standard deviation is $\frac{5}{1.25} = 4$.

9.   C, E

The greatest known value in the set is 14 and the least is -1, so the range without x is $14 - (-1) = 15$. Since the range with x is 17, the value of x must be either greater than 14 or less than -1. So, on the low end, $14 - x = 17$, in which case $x = -3$. On the high end, $x - (-1) = 17$, so the other possible value of x is 16. **(C)** and **(E)** are correct.

10.   B, C, D, E

Examine the two extreme cases for the number of teaches who could be dual-certified. The formula for overlapping sets is Total = Group A + Group B − Both + Neither. So, $30 = 14 + 20 -$ Both + Neither. Since Neither cannot be a negative number, the lower limit for Both is $14 + 20 - 30 = 4$. The logical upper limit for Both is 14, the number of teachers who could be certified in both if all 14 science-certified teachers are math certified. **(B)**, **(C)**, **(D)**, and **(E)** are all within these lower and upper limits.

Counting Methods and Probability Explanations

1.   A

Since the probability of scoring a point is 0.5, the probability of not scoring a point is $1 - 0.5 = 0.5$. There are $2^2 = 4$ equally likely outcomes of 2 tosses, 2 of which result in 1 point. Therefore, the probability of scoring exactly 1 point is $\frac{2}{4} = 0.5$. There are $2^4 = 16$ possible outcomes of 4 tosses. Since the successful tosses could occur on any 2 of the 4 tosses, the number of outcomes that result in two points is $_4C_2 = \frac{4!}{2!(4-2)!} = \frac{4 \times 3 \times 2 \times 1}{2 \times 1(2 \times 1)} = 6$. So the probability of exactly 2 points is $\frac{6}{16} = 0.375$. **(A)** is correct.

2.   A

For Quantity A, use the fact that the probability of something happening equals 1 minus the probability of it not happening: $P(A) = 1 - P(\text{Not } A)$. The probability of rolling a 5 or higher is $\frac{1}{3}$: two possibilities (5 or 6) divided by six total possibilities. The probability of rolling two 5s or higher is therefore $\frac{1}{3} \times \frac{1}{3} = \frac{1}{9}$. So the probability that the two dice *won't* both be a 5 or higher—i.e., that at least one of them be lower than a 5—is $1 - \frac{1}{9} = \frac{8}{9}$.

Use the same principle for Quantity B. The probability that Raghu *does* roll the same number twice is $\frac{1}{6}$. (The first die can be any number, and there's a 1 in 6 chance that the second die will roll the same number.) So the probability that Raghu *doesn't* roll the same number twice is $1 - \frac{1}{6} = \frac{5}{6}$. Quantity A is greater.

3. B

To compare the quantities, calculate both values. For Quantity A, there are 6 choices for the first object, 5 for the second, and 4 for the third, so the total possible permutations are $6 \times 5 \times 4 = 120$. For combinations of k objects selected from among n objects, the formula is $_nC_k = \dfrac{n!}{k!(n-k)!} = \dfrac{9!}{4!(5!)}$. This simplifies to

$$\frac{9 \times 8 \times 7 \times 6 \times \cancel{5} \times \cancel{4} \times \cancel{3} \times \cancel{2} \times \cancel{1}}{4 \times 3 \times 2 \times 1 \times \cancel{5} \times \cancel{4} \times \cancel{3} \times \cancel{2} \times \cancel{1}} = \frac{9 \times 8 \times 7 \times \cancel{6}}{4 \times \cancel{3} \times \cancel{2} \times \cancel{1}} =$$

$9 \times 2 \times 7 = 126$. **(B)** is correct.

4. B

Use the multiplication principle to determine the value of each quantity. For Quantity A, the only way to meet the conditions is to select exactly 1 game from each category. Per the multiplication principle:

Quantity A $= 3 \times 5 \times 7 = 105$

For Quantity B, consider the 2 bidding games separately from the other two. There are 3 ways to select 2 bidding games out of 3. (Selecting 2 games out of 3 is the same as selecting 1 game out of 3 to reject.) From the remaining $5 + 7 = 12$ non-bidding games, there are $_{12}C_2 = 12 \times 11 \div 2 = 66$ possible selections. Per the multiplication principle, the total number of possibilities is therefore $3 \times 66 = 198$, and Quantity B is greater.

5. D

Solving this question requires finding Percy's odds of striking the bullseye on his first throw, then increasing that probability by 40% on each of his second and third throws. Finally, the three probabilities need to be multiplied together because it is an AND scenario: the goal is for Percy to throw a bullseye on the first throw AND on the second throw AND on the third throw. Calculate the probability for each throw:

First throw: $\dfrac{1}{5} = 20\%$

Second throw: $20\% \times 1.4 = 28\%$

Third throw: $28\% \times 1.4 = 39.2\%$

Since the answer choices are widely spaced, you can estimate the result by multiplying $0.2 \times 0.3 \times 0.4 = 0.024$, which is 2.4% . Only **(D)** is close to this value.

6. 96

Solving the problem hinges on recognizing that the AB and EF pairings should be treated as blocs when setting up the slots. Draw four slots rather than six: one for AB, one for C, one for D, and one for EF. Next, apply the multiplication principle: $4 \times 3 \times 2 \times 1 = 24$. However, this is not the final answer because there are two ways to arrange the AB pairing (AB or BA) and two ways to arrange the EB pairing (EF or FE). Multiplying these two options for each pair yields $24 \times 2 \times 2 = 96$.

7. B, C

Due to overlap, there are three ways the beards and glasses in the room can be distributed:

Option A: 2 people have glasses only; 2 people have beards only; 1 person has both

Option B: 1 person has glasses only; 1 person has a beard only; 2 people have both; 1 person has neither

Option C: 3 people have both glasses and beards; 2 people have neither

Choice (A) is incorrect because its probability is 60% in Option C (3 out of 5).

Choice **(B)** is correct because there are at most 2 people out of 5 (40%) who have neither glasses nor a beard (Option C).

Choice **(C)** is correct because there are at most 2 people out of 5 (40%) who have glasses but not a beard (Option A).

Choice (D) is incorrect because its probability is higher than 50% in all three options. For example, in Option C, the only way to avoid a beard or glasses is to pick exactly the two people who have neither glasses nor a beard. The likelihood of this happening is 10% (1 possible pairing divided by 10 total pairings), so the probability of it *not* happening is 90%. (Note: to get the number of pairings, take $_5C_2 = 5 \times 4 \div 2 = 10$.)

Choice (E) is incorrect because its probability is 100% in Option A, where everyone in the room has either glasses or a beard or both.

8. B

First consider the manner in which the groups can line up. Since there are 3 groups, the number of ways in which the groups can line up is $3! = 6$. Within each group, although there are 4 members, the group leader must be in the first position. So, for each group there are $3! = 6$ ways to line up. Altogether there are $6(6 \times 6 \times 6) = 1{,}296$ ways that the children could line up.

9. C

Because factorials are products of sequential integers, this question cannot easily be answered algebraically. Backsolving would be an excellent approach. Try (B):

$$_{12}C_3 = \frac{12!}{3!(9)!} = \frac{12 \times 11 \times 10}{3 \times 2 \times 1} = 2 \times 11 \times 10 = 220$$

Try (D):

$$_{12}C_5 = \frac{12!}{5!(7)!} = \frac{\cancel{12} \times 11 \times \cancel{10} \times 9 \times 8}{\cancel{5} \times \cancel{4} \times \cancel{3} \times \cancel{2} \times 1} = 11 \times 9 \times 8 = 792$$

So **(C)** must be correct. For the record:

$$_{12}C_4 = \frac{12!}{4!(8)!} = \frac{12 \times 11 \times 10 \times 9}{4 \times 3 \times 2 \times 1} = 11 \times 5 \times 9 = 495$$

10. C

Because the purple dolls can't go on the ends or be adjacent to each other, they must occupy positions 2, 4, and 6. The remaining four dolls must occupy positions 1, 3, 5, and 7. The number of ways to arrange the 3 purple dolls across 3 positions is $3! = 6$. The number of ways to arrange the 4 non-purple dolls across 4 positions is $4! = 24$. So the total number of possibilities is $6 \times 24 = 144$, choice **(C)**.

Lines and Angles Explanations

1. A

To solve this question, first find the degree measures for angles q, t, and r. Line N is perpendicular to both line L and line M, so angle r is 90°. Angle t and the 35° angle form a straight line, so angle t must be $180° - 35° = 145°$. Line K is a transversal crossing parallel lines, so angle q and the 35° angle are equal. Comparing Quantity

A, $2(35°) = 70°$, to Quantity B, $145° - 90° = 55°$, Quantity A is greater, and **(A)** is correct.

2. C

At first glance, solving for all of the four angles might seem like the only viable option, but strategic use of the rules for straight lines will get you to the answer much faster. Lines T and W are parallel, which means that angles j and m are supplementary (that is, they sum to 180°), and the same logic applies to angles k and l because lines U and V are also parallel. Substituting this information makes Quantity B $180° + 180° = 360°$. **(C)** is correct.

3. D

Don't fall for the trap! The centered information does not provide the exact length from G to J, so an exact value for x cannot be found, only a range of values. The smallest integer value that works for x is 1, in which case GH is 8, IJ is 12, and GJ is 21. The largest integer value that works for x is 8 (so that GH can be at least 1), in which case GH is 1, IJ is 5, and GJ is 14. In the first scenario, Quantity A is $21 - 1 = 20$, while in the second scenario it is $14 - 8 = 6$, which proves that Quantity A can be greater or less than Quantity B. **(D)** is correct.

4. A

"Bisect" means to divide an angle or line segment into two equal parts, and "complement" refers to angles that total 90°. For Quantity A, since the 116° angle and angle p are vertical angles, angle p is 116°, and bisecting angle p would create two angles that are 58° each. For Quantity B, angle q is the same as angle s, and angle s can be found by setting $116° + s° + 22° = 180°$ because those three angles form a straight line. Solving for angle s yields $180° - 116° - 22° = 42°$, which means that angle q is 42°. The complement of angle q is $90° - 42° = 48°$. Comparing Quantity A, 58°, to Quantity B, 48°, Quantity A is greater, and **(A)** is correct.

5. E

Notice that $\angle AOE$ and $\angle BOD$ are vertical angles, and therefore must have equal measures. $\angle BOD$ is made up of one angle with a measure of 105°, and a second angle with a measure of 40°; it must have a measure of $105° + 40°$, or 145°. Therefore, $\angle AOE$ must also have a measure of 145°. **(E)** is correct.

6. C

$\angle AFD$ is a straight angle. The angle marked 40°, the right angle, and the angle marked $x°$ together form $\angle AFD$; therefore, they must sum to 180°.

$$x + 90 + 40 = 180$$
$$x + 130 = 180$$
$$x = 50$$

(C) is correct.

7. D

The sum $v + w + x + y$ must equal 180 since the angles with these measures together form a straight line. Because the question asks for the value of y, define all variables in terms of y. If $w = 2x$ and $x = \dfrac{y}{3}$, then $w = \dfrac{2y}{3}$. Similarly, $v = 2w$, so $v = 2\left(\dfrac{2y}{3}\right)$ or $\dfrac{4y}{3}$. Substitute the angles in terms of y into the equation:

$$v + w + x + y = 180$$
$$\frac{4y}{3} + \frac{2y}{3} + \frac{y}{3} + y = 180$$
$$\frac{7y}{3} + y = 180$$
$$\frac{10y}{3} = 180$$
$$y = \frac{3}{10} \times 180 = 3 \times 18 = 54$$

(D) is correct.

8. 107

Sometimes along with transferring the diagram to the scratch paper, you will need to add a missing piece of information to the drawing. In this case, line segment CO should bisect $\angle AOB$. The degree measure of $\angle AOB$ can be found by subtracting 34 from 180: $180° - 34° = 146°$. Dividing that angle in half makes $\angle COB$ equal to 73°. At this point, the diagram on the scratch paper should look like this:

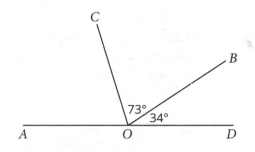

The final step is to add $\angle COB$ and $\angle BOD$, $73° + 34° = 107°$, so $\angle COD$ is **107°**. Always remember that, unless it is specifically stated, you cannot assume that GRE geometry diagrams are drawn to scale.

9. B

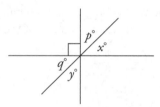

Before looking at the choices, see what information you can get from the diagram. Angles p and x together are supplementary to the right angle, so p and x together must form a right angle. The same is true for angles q and y. There are also these two pairs of vertical angles: $p = y$ and $x = q$. Now look at the three statements.

(A) $p = x$ and $q = y$. This will be true only if $p = 45$. Since you have no way of knowing the exact measure of p, this could be true but doesn't have to be. Eliminate.

(B) $x + y = 90$. This is true since $q + y = 90$ and $x = q$. **(B)** is correct.

(C) $x = y = 45$. There is no indication from the diagram that the angles x and y must have the same degree measure. This statement does not have to be true. Eliminate.

Only **(B)** is correct.

10. A

The angle marked $(2x - 20)°$ and the angle marked $3x°$ together form a straight angle. This means that the sum of their degree measures must be 180.

$$(2x - 20) + (3x) = 180$$
$$2x - 20 + 3x = 180$$
$$5x = 200$$
$$x = \frac{200}{5} = 40$$

Triangles Explanations

1. B

Notice that each marked angle makes a pair of vertical angles with one of the interior angles of the triangle.

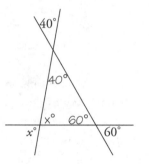

Since these marked angles have the same degree measure as the corresponding interior angles, the sum of their measures must equal 180.

$$x + 40 + 60 = 180$$
$$x = 180 - 100$$
$$x = 80$$

2. E

Angle $x°$ is supplementary to $\angle ABD$, and $\angle ABD$ is an interior angle of $\triangle ABD$. The sum of the measures of the 2 known angles in $\triangle ABD$ is $20° + 40° = 60°$. Therefore, the third angle, $\angle ABD$, must have a measure of $180° - 60°$, or $120°$. So $x = 180 - 120$, or 60.

A quicker way to get this solution is to remember that the measure of an exterior angle is equal to the sum of the measures of the two remote interior angles. Angle x is an exterior angle, so $x = 20 + 40$, or 60.

3. C

Since the angle marked $x°$ and the angle marked $y°$ together form a straight angle, their measures must sum to $180°$.

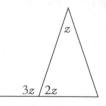

Substitute in $2z$ for x and $3z$ for y, and solve for z.

$$x + y = 180$$
$$2z + 3z = 180$$
$$5z = 180$$
$$z = \frac{1}{5} \cdot 180 = 36$$

4. E

Since BC is parallel to AD, $\angle GBF$ must have the same degree measure as x (since there are two parallel lines cut by transversal AG). Consider $\triangle BFG$ and $\triangle DCF$. The interior angles of these two triangles at point F must have the same degree measure since they are vertical angles. In addition, each triangle has a $60°$ angle. Since these are two triangles with two pairs of equal angles, the third pair of angles must be equal, too. The third angle in $\triangle DCF$ has measure $70°$; therefore, $\angle GBF = x° = 70°$.

5. A, B

Evaluate each choice individually. For (A), $x > 50$, you could solve for the value of x, but it's easier to ask "could x be 50?" If x were 50, then the triangle would have two $50°$ angles and a third angle $15°$ less than $50°$. But this would make the total less than $180°$. Therefore, x must be greater than 50, and **(A)** is correct.

For (B), recall that the shortest side of a triangle will always be opposite the angle of smallest measure. Two of the angles have degree measure x; the third, $\angle CBA$, has a degree measure less than that, $x - 15$. Thus $\angle CBA$ is the smallest angle, so the side opposite it, side AC, must be the shortest side. Since CB has length 10, AC must be less than 10. **(B)** is correct.

For (C), note that $\angle ACB$ and $\angle BAC$ both have a measure of $x°$, so $\triangle ABC$ is isosceles. Therefore, AB has the same length as CB (they're opposite the equal angles). Since BC has a length of 10, AB must also have a length of 10. (C) is incorrect.

6. E

First, solve for the length of BC, the shortest side, then find the length of AB and the length of AC using the Pythagorean theorem.

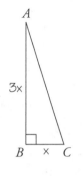

The area of any right triangle equals one-half the product of the legs. If BC has a length of x, then AB has a length of $3x$. The area of the triangle is one-half their product, or $\frac{1}{2}(x)(3x)$. This equals 6.

$$\frac{1}{2}(x)(3x) = 6$$
$$3x^2 = 12$$
$$x^2 = 4$$
$$x = 2$$

BC has a length of 2. So AB, which is $3x$, is 6. Now use the Pythagorean theorem to find AC:

$$AC^2 = AB^2 + BC^2$$
$$AC^2 = (6)^2 + (2)^2$$
$$AC^2 = 36 + 4$$
$$AC = \sqrt{40} = \sqrt{4 \cdot 10} = \left(\sqrt{4}\right)\left(\sqrt{10}\right) = 2\sqrt{10}$$

7. D

Draw a diagram so that the picture is more clear:

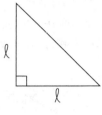

In an isosceles right triangle, both legs have the same length. Therefore:

$$\text{area} = \frac{1}{2}l \times l = \frac{l^2}{2}$$

Given that the area is 32, set up an equation to solve for l:

$$\frac{l^2}{2} = 32$$
$$l^2 = 64$$
$$l = 8$$

Remember, the ratio of the length of the legs to the length of the hypotenuse in any isosceles right triangle is $1 : \sqrt{2}$.

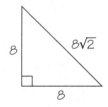

Since the legs have a length of 8, the hypotenuse is $\sqrt{2}$ times 8, or $8\sqrt{2}$.

An alternative is to use the Pythagorean theorem to find the hypotenuse:

$$\text{hyp}^2 = 8^2 + 8^2$$
$$\text{hyp}^2 = 64 + 64$$
$$\text{hyp}^2 = 128$$
$$\text{hyp} = \sqrt{128} = \sqrt{64 \cdot 2} = 8\sqrt{2}$$

8. B

If $\angle DBA$ has a measure of 60°, $\angle CBD$, which is supplementary to it, must have a measure of $180 - 60$, or 120°.

$\angle DCB$ has a measure of 30°; that leaves $180 - (120 + 30)$, or 30 degrees for the remaining interior angle: *BDC*.

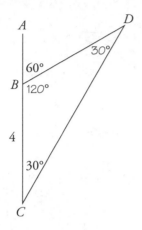

Since $\angle BCD$ has the same measure as $\angle BDC$, $\triangle BCD$ is an isosceles triangle, and the sides opposite the equal angles will have equal lengths. Therefore, *BD* must have the same length as *BC*, or 4.

9. E

One of the given sides is the hypotenuse, which is the longest side of a right triangle. So it must be the larger value, $\frac{d}{3}$. Use the Pythagorean theorem to solve for the unknown side, which you can call *x*.

$$(\text{hypotenuse})^2 = (\text{leg})^2 + (\text{leg})^2$$
$$\left(\frac{d}{3}\right)^2 = \left(\frac{d}{4}\right)^2 + x^2$$
$$\frac{d^2}{9} = \frac{d^2}{16} + x^2$$
$$\frac{d^2}{9} - \frac{d^2}{16} = x^2$$
$$\frac{16d^2 - 9d^2}{144} = x^2$$
$$\frac{7d^2}{144} = x^2$$
$$x = \frac{d\sqrt{7}}{12}$$

Another way to solve this that avoids algebra is to pick a number for *d*, such as 12, since that is divisible by both 3 and 4. Then the two sides have length $\frac{12}{3}$, or 4, and $\frac{12}{4}$, or 3. The hypotenuse must be 4, and 3 must be a leg. Now use the Pythagorean theorem to find the other leg:

$$(\text{leg}_1)^2 + (\text{leg}_2)^2 = (\text{hyp})^2$$
$$(\text{leg}_1)^2 + (3)^2 = (4)^2$$
$$(\text{leg}_1)^2 + 9 = 16$$
$$(\text{leg}_1)^2 = 7$$
$$\text{leg}_1 = \sqrt{7}$$

Now plug in 12 for *d* into each answer choice; any choice that does not equal $\sqrt{7}$ can be eliminated.

$$\frac{5 \times 12}{12} = 5 \text{ Discard.}$$
$$\frac{12}{\sqrt{7}} \neq \sqrt{7} \text{ Discard.}$$
$$\frac{12}{5} \neq \sqrt{7} \text{ Discard.}$$
$$\frac{12}{12} = 1 \text{ Discard.}$$
$$\frac{12\sqrt{7}}{12} = \sqrt{7} \text{ Correct.}$$

10. A

The Pythagorean theorem states that the sum of the squares of the legs is equal to the square of the hypotenuse, or, in this case: $x^2 + (x + 2)^2 = (2x - 2)^2$.

Expand this equation and set the resulting quadratic equal to 0:

$$x^2 + x^2 + 4x + 4 = 4x^2 - 8x + 4$$
$$12x = 2x^2$$
$$2x^2 - 12x = 0$$
$$2x(x - 6) = 0$$

When the product of two factors is 0, one or both must equal 0. So either $2x = 0$, in which case $x = 0$, or $x - 6 = 0$, in which case $x = 6$. But *x* is the length of one side of a triangle, which must be a positive number. This means that *x* must equal 6, which makes triangle *ABC* a 6:8:10 right triangle.

Another way to do this problem is to try plugging each answer choice into the expression for x, and see which one gives side lengths which work in the Pythagorean Theorem. Choice (**A**) 6 when substituted for x results in 6, 8, and 10 (a Pythagorean triplet) for the three sides of the triangle, so it must be correct.

Polygons Explanations

1.   A

The formula for the sum of the interior angles of a polygon is $(n-2)(180°)$. Since a pentagon has 5 sides, the sum of the interior angles is $(5-2)(180°) = 540°$. If the pentagon is a regular pentagon, all the sides are equal, so each of the angles is $\dfrac{540°}{5} = 108°$, which is greater than 105°. If the pentagon is not regular, then at least one angle would have to be greater than 108°, so (**A**) is correct.

2.   B

The garden's radius is half its diameter, or 20 feet. Since the walkway is 10 feet wide, the radius of the outer circumference of the walkway is $20 + 10 = 30$ ft. Use the formula for the area of a circle, $a = \pi r^2$, to compare the two quantities. The area of the garden is $\pi(20)^2 = 400\pi$. Since the garden lies in the middle of the walkway, the area of the walkway can be determined by subtracting the area of the garden from the area of a circle formed by the outer circumference of the walkway. This is $\pi(30)^2 - \pi(20)^2 = 900\pi - 400\pi = 500\pi$. So, the area of the walkway is greater than that of the garden.

3.   C

Since angles BCD and CDA are both right angles, BC and AD are parallel, and quadrilateral $ABCD$ is a trapezoid. The area of a trapezoid is $\dfrac{b_1 + b_2}{2}(h)$, where b_1 and b_2 are the lengths of the bases and h is the height. A perpendicular line dropped from B to side AD would be the height. Since the angle at A is 45°, the height is one side of a 45-45-90 isosceles right triangle with a hypotenuse of 8. Thus, the height of the trapezoid is $4\sqrt{2}$. (If you didn't recall the side ratios of an isosceles right triangle, you could have calculated the value using the Pythagorean theorem.) This also means that AD is $4\sqrt{2}$ longer than BC, which is $10\sqrt{2} + 4\sqrt{2} = 14\sqrt{2}$. So the area of $ABCD$ is

$\dfrac{10\sqrt{2} + 14\sqrt{2}}{2}(4\sqrt{2}) = 12\sqrt{2}(4\sqrt{2}) = 96$. The two quantities are equal.

4.   B

Drawing a sketch can help you work through this question.

5.   A

Keep in mind that the measures of the interior angles of a quadrilateral sum to 360°. Then note that the angles marked 75° and 60° are both supplementary to the two unmarked interior angles in the diagram. The angle supplementary to the 75° angle must have a measure of $180 - 75$, or 105°. The angle supplementary to the 60° angle must have a measure of $180 - 60$, or 120°.

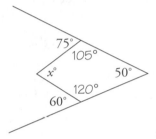

Now that you know the measures of three of the interior angles, you can set up an equation to solve for x:

$$x + 105 + 50 + 120 = 360$$
$$x + 275 = 360$$
$$x = 360 - 275 = 85$$

6.   C

The bases of $\triangle AEB$ and $\triangle ACD$ both have the same length, since $AB = CD$. So you just need to find the relationship between their respective heights. AC and BD intersect at the center of the rectangle, which is point E. Therefore, the perpendicular distance from E to side AB is half the distance from side CD to side AB. This means that the height of $\triangle AEB$ is half the height of $\triangle ACD$. So the area of $\triangle ACD$ is twice the area of $\triangle AEB$: $2 \times 8 = 16$.

7. B

The sum of the lengths of all four sides of the rectangle is $6w$. The two short sides add up to $\dfrac{w}{2} + \dfrac{w}{2}$, or w. This leaves $6w - w$, or $5w$, for the **sum** of the other two sides. So **each** long side is $\dfrac{1}{2}(5w)$, or $\dfrac{5}{2}w$. Therefore:

$$\text{Area} = \left(\frac{w}{2}\right)\left(\frac{5w}{2}\right) = \frac{5w^2}{4}$$

8. B

A good way to solve this problem is to pick a value for the length of a side of square A. Use numbers that will be easy to work with, such as 10 for the length of each side of square A. The length of each side of square B is 100% greater, or twice as great as a side of square A. So the length of a side of square B is 2×10, or 20. The length of each side of square C is 50% greater, or $1\dfrac{1}{2}$ times as great as a side of square B.

So the length of a side of square C is $1\dfrac{1}{2} \times 20$, or 30. The area of square A is 10^2, or 100. The area of square B is 20^2, or 400. The sum of the areas of squares A and B is $100 + 400$, or 500. The area of square C is 30^2, or 900. The area of square C is greater than the sum of the areas of squares A and B by $900 - 500$, or 400. The percent that the area of square C is greater than the sum of the areas of squares A and B is $\dfrac{400}{500} \times 100\%$, or 80%.

9. D

If a rectangle has perimeter 10, what could its dimensions be? Perimeter $= 2L + 2W$, or $2(L + W)$. The perimeter is 10, so $2(L + W) = 10$, or $L + W = 5$. Since L and W must be integers, there are two possibilities: $L = 4$ and $W = 1$ ($4 + 1 = 5$), or $L = 3$ and $W = 2$ ($3 + 2 = 5$). Let's consider each case separately. If $L = 4$, then how many of these rectangles would fit along the length of the larger rectangle? The length of the larger rectangle is 60: $60 \div 4 = 15$, so 15 smaller rectangles would fit, if they were lined up with their longer sides against the longer side of the large rectangle. The width of the smaller rectangles is 1, and the width of the large rectangle is 24. Because $24 \div 1 = 24$, it follows that 24 small rectangles can fit against the width of the large rectangle. The total number of small rectangles that fit inside the large rectangle is the number along the length times the number along the

width: $15 \times 24 = 360$. In the second case, $L = 3$ and $W = 2$. $60 \div 3 = 20$, so 20 small rectangles fit along the length; $24 \div 2 = 12$, so 12 small rectangles fit along the width. So the total number of small rectangles is 20×12, or 240. The first case yields the greatest number: 360.

10. B, C, D

The perimeter of a rectangle is 2(length + width) and the area is length × width. Since the perimeter of this rectangle is 24, the length and width must sum to half that, which is 12. When given a range of values in a question, start by picking a number that is the extreme allowable value. In this case, that means picking 2 for the width. For that value, the length is $12 - 2 = 10$, and the area is $2 \times 10 = 20$. Now try a greater width, such as 4. This equates to a length of 8 and an area of 32. The width cannot exceed the length, so the maximum value of the width occurs when the rectangle is a square with sides of 6 and an area of 36. Since area increases as width increases, 20 is the minimum value of the area of the rectangle and 36 is the maximum. Choices **(B)**, **(C)**, and **(D)** fall within this range.

Circles Explanations

1. B

First find the radius in order to get the circumference. Given that the area is 64π, use the area formula to get the radius:

$$\text{Area} = \pi r^2 = 64\pi$$
$$r^2 = 64$$
$$r = 8$$

The circumference, which is $2\pi r$, is $2\pi(8)$, or 16π.

2. B

Use the following proportion:

$$\frac{\text{length of arc}}{\text{circumference}} = \frac{\text{measure of arc's central angle}}{360°}$$

to solve for x. The measure of the arc's central angle is x degrees and the length of the arc is $\dfrac{1}{8}$ of the circumference. So:

$$\frac{1}{8} = \frac{x}{360}$$
$$x = 45$$

3.   D

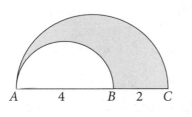

Approach I:

The area of the shaded region equals the difference in the areas of the two semicircles. To find the fraction of the larger semicircle that the shaded region occupies, first find the area of the shaded region, then divide this by the area of the larger semicircle. The area of a semicircle is $\frac{1}{2}$ the area of the whole circle, or $\frac{1}{2}\pi r^2$. The larger semicircle has a diameter of 6 and a radius of 3, so its area equals $\frac{1}{2}\pi r^2 = \frac{1}{2}\pi(3)^2$, or $\frac{9}{2}\pi$. The smaller semicircle has a diameter of 4 and a radius of 2, for an area of $\frac{1}{2}\pi(2)^2$, or 2π. The area of the shaded region equals

$$\frac{9\pi}{2} - 2\pi = \frac{9\pi}{2} - \frac{4\pi}{2} = \frac{5\pi}{2}$$

The fraction of the larger semicircle the shaded region occupies is

$$\frac{\frac{5\pi}{2}}{\frac{9\pi}{2}} = \frac{5\pi}{2} \times \frac{2}{9\pi} = \frac{5}{9}$$

Method II:

Avoid most of this work by exploring the ratios involved here. Any two semicircles are similar. The ratio of AB to AC is $4:6$ or $2:3$. The ratio of all linear measures of the two circles, including circumference and radius, will also have this ratio. The area ratio will be the square of $\frac{2}{3}$, so the small semicircle has $\frac{4}{9}$ the area of the large semicircle, leaving $\frac{5}{9}$ of the area of the large semicircle for the shaded region.

4.   E

Sketch a diagram:

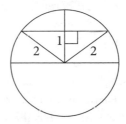

Since the radius of the circle is 2, the end-points of the line segment are both 2 inches from the center. The line segment can be seen as the legs of two right triangles, each of which has a hypotenuse of 2 and a leg of 1. Call the other leg of these triangles, which is half the length of the line segment in the question, x. Using the Pythagorean theorem, $1^2 + x^2 = 2^2$, so $x^2 = 3$ and $x = \sqrt{3}$. The total length of the line segment is twice this, or $2\sqrt{3}$.

5.   B

Since the diameter of the semicircle around AB is given, begin with this semicircle. The radius of semicircle AB is $\frac{1}{2}(4)$, or 2. The area of a semicircle is half the area of the circle, or $\frac{1}{2}\pi r^2$. So the area of semicircle AB is $\frac{1}{2}\pi(2)^2$, or 2π. $BC = 2AB$, so $BC = 2(4)$, or 8.

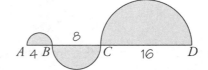

The radius of semicircle BC is 4, so the area of semicircle BC is $\frac{1}{2}\pi(4)^2$, or 8π. $CD = 2BC$, so $CD = 2(8)$, or 16. The radius of semicircle CD is 8, so the area of semicircle CD is $\frac{1}{2}\pi(8)^2$, or 32π. Add the three areas together: $2\pi + 8\pi + 32\pi = 42\pi$.

6. A

Use the area of circle O to find the radius, which is OB. Then AB is just the difference of the lengths of OB and OA. Since the area of the circle is $100\pi = \pi r^2$, the radius must be $\sqrt{100}$, which is 10. Radius OC, line segment CA, and line segment OA together form a right triangle. Notice that 10 is twice 5 and 6 is twice 3, so right triangle AOC has sides whose lengths are in a 3:4:5 ratio. OA must have a length of twice 4, or 8. AB is the segment of radius OB that's not a part of OA; its length equals the length of OB minus the length of OA, or $10 - 8 = 2$.

7. C

Each leg of right triangle XOY is also a radius of circle O, so the area of $\triangle XOY$ is $\frac{1}{2}(r)(r)$, or $\frac{r^2}{2}$, and the area of circle O is πr^2. Use the area of $\triangle XOY$ to find r^2, and then multiply r^2 by π to get the area of the circle.

$$\text{Area of } \triangle XOY = \frac{r^2}{2} = 25$$

$$r^2 = 50$$

Area of circle $O = \pi r^2 = \pi(50) = 50\pi$

Note that it's unnecessary (and extra work) to find the actual value of r, since the value of r^2 is sufficient to find the area.

8. D

Pick a value for the diameter of the circle. If the diameter is 4, then the radius is 2, which means that the area is $\pi(2)^2$, or 4π. Increasing the diameter by 50% means adding on half of its original length, so the new radius is 3, which means that the area of the circle is now $\pi(3)^2$, or 9π. The percent increase is $\frac{9\pi - 4\pi}{4\pi} \times 100\% = \frac{5\pi}{4\pi} \times 100\%$, or 125%.

9. D

Call the end-points of the arc A and B and the center of the circle C. Major arc AB represents $\frac{3}{4}$ of $360°$, or $270°$. Therefore, minor arc AB is $360° - 270°$, or $90°$. Since AC and CB are both radii of the circle, $\triangle ACB$ must be an isosceles right triangle:

Major arc AB, which takes up $\frac{3}{4}$ of the circumference, has a length of 12π, so the entire circumference is 16π. The circumference of any circle is 2π times the radius, so a circle with circumference 16π must have radius 8. The ratio of a leg to the hypotenuse in an isosceles right triangle is $1:\sqrt{2}$. The length of AB is $\sqrt{2}$ times the length of a leg, or $8\sqrt{2}$.

10. D

Connect the centers of the circles O, P, and Q as shown below. Each leg in this right triangle consists of two radii. The hypotenuse consists of two radii plus the diameter of the small circle.

The total area of the four large circles is 36π, so each large circle has area 9π. Since the area of a circle is πr^2, the radii of the large circles all have length 3.

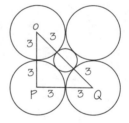

Therefore, each leg in the isosceles right triangle OPQ is 6. The hypotenuse then has length $6\sqrt{2}$. (The hypotenuse of an isosceles right triangle is always $\sqrt{2}$ times a leg.) The hypotenuse is equal to two radii of a large circle plus the diameter of the small circle, so $6\sqrt{2} = 2(3) + 1$ diameter. Thus, the diameter is $6\sqrt{2} - 6$.

Multiple Figures Explanations

1. A

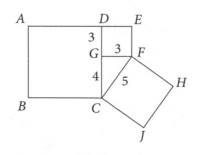

In order to determine the area of square *FCJH*, find the length of side *FC*, which is the hypotenuse of $\triangle FGC$. Since *ABCD* has area 49, which is the length of a side squared, each side must have length $\sqrt{49}$, or 7. Therefore, *DC* has length 7. Since *DEFG* has area 9, side *FG* must have length $\sqrt{9}$, or 3. *DG* is a side of the same square, so its length is also 3. The length of *CG* is the difference between the length of *DC* and the length of *DG*: $7 - 3 = 4$. Given that the lengths of the legs of $\triangle FGC$ are 3 and 4, it is a 3-4-5 right triangle. So *CF* has length 5. The area of square *FCJH* is the square of the length of *CF*: $5^2 = 25$.

2. E

The three right angles define three sectors of the circle, each with a central angle of 90°. Together, those three sectors account for $\dfrac{270°}{360°}$, or $\dfrac{3}{4}$ of the area of the circle, leaving $\dfrac{1}{4}$ of the circle for the shaded regions. The total area of the circle is $\pi(8^2) = 64\pi$, so the area of the shaded regions is one-fourth of that, 16π.

3. B

The area of a square with side *x* is x^2. The area of a circle with radius *r* is πr^2. Since the two areas are equal, set up the equation $x^2 = \pi r^2$ and solve for $\dfrac{x}{r}$:

$$\frac{x^2}{r^2} = \pi$$

$$\frac{x}{r} = \sqrt{\pi}$$

4. D

Notice that both squares share a side with right triangle *CDE*. Since square *CEFG* has an area of 36, *CE* has a length of $\sqrt{36}$, or 6. Since right triangle *CDE* has a 45° angle, *CDE* must be a 45-45-90 isosceles right triangle. Therefore, *CD* and *DE* are the same length, designated as *x* on the sketch below:

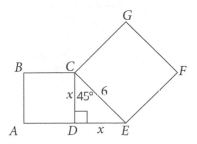

5. B

The diameter of the circle is 5, so the radius is $\dfrac{5}{2}$ and the area is $\pi\left(\dfrac{5}{2}\right)^2$ or $\dfrac{25}{4}\pi$. This is equal to the area of the triangle. Given that the base of the triangle is 5, solve for the height using the formula for the area of a triangle, $\dfrac{1}{2}bh$:

$$\frac{1}{2}(5)(h) = \frac{25}{4}\pi$$

$$5h = \frac{25}{2}\pi$$

$$h = \frac{5}{2}\pi$$

The question asks for the area of square *ABCD*, which will be x^2. Use the Pythagorean theorem to solve for x^2 (you don't need to find *x*, since the question asks for the area, which is x^2).

$$(\text{leg})^2 + (\text{leg})^2 = (\text{hypotenuse})^2$$

$$x^2 + x^2 = 6^2$$

$$2x^2 = 36$$

$$x^2 = 18$$

6. E

Each side of square *EFGH* consists of 2 radii of the quarter-circles, so the radius of each quarter-circle is half the length of the square's sides. The four quarter-circles together are equivalent to a whole circle with a circumference of $4 \times \pi = 4\pi$. Use the circumference formula to solve for the radius of each quarter-circle:

$$\text{Circumference} = 2\pi r = 4\pi$$

$$r = 2$$

So each side of square *EFGH* has length $2 \times 2 = 4$. Therefore, the perimeter of the square is $4(4) = 16$.

7. C

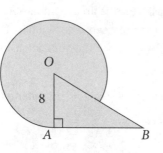

The total area of the shaded region equals the area of the circle plus the area of the right triangle minus the area of overlap. The area of circle O is $\pi(8)^2$, or 64π. The area of right triangle OAB is 32. The area of overlap is a sector of the circle. In order to determine that value, start by finding the measure of $\angle AOB$, the central angle of the sector.

The area of right triangle OAB is 32, and the height is the radius. So $\frac{1}{2}(8)(AB) = 32$, so $AB = 8$. Since $AB = OA$, $\triangle OAB$ is an isosceles right triangle. Therefore, $\angle AOB$ has a measure of $45°$. So the area of the sector is $\frac{45}{360}(64\pi) = \frac{1}{8}(64\pi)$, or 8π. Thus, the total area of the shaded region is $64\pi + 32 - 8\pi = 56\pi + 32$.

8. E

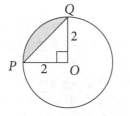

The area of the shaded region is the area of the quarter-circle (sector OPQ) minus the area of right triangle OPQ. The radius of circle O is 2 and $\triangle POQ$ is a right triangle, so the area of the quarter-circle is

$$\frac{90}{360}\pi r^2 = \frac{1}{4} \times \pi(2)^2 = \frac{1}{4} \times 4\pi = \pi$$

Each leg of the triangle is a radius of circle O, so the area of the triangle is

$$\frac{1}{2}bh = \frac{1}{2} \times 2 \times 2 = 2$$

Therefore, the area of the shaded region is $\pi - 2$.

9. D

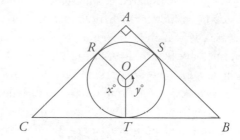

A line tangent to a circle is perpendicular to the radius of the circle at the point of tangency. Since AC is tangent to circle O at R and AB is tangent to circle O at S, $\angle ARO$ and $\angle ASO$ are each $90°$ angles. Thus, three of the angles in quadrilateral $RASO$ are right angles, so the fourth, $\angle ROS$, must also be a right angle. $\angle ROS$, $x°$, and $y°$ sum to $360°$, so $x + y = 360 - 90 = 270$.

10. B

The total area of the shaded regions equals the area of the sector of the circle minus the area of the rectangle. Since $\angle AOB$ is $90°$, the length of arc AB, 5π, is a quarter of the circumference of circle O; so the whole circumference is 20π. Because circumference is $2\pi r$, the radius of the circle is 10, as shown in the diagram below. So, $OC = 10 - 4 = 6$, which means that $\triangle OEC$ is a 6:8:10 right triangle and $EC = 8$.

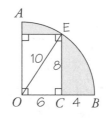

The area of the rectangle is $l \times w = 8 \times 6 = 48$. The area of the sector is $\frac{90}{360}(\pi)(10)^2 = 25\pi$. So the total area of the shaded regions is $25\pi - 48$.

The length of each side of the square is given as s, which is also the diameter of the smaller circle.

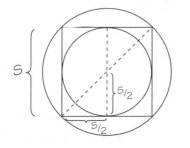

This means that the radius of the smaller circle is $\frac{s}{2}$, so its area is $\left(\frac{s}{2}\right)^2$, or $\frac{s^2}{4}\pi$. A diagonal of the square is the diameter of the larger circle. The diagonal divides the square into two isosceles right triangles, where each leg has length s. So the length of the diagonal is $s\sqrt{2}$, and the radius of the larger circle is $\frac{s\sqrt{2}}{2}$. The area of that circle is $\pi\left(\frac{s\sqrt{2}}{2}\right)^2 = \frac{s^2}{2}\pi$. The area of the smaller circle is $\frac{s^2}{4}\pi$, so the area of the larger circle is twice the area of the smaller circle, which is a 2:1 ratio.

Uniform Solids Explanations

1. A

The area of insulation is the surface area of a cylinder with a 1-in. diameter and a length of 3 feet, which is 36 in. The formula for the surface area of a cylinder (without the ends) is πdh, which is $\pi(1)(36) = 36\pi$. Quantity B, 108 in^2, is 3×36 in^2. Since π is a bit greater than 3, Quantity A is greater than Quantity B.

2. B

The volume of any uniform solid is the area of the base times the height. Since the base of solid A is a triangle, that area is $\frac{1}{2}bh$. The height of that equilateral triangle splits it into two 30-60-90 triangles, each with a base of 2 and a hypotenuse of 4. The side lengths of a 30-60-90 triangle are in the ratio $x : x\sqrt{3} : 2x$, so the height of each of the two 30-60-90 triangles is $2\sqrt{3}$. So the area of the base of solid A is $\frac{1}{2}(4)(2\sqrt{3}) = 4\sqrt{3}$, and the volume is $4\sqrt{3} \times 10\sqrt{3} = 40 \times 3 = 120$. The area of the base of solid B is $4 \times 3 = 12$. Rearrange the formula for the volume of a uniform solid to height $= \frac{\text{volume}}{\text{area of base}}$. So, the height of

solid B is $\frac{120}{12} = 10$ inches. This is less than 12 inches, so **(B)** is correct.

3. A

Express the volume of a cylinder with radius r and height h first. (Call it cylinder A.)

Volume $=$ area of base $\times$ height $= \pi r^2 h$

For the cylinder with radius h and height r (cylinder B),

Volume $= \pi h^2 r$

The ratio of the volume of A to the volume of B is $\frac{\pi r^2 h}{\pi h^2 r}$. Cancel the factor πrh from both numerator and denominator, leaving $\frac{r}{h}$.

4. B

The volume of a rectangular solid is equal to the product $l \times w \times h$. So, the volume of the rectangular solid is $16 \times 8 \times 4$, and this must equal the volume of the cube as well. The volume of a cube is the length of an edge cubed, so you can set up an equation to solve for this length (call it e for edge):

$$e^3 = 16 \times 8 \times 4$$

To avoid the multiplication, break the 16 down into 2×8:

$$e^3 = 2 \times 8 \times 8 \times 4$$

Now combine 2×4 to get another 8:

$$e^3 = 8 \times 8 \times 8$$
$$e = 8$$

The length of an edge of the cube is 8.

5. B

Since 16 cubic meters represents 25%, or $\frac{1}{4}$, of the volume of the whole cube, the cube has a volume of 4×16, or 64 cubic meters. The volume of a cube is the length of an edge cubed, so $e^3 = 64$. Therefore e, the length of an edge, is 4.

6. B

This figure is an unfamiliar solid, so don't try to calculate the volume directly. Since the solid in question is half of a cube, visualize or sketch the other half lying on top of the solid forming a complete cube.

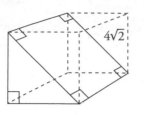

The diagonal with length $4\sqrt{2}$ forms an isosceles right triangle with two of the edges of the cube, which are the legs of the triangle. In an isosceles right triangle, the hypotenuse is $\sqrt{2}$ times each of the legs. Here the hypotenuse has length $4\sqrt{2}$, so the legs have length 4. So the volume of the whole cube is $4 \times 4 \times 4$, or 64. The volume of the solid in question is one-half of this, or 32.

7. C

From the situation described, the volume of the milk in the cylinder must be the same volume as the rectangular container, which is $4 \times 9 \times 10$, or 360 cubic inches. The volume of a cylinder equals the area of its base times its height, or $\pi r^2 h$. Since the diameter is 6 inches, the radius, r, is 3 inches. Now you're ready to set up an equation to solve for h (which is the height of the milk):

$$\pi(3)^2 h = 360$$

$$h = \frac{360}{9\pi} = \frac{40}{\pi}$$

8. E

It may be helpful to draw a quick diagram, like this one:

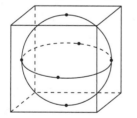

The sphere will touch the cube at six points. Each point will be an endpoint of a diameter and will be at the center of one of the cubic faces. So the diameter extends directly from one face of the cube to the other and is perpendicular to both faces that it touches. This means that the diameter must have the same length as an edge of the cube. The cube's volume is 64, so each edge has length $\sqrt[3]{64}$, or 4. Thus, the diameter of the sphere is 4, which means that the radius is 2.

9. B

The given conditions narrow down the possibilities for the solid's dimensions. The volume of a rectangular solid is length × width × height. Since one of these dimensions is 4, and the volume is 24, the other two dimensions must have a product of $\frac{24}{4}$, or 6. Since the dimensions are integers, there are two possibilities: 2 and 3 ($2 \times 3 = 6$), or 1 and 6 ($1 \times 6 = 6$). Work with either possibility to determine the total surface area. If the result matches an answer choice, you can stop (the question merely asks for what "could be" a valid result). If your first test does not match an answer choice, try the other possibility. Testing 4, 2, and 3 yields:

$$\begin{aligned} \text{Surface area} &= 2lw + 2lh + 2wh \\ &= 2(4)(2) + 2(4)(3) + 2(2)(3) \\ &= 16 + 24 + 12 = 52 \end{aligned}$$

Since choice (**B**) is 52, that is the correct answer to this question that only requires a single credited response.

10. A, B, C

Assess each statement one at a time.

Statement A:

Intuitively or visually, you might be able to see that *FD* and *GA* are parallel. It's a little trickier to prove mathematically. Remember, two lines are parallel if they're in the same plane and if they do not intersect. Imagine slicing the cube in half, diagonally (as in question 6) from *FG* to *AD*.

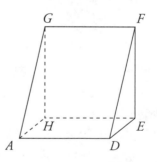

The diagonal face will be a flat surface, with sides *AD*, *FD*, *FG*, and *GA*. So *FD* and *GA* are in the same plane. They both have the same length, since each is a diagonal of a face of the cube. *FG* and *AD* also have the same length, since they're both edges of the cube. Since both pairs of opposite sides have the same length, *ADFG* must be a parallelogram. (In fact, it's a rectangle.) So *FD* and *GA*, which are opposite sides, are parallel.

Statement B:

$\triangle GCF$ is half of square $BCFG$, and $\triangle AHD$ is half of square $ADEH$. Both squares have the same area, so both triangles must also have the same area.

Statement C:

Draw in diagonals AE and AF to get right triangle AEF. Also draw in diagonals HD and GD to get right triangle DHG.

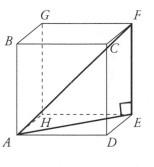

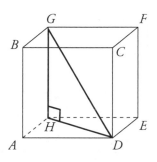

AE and HD are both diagonals of the same square, so $AE = HD$. FE and GH are both edges of the cube, so $FE = GH$. Since right triangle AEF and right triangle DHG have corresponding legs of the same length, they must also have hypotenuses of the same length. AF and GD are the respective hypotenuses, so $AF = GD$.

Therefore, all three statements are true.

Coordinate Geometry Explanations

1. A

Since points A and B have the same y coordinate, they form a horizontal line segment of length $3 - (-5) = 8$. Likewise, B and C have a common x coordinate, so they make a vertical line segment that is $2 - (-2) = 4$ units long. Therefore, AB and BC are at a right angle, and they form the base and height of right triangle ABC. The area of a triangle is $\frac{1}{2}bh$, which is $\frac{1}{2}(8)(4) = 16$. Quantity A is greater than Quantity B.

2. B

Rearrange the second equation to $y = -x + 9$. At the point where the two lines intersect, their coordinates will be the same, so set the two equations for y equal to each other: $\frac{x}{2} + 3 = -x + 9$. This simplifies to $\frac{3x}{2} = 6$, so $x = 4$. Plug this value for x into $y = \frac{x}{2} + 3$ to get $y = 2 + 3 = 5$. (You could have chosen to use the other equation instead; the result of $y = 5$ is the same.) Thus, the y coordinate of the point of intersection is greater than the x coordinate.

3. A

Determine the equation for line Z in slope-intercept form to find the y-intercept. At the point where $x = 4$, the y-coordinate of the known line is $3(4) - 9 = 3$. The slopes of perpendicular lines are negative reciprocals, so the slope of line Z is $-\frac{1}{3}$. Since line Z passes through the point $(4, 3)$, set up the equation $3 = -\frac{1}{3}(4) + b$. So, $b = 3 + \frac{4}{3} = 4\frac{1}{3}$. This is greater than 4, so (**A**) is correct.

4. C

When a point with coordinates (x, y) is reflected over the x-axis, the coordinates of the reflection will be $(x, -y)$. Substitute a and b for x and y and the coordinates of P' are $(a, -b)$. So $d = -b$, which means that $-d = b$, and the quantities are equal.

5. D

Just try the choices until you find one that satisfies the equation. In each case, substitute the first value in the pair for x and the second value for y into the expression $3x - 2y$ and see whether it equals 4:

(A) $3(0) - 2(2) = 0 - 4 = -4$. No good.

(B) $3(1) - 2(4) = 3 - 8 = -5$. Even worse.

(C) $3(2) - 2(0) = 6 - 0 = 6$. Nope.

(D) $3(2) - 2(1) = 6 - 2 = 4$. This is it.

For the record:

(E) $3(2) - 2(4) = 6 - 8 = -2$. No good.

6. D

In order to find the area of the circle first find the radius, which is the distance from the center to any point on the circumference of the circle. For instance, to find the distance from the center to point (3, 3), drop a perpendicular line segment from (3, 3) to the x-axis. This creates a right triangle with the radius of the circle as the hypotenuse.

The length of the base of the triangle is the distance from the origin to the perpendicular—the same as the x-coordinate of the point, or 3. Similarly, the other leg has length 3—the y-coordinate of (3, 3). This is an isosceles right triangle; therefore, the hypotenuse has length $3\sqrt{2}$. Use this value of the radius to find the area of the circle:

$$\text{Area} = \pi r^2$$
$$= \pi\left(3\sqrt{2}\right)^2$$
$$= 18\pi$$

7. C

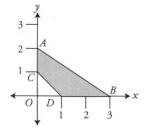

To find the area of the shaded region, subtract the area of right triangle COD from the area of right triangle AOB. OB lies along the x-axis, so its length is simply the difference in

x-coordinates between O and B: $3 - 0 = 3$. Similarly, the length of OD is $1 - 0$, or 1. OA lies along the y-axis, so its length is the difference in y-coordinates between O and A: $2 - 0 = 2$. Similarly, the length of OC is $1 - 0$, or 1. Now calculate the areas of the triangles:

$$\text{Area of } \triangle AOB = \frac{1}{2}(3)(2) = 3$$
$$\text{Area of } \triangle COD = \frac{1}{2}(1)(1) = \frac{1}{2}$$

Find the difference in areas, which is the area of the shaded region:

$$3 - \frac{1}{2} = 2\frac{1}{2} = \frac{5}{2}$$

8. A

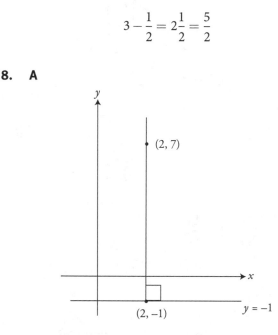

With questions like this it's often helpful to start by drawing a diagram.

The line with equation $y = -1$ is parallel to the x-axis, one unit below it. The shortest distance from the point (2, 7) to the line $y = -1$ is a line segment perpendicular to the line. (The shortest segment between a point and any line is always perpendicular to the line.) A perpendicular dropped from the point to the line will meet the line at the point $(2, -1)$, directly below (2, 7). Since both points have the same x-coordinates, the distance between the points is the difference of the y-coordinates: $7 - (-1)$, or 8.

9. E

If the line $y = 7x + d$ passes through point $(-3, 4)$, then $x = -3$ and $y = 4$ must satisfy the equation. Just plug in those values to find the value of d:

$$y = 7x + d$$
$$4 = 7(-3) + d$$
$$4 = -21 + d$$
$$4 + 21 = d$$
$$d = 25$$

10. E

First, use the given x and y values to find the slope of the line.

$$m = \frac{\text{change in } y}{\text{change in } x} = \frac{-1 - (-7)}{6 - 2} = \frac{6}{4} = \frac{3}{2}$$

The equation of the line must be in the form $y = \frac{3}{2}x + b$. At this point, you can already eliminate choices (A), (B), and (C), since they have different slopes. To find b in the equation $y = \frac{3}{2}x + b$, substitute in the values from one of the given points. It doesn't matter which point; try $(6, -1)$.

$$y = \frac{3}{2}x + b$$
$$-1 = \frac{3}{2}(6) + b$$
$$-1 = 9 + b$$
$$-10 = b$$

The equation is $y = \frac{3}{2}x - 10$, choice **(E)**.

CHAPTER 10

Additional Verbal Practice

Short Verbal

Text Completion Practice Set

Directions: Select one choice for each blank to best match the surrounding context.

1. While the yearly migration of monarch butterflies from the northern United States to Mexico is well-known, the fact that their milkweed diet makes them poisonous is an _____ trait with which few people outside the field of lepidopterology are familiar.

    (A) itinerant
    (B) innocuous
    (C) infamous
    (D) obscure
    (E) anodyne

2. Discovered almost four centuries ago, the Rosetta Stone long intrigued scholars who sought to _____ the hieroglyphics contained on the stone by comparing them to the previously translated common Egyptian and Greek texts also included on the stone.

    (A) confuse
    (B) decipher
    (C) redact
    (D) generate
    (E) degenerate

3. The late composer and conductor extraordinaire Leonard Bernstein sought to help music lovers of all types better appreciate and experience the _____ aspect of music; his book, *The Joy of Music,* is solidly focused on the science behind both composition and performance.

    (A) intellectual

    (B) emotive

    (C) simplistic

    (D) minimalistic

    (E) controversial

4. In his theory of psychosocial development, psychologist and psychoanalyst Erik Erikson challenges the notion that childhood should be an _____ time by claiming that each stage of human development, from infancy through old age, is fraught with psychosocial conflict that must be overcome for one to advance successfully.

    (A) edifying

    (B) abstract

    (C) idyllic

    (D) incorruptible

    (E) analytical

5. Observe how _____ is "common knowledge"; for centuries it has been accepted as fact that rats spread the plague known as the "Black Death" in medieval Europe, but upon the publication of a single study implicating human-borne vectors (lice, in this case), numerous respected journalistic outlets rashly proclaimed the rat wholly vindicated from blame.

    (A) incomprehensible

    (B) unwavering

    (C) pragmatic

    (D) fickle

    (E) impractical

6. Many novels that are banned from public consumption due to their controversial subject matter find broad acceptance among varied audiences only a few years later; that which is considered _____ by one generation is often swiftly embraced by the next.

    (A) prevailing

    (B) equivocal

    (C) passable

    (D) puerile

    (E) contentious

7. It is not _____ that many beginning geography students are awed by the Nile in northern Africa, as that river is generally considered the longest in the world and is significantly longer than the second longest river in Africa, the Congo. Interestingly, though, students tend to be _____ the fact that the Congo, which is as much as 20 times deeper than the Nile, is the deepest river in the world.

Blank (i)		Blank (ii)	
A	unremarkable	D	nonchalant about
B	unanticipated	E	impressed by
C	uninstructive	F	cognizant of

8. As much as the Enlightenment was driven by great thinkers who valued that which was reasonable and _____, the Romantic period that followed was ushered in by poets and artists who prized imagination and subjective experience above all else. The elevation of the individual over society and emotion over rationality led to an upheaval of various social norms, as many of the Romantic period's most noteworthy figures _____ the rules of decorum held dear by previous generations.

Blank (i)		Blank (ii)	
A	intuitive	D	bolstered
B	empirical	E	distilled
C	esoteric	F	flouted

9. Public opinion surveying is both an art and a science that in the hands of a novice can yield highly questionable results; would anybody _____ in the intricacies of public polling intuitively understand that merely swapping the order of the questions in a two-question survey could _____ increase the percentage of respondents who answer "yes" to both questions?

Blank (i)		Blank (ii)	
A	educated	D	substantially
B	uninitiated	E	marginally
C	steeped	F	inconceivably

10. Filmed on a _____ budget and edited at breakneck speed, the documentary nonetheless _____ the Cannes critics with its trenchancy and verve.

Blank (i)		Blank (ii)	
A	paltry	D	disappointed
B	lavish	E	impressed
C	magnanimous	F	disillusioned

11. It's not uncommon for a single individual to have a _____ influence on the development of an artist. Certainly, Isaac Albéniz published and performed quality piano compositions early in his career, but these weren't the works that would be studied by successive generations of musicians and recognized as evoking the spirit of Spain. It was only after meeting Felip Pedrell in 1890 that Albéniz sought _____ from traditional Spanish folk music and incorporated some of its elements into his compositions.

Blank (i)			Blank (ii)	
A	nugatory		D	impetus
B	pivotal		E	invigoration
C	baleful		F	inspiration

12. In the 1930s, many in America, England, and France, including such prominent luminaries as Hemingway and Picasso, considered their countries' neutrality in the Spanish Civil War to be _____ to the cause of freedom, as Franco's Nationalist forces were being supported by Nazi Germany and Fascist Italy. However, the Allies' _____ in refusing to aid the Republic's defenders should be traced to an unremitting distrust of Communism, as the Republican forces were themselves being supported by the Soviet Union and a leftist regime in Mexico.

Blank (i)			Blank (ii)	
A	inimical		D	malleability
B	enigmatic		E	perfidy
C	indispensable		F	intransigence

13. First published in 1649, Pacheco's _____ treatise contains not only chapters outlining iconography and technique, but also commentary on contemporary painters that now _____ our most comprehensive information on these artists, as well as the most thorough discussion available on Baroque aesthetics.

Blank (i)			Blank (ii)	
A	inconsequential		D	commends
B	invaluable		E	compels
C	insuperable		F	comprises

14. For much of history, scientific thinkers took for granted the existence of a luminiferous ether—an invisible medium for the propagation of light that supposedly _____ the universe. In the nineteenth century, belief in luminiferous ether's existence was almost absolute; the ether was _____ by nearly everyone working in the field of physics. The reason for this was that the ether provided a way to explain how light waves could travel through empty space, something that, it was believed, waves could not do. It should come as no shock, then, that Albert Michelson won the Nobel Prize in physics for his role in the Michelson-Morley experiments, the surprising results of which _____ the long held belief in the ether and helped open the door for a new way of thinking about light and the universe.

Blank (i)		Blank (ii)		Blank (iii)	
A	unified	D	quantified	G	explicated
B	permeated	E	eschewed	H	undermined
C	mirrored	F	venerated	I	derided

15. In the late 9th century, Alfred the Great, King of Wessex, _____ a law code that included case law from the codes of previous Saxon kings and from the Mosaic law of the Old Testament. This code, prefaced by a summary of biblical law, _____ the elements of Alfred's legal system, which was founded on mercy and equality in judgment and often necessitated the interpretation of nuanced legal precedents for application to the specific facts in each case. This contrasted sharply with earlier codes based on Roman legal principles, the basis for civil law, which attempted to prescribe _____ for every situation. As the rule of Wessex spread to include all English speakers in the British Isles, Alfred's code became the foundation of English common law.

Blank (i)		Blank (ii)		Blank (iii)	
A	dissembled	D	cooperated	G	hypotheses
B	promulgated	E	enumerated	H	defectors
C	mitigated	F	undermined	I	judgments

16. With no reliable way to examine internal activity or malignancies of the human brain, early practitioners of psychology relied only on outward _____ to diagnose and treat mental disorders. Some of the more enterprising pioneers in this field performed autopsies on deceased patients but gained few insights from these _____. Major technological breakthroughs in the second half of the 20th century _____ the field forever. The development of magnetic resonance imaging (MRI) in the 1970s and 1980s, for example, provided a view inside the living brain.

Blank (i)		Blank (ii)		Blank (iii)	
A	stipulations	D	investigations	G	altered
B	juxtapositions	E	characteristics	H	stagnated
C	manifestations	F	authorities	I	reinforced

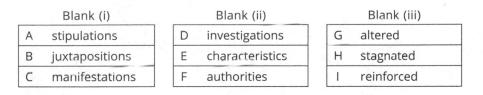

17. Writers of children's literature should not coddle their readers; instead, authors should expose children to the _____ of the adult world. When a child first experiences evil, disappointment, or even death, through the relative safety of the page, he or she will be somewhat _____ the pain of real loss. The _____ reality of uncensored fairy tales affirms this point: many stories from the Brothers Grimm and Hans Christian Andersen, though intended for children, involve cruelty and violence.

Blank (i)		Blank (ii)		Blank (iii)	
A	vicissitudes	D	fixated on	G	entertaining
B	eccentricities	E	amused by	H	macabre
C	hypocrites	F	inured to	I	skeptical

18. When most people hear the word *bacteria*, they think of pathogens that cause illness. Nevertheless, human beings have relied on the power of _____ bacteria to ferment foodstuffs for millennia. Yogurt, for example, is _____ using a culture of *Lactobacillus bulgaricus* and other bacteria, which ferment the lactose in milk to produce lactic acid, giving yogurt its characteristic tang. Other common bacteria-fermented foods include sauerkraut, sourdough bread, miso, and many others. Indeed, only a minority of bacteria cause disease, so the common perception of bacteria as _____ is incorrect.

Blank (i)		Blank (ii)		Blank (iii)	
A	beneficial	D	enhanced	G	assiduous
B	formidable	E	produced	H	nefarious
C	temperate	F	rejected	I	capricious

19. As is the case with _____ styles of dance—ballet, ballroom, and disco, just to name a few—break dancing has its origins in a much earlier form of dancing. The Swedish dance step known as the Giesse Harad Polksa, or salmon district dance, required both _____ skill and an uncanny sense of _____. Mimicking the leaps and movements of a salmon seeking to return to its spawning ground, the dancer would also spin on his head while carefully tracing a circle in the air with his legs.

Blank (i)		Blank (ii)		Blank (iii)	
A	multifaceted	D	aerobic	G	equitation
B	myriad	E	anachronistic	H	equipoise
C	exiguous	F	acrobatic	I	equivocation

20. While predicting dire economic and social consequences to coastal communities from rising sea levels resulting from _____ climate change caused by the burning of fossil fuels, scientists concede that such impacts could be _____ through massive investments in sea walls and other heavy infrastructure, though this would _____ the severe harm to natural ecosystems and species of wildlife.

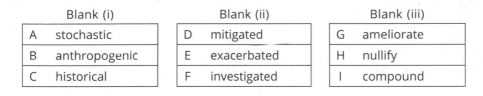

Blank (i)		Blank (ii)		Blank (iii)	
A	stochastic	D	mitigated	G	ameliorate
B	anthropogenic	E	exacerbated	H	nullify
C	historical	F	investigated	I	compound

Sentence Equivalence Practice Set

Directions: Select <u>two</u> answer choices that conform to the context and that create sentences with similar meanings.

1. Though _____ mathematics is essential for work in the sciences, it will not replace critical thinking or creative problem-solving skills.

   A fluency in

   B fixation on

   C cooperation with

   D misuse of

   E obsession with

   F command of

2. The appropriate application of a maxim to a given scenario depends more on careful selectivity than on tapping into some arcane store of universal _____: for every instance of "Fortune favors the bold," there exists a counterexample of "Fools rush in where angels fear to tread."

   A alacrity

   B verities

   C veracity

   D discrepancy

   E familiarity

   F obduracy

3. The majestic cathedrals of medieval Europe stand as testaments not only to the _____ of the architects but also to the power of the rulers and the devotion of the populace.

   [A] apathy
   [B] prowess
   [C] complexity
   [D] popularity
   [E] expertise
   [F] complacence

4. Anarchists contend that government is by definition the repression of natural human desire, and their ideological rivals concur; it is over the _____ of this definition that the two groups clash: only the anarchists believe that government should be abolished.

   [A] semantics
   [B] etiology
   [C] ramifications
   [D] phraseology
   [E] expression
   [F] implications

5. The disturbance regime of any ecosystem is _____ by the relative frequencies of small-scale perturbations, such as a few trees downed by a windstorm, and large-scale perturbations, such as multiple acres of forest burned in a fire, that drive its ecological processes.

   [A] mitigated
   [B] supplanted
   [C] characterized
   [D] contradicted
   [E] obfuscated
   [F] dictated

6. Learning science, a nascent, interdisciplinary, research-based field that explores how individuals best acquire and retain new information, holds significant implications for curriculum design and may undermine _____ conceptions of education.

   [A] effective
   [B] orthodox
   [C] rudimentary
   [D] advantageous
   [E] pedagogical
   [F] established

7. Rembrandt's etching plates outlived their creator, and although they require maintenance and reconstruction by technicians to areas worn down over time, pictures created from them after his death are arguably considered _____, yet in reality are far less sought after by aficionados of his art.

    A valuable

    B priceless

    C tainted

    D authentic

    E originals

    F sullied

8. Hilaire Belloc was widely known and lauded as a prolific writer, orator, and poet: though he published more than 150 books and debated with such intellectual luminaries as G.K. Chesterton and George Bernard Shaw, he retained a flair for the _____, as evinced by his *Cautionary Tales for Children,* including "Godolphin Horne, Who was cursed with the Sin of Pride, and Became a Boot-Black," and "Franklin Hyde, who caroused in the Dirt and was corrected by His Uncle."

    A farcical

    B erudite

    C ridiculous

    D macabre

    E learned

    F copious

9. Literature, like fashion and architecture, often features _____: the domestic novel, for example, originated with Catharine Sedgwick's *A New-England Tale* in 1822, quickly rose to prominence, and all but disappeared after 1870.

    A repetitions

    B vogues

    C trends

    D cycles

    E characters

    F nadirs

10. The evolutionary journey of practically every major animal phyla started with the Cambrian explosion; "explosion" likely seems an _____ designation to most lay people as it represents a period covering millions of years.

    [A] inapt

    [B] insidious

    [C] important

    [D] obstreperous

    [E] incongruous

    [F] obsolete

11. Handel's *Messiah* is perhaps the most recognizable example of oratorio, a musical composition that typically features religious themes and, unlike opera with all its pageantry, _____ the use of costumes, scenery, and action in an attempt to preserve the audience's attention to the transcendent.

    [A] includes

    [B] embraces

    [C] forgoes

    [D] sabotages

    [E] eschews

    [F] accentuates

12. Excellent examples of cartography rendered using modern Geographic Information Systems, known as GIS, not only provide vital and practical geographic information but also _____ aesthetic appeal.

    [A] minimize

    [B] personify

    [C] delegitimize

    [D] effect

    [E] furnish

    [F] rectify

13. Many enterprising individuals had bright ideas and conducted experiments during the Industrial Revolution, but only those with considerable _____ reached the point at which they could show off a practical invention they had created.

    [A] dauntlessness

    [B] persistence

    [C] integrity

    [D] ingenuity

    [E] sagacity

    [F] tenacity

14. Integration and differentiation operate as parallel yet inverse mathematical processes; thus, differentiating a function and then integrating the resulting function _____ the original function.

  A yields

  B concedes

  C negates

  D approximates

  E replicates

  F dissembles

15. Charles Darwin's achievement lies not in being the first to postulate the concept of the evolution of species—indeed, Darwin's own grandfather and many others espoused the idea—but rather, in his exhaustive compilation of evidence, prodigious _____ of the theory in his tome *On The Origin of Species*, and lucid articulation of a mechanism (i.e., natural selection) by which evolution advanced.

  A renunciation

  B contrivance

  C attenuation

  D exposition

  E revitalization

  F enunciation

16. The distinctive goal of an institution is its primary goal, whatever _____ functions the institution may carry out.

  A organizational

  B societal

  C ancillary

  D regulatory

  E appurtenant

  F incongruous

17. In all likelihood, Holst attended an early performance of Schoenberg's *Five Orchestral Pieces* and was _____, for he originally titled his own *The Planets*, composed soon after Schoenberg's work, *Seven Pieces for Large Orchestra*.

  A disturbed

  B envious

  C discouraged

  D overjoyed

  E impressed

  F captivated

18. As the rise of internet commerce eliminated millions of retail jobs but mitigated the consequences on the employment market by amplifying the number of warehouse, call center, and delivery positions, the proliferation of self-driving vehicles will, in turn, _____ the need for many delivery drivers and long-haul truckers, while compensating those losses with employment opportunities in the computer science, engineering, and technical support fields.

    A nullify

    B attenuate

    C ameliorate

    D amplify

    E obviate

    F relinquish

19. Author Milan Kundera _____ the waves of euphoria and disillusionment roiling Czechoslovakia in the wake of its home-grown socialist revolution, subsequent Soviet invasion, and resultant democratic counter-revolution to produce exquisite novels profoundly examining the human condition, especially through the eyes of a Czech émigré.

    A flouted

    B wielded

    C anthropomorphized

    D explored

    E transcended

    F scrutinized

20. While many researchers reuse gel electrophoresis buffer solutions, which provide a supply of ions to allow for conductivity and reduce pH changes caused by the electrical field, even one long use can significantly _____ the buffering capacity of the solution.

    A catalyze

    B regulate

    C deplete

    D enhance

    E diminish

    F stimulate

Reading Comprehension Practice Set

Directions: Each passage is followed by questions based on its content. After reading a selection, choose the best response(s) to each question. Your replies should based on what is *stated* or *implied* in the passage.

Questions 1–2 refer to the following stimulus.

Contrary to popular conception, extinct reptiles like *Pterodactylus* were not actually dinosaurs, but members of a related but distinct group known as pterosaurs. These two groups diverged from a common ancestor during the geological period known as the Triassic. Further, while well-known dinosaurs such as *Tyrannosaurus* and *Triceratops* were landbound, pterosaurs possessed the power of flight. Using wings composed of unique membranes attached to their elongated fourth fingers, this diverse and successful group commanded skies around the prehistoric world for more than one hundred million years. Research suggests that pterosaur wings may have had terrestrial utility as well: some pterosaurs could use them to ambulate, hunting and travelling alongside the likes of *Tyrannosaurus*.

1. Which of the following could reasonably be concluded based on the information in the passage?

   (A) Pterosaurs likely outnumbered dinosaurs before each group became extinct.

   (B) *Tyrannosaurus* was more closely related to pterosaurs than other dinosaurs were.

   (C) Pterosaurs and dinosaurs had a symbiotic relationship.

   (D) Research suggests that pterosaurs survived much longer than previously thought.

   (E) *Pterodactylus* and *Triceratops* share a common ancestor.

2. In the context of the passage, the word "terrestrial" most nearly means:

   (A) extinct

   (B) related to the ground

   (C) a feature common to all reptiles

   (D) useful for communicating with other species

   (E) coming from planet Earth

Questions 3–4 refer to the following stimulus.

The language Esperanto was created by Polish ophthalmologist L.L. Zamenhof (1859–1917) to foster international communication and understanding. Zamenhof, raised in an environment of distrust and misunderstanding among Poles, Jews, Russians, and Germans, believed that a newly constructed language could be more politically neutral than a natural language. He also hoped that Esperanto would be relatively easy for learners to acquire as a second or third tongue. Once Zamenhof published Esperanto's foundational text *Unua Libro* in 1887, the language began to gain speakers throughout the world.

Since the nineteenth century, the Esperanto movement has not been without its setbacks: in Nazi Germany and the Soviet Union, for instance, the ruling parties believed that Esperanto might foster international conspiracies, and in some cases executed its speakers. Today, however, while Esperanto may not be the lingua franca of the United Nations, it continues to be used by enthusiasts who, by some estimates, number in the millions. These enthusiasts gather together from diverse countries to participate in conferences and produce original music, films, and literature in Esperanto. Some "Esperantists" have even raised their children with the language, leading to generations of native Esperanto speakers.

3. Which of the following could best serve as a title to the passage?

    (A) The Contributions of L.L. Zamenhof to Linguistics
    (B) An Analysis of Esperanto: Grammar and Vocabulary
    (C) Solutions to International Misunderstanding
    (D) Esperanto: A Living Experiment
    (E) Esperanto: An International Conspiracy

4. Consider each of the choices separately and select all that apply.

    Which of the following can be correctly inferred from the passage?

    [A] Had it not been for persecution by authoritarian regimes like Nazi Germany, Esperanto would be used commonly today in the United Nations.
    [B] Esperanto succeeded at least partially in achieving Zamenhof's goals.
    [C] Children raised speaking Esperanto will learn the language with less effort than they would other languages.

Questions 5–6 refer to the following stimulus.

In his scholarly text *The Cheese and the Worms* (1976), Carlo Ginzburg unpacks Renaissance-era culture through the lens of an Italian miller named Menocchio. This text is often considered seminal in the field of *microhistory*, or history with an extended focus on a limited subject—in this case, a well-read peasant who was tried and executed for heresy by the Inquisition. A figure of Menocchio's obscurity would be fortunate to receive terse treatment from a traditional work of history. However, Ginzburg's microhistory extrapolates from court records to form a robust picture of how Menocchio must have seen the world as he developed his idiosyncratic (and in the eyes of the Inquisition, blasphemous) ideas about cosmology. According to Menocchio, for instance, the universe curdled into being like cheese from milk.

5. In the context of the passage, the word "terse" most nearly means

    (A) rude.
    (B) equitable.
    (C) arcane.
    (D) brief.
    (E) benevolent.

6. Which of the following is the primary purpose of the passage?

    (A) To characterize the historical tastes of Carlo Ginzburg.
    (B) To summarize the controversial views of Menocchio.
    (C) To outline the controversial aspects of *The Cheese and the Worms*.
    (D) To describe *The Cheese and the Worms* as an example of microhistory.
    (E) To reject the intolerance and cruelty of the Inquisition.

Questions 7–8 refer to the following stimulus.

The contemporary writer of a short story or novel can choose from a variety of narrative perspectives, or points of view. One option is the *third person omniscient*, in which the narrator is all-knowing and likely does not represent any one character. This option was extremely popular historically, and deployed to great effect by writers from Charles Dickens to Jane Austen. To the modern reader, however, the third person omniscient can come across as old-fashioned or cloying. As such, more prevalent now is the *third person limited*, in which the writer only provides details and knowledge that a single character would have. The rise of third person limited should come as no surprise: in the modern age, we expect more psychological depth of our literature, and do not find stories believable unless they are rooted in subjective experience.

7. According to the author, all of the following are true of *third person omniscient* EXCEPT:

    (A) It offers little opportunity for any psychological depth.

    (B) The narrator is all-knowing.

    (C) It is a perspective that can be used by the modern writer.

    (D) It was used by Charles Dickens.

    (E) It is currently uncommon compared to *third person limited*.

8. What is the purpose of the highlighted sentence in the passage?

    (A) It provides a viewpoint which the writer subsequently argues against.

    (B) It presents a historical point of comparison.

    (C) It is evidence for the passage's conclusion.

    (D) It is the author's thesis.

    (E) It provides context for the passage's main ideas.

Questions 9–12 refer to the following stimulus.

While many influences determine local air movements, large-scale motion of winds over the earth's surface depends primarily on only two factors. The first is differential heating. Equatorial air absorbs more solar energy than air at higher latitudes. Thus equatorial air rises, and cool air from higher latitudes flows under it, while the equatorial air flows toward the poles. Eventually it cools and sinks, continuing as surface wind. Hence, surface winds move toward the equator at low altitudes and toward the poles at higher altitudes.

Global wind motions are also affected by the Coriolis effect, which influences objects moving within a rotating system such as the earth. Objects on the earth's surface move eastward at the same speed as the earth's rotation—about 1,000 miles per hour at the equator, basically zero at the poles. An air mass that has moved north or south from the equator retains its inertial velocity, but the earth it passes over is moving more slowly. Hence, the air is deflected to the east. Winds from the poles toward the equator, on the other hand, have a low velocity compared to the areas they pass over; they are deflected toward the west.

9. The author is primarily concerned with

    Ⓐ summarizing evidence.
    Ⓑ explaining phenomena.
    Ⓒ outlining opposing views.
    Ⓓ offering hypotheses.
    Ⓔ recording scientific observations.

10. Consider each of the choices separately and select all that apply.

    According to the passage, winds near the equator usually do which of the following?

    A They absorb solar energy at an unvarying rate.
    B They flow toward the equator near the earth's surface and away from it at higher altitudes.
    C They rush toward the east faster than the earth's rotation.

11. The passage suggests that if the Coriolis effect did not exist, high-altitude wind near the equator would do which of the following?

   (A) It would not appear to move, because it would flow east at the same speed as the earth

   (B) It would flow west faster than the earth's rotation

   (C) It would flow directly north or south from the equator

   (D) It would remain stationary and mix with the warmer air from higher latitudes

   (E) It would be deflected more toward the east than air near the poles

12. The author would describe global air movements, in comparison with local winds, as

   (A) less regular.

   (B) less well understood.

   (C) less interesting.

   (D) more predictable.

   (E) basically similar.

Questions 13–18 refer to the following stimulus.

The two essays in which Virginia Woolf pursues women's role in art and politics have traditionally been seen as problematical adjuncts to her novels. While *A Room Of One's Own*, with its acerbic wit, has been given grudging respect, the outspokenly programmatic *Three Guineas* has been dismissed as a pacifist-feminist tract. No doubt these essays lack the subtlety and superb control of the novels, but to a recent generation of critics they remain significant because they anticipated many of the concerns of contemporary feminism.

A *Room of One's Own* (1929) is written in the form of a lecture "delivered" at a fictitious women's college. Woolf begins by contrasting the paltry luncheon given at the college with the luxurious fare offered at a nearby men's university. The difference symbolizes more profound disparities which—Woolf now comes to her main point—bear directly on the fortunes of women artists. For the woman author, financial independence, opportunities for education, tranquility, and privacy are necessary preconditions, without which women are unlikely to produce works of genius. Great art can never be expected from "labouring, servile, or uneducated people." (Among modern feminists, Tillie Olsen makes a similar point in *Silences*, though without Woolf's undertone of class condescension.) When a woman obtains a room of her own, in all its senses, she may, according to Woolf, develop what Coleridge termed "the androgynous mind," one which, having united its "male" and "female" sides, "transcends and comprehends the feelings of both sexes."

In *Three Guineas* (1938), Woolf's central argument, again foreshadowing a key contention of later feminism, is that the process of changing gender restrictions in the public world and in the private individual are interdependent. Issues such as childrearing (which she felt should be a shared responsibility) and professional equality between the sexes are not separate considerations, but rather different aspects of the same problem. Woolf also attempts to define women's responsibilities in the larger political world. Discussing the probability of another world war, she argues that women with jobs in manufacturing should refuse to produce arms for use in a male-instigated debacle. Both at the time and since, many readers have found this argument naive. One working-class reader, Agnes Smith, wrote Woolf that the book was decidedly class-bound; working women could hardly afford to jeopardize their employment for a pacifist ideal. Current feminist critics accept the validity of Smith's point—indeed, they acknowledge that it exposes a limitation of Woolf's feminism generally—but they also note that the mild derision which greeted *Three Guineas* from the male establishment was typical of the reception often given a woman thinker's ideas.

13. As used by Woolf, the phrase "a room of one's own" apparently refers to all of the following EXCEPT

  (A) freedom from economic insecurity.

  (B) separation of the "male" and "female" sides of consciousness.

  (C) educational opportunities for women equal to those available to men.

  (D) personal autonomy.

  (E) the ability to work without distractions.

14. Judging from the second paragraph, which of the following assumptions did Woolf make in the discussion of women writers?

  (A) The mind can be characterized as having masculine and feminine aspects.

  (B) All great authors have come from economically privileged backgrounds.

  (C) There have been no truly great women writers in the past.

  (D) Artistic development is independent of formal education.

  (E) Investigation of feelings and emotions is the most important goal of literature.

15. The passage provides information to answer which of the following questions?

  (A) Why did Woolf write *A Room Of One's Own* as a lecture when in fact it was not?

  (B) Why did Woolf's tone in *Three Guineas* shift from her tone in *A Room of One's Own*?

  (C) How did Woolf struggle against male prejudice in her writing career?

  (D) What conditions foster the development of the "androgynous mind"?

  (E) What were readers' responses to the ideas in *A Room of One's Own*?

16. The author would likely state that, in comparison to her novels, Woolf's essays on feminist themes are regarded as more

  (A) original.

  (B) familiar to the public.

  (C) accepted by critics.

  (D) artistically disciplined.

  (E) blunt and direct.

17. Consider each of the choices separately and select all that apply.

    It can inferred from the passage that *A Room Of One's Own* and *Three Guineas* are similar in which of the following respects?

    A   Both discuss social issues in terms of artistic development.

    B   Neither presents specific ways in which women can fight a male-dominated society.

    C   Both deal implicitly with the concerns of economically advantaged women.

18. Which of the following provides the most appropriate title for the passage?

    (A) Virginia Woolf: Pacifist Pioneer

    (B) The Genesis of Virginia Woolf's Feminism

    (C) A Precursor of Modern Feminism

    (D) Virginia Woolf's Marriage of Art and Politics: A Critical Evaluation

    (E) The Myth of Virginia Woolf's Feminism

Questions 19–22 refer to the following stimulus.

Satire attained a dominating position between 1660 and 1730 that it had not had before. As an oblique expression of the writer's wish to reform society, or as the somewhat baser tool of his scorn and ridicule, Restoration satire had diverse targets. Political parties, religious sects, and fashionable philosophies were as much the delights of satirists as were topical gossip and assorted fops, pedants, and bigots.

Pope's mock heroic epic, *The Rape of the Lock*, probes the excesses of romantic etiquette: Lady Belinda's tresses are cropped by a suitor while she lingers over her coffee. According to Samuel Johnson, such an incident was a questionable topic for poetic treatment: "The subject of the poem is an event below the common incidents of common life." Yet the frivolous subject matter provides the ideal setting for a gentle lambasting of traditional epic machinery and a delicate exposure of the romantic conventions of the day.

19. Consider each of the choices separately and select all that apply.

     The passage supports which of the following statements concerning satire?

     [A] Satirists may focus both on the foibles of individuals and on larger, societal ills.
     [B] Satire could be used to mock poetic conventions.
     [C] Satire often served as a formidable weapon for personal revilement.

20. According to the description in the passage, which of the following would be a satiric work?

     (A) a polemic decrying Calvinism
     (B) a vigorous denial of Lockean ethics
     (C) an exposé of patronage at the court of Charles II
     (D) a fanciful description of a mythical land
     (E) a cleverly disguised attack on an academic

21. The author would most likely argue that Johnson's criticism of *The Rape of the Lock* shows

    (A) a narrow conception of the appropriate content of poetry.

    (B) an obsession with minor stylistic flaws at the expense of an appreciation of the work as a whole.

    (C) a failure to realize that the work is intentionally humorous.

    (D) a belief that the work mocks the dignity of everyday life.

    (E) an outdated code of values.

22. The passage implies which of the following about the period before 1660?

    (A) Satire dealt only with subjects of political and religious importance.

    (B) Readers objected to satirists' mocking of conventional values.

    (C) The conventions of heroic poetry were considered above criticism.

    (D) Satire was seen as only one among several important literary genres.

    (E) Because there was greater political freedom, writers could express political ideas directly rather than through satire.

Questions 23–26 refer to the following stimulus.

In some circles, Mendelssohn's reputation diminished rapidly after his death in 1847. By 1852, he was already regarded by many as "the object of pitying disparagement." European musical audiences, newly enamored with the expansiveness of Wagner's *Tristan and Isolde*, soon found Mendelssohn's music too restrained and academic.

As time progressed, post-Wagnerian anti-Romanticism did little to salvage the composer's standing. Proponents of Schoenberg and his twelve-tone serialism regarded Mendelssohn as a quaint, conservative composer who crafted superficial, "tenderly sentimental" music.

Such "arbiters" as these have moved far too illiberally to certain conclusions. The atmospheric melodic beauty of the *Overture to A Midsummer Night's Dream* shows the imprint of an original mind, anticipating the orchestral achievement of Rimsky-Korsakov. At the time of its composition, Mendelssohn's *Octet* displayed unexampled lightness and rhythmic effect; his impressionistic *Hebrides Overture* inspired the painting of Turner. And Mendelssohn's greatest pictorial works, the *Scottish* and *Italian* symphonies, constantly reveal new vistas. The work of one of the first, great nineteenth-century Nature composers, Mendelssohn's music simply endures; critics would do well to ask why.

23. It can be inferred that the author apparently regards certain critics of Mendelssohn as

(A) ignorant and ill bred.

(B) shortsighted and ungenerous.

(C) brilliantly perceptive.

(D) cowardly and overcautious.

(E) ambitious and insincere.

24. The author refers to the proponents of Wagner and Schoenberg in the first two paragraphs primarily in order to

(A) explain the differences between the two groups' musical tastes.

(B) make the point that the critics of Mendelssohn have also failed to appreciate the work of other great composers.

(C) introduce the idea that the music critics of a given period usually lack sensitivity toward earlier composers.

(D) illustrate how some people have unjustly neglected the musical achievement of Mendelssohn.

(E) contrast the musical ideas of Wagner and Schoenberg to those of Mendelssohn.

25. Consider each of the choices separately and select all that apply.

    On the basis of the passage, the author would be likely to say that Mendelssohn's music

    [A] was constrained by traditional forms and styles.

    [B] was innovative and influential.

    [C] should be judged on its own terms, not according to the standards of later taste.

26. The author's argument in favor of Mendelssohn is primarily developed by

    (A) appealing to the authority of post-Wagnerian anti-Romantic critics.

    (B) citing examples that demonstrate Mendelssohn's originality and skill.

    (C) pleading that Mendelssohn has been unfairly measured against far greater composers.

    (D) pointing out that Mendelssohn's critics have focused on unrepresentative aspects of his work.

    (E) favorably comparing Mendelssohn's achievements to those of admired composers like Rimsky-Korsakov and Wagner.

Questions 27–30 refer to the following stimulus.

Desert plant populations have evolved sophisticated physiological and behavioral traits that aid survival in arid conditions. Some send out long, unusually deep taproots; others utilize shallow but widespread roots, which allow them to absorb large, intermittent flows of water. Certain plants protect their access to water. The creosote bush produces a potent root toxin that inhibits the growth of competing root systems. Daytime closure of stomata exemplifies a further genetic adaptation; guard cells work to minimize daytime water loss, later allowing the stomata to open when conditions are more favorable to gas exchange with the environment.

Certain adaptations reflect the principle that a large surface area facilitates water and gas exchange. Most plants have small leaves, modified leaves (spines), or no leaves at all. The main food-producing organ is not the leaf but the stem, which is often green and non-woody. Thick, waxy stems and cuticles, seen in succulents such as cacti and agaves, also help conserve water. Spines and thorns (modified branches) protect against predators and also minimize water loss.

27. Consider each of the choices separately and select all that apply.

    The passage refers to the spines and thorns of desert plants as

    A genetically evolved structural adaptations that protect against predation.

    B genetic modifications that aid in the reduction of water loss.

    C structures that do not participate directly in food production.

28. Consider each of the choices separately and select all that apply.

    The author suggests that the guard cells of desert plants act to do which of the following?

    A facilitate gas and water exchange between the plants and their surroundings

    B cause the stomata of desert plants to remain closed during daytime hours

    C respond to sudden, heavy rainfalls by forcing the plants' stomata to open

29. The passage suggests that which of the following weather-related conditions would most benefit plants with shallow root systems?

   (A) an unusually prolonged drought

   (B) a windstorm

   (C) a flash flood

   (D) a light spring rain

   (E) a winter snowfall

30. The information in the passage about the adaptations of desert plants to their environment would tend to support the statement that

   (A) the rate of genetic evolution is greater in the desert than in more temperate surroundings.

   (B) structures in a plant that usually perform one function may, under certain conditions, perform different functions.

   (C) the amount of leaf surface area is far less critical for non-desert plants than for desert plants.

   (D) desert plants do not have many physiological and behavioral traits in common with other plants.

   (E) desert plants could probably adapt to life in a variety of harsh ecosystems.

Reasoning Practice Set

> **Directions:** Select one choice for each question in accord with your analysis of the argument that precedes it.

The country of Tolespinia uses the currency *pecunium*. Though the conversion rate varies, one *pecunium* is worth approximately one tenth of a US dollar at the time of this writing. Every year, a prominent magazine in Tolespinia publishes a report of the total value of the investment portfolios from the highest-grossing companies in the country. Based on the latest report, and despite some concerns about the overall health of the Tolespinian economy, one financial adviser argues that foreign and domestic investors would do well to increase their existing investments and explore new investment opportunities. After all, the total value of the listed portfolios has increased from $97.5 million (US dollars) ten years ago to well over $200 million in this year's issue. Clearly, the adviser states, this shows that investment in the Tolespinian stock market will guarantee significant returns.

1. Which of the following, if true, most undermines the financial advisor's argument?

    (A) Some economists in Tolespinia predict that decreased unemployment may lead to greater financial stability within the next twelve months.

    (B) The magazine's report previously included the twenty highest-grossing companies in Tolespinia but was recently expanded to include the fifty highest-grossing companies.

    (C) A neighboring country's economy has suffered from a lack of foreign investment and is facing a financial collapse.

    (D) Twelve years ago, the exchange rate for *pecunium* to US dollars was expected to increase significantly over the next decade.

    (E) In response to economists' concerns about the overall health of the economy, Tolespinia's parliament is considering legislation that would directly affect the stability of the stock market.

The work of a translator is more closely related to that of an author or artist than it is to that of a transcriptionist. This is equally true whether the original work was poetry or prose. Requirements of meter for the former and nuances of meaning for both demand not only interpretation but also adaptation. Were a translation to be translated back into its original language, the result would little resemble the primary work. For this reason, a translation is best understood as an original work.

2.   Which of the following, if true, most strengthens the author's conclusion?

   (A) Writing an original work requires creativity and the ability to generate ideas.
   (B) Successful playwrights are often celebrated only when their plays are performed.
   (C) Most writers and translators work for years to develop their ability before they achieve commercial success.
   (D) Many words and phrases, especially idioms, lack exact equivalents in other languages.
   (E) Some translations are acclaimed for their accuracy while others are praised for their beauty.

As modern cities continue to experience a population boom, the highly scientific process of optimizing the flow of traffic in metropolitan areas will become an even more critical task for civil engineers. Those who live and work in cities depend on these professionals to design, develop, and maintain functional urban communities by weighing numerous considerations simultaneously. The size of the population, the different means of transportation used, the diversity and required maintenance of the infrastructure, as well as the projected growth and expansion across the surrounding regions are all factors that come to bear on decisions that impact a city's traffic patterns. Additionally, civil engineers must prepare for the ways in which unusual events, such as citywide emergencies or major sporting events, may result in traffic disruptions. Traffic plans must meet the needs of the current population, while also anticipating the demands of the future population.

By using sophisticated computer modeling programs, civil engineers can create highly detailed models that allow them to run a nearly infinite number of traffic scenarios and predict the impact of specific solutions. Traffic sensors and satellite imagery also provide valuable, real-time data that track fluctuating traffic patterns. Despite the many high-tech tools at their disposal, civil engineers should be careful not to overlook the value of low-tech solutions, which can often produce the greatest benefits for traffic challenges. For example, numerous studies have shown that incorporating roundabouts or traffic circles into areas that traditionally experience high traffic congestion can considerably improve traffic flow. These structural solutions also have been shown to reduce traffic accidents involving both vehicles and pedestrians by a noteworthy margin.

3. In the passage above, the two highlighted portions play which of the following roles?

   (A) The first is a counterpoint to the author's conclusion, while the second provides a subsidiary conclusion.

   (B) The first paraphrases a conclusion made earlier in the passage, while the second describes a cause-and-effect relationship that supports a second main conclusion.

   (C) The first provides background information to give context to the author's primary conclusion, while the second offers a premise in support of the author's primary conclusion.

   (D) The first provides the author's main conclusion, while the second describes the position against which the author is arguing.

   (E) The first describes a premise in support of the author's primary conclusion, while the second offers evidence in support of the author's second main conclusion.

Beer drinkers who have developed a taste for artisanal microbrews are far more likely than those who favor mass-produced corporate beer brands to refuse to consume a type of beer other than the one they typically prefer. Thus, since we want to limit the number of different beers served at our establishment, focusing solely on microbrews will better serve our patrons than our current menu of predominantly corporate brands.

4.   Which of the following would most undermine the argument above?

   (A)   Some drinkers of mass-produced, corporate beer brands are more adamant regarding their preference than most of those who typically drink artisanal microbrews.

   (B)   The vast majority of beer drinkers in the country typically drink mass-produced, well-known corporate brands.

   (C)   Many beer drinkers do not have any strong allegiance to either artisanal microbrews or to well-known corporate brands.

   (D)   Almost all beer drinkers who consume an average of four or more beers in a typical week can identify a single favorite beer variety in response to a survey question.

   (E)   The popularity of artisanal microbrews has plateaued after increasing steadily for almost a decade.

The declining birth rate will wreak havoc on our economy and national budget as fewer young workers will be burdened with supporting the growing numbers of retirees. On the other hand, in as little as two decades, due to the growing trend of older workers holding on to their jobs longer and the accelerating mechanization of labor, substantial numbers of young and prime-age workers will be unable to find employment, probably necessitating the implementation of some sort of universal basic income (in essence, providing everybody, whether they work or not, a living wage). Still, maintaining the health of the economy into the future depends upon reversing the decline in the birth rate to produce more young workers.

5.   Which of the following is an assumption upon which the argument above depends?

   (A)   Youth and young adult unemployment is not a serious problem.

   (B)   When older workers hold on to their jobs until later in life than was common in the past, the overall effect on the economy is detrimental.

   (C)   The potential benefit of additional young workers contributing to the economy is not outweighed by the potential burden of providing universal basic income to a growing population.

   (D)   A decline in the birth rate will not have significant benefits for the ecological sustainability of human life on earth.

   (E)   Implementation of a universal basic income will likely reverse the trend towards older workers holding on to their jobs longer.

It is well established that the translocation by humans of small mammals to isolated islands previously devoid of such animals has resulted in the decimation of countless species of birds that evolved in the isolation of predators. Curiously, it has recently been discovered that the population of one particular species of island bird plummeted dramatically after the arrival of humans, even though, due to its unique nesting habits, it was not subject to predation by mammals. Thus, the arrival of humans must have resulted in the decline of this bird species in some way unrelated to the concurrent arrival of small mammals brought by the people.

6. Which of the following would most weaken the conclusion in the argument above?

(A) The types of small mammals brought to this particular island are not voracious predators of birds.

(B) The bird discussed in the argument has an evolutionary competitive advantage over other species of birds on the island.

(C) Parasites carried to the island on small mammals brought by humans are vectors for avian diseases not previously found on the island.

(D) Human agriculture on the island uses large quantities of pesticides and herbicides known to be harmful to birds.

(E) To date, the harmful effects of climate change have not been conclusively linked to declines in island bird species.

A sense of humor is a uniquely human characteristic, and while nobody considers himself or herself devoid of it, it is widely acknowledged that few people can make others laugh on a regular basis. Furthermore, all people believe that at least some of the individuals they know are thoroughly humorless. If we generously assume that the majority of the public is immune to self-delusion in these matters, then it must be the case that most people _____.

7. Which of the following most logically completes the argument above?

(A) are lying when they say that they have a sense of humor

(B) do not consider a sense of humor a uniquely human characteristic

(C) cannot agree on what it means to have a sense of humor

(D) believe that having a sense of humor does not require making others laugh

(E) apply a different definition of "sense of humor" to others than they do to themselves

Lunches served at a local school have long been criticized for being neither tasty nor nutritious. As a result, one suggestion parents commonly bring before the school board is to hire better chefs. What these parents do not understand is that the school's narrow food budget prevents the chefs from making the meals they want to make. Further straining the budget by hiring prestigious culinary staff would only make the current situation worse. If the parents of this community are as committed to healthier, better-tasting lunches as they claim, then they will have to accept paying higher taxes to enlarge the budget of the school lunch program.

8. Which of the following, if true, would most strongly support the argument?

    Ⓐ In recent elections, the school district's residents have consistently voted in favor of small tax increases to increase the school's budget.

    Ⓑ The sole deciding factor in determining whether the current chefs can make better tasting, healthier meals is the amount of money available for purchasing ingredients.

    Ⓒ Making cuts to the food ingredient budget that would enable the school to hire better chefs would not prevent those chefs from making meals that are better-tasting and more nutritious.

    Ⓓ Because the food labor market is more competitive now than it was when the current chefs were hired, the school could hire more talented chefs without significantly impacting the existing budget.

    Ⓔ Because the school district is in a remote area, the ingredients available to the school's chefs are of universally low quality.

As the attainment of an undergraduate degree becomes increasingly ubiquitous among young adults, most entry-level positions available at major corporations now require that an applicant possess at least a bachelor's degree before considering his or her application. Judging by this trend, those who do not pursue higher education after the completion of their secondary studies will find that their prospects for future employment are greatly diminished.

9. Which of the following, if true, would most weaken the argument above?

    Ⓐ Many positions at major corporations now require that applicants possess a graduate degree in a specialized field.

    Ⓑ Students who do not complete undergraduate degrees often prepare for skilled work not sought by major corporations.

    Ⓒ Most major corporations are eager to hire students who have undergraduate degrees in business or related fields.

    Ⓓ Most entry-level jobs utilize skills that students develop in secondary school.

    Ⓔ Only a small percent of the entry-level positions available to young adults are offered by major corporations.

Most knowledge about dinosaurs comes from fossils, but this reliance leads to an incomplete understanding of dinosaur anatomy and habits. Fossils typically preserve only a portion of the deceased organism—usually only the portion that was partially mineralized during life, such as the bones and teeth of vertebrates or the exoskeletons of invertebrates. The discovery of a "mummified" brachylophosaurus has revolutionized the field of paleontology because this specimen preserves the skin and internal organs of the dinosaur. This discovery reveals new information about the dinosaur's diet, mode of locomotion, and environment. Indeed, it has been described as a "quantum leap" in paleontology.

10. In the argument above, the two highlighted portions play which of the following roles?

Ⓐ The first is a judgment made by the author about a given explanation; the second offers evidence for that judgment.

Ⓑ The first describes a limitation of a certain mode of inquiry; the second offers an explanation for the author's conclusion.

Ⓒ The first sums up the final conclusion of the argument; the second sums up the subsidiary conclusion.

Ⓓ The first describes the reason for the author's objection to a given line of inquiry; the second states a contradictory conclusion.

Ⓔ The first expresses a conclusion that runs counter to the author's conclusion; the second is the author's conclusion.

Issue Essay Practice Set

> **Directions:** Take 30 minutes to outline and draft a response to the prompt. Be sure to follow the specific instructions provided. Support your position with evidence and examples. These may be taken from your college coursework or other reading as well as from your own experience.
>
> You should think through the complexities of the issue and organize your thoughts before you start to write. Also remember to save a couple of minutes to proofread.

1. Claim: All college students, regardless of their majors, should be required to take several courses in the sciences.

   Reason: Non-science majors are likely to benefit more from such courses than they would from taking additional courses in their own majors.

   Write a response that explains your position on the claim and on the reason that supports the claim.

2. The best way to learn about a society is to study its great works of art.

   Write a response that explains the extent to which you agree or disagree with the statement. Discuss the considerations that impact your position.

Argument Essay Practice Set

> **Directions:** Take 30 minutes to outline and draft a response to the prompt. Be sure to follow the specific instructions provided. Note that your task is to analyze the argument given, **not** to describe your own opinions. Support your analysis with evidence and/or examples.

1. The following appeared as part of a business memorandum from the marketing department of a railway company.

    "In recent years, the number of passengers riding on our railways has steadily fallen. However, we have surveyed commuters living in the major cities where we operate and come up with a strategy that can reverse the trend and increase our profits. Over 90% of survey respondents indicated that they were "highly concerned" with the ecological impact of commuting by car. To take advantage of this consumer concern, we recommend a new marketing initiative in which our print, internet, and in-train advertisements would all emphasize the ecological benefits of traveling by train."

    Write a response discussing the questions that would need to be asked in order to evaluate the recommendation. Discuss how the answers to these questions would help determine how likely the recommendation is to have the intended outcome.

2. The following appeared in a memorandum from the director of an aquarium.

    A year ago, we switched one of our tanks of sparrowfish from a dry flake diet to a diet of live brine shrimp. The sparrowfish in this tank lived longer on average than the sparrowfish in other tanks, all of which continued to receive dry flakes alone. Further, the shrimp-fed fish grew on average to larger sizes than the flake-fed fish. The best explanation for this disparity is that live brine shrimp meet the nutritional requirements of sparrowfish better than dry flakes do.

    Write your own response describing one or more explanations that could challenge the provided explanation. Discuss how your alternative explanation(s) would reasonably account for the evidence presented in the argument.

Text Completion Answer Key

1. **D**	6. **E**	11. **B, F**	16. **C, D, G**
2. **B**	7. **B, D**	12. **A, F**	17. **A, F, H**
3. **A**	8. **B, F**	13. **B, F**	18. **A, E, H**
4. **C**	9. **B, D**	14. **B, F, H**	19. **B, F, H**
5. **D**	10. **A, E**	15. **B, E, I**	20. **B, D, I**

Sentence Equivalence Answer Key

1. **A, F**	6. **B, F**	11. **C, E**	16. **C, E**
2. **B, C**	7. **D, E**	12. **D, E**	17. **E, F**
3. **B, E**	8. **A, C**	13. **B, F**	18. **A, E**
4. **C, F**	9. **B, C**	14. **A, E**	19. **D, F**
5. **C, F**	10. **A, E**	15. **D, F**	20. **C, E**

Reading Comprehension Answer Key

1. **E**	9. **B**	17. **C**	25. **B**
2. **B**	10. **B**	18. **C**	26. **A, B, C**
3. **D**	11. **C**	19. **E**	27. **A, B**
4. **B**	12. **D**	20. **A**	28. **C**
5. **D**	13. **B**	21. **D**	29. **B**
6. **D**	14. **A**	22. **B**	
7. **A**	15. **D**	23. **D**	
8. **E**	16. **E**	24. **B, C**	

Reasoning Answer Key

1. **B**	4. **B**	7. **D**	9. **E**
2. **D**	5. **C**	8. **B**	10. **B**
3. **B**	6. **C**		

Answers and Explanations

Text Completion Explanations

1. D

This sentence begins with the detour road sign "while," which signals that there will be contrasting ideas in this sentence. The beginning of the sentence identifies something that is well-known, so the end of the sentence must reference a trait that is "not well-known." Using that phrase as a prediction leads to **(D)** *obscure,* which means "not widely known," as the match. (B) *innocuous* and (E) *anodyne* both mean "innocent," so neither choice matches the prediction. (A) *itinerant* means "to roam from place to place"; while this may remind you of the monarch's migration, it does not describe the trait—being poisonous—with which few people are familiar. (C) *infamous* means "well-known for a negative reason," and thus does not contrast with "well-known"; when part of the definition does not match the prediction, the choice is incorrect.

2. B

The sentence points out that the Rosetta Stone contains information written in hieroglyphics, common Egyptian, and Greek. The blank in the sentence requires a word that describes what scholars who were "intrigued" by the stone hoped to do by comparing the hieroglyphic text to the common Egyptian and Greek texts that had already been translated. Good predictions for the blank include "translate," "comprehend," or "understand," making **(B)** *decipher* a great match; it means "to find the meaning of something." The scholars certainly do not want to make the hieroglyphics harder to understand, so (A) *confuse* can be eliminated. (C) *redact* means "to put something down in writing" or "to remove text from a document before it is released to the public"; both definitions fail to match the prediction. (D) *generate* and (E) *degenerate* might seem to be opposites, but the former means "to create something," while the latter means "to make something worse or weaker," and neither of those choices match the prediction.

3. A

In this sentence, the semicolon is a useful straight-ahead road sign that suggests alignment between Bernstein's educational goals and the specific focus of his book. The second part of the sentence points out that *The Joy of Music* concentrates on the science behind music. This suggests that Bernstein wanted listeners to go beyond the emotional and aesthetic experience of music, and comprehend its "technical" or "logical" aspects as well. Both of those words make great predictions. The best match for the prediction is **(A)** *intellectual,* meaning "thinking about something in a logical instead of emotional way." (B) *emotive* means "expressing emotions," the opposite of the prediction. (C) *simplistic* and (D) *minimalistic* are similar and can both be defined as "in a simple or uncomplicated way"; neither term fits the blank describing Bernstein's educational goals. The sentence doesn't indicate that Bernstein was trying to spark arguments or debates, so eliminate (E) *controversial* as well.

4. C

The keyword "challenges" acts as a detour road sign, contrasting a particular view of childhood with Erikson's claim that even the youngest of children must deal with conflict. A period of time that is free from conflict can be described as "happy and peaceful," a prediction that matches **(C)** *idyllic.* Erikson's theory indicates that psychosocial conflicts are ultimately beneficial for people, so they are not in contrast to (A) *edifying,* which means "that which can improve one's character." (B) *abstract*—meaning "theoretical"—does not fit the context of the blank. Eliminate (D) *incorruptible* as there are no clues indicating that psychosocial conflicts have a corrupting or morally degrading influence. (E) *analytical*—meaning "logical" or "scientific"—is not supported by any clues in the sentence.

5. D

This sentence was written by an author exasperated by how quickly some media outlets abandoned a scientific belief considered "common knowledge" following a single contradictory study. The blank requires an adjective that describes being too willing to abandon a belief quickly. The correct answer, **(D)** *fickle,* means "disloyal or likely to change." (B) *unwavering* is the opposite, meaning "steadfast or not subject to change." (A) *incomprehensible* means "unable to be understood." There appears to be some debate as to whether rats or human-borne lice caused the plague, but those two positions are stated pretty simply. "Incomprehensible" does not describe the author's concern that a long-standing position is being abandoned hastily. (C) *pragmatic* means "practical;" neither it nor its antonym (E) *impractical* match this author's concern.

6.   E

The semicolon in this sentence acts as a straight-ahead road sign, drawing a parallel between the first independent clause and the second. The first independent clause states that some initially controversial books become socially acceptable over a short period of time. The second clause offers a general principle that explains why this is so. Based on this parallel structure, predict that the missing word means something like "controversial." This prediction matches (E) *contentious*, which means "likely to provoke an argument." Since the missing word must have a negative connotation, eliminate (A) *prevailing*, which has the neutral meaning "current." (B) *equivocal* means "ambiguous," which does not fit the context of the blank. (C) *passable* means "acceptable" and is the opposite of the predicted meaning. (D) *puerile* may be a tempting choice as it has the required negative connotation; this word, however, means "immature" rather than "controversial."

7.   B, D

The word "as" in the first sentence is the key to understanding the first blank. The Nile is the longest river in the world, and "as" indicates that this superlative is the reason students are awed. It's foreseeable that students might be awed by this. You might predict "not surprising" or "expected," but watch out for the double negative. The blank is preceded by "not," so the word that fits must mean "surprising" or "unexpected." (B) *unanticipated* is a great match. (A) *unremarkable*, when read in to the sentence, forms "It is not unremarkable..." In other words, it's remarkable—the opposite of what is needed. Similarly, (C) *uninstructive*, when read into the sentence, becomes "not uninstructive"; in other words, it is instructive, meaning it "carries a lesson" or "provides knowledge." The sentence, however, isn't dealing with whether anything is learned from the students' awe, which was in any case expected.

The second sentence describes how the Congo is the deepest river in the world, much deeper than the Nile. One might expect that this, too, would awe students. The second sentence presents a contrast, however, as indicated by

"[i]nterestingly, though..." Predict, therefore, that the word in the blank means that students are not at all awed by the Congo's depth. They might be "unmoved by" or "apathetic about" the fact. (D) *nonchalant about*, or "indifferent to, unconcerned by" is a nice match. (E) *impressed by* is the opposite of what is expected here. Students may or not be (F) *cognizant of*, or "mindful of," the Congo's depth, but either way there is no contrast with the awe presented in the first sentence.

8.   B, F

The first blank is connected to the term "reasonable" by the straight-ahead road sign "and" and is set in contrast to "imagination" and "subjective experience." Predict that the missing word means something like "factual." This prediction matches (B) *empirical*, which means "evidence-based." (A) *intuitive* means "instinctive" and is opposed to the predicted meaning of the missing word. (C) *esoteric* refers to something that is "meant to be understood by only a select group of people." This definition does not fit the predicted meaning of "observable fact."

In the second sentence, the blank describes what some noteworthy figures of the Romantic period did to the rules of decorum, or good behavior, that were valued by older generations. Given that this was described earlier in the sentence as an "upheaval of social norms," predict that some Romantics "violated" the rules of decorum. This prediction matches (F) *flouted*, which means "disobeyed." (D) *bolstered* means "supported," which is the opposite of the prediction. (E) *distilled* means "took the most important aspects of something" and is not supported by the context in the sentence.

9.   B, D

The vocabulary in the sentence and the answer choices is not all that challenging; however, if one doesn't focus on the intent and structure of the sentence overall it is easy to fall for a trap answer. Looking narrowly at the vicinity of the first blank, "anybody *educated* in the intricacies of" (A) and "anybody *steeped* in the intricacies of" (C) sound familiar and tempting. However, both describe the opposite of the "novice" the author discusses in the first clause. The clue "novice" and the semicolon (a straight-ahead road sign) yield a prediction of "inexperienced" for the first blank, so (B) *uninitiated* is correct answer here. The author believes that somebody lacking a fundamental knowledge of public opinion surveys would *not* suspect that "merely" swapping the order of questions would produce the change in results described by the second blank. Thus, the resulting increase must be "large" or "colossal." That leads to **(D)** *substantially*. (F) *inconceivably* does not work because to the author (and others knowledgeable in public surveys) such a result is not only conceivable, but unsurprising. A *marginal* change (E) would not be a counterintuitive result of a "mere" switch of question order.

10. A, E

The detour road sign "nonetheless" indicates a contrast between the two missing words. Either the budget was large but the critics were disappointed, or the budget was small but the critics were pleasantly surprised. The clue at the end of the sentence, "trenchancy and verve," settles it in favor of the second of these options. All you need to do is to recognize "trenchancy and verve" as a positive description. (For the record, "trenchancy" means "penetrating insight," while "verve" means "liveliness" or "vitality.") The correct answers are **(A)** *paltry*, which means "meager" or "small," and **(E)** *impressed*. Choices (B) *lavish*, or "abundant," (D) *disappointed*, and (F) *disillusioned*, which is a synonym for *disappointed*, are all opposites of what you need. Choice (C) *magnanimous* means "generous," but it is generally used to refer to people, not things (such as budgets).

11. B, F

The second sentence distinguishes Albéniz's earlier works from those that had a lasting impact and reflected Spanish culture. The third sentence explains that the influence of Pedrell was responsible for the difference. Thus, the influence described by the first blank must have been "profound," "significant," or "positive." This leads to **(B)** *pivotal*, or "having a central role or effect" as the correct answer. (A) *nugatory*, or "inconsequential," is the opposite of what is needed here. (C) *baleful*, or "destructive in influence," has the right strength but the wrong charge. The influence discussed in these sentences is a positive one.

For the second blank, note that Albéniz's later compositions would be recognized as "evoking the spirit of Spain" and would incorporate elements of Spanish folk music. Thus, predict that Albéniz sought "ideas," "stimulation," or "vision" from traditional Spanish folk music. **(F)** *inspiration* is the closest fit, and is the correct answer. (D) *impetus*,

or "impulse, incentive" is incorrect because it was meeting Pedrell that served as Albéniz's impetus to change his music. The Spanish folk music was the tradition to which Albéniz turned to once he decided to change, but he didn't seek the impetus from the folk music itself. (E) *invigoration*, or "fullness of life and energy," is incorrect because there is nothing in the sentences to indicate that Albéniz was looking for life and energy, whether for himself or for his compositions.

12. A, F

A good prediction for the first blank would be that refusing to aid a government under siege from allies of Nazi Germany would be "harmful" to the cause of freedom, which is **(A)** *inimical*, meaning "unfriendly or hostile to." (C) *indispensable*—meaning "totally necessary"—is the opposite. (B) *enigmatic*—meaning "mysterious" or "puzzling"—does not fit the sentence; while American, English and French supporters of the Spanish Republic might have been puzzled by their countries' neutrality, it does not make sense to say "puzzling to the cause of freedom."

The second blank must be an adjective in line with the Allies' "*unremitting* distrust." Predict a word like "steadfastness," which leads to choice **(F)** *intransigence*, meaning "uncompromising." (D) *malleability*—which describes a person or thing as "changeable"—is the opposite. (E) *perfidy* means "faithlessness or treachery" and does not align with the notion that the Allies based their refusal to support the Republic on a stubborn distrust of the Republican forces' Soviet backers.

13. B, F

The first missing word describes Pacheco's treatise. A treatise that contains information on iconography, technique, and contemporary painters sounds *broad* and *significant*. This description is confirmed after the second blank, when it turns out that the treatise is "our most comprehensive information" on these subjects. The word in the first blank will definitely have a positive charge. The only choice with a positive charge is **(B)** *invaluable*, which means "priceless." (A) *inconsequential*, or "unimportant," is the opposite of what you need, while (C) *insuperable*, meaning "insurmountable" or "impossible to overcome," doesn't fit the context of this significant treatise.

The the second blank must be an verb describing what Pacheco's commentary achieves. Predict something like "constitutes" or "makes up." That's **(F)** *comprises*. If you couldn't make a prediction, or didn't know the meaning of the word "comprises," you could still get to this answer by ruling out the other choices. (D) *commends* means "praises"; it doesn't make sense to say that commentary published in 1649 *now* praises *our information*. (E) *compels* means "to force someone to do something"; that's not something that a commentary can do to information.

14. B, F, H

Consider together the several statements made about the luminiferous ether: Its existence was simply taken for granted by scientific thinkers. Belief in it was almost absolute. It provided great explanatory power with regard to how light traveled. This means the second blank should be a positively charged verb that describes how past physicists related to the ether. **(F)** *venerated*, or "regarded with reverential respect," is a great match, and is the correct answer for this blank. (D) *quantified*, or "measured," is incorrect because its charge isn't positive enough, and there is nothing in the sentences to support the idea that scientists measured the ether. The first sentence, in fact, says that scientists assumed its existence. (E) *eschewed*, or "shunned," is the opposite of what is needed here.

The Michelson-Moreley experiments had "surprising" results and led to a "new way" of thinking about light and the universe. In relation to the ether, one can predict that these experiments must have "weakened" or even "ruined" the long-held belief in its existence. This leads to **(H)** *undermined*—meaning "weakened"—as the correct answer for the third blank. (I) *derided*, or "ridiculed, insulted," has the correct negative charge, but the wrong attitude. The sentences merely imply a matter-of-fact weakening of the belief, not insult or ridicule. (G) *explicated*, or "gave a detailed explanation of," doesn't fit with the clues. Since the results of the experiments were surprising and led to new ways of thinking, the third blank calls for a weakening of past beliefs, not an explanation of them.

As for the first blank, since the ether was believed to be a medium that allowed for light to travel in empty space, predict that the blank means that it "filled" the universe. This makes **(B)** *permeated*, or "diffused throughout," the correct answer. While (A) *unified*, or "made into a coher-

ent whole," and (C) *mirrored*, or "reflected or resembled," may sound science-like, there is no support for either of these ideas in the other sentences.

15. B, E, I

The first sentence gives details about a new law code that included case law from other sources. As the sovereign, King Alfred would have "developed" or "decreed" this legal code. **(B)** *promulgated* means "promoted," "made widely known," or "put into effect by decree," and is the correct answer. (A) *dissembled* means "disguised" or "concealed," so it's the opposite of what you need. (C) *mitigated* means "made less serious," which doesn't fit the context—there's no indication that Alfred reduced the impact of the new code.

For the second blank, the new code would have outlined the details of Alfred's legal system. That prediction matches **(E)** *enumerated*, which means "listed." (D) *cooperated* doesn't work within the sentence, since "cooperate" can't take a direct object. (F) *undermined* means "damaged" or "weakened." This is the opposite of the blank's meaning.

The third blank relates to Roman law, which "contrasted sharply" with Alfred's code, in which the role of case law "often necessitated the interpretation of nuanced legal precedents for application to the specific facts in each case." This blank, then, is a noun for something that does not require interpretation and application. The verb "prescribe" provides a hint: it means "state as a rule." Use that to make a loose prediction, such as "rules," and stay flexible in the answer choices. **(I)** *judgments* matches the legal context and is correct. (G) *hypotheses* means "proposed explanations that require proof," so this does not match. (H) *defectors* means "people who have abandoned their country." This does not make sense in the context of what laws would prescribe.

16. C, D, G

Early psychologists had "no reliable way" to look at the brain's internal activity, so they must have used the external "symptoms" or "signs" to assess and treat mental disorders. **(C)** *manifestations* is a match. (A) *stipulations* means "demands or requirements in an agreement or contract," and so, has no place in this context. (B) *juxtapositions* is an example of challenging vocabulary. It means "two things placed next to each other." The sentence, however, does not describe two things that could be placed next to each other. Eliminate (B).

From the first blank, you know that early psychologists relied on the outward symptoms of mental disorders. The second blank refers to the internal *autopsies* used by the "more enterprising pioneers" to learn more about the human brain. Predict "operations" or "examinations." That matches **(D)** *investigations*. Eliminate (E) *characteristics*, or "features," because it does not fit the blank's context: the sentence does not provide details about any "features" these autopsies revealed. Note the detour key word "but," which indicates that the autopsies provided "few insights." Eliminate (F) *authorities,* meaning "experts," because the word in the blank must refer to the autopsies, and not to the early pioneers who performed them.

The third blank describes the effect of "major technological breakthroughs" on the field of psychology. It will contrast with the early investigations, which yielded little information. The word that goes in this blank should mean "changed." **(G)** *altered* matches and is correct. (H) *stagnated* is exactly the opposite of the prediction, since it means "stopped developing." (I) *reinforced* comes close, but it means "buttressed" or "strengthened." This does not match because the sentence indicates major changes from "technological breakthroughs."

17. A, F, H

The first sentence implies a contrast but does not state it directly. The author says that children's authors should not protect their readers but should instead "expose" them to some aspects of the adult world. The clue "coddle" contrasts with the second part of this sentence, so predict "realities" or something similar with a negative charge, such as "hardships" or "troubles." Some difficult vocabulary in the answer choices may require the process of elimination. If you are not familiar with **(A)** *vicissitudes*, move on to the other answer choices. Eliminating the two wrong answer choices can still yield the right answer. (B) *eccentricities*, or "things that are strange," is inconsistent with clues later in the sentence. An author would not describe "evil, disappointment, or even death" as mere "eccentricities." (C) *hypocrites* means "people who say one thing and do another," so it is too specific for the blank. Hypocrites certainly exist in the adult world, but the sentence does provides no clues to support this choice.

It is also inconsistent with the later clues, which are strongly negative. By process of elimination, then, **(A)** *vicissitudes* is the match. It means "changes of circumstances, usually ones that are unwelcome or unpleasant." This is consistent with the context of the sentence, since "evil, disappointment, or even death" represent unwelcome changes.

The third blank has clear clues and offers the next best opportunity to predict and match. In the first sentence, the author recommends exposing young readers to the difficult realities of the adult world. This final sentence provides additional context: the fairy tales are "uncensored" and "involve cruelty and violence." This blank, which describes the reality of these fairy tales, should have a similarly negative connotation. **(H)** *macabre* means "disturbing because it depicts death" and matches exactly. (G) *entertaining* may describe your experience with fairy tales, but does not match the negative clues in the sentence. (I) *skeptical* means "not easily convinced," and would describe a person, not "reality."

As for the second blank, the author of this sentence wants children's authors to use the "relative safety" of written stories to expose children to the tough realities of adult life. The author suggests that this will "protect" children against the "pain of real loss." That matches **(F)** *inured to*, which means "accustomed to pain." (D) *fixated on* runs counter to the author's meaning: early exposure will protect children from pain, not cause them to obsess over it. (E) *amused by* goes too far: the author does not suggest that children will find hardship funny, just that they'll be better able to deal with it.

18. A, E, H

The detour road sign "nevertheless" sets up a contrast with the common view from the first sentence: most people think of the bacteria that cause illness, but human beings have "relied" on "good" bacteria for thousands of years. **(A)** *beneficial* matches that prediction. (B) *formidable* means "powerful" and fails to produce the necessary contrast with the view of bacteria as causing illness. (C) *temperate* means "moderate," but the sentence does not suggest that the bacteria are "average in intensity." Instead, the author emphasizes the "power" of these bacteria and human reliance on it.

The second blank is part of the example: yogurt comes from a culture of beneficial bacteria. Predict "made" or "created." **(E)** *produced* is correct. (F) *rejected* is not consistent with the author's positive tone: the author just described the positive effects of bacteria, and the straight-ahead road sign "for example" continues that tone. (D) *enhanced* matches the positive tone of the sentence. This word, however, means "made better." The sentence indicates that bacteria change milk into yogurt, not that bacteria improve yogurt.

The last sentence contrasts "the common perception of bacteria" with the fact that "only a minority of bacteria cause disease." This contrast, along with the first part of the first sentence, leads to the prediction that people perceive bacteria to be "harmful." (H) *nefarious* means "wicked," so it matches the negative context. (G) *assiduous* means "showing great care," and it is not consistent with the author's negative tone. Finally, (I) *capricious* means "changing moods or behavior suddenly." The author demonstrated that people have relied on bacteria "for millennia," so there's no reason to believe that bacteria change suddenly.

19. B, F, H

Start with the first blank, for which the word "as" serves as a straight-ahead road sign. The information between the dashes conveys that the three named examples are but "a few" of the dance styles that have early origins. This implies that there are "many" such styles. That prediction works well with (B) *myriad*, which means "numerous." (A) *multifaceted* has a prefix that might make it seem to be a good fit, but the sentence does not imply that *each* style has "many different aspects" to it, just that there are many different dance styles with early origins. (C) *exiguous* means "few" and is thus the opposite of the prediction.

The second and third blanks describe the dancer's skill set, and the third sentence provides details helpful for predicting the words that will fill the blanks. The dancer is described as "leaping and moving like a salmon" and "spinning on his head while tracing a circle with his feet" Good predictions would be "body control" for the second blank and "coordinated" for the third. Based on those predictions (F) *acrobatic,* which means "performing gymnastic feats that require skillful body control," and (H) *equipoise,* which means "equilibrium and balance," are the correct

answers. (D) *aerobic* relates to "any activity that increases the body's demand for oxygen," which does not capture the body control required by this dance, while (E) *anachronistic* does not work because it means "something that seems to belong in the past and does not fit in with the present." Since they are not close to the prediction of "coordinated", (G) *equitation*, meaning "the art of riding on horseback," and (I) *equivocation*, meaning "prevarication" or "intentional ambiguity to conceal the truth," are both incorrect.

20. B, D, I

The road signs come from the phrase "While predicting [bad things] . . . scientists concede _____ . . ." Thus, the second blank is a good place to start and should indicate that the bad things might not be as bad as predicted. So (D) *mitigated*, which means to lessen a negative consequence, fits. (E) *exacerbated*—meaning "make worse"—is the opposite. While (F) *investigated* could fit the sentence up to that point, reading further eliminates it from consideration since investigation is not the purpose of building heavy infrastructure.

The next road sign, "though," indicates a need to change directions. So while some harm to coastal communities may be mitigated, the third blank requires a word indicating that harm to wildlife either can't be mitigated or would be made worse. Thus, (I) *compound* is correct. Both (G) and (H) are the opposite of what the structure demands. *Ameliorate* is synonymous with *mitigate*, while *nullify* goes further and suggests the harms would be completely eliminated or compensated for.

The first blank requires an adjective to describe "climate change," which we are told subsequently is "caused by the burning of fossil fuels." Since people are burning fossil fuels, (B) *anthropogenic* is correct. The root *anthro* indicates "people" (think "anthropology"—the study of humans) and *genic* indicates "origin" (think "genesis"). (A) *stochastic* is incorrect because it means "random" or "resulting from chance events" and (C) *historical* is incorrect because the passage refers to predictions for the future from an ongoing event.

Sentence Equivalence Explanations

1.   A, F

The blank describes something about mathematics that is "essential" for scientists. The author contrasts this necessity with the additional need for critical thinking and creative problem-solving skills, but that contrast is not necessary for the meaning of the blank. Predict "skill in" or "ability in" and look for the two matching answer choices. **(A)** *fluency in* and **(F)** *command of* both describe strong ability and are correct. (B) *fixation on* and (E) *obsession with* are synonyms of each other, but the sentence does not suggest that math should fill the minds of scientists. Perhaps scientists need to cooperate with mathematicians, but (C) *cooperation with* mathematics does not make logical sense. Finally, nothing in the sentence suggests the negative tone of (D) *misuse of*.

2.   B, C

This author seems to have a low opinion of pithy sayings. She claims that the appropriate use of a saying depends on "careful selectivity" in matching it to a specific situation rather than on something else more universal. "Truth" would be a good prediction. (A) *alacrity* means "speed," so it is not relevant to choosing the right saying for a given situation. **(B)** *verities* and **(C)** *veracity* are both related to truth and match the context of the sentence. These are the correct answers. (D) *discrepancy* is a lack of compatibility between two things. This describes the contradictory maxims, but is not appropriate for the blank. (E) *familiarity* might help someone consider available maxims, but the author says appropriate application does not depend on the word in the blank. (F) *obduracy* is "stubbornness," which is not relevant to the application of maxims.

3.   B, E

This sentence starts with a strongly positive word, "majestic." The author claims that the amazing cathedrals are "testaments" to a quality or characteristic of the architects. Predict "ability," "talent," or perhaps something like "experience." **(B)** *prowess* and **(E)** *expertise* both match. (A) *apathy* and (F) *complacence* both describe a lack of investment or care. These negative terms would not be characteristic of architects who create "majestic" works. (C) *complexity* and (D) *popularity* might describe the cathedrals themselves, but do not describe the architects, and neither matches any other word among the choices.

4.   C, F

The ideological rivals of anarchists would "agree", according to the first clause of the sentence, that government is responsible for the "repression of natural human desire," but "only the anarchists" believe that government should be abolished. The rival group, then, does not believe this. It's the outcome of the definition of government that the two groups disagree about. The missing word must mean something like "logical consequences." **(C)** *ramifications* and **(F)** *implications* match this prediction and are the correct answers. (A) *semantics* can mean either "the study of language" or "the meaning of a word or phrase." The second of these meanings might be tempting, but the two groups don't disagree over meaning or definition; rather, they diverge over the results of viewing government in this way. (B) *etiology* means the "cause" or "origin" of something; the two groups aren't disagreeing about the origin of the definition of government. (D) *phraseology* and (E) *expression* both refer to the way words are arranged, and once again, this is not the source of the two groups' disagreement.

5.   C, F

There is no change of direction in this sentence. Initial predictions for the blank could include "deliniated," "determined" or "defined." Both **(C)** *characterized* and **(F)** *dictated* would produce sentences that indicate that the frequency and type of destructive events in an ecosystem determine the type of "disturbance regime" present in that ecosystem. (A) *mitigated* means that a harmful impact is lessened; it sounds unlikely that destruction caused by windstorms and forest fires lessens the harmful impact of a "disturbance regime." None of (B) *supplanted*, meaning "replaced," (D) *contradicted*, or (E) *obfuscated*, meaning "made unclear" or "confused," fit the sentence or have a partner that could yield an equivalent sentence.

6.   B, F

This sentence introduces a new ("nascent") field that involves several subjects ("interdisciplinary") and studies how people learn. According to the author, this field holds "significant implications" for the way educational courses are designed. The straight-ahead road sign "and" reveals that the sentence continues in the same direction.

Predict that the correct answers will contain adjectives indicating that this innovative new field may weaken or undermine "long-held" or "traditional" ideas of education. **(B)** *orthodox* and **(F)** *established* are correct because they mean "traditional" or "customary." You may be more familiar with the religious sense of *orthodox*, meaning "devout" or "conservative," but it also carries a general meaning of "accepted" or "traditional." Both (A) *effective* and (D) *advantageous* have positive charges—and they match one another—but using them to describe the views learning science is displacing would produce an illogical sentence by claiming that learning science is attacking good educational practices. (C) *rudimentary* means "simple" or "basic." It often has a negative connotation, and it is incorrect here because the author does not imply that learning science will change only the simplest conceptions of education, and because it has no match among the other choices. (E) *pedagogical*, meaning "related to teaching," matches the topic of the sentence but has no pair among the answer choices.

7.   D, E

You first learn that Rembrandt created etching plates. The missing word describes how pictures created from the plates after Rembrandt's death are evaluated. Two detour road signs help define the missing word. The first, "although," indicates that the plates are considered in some way despite the fact that technicians have retouched and repaired the plates. The second, "yet," tells you that even though the pictures are considered in this way, they aren't very popular with collectors. This may allow you to predict the correct answers almost word for word. The correct choices, **(D)** *authentic* and **(E)** *originals,* create logical, equivalent sentences by describing the pictures as "original Rembrandts" and "authentic Rembrandts," in contrast to the works being considered copies, forgeries, or replicas. (C) *tainted* and (F) *sullied* also create equivalent sentences, but they do not contrast with the fact that the plates have been retouched and repaired. (A) *valuable* and (B) *priceless* are potentially equivalent as well, but if these works are not sought after by collectors, they must be worth less, not more.

8.   A, C

The sentence introduces Hilaire Belloc, who wrote a great many books and "debated with intellectual luminaries." The detour road sign "though" contrasts Belloc's highbrow credentials with the word in the blank describing his "flair for" something revealed ("evinced") by his children's book. That contrast and the example titles are key to a prediction: Belloc has a flair for the "goofy" or "lowbrow." **(A)** *farcical* means "absurd or ridiculous," which matches the prediction and works in the context of the sentence. **(C)** *ridiculous* has a similar meaning and is also correct. (B) *erudite*, meaning "knowledgeable" or "cultivated" and (E) *learned* are both related to Belloc's intellect. These choices might be tempting if you missed the detour road sign. (D) *macabre* means "disturbing or horrifying; related to death or injury," but this does match the context of the sentence. Neither becoming a boot-black—that's just an old fashioned word for a person who shines shoes— nor being corrected by an uncle is severe enough to be called "macabre." (F) *copious*, which means "ample" or "extensive," might relate to Belloc's "prolific" writing, but it does not fit the clues for this blank. Watch out for wrong answers that describe something else in the sentence.

9.   B, C

Before the blank, this sentence compares literature to fashion and architecture. That doesn't provide enough information to make a prediction, so you should look after the blank for additional clues. The author provides an example from literature: a specific genre started in 1822, "quickly" became popular, and "all but disappeared" within 50 years. The domestic novel, then, was a "fad" or "short-lived style." **(B)** *vogues* and **(C)** *trends* match this prediction. Literature does feature (E) *characters*, but this does not match the example, and would not apply to fashion and architecture. (A) *repetitions* and (D) *cycles* are similar in meaning, and both are wrong for the same reason: the sentence says that the domestic novel "all but disappeared after 1870," and provides no evidence that it ever came back into favor after its 50-year run. (F) *nadirs*—which means "lowest levels"—implies a strongly negative evaluation of the domestic novel that the author does not include.

10. A, E

The blank describes the way most people—"lay people," by the way, refers to non-experts—will perceive the term "explosion" when scientists apply it to a period of millions of years. Something last that long would likely strike most people as slow and gradual, so the blank must mean "inappropriate," "ill suited," or "off base." Both **(A)** *inapt* and **(E)** *incongruous* mean "inappropriate" and are correct. Neither (C) *important* nor (F) *obsolete*, meaning "outdated, no longer of use," matches the prediction. (B) *insidious* means "treacherous" or "deceitful," and carries a connotation too strong to match "inappropriate" or "ill suited." (D) *obstreperous* means "unruly," and doesn't make sense in this context.

11. C, E

The author cites Handel's *Messiah* as an example of oratorio, whose production is contrasted with the "pageantry" (meaning "pomp" or "splendor") of opera. To keep the audience focused on "the transcendent," then, the author is suggesting that oratorio would "avoid" distractions such as costumes. **(C)** *forgoes* ("omits") matches nicely. **(E)** *eschews* ("avoids using") is the second correct choice. (A) *includes* and (B) *embraces* are both positive, so they do not match the context of the sentence, which implies that costumes get in the way of an oratorio's goal. (F) *accentuates*—meaning "makes more noticeable"—is wrong for the same reason, since it has an even stronger positive charge. (D) *sabotages* means "deliberately destroys or damages" and is too strongly negative for this sentence; the author makes no suggestion that costumes and props are deliberately damaged.

12. D, E

The phrasing "not only . . . but also" is *not* a detour road sign. "Not only . . . but also" is a means of emphasizing a second, and more dramatic or unexpected, aspect that differs from or simply goes beyond the first thing mentioned. So, in this sentence, you should read it as implying that "[e]xcellent examples . . . *provide* vital and practical geographic information and also, perhaps unexpectedly, *provide* aesthetic appeal." Using "provide" or "supply" as your prediction, you can spot **(D)** *effect* and **(E)** *furnish* as the correct answers. "Effect" (used here in its verb form) means to cause or bring about. Don't confuse it with "affect," meaning to impact. You may be used to seeing the word "furnish" in the context of decorating a room with furniture. but it also means to provide or supply more generally. (A) *minimize* fits the sentence structure and you might have clung to it to if you interpreted "but also" as a detour road sign. Note, however, that *minimize* neither fits the author's meaning nor does it have a match in the list. None of the remaining choices fit logically into the sentence. (B) *personify* means "represent" or "embody." (C) *delegitimize* means "remove authority or legal status." (F) *rectify* means "to make right."

13. B, F

The sentence contrasts people who had ideas and took some action with those who made it far enough to create a practical invention. Consider traits the latter group might have had that the first group lacked. The language "reached the point" leads to the prediction that such people probably needed great "determination" or "diligence" in order to keep working until they had invented something practical. **(B)** *persistence* and **(E)** *tenacity* mean "perseverance" or "determination" and are therefore correct. (A) *dauntlessness*—meaning "fearlessness" or "courage"—is a positive trait that may benefit inventors, but it doesn't match the clues, nor is there another word among the choices that would give the same meaning to the sentence. (C) *integrity*, or "firm adherence to a code of moral values," is another positive trait that is not suggested by the clues in the sentence. (D) *ingenuity*, or "inventiveness," is certainly a trait one might expect of inventors, but it doesn't fit with the sentence's emphasis on "reaching the point," and it has no partner among the choices that would produce and equivalent meaning. (D) *sagacity*—meaning "wisdom"—suggests discernment and good judgment. This is a positive trait, of course, but doesn't fit the sentence's clues.

14. A, E

The sentence describes two mathematical operations. The key phrase indicates that these two processes are "parallel yet inverse," and the semicolon acts as a straight ahead road sign meaning that the second clause matches the first. To get a handle on "parallel but inverse," picture two bridges that run right next to one another in opposite directions. Taking one bridge and then turning right around and taking the other will bring you back to where you started. So a good prediction for the blank would be "reproduces" or "duplicates." That leads to **(E)** *replicates*, and given the blank's context, **(A)** *yields* produces an equivalent sentence. While *yields* means "produces" and *replicates*, meaning "produces a copy," is more specific, the phrase "yields the original function" is equivalent to "replicates the original function."

(D) *approximates* works within the structure of the sentence, but would not produce an equivalent sentence with either *yields* or *replicates*. Those words demand an identical (and not merely a close) result. (F) *dissembles*—meaning "gives a false impression" or "conceals the truth"—does not fit the sentence and cannot be a match to *approximates* or any of the other words. If you got turned around while parsing the sentence, you might have liked (C) *negates*. However, it has no match among the remaining choices and thus must be eliminated.

15. D, F

The sentence indicates that Darwin did not invent the theory of evolution, so the blank will be a noun describing what he did with the theory in his well-known book. A prediction could be "explanation" or "presentation." **(D)** *exposition* and **(F)** *enunciation* both match the prediction. You may be familiar with "enunciation" in reference to the clear pronunciation of words; it also is used to refer to the articulation of a position or declaration of a theory. (A) *renunciation*—meaning "repudiation" or "disavowal"—and (C) *attenuation*—meaning "weakening" or "reduction"—are contrary to the meaning of the sentence. (B) *contrivance*—meaning "invention"—does not work because the sentence indicates that Darwin did not invent or come up with the theory. (E) *revitalization*—meaning "restoration"—could indicate that Darwin had resurrected an old theory; however, the sentence doesn't indicate that Darwin's book restored a once popular theory, nor does this word have a partner among the remaining choices.

16. C, E

The word "whatever" is a subtle detour road sign indicating that the functions noted in the second part of the sentence are distinct from and in contrast to an institution's "primary goal." Thus, "secondary" or "additional" would be a good predictions for the word in the blank. (B) *ancillary*, or "subordinate, subsidiary," and **(E)** *appurtenant*, or "auxiliary," are good matches and are the correct choices. Incorrect choices (A) *organizational*, (B) *societal*, and (D) *regulatory* all describe possible functions of an institution,

but none of them logically contrasts with "primary." (F) *incongruous* means "incompatible" or "unsuitable." This word is out of sync with the sentence, which allows for all of an institution's goals and functions to be compatible.

17. E, F

The word "for" after the comma is a clue that what follows is a reason to believe that Holst saw a performance of Schoenberg's new work and reacted in the way described by the word in the blank. The reason given is that Holst's original title for his new work was very similar to the title of Schoenberg's work. This suggests that Holst's reaction to Schoenberg's work was positive, so predict that Holst was "influenced" or "moved" by the composition. **(E)** *impressed* and **(F)** *captivated* are both good matches that give the sentence similar meanings and are therefore the correct answers. (A) *disturbed* and (C) *discouraged* are both negative words that don't fit in with the clues given by the second part of the sentence. Arguably, (B) *envious* leads to a logical, although negatively charged, sentence. Still, there is no other choice that would give the sentence a similar meaning. (D) *overjoyed* might describe Holst's feelings after attending the performance, but it expresses an emotion too strong to fit with the rest of the sentence. Moreover, no other word among the choices would give the sentence an equivalent meaning.

18. A, E

The straight ahead road signs "[a]s" and "in turn" indicate that the author is presenting an analogy between what happened in the past with the rise of internet commerce and what will happen in the future with the rise of self-driving vehicles. The pattern of "eliminated . . . but mitigated" will be repeated. The second half of the analogy has "_____ . . . while compensating." "Compensating" matches "mitigated," so the blank should match "eliminated". Thus, **(A)** *nullify*—meaning "render useless"—and **(E)** *obviate*—"render unnecessary"—are correct.

If you looked at the blank only in the context of the second half of the sentence and ignored the first half of the analogy, (B) *attenuate*—meaning "to weaken or lessen"—might appear to fit. It does not, however, equate to "eliminate" in a way that matches the pattern of the analogy nor does it match "nullify" or "obviate" as well as they match each other. (C) *ameliorate* is synonymous with "mitigate" and "compensate," but the word in the blank must be at odds with those terms. Similarly, (D) *amplify* means the opposite of what the word in the blank must be. (F) *relinquish* means "to give up control." It does not make sense to state that the "proliferation of self-driving vehicles" will *relinquish* jobs that people are doing. The workers would be the ones *relinquishing* the jobs.

19. D, F

The blank requires a verb indicating that Kundera used the tumultuous times in Czechoslovakia to gain information and insights into human nature that provide material for his novels. A good prediction would be "studied" or "examined." **(D)** *explored* and **(F)** *scrutinized* are the correct answers.

(A) *flouted* means disregarded, which is the opposite of the intended meaning. (B) *wielded* means used. (C) *anthropomorphized* describes a literary device in which the author attributes human traits to non-human entities. Nothing here suggests that Kundera attributed human traits to the "waves of euphoria and disillusionment" that inspired his novels. (E) *transcended* might work; in the case, the sentence would mean that Kundera overcame the turmoil in his homeland to write profound novels. The problem is that no word among the remaining choices produces an equivalent sentence.

20. C, E

The first word of the sentence, "[w]hile," acts as a detour road sign, but the detour does not occur until much later in the sentence. Before the detour is taken, the sentence relates several facts that only someone with a strong science background could be expected to understand. The GRE does *not* expect students to understand the terminology here. Instead, it expects students to avoid the terminology and focus on the simple subjects and verbs. The detour sign at the beginning of the sentence implies that even though many researchers reuse buffer solutions, they probably should not. Since buffer solutions "provide a supply" of something, you can predict that even one long use can "lower" or "reduce" that supply. This leads to **(C)** *deplete* and **(E)** *diminish* as the correct answers. (A) *catalyze* sounds scientific, but it doesn't fit here because its meaning—to "bring about" or "increase the rate" of a chemical reaction—is the opposite of what the blank needs to say. (D) *enhance* and (F) *stimulate* also have positive charges, and are therefore incorrect. (B) *regulate* is not supported by the contrast in the sentence.

Reading Comprehension Explanations

Pterosaur Passage

Topic and Scope: Pterosaurs—divergence from dinosaurs and distinguishing characteristics.

Purpose: To describe how pterosaurs are distinct from dinosaurs, particularly in their modes of movement.

1. E

It's difficult to make a prediction based on this Inference question, so evaluate the answer choices one by one. (A) is unsupported; while the passage tells you that pterosaurs were "diverse" and "successful," there is no indication of how their numbers compared to those of dinosaurs. (B) is unsupported as well. Nothing in the passage suggests that *Tyrannosaurus* was more or less closely related to pterosaurs than other dinosaurs were. (C) is extreme. Although pterosaurs may have lived "alongside" dinosaurs, the passage does not claim that their relationship was "symbiotic," or even mutually beneficial. (If you were unsure about the meaning of "symbiotic," you would have been best off moving on to evaluate the remaining choices.) (D) is wrong because while the passage states that pterosaurs existed for more than one hundred million years, it says nothing about how this figure compares to previous estimates. This leaves (**E**) as correct. The passage refers to *Pterodactylus* as a species of pterosaur, and to *Triceratops* as a species of dinosaur, and further states that dinosaurs and pterosaurs share a common ancestor. It follows that *Pterodactylus* and *Triceratops* share a common ancestor.

2. B

This is a Vocabulary-in-Context question. The third sentence describes how pterosaur's wings were used to fly, and the fourth suggests that they "had terrestrial utility as well." Predict, then, that the correct answer will define "terrestrial utility" in a way that contrasts with flight. The information that pterosaurs could "ambulate" gives the rest of the picture: their wings could be used to walk. This suggests that "terrestrial" has something to do with the ground, and (**B**) *related to the ground* fits that prediction. (E) *coming from planet Earth* is another possible meaning of *terrestrial*, but does not contrast with the idea of flight or otherwise fit the passage. (A) *extinct* doesn't match the prediction: while pterosaurs are extinct, this has nothing to do with what their wings were used for. There is nothing

in the passage to suggest that wings were *common to all reptiles*, as (C) implies. Although the final sentence states that pterosaurs "traveled alongside" dinosaurs, it does not indicate that the two classes of creatures communicated, so (D) *useful for communicating with other species* is out.

Esperanto Passage

Par 1: Zamenhof invented Esperanto for international communication and ease of use; it gained speakers after publication of *Unua Libro.*

Par. 2: Speakers executed by Nazis and Soviets; millions of speakers today; original culture and literature; native speakers.

Topic and Scope: Esperanto. Specifically, its origins, history, and current state.

Purpose: Describe the reasons why Zamenhof invented Esperanto; outline its setbacks and successes.

3. D

This is a Global question, asking you to pick an appropriate title for the passage. Simply consult your T/S/P to find the passage's main idea, and predict that the answer should relate to why Esperanto was formed, what happened to it, and how it currently exists. (**D**) does this, and is the correct answer. (A) misses the mark; the passage focuses on the language Esperanto, not its creator's "contributions to linguistics." (B) fails because the passage never focuses on Esperanto's grammar or vocabulary. (C) is far too broad; this passage is about Esperanto in particular, not "solutions to international misunderstanding" in general. (E) is too narrow; one sentence in the second paragraph claims that some viewed Esperanto as a conspiracy, but this is not the point of the passage.

4. B

Evaluate each choice to crack this all-that-apply Inference question. Refer to your passage map to guide your research. (A) describes a cause-and-effect relationship that is not supported by the passage. Paragraph 2 tells you that Esperanto suffered setbacks at the hands of Nazi Germany, and that it "may not be the lingua franca of the United Nations." However, nothing in the passage suggests that these setbacks *caused* Esperanto's failure to become the U.N.'s common tongue.

You can determine that (**B**) is correct by comparing Zamenhof's goals, listed in paragraph 1, to its successes, listed in paragraph 2. Zamenhof wished to "foster international communication," which is consistent with the fact that Esperanto enthusiasts "gather together from diverse countries to participate in conferences and produce original music, films, and literature in Esperanto."

(C) distorts the passage. Paragraph 1 tells you that Zamenhof wanted Esperanto to be easy to pick up as a second or third language, and Paragraph 2 tells you that some children have been raised with it. However, nothing in the passage supports a claim that these children learn Esperanto with "less effort" than they would learn other languages.

The Cheese and the Worms Passage

Topic and Scope: The Cheese and the Worms, including its subject (Menocchio) and methods (microhistory).

Purpose: To describe *The Cheese and the Worms* as microhistory.

5. D

This is a Vocabulary-in-Context question. The word "terse" means "brief" or "rude." Even if you know this, take care in researching this word's context in the passage—since *brief* is choice (D) and *rude* is choice (A). The passage uses the key word "however" to contrast the treatment Menocchio would be "lucky" to get in a traditional history with the "robust" (or thorough) picture that appears in *The Cheese and the Worms.* For this contrast to make sense, the writer must be using "terse" to mean "short" or "quick." This leads to (**D**), the correct answer. Nothing in the passage suggests that a traditional history would treat Menocchio's story unfairly (just briefly), so (B) *equitable* does not fit, nor does the term "equitable" match "terse" in any way. (C) *arcane* ("obscure") and (E) *benevolent* ("kindly") also fail to define "terse" and do not fit the context of the word in the passage.

6. D

This is a Global question, so refer to your T/S/P summaries. You should expect the correct answer to address *The Cheese and the Worms* as an example of microhistory. Only (**D**) matches this prediction. (A) misses the mark by focusing on Ginzburg's views; the passage tells you that he wrote *The Cheese and the Worms,* but provides no information about his opinions. The passage describes one of Menocchio's views in the final sentence, but this is not the focus of the passage, so (B) is out. The passage never indicates that *The Cheese and the Worms* is controversial—only that it differs in a crucial respect from traditional history—so eliminate (C). The passage describes a book, and issues no call to action on its subject matter, so (E)'s language—"[t]o reject" and "intolerance and cruelty"—is off base.

Narrative POV Passage

Topic and Scope: Narrative POV; specifically, 3rd person omniscient and 3rd person limited.

Purpose: To describe the usage and changing popularity of these POVs. 3rd person omniscient was popular historically, but is less popular than 3rd person limited presently.

7. A

This "except" Detail question asks you to find a statement about third person omniscient that is *not* supported by the passage. Researching the passage reveals that this point of view refers to an all-knowing narrator, that it was used by Dickens and Austen, and that it has become less popular than third person limited. This allows you to eliminate (B), (D) and (E). The passage also describes third person omniscient as an "option" for contemporary short story writers and novelists. Therefore, (C) must be true, and so is not the correct answer. This leaves (**A**), the correct answer. Although the passage implies that third person limited is better at delivering psychological depth, it is extreme to claim that third person omniscient offers "little opportunity" for "any."

8. E

This is a Logic question, so research the passage to determine the role of the highlighted sentence. Here, the highlighted sentence introduces the concept of authorial points of view in order to set up a more targeted discussion of the third person omniscient and third person limited. Skimming the answer choices, only (**E**) fits. For the record, nowhere does the passage argue against the information in this sentence, so (A) is out. The sentence is not used as a point of comparison, eliminating (B). Based on your prediction, you know that the sentence is context or background, not evidence or conclusion, so eliminate (C) and (D) as well.

Global Winds Passage

Par. 1: Local air movements are complicated, but large-scale movements depend on only two factors. First factor: differential heating.

Par. 2: Second factor: Coriolis effect.

Topic and Scope: Wind; specifically, why winds move the way they do on a large scale.

Purpose: To explain the mechanisms that control large scale wind motion.

9. B

This is a Global question. **(B)** fits the passage best; the author is describing and explaining observable phenomena. (A) would require some statement that the facts the author mentions are proof or support for a theory. (C) mischaracterizes the passage; the author presents only one view (containing two complementary factors). (D) distorts the passage, which presents the explanation as accepted consensus, not as a hypothesis. (E) is incorrect; the author records no observations and discusses the subject without any reference to specific data.

10. B

Here is a straight Detail question. Go to the points in the passage at which the behavior of winds near the equator is described (namely, at the end of each paragraph).

(B) is easy to verify; it rephrases material in the fourth and sixth sentences of paragraph 1. (A) and (C) are easy to rule out because they contain exaggerated or absurd ideas. Watch for these—the GRE will often make a potentially tricky choice clearly wrong by using one plainly foolish word. In (A), the word is *unvarying*—why would the rate be unvarying? It should at least vary between night and day, and at different times of the year; in any case, the idea of "unvarying" never appears in the passage. In (C), "rush" should stand out; whatever the winds do, it isn't this. Moreover, winds moving from the poles toward the equator are deflected to the west.

11. C

Here's a difficult Inference question. The Coriolis effect may be hard to understand if you're not familiar with it. Reread the second paragraph, the portion of the passage that describes the Coriolis effect.

In paragraph 2, you're told that the Coriolis effect *deflects* the winds. So, if there were no Coriolis effect, they would simply rise and flow away from the equator—either north or south, since the equator has two sides (choice **(C)**).

Eliminate the other answer choices. (A) is tricky; the wind's speed *would* match that of the earth, initially, but it leaves out differential heating, which causes the wind to move away from the equator. (B) and (D) are contrary to the passage: winds flowing away from the equator are deflected east, not west, and the wind would not remain stationary, because of differential heating. The wording of (E) may be a little confusing, but nothing in the passage *supports* it; according to the passage, the earth is moving eastward at its highest speed near the equator, so the air's eastward motion would diverge least from the earth's at the equator. (E) must be false.

12. D

This is an Inference question. The passage's first sentence specifies that "many" influences determine local winds, while only two determine global air movements. Logically, the interaction of "many" factors is harder to predict, so **(D)** is correct.

(A) contradicts the passage—the author's point is that global air movements are quite regular.

(B) is unsupported in the passage: global winds seem to be quite well understood, and there is no basis for a comparison with local winds on this point.

(C) would depend on what one is interested in, wouldn't it? The passage provides no basis for this choice.

(E) is false: you're not told about local air movements, but the first sentence (and common sense) suggests that they're quite different from the regular movements of the large-scale global winds.

Virginia Woolf Passage

Par. 1: Introduces the essays.

Par. 2: Describes *A Room of One's Own* and its arguments.

Par. 3: Describes *Three Guineas* and provides some criticism of this work.

Topic and Scope: Virginia Woolf; specifically, two of her essays that deal with feminist issues.

Purpose: To evaluate these essays, giving a synopsis of and critical reaction to the ideas contained in each.

13. B

For this Detail question, go to paragraph 2, in which the preconditions needed for women to produce works of genius, which are then figuratively summed up as "a room of [one's] own, in all its senses," are described. These preconditions provide our wrong answers. (A) and (C) are virtual paraphrases of "financial independence" and "opportunities for education," respectively. If a writer is no longer "labouring and servile," she is then relatively autonomous, as in (D). (E) refers to the need for "tranquility and privacy." That leaves **(B)**, the correct choice, which describes something to be *overcome* after one obtains a "room of one's own."

14. A

This is an Inference question. According to paragraph 2, one goal of a woman writer is to develop an "androgynous mind," one that has united "male" and "female" characteristics. Thus Woolf's assumption is that there is a division of mental processes according to gender, one which is "transcended" by genius. The assumption in **(A)** is required for Woolf's discussion to make sense.

(B) makes an all-inclusive generalization that distorts Woolf's emphasis on financial security; it implies that no great artists have come from lower class backgrounds—a distortion of the idea that women writers must gain financial security.

(C) is unsupported in the passage. That Woolf would think there has never been a great woman writer is implausible; paragraph 2 merely says that without financial independence, women are *unlikely* (not unable) to produce great art.

(D) is contrary to Woolf's argument; she is saying that education is needed for women to become great writers.

(E) mistakes one goal of the "androgynous" mind (comprehending the feelings of both sexes) for the *main* goal of all literature.

15. D

This is a Detail question. The conditions for the development mentioned in **(D)** are discussed in paragraph 2. If a woman author obtains a room of her own in all its meanings (education, financial independence, etc.), she may then go on to develop an "androgynous" mind.

(A) goes too far, since the passage provides no information on why Woolf used the "lecture" format in *A Room of One's Own.*

(B) is also unmentioned; although a tone shift between *A Room of One's Own* and *Three Guineas* is implied by the terms used to describe them (paragraph 1), the reason for the change is not specified.

(C) is out since the passage notes only one example of apparent male prejudice against Woolf—the response to *Three Guineas* ("mild derision")—and says nothing about Woolf's reaction to it.

(E) is tricky. You are told how the public reacted to *Three Guineas,* but not to the ideas in *A Room of One's Own.*

16. E

This is another Detail question. The novels are mentioned only in the first paragraph, where the author concedes that the essays "no doubt . . . lack the subtlety" of the novels. In comparison to her novels, then, Woolf's essays are "unsubtle." This idea is expressed in **(E)**.

17. C

This is a lengthy Inference question that requires you to skip between the second and third paragraphs.

Take the answers one at a time. You can see (A) is not true; only *A Room of One's Own* discusses artistic development. (B) is also incorrect; specific ways of fighting against male domination are brought up only in *Three Guineas* (pacifist action against a "male-instigated" war). **(C)** is correct. As paragraph 2 makes clear, *A Room of One's Own* discusses the achievement of financial independence by women who already possess some education and freedom from poverty; that essay's fictitious academic setting underlines this point. *Three Guineas,* as demonstrated by the criticism of Agnes Smith, was "class-bound"—relevant mainly to non-working-class women. The author refers to this as a "limitation of Woolf's feminism generally," further strengthening (C).

18. C

This is a type of Global question. A "best title" question asks you to identify the main theme of the passage, which is what a good title will focus on. Here, the last sentence of paragraph 1 states the theme: Woolf's essays are valuable because of their "anticipation . . . of contemporary feminism." This idea is directly paraphrased in correct choice **(C)**. Don't worry that this choice doesn't mention Woolf; it focuses squarely on what the author says about Woolf. The remainder of the passage surveys two aspects of Woolf's feminism, both of which foreshadow present-day feminism, as paragraph 3 states directly and as the reference to Tillie Olsen in paragraph 2 suggests.

(A) focuses on supporting detail—pacifism—a relatively minor issue in the passage.

(B) is unsupported in this passage. The passage does not address the genesis (in other words, the origin) of Woolf's feminist ideas.

(D) is half right, half wrong. The creation of art is discussed only in *A Room of One's Own*, not in *Three Guineas*.

(E) is too critical. Woolf's feminism is taken seriously and is not criticized as a myth.

Restoration Satire Passage

Par. 1: Introduction to Restoration satire and what it allowed writers to do.

Par. 2: Criticism of *The Rape of the Lock* and defense of the poem.

Topic and Scope: Satire between 1660–1730, particularly Pope's *The Rape of the Lock*.

Purpose: To outline how satire achieved a dominating position (it provided a new means of lambasting society)

Because this is a Detail question, evaluate the answers one at a time with reference to the passage text.

(A) summarizes the diverse targets of satire, as detailed in the second and third sentences of paragraph 1.

(B) is supported by the example of *The Rape of the Lock*, in paragraph 2.

(C) goes back to paragraph 1. Satire was used as a tool for scorn and ridicule, and "fops, pedants, and bigots" were among its targets.

19. E

Here is an Inference question asking you to apply a term—in this case, "satire"—defined in the passage. According to the passage, satire is both an "oblique" (in other words, indirect) way of suggesting the need for social change, and a "baser" method of personal attack and vilification. **(E)** satisfies the latter part of this definition, as its target is a person. It also brings in the notion of using an indirect method, although this does not seem to be requisite in a work satirizing a person. The last sentence of paragraph 1 also supports this choice; a list of "pedants" (scholars or teachers) might well have included an academic. All the other choices fail to make the proper distinctions. (A), (B), and (C) emphasize the idea of social reform, without the equally important qualification of making their points indirectly. They are earnest, direct approaches and hence not satirical. (D) is a genre that could be used for satire, but is not necessarily satirical in nature.

20. A

This Inference question asks you for author's position on Johnson's criticism. Research the author's rebuttal to Johnson's critique in the final paragraph. Johnson criticizes the *subject matter* of Pope's mock epic: he thinks it too "common." The sentence following the quote offers the author's disagreement with this assessment (signaled with the key word "yet"). The author claims that Pope used both the triviality of his subject and his mock serious treatment of it to make a social comment on the "excesses of romantic etiquette." The implication is that Johnson ignored the uses Pope made of his subject matter in poetry. Alternatively, one can write poetry about common life. Either way, **(A)** correctly makes the point that Johnson presupposes a narrow definition of the medium.

(B) is untrue; the passage characterizes Johnson's critique as addressing the subject matter, not the style, of Pope's satiric poem.

(C) and (E) are unsupported in the passage. Nowhere does the author suggest that Johnson misunderstood Pope's intention, or suggest that Johnson's views were particularly old-fashioned.

(D) distorts Johnson's meaning. If anything, his criticism reveals a contempt for ordinary life, not an idea of its "dignity."

21. D

This is another Inference question. If, as the first sentence says, satire had a "dominating position between 1660 and 1730 that it had not had before," then before 1660 it did not have a dominant position; (**D**) states this idea in different words.

The other choices pick up on details about post-1660 satire scattered throughout the passage—its use of topical and personal as well as political and religious topics, in (A), Pope's satire of romantic conventions and the conventions of epic or heroic poetry, (B) and (C), and satire as an oblique weapon of reform, (E). But the passage provides no basis for a pre- versus post-1660 comparison on any of these points. (E) is worth noting as a slightly cumbersome, plausible-sounding statement that has no basis in the passage; the GRE uses this type of answer choice often. The opening generalization in (E) is questionable, and the passage never suggests that writers used satire for political expression because more open expression was forbidden.

Mendelssohn Passage

Par 1: What happened to Mendelssohn's reputation just after he died: people liked Wagner better.

Par 2: How later schools of thought liked him even less.

Par 3: Author argues that these judgments are too harsh; offers examples to show that Mendelssohn's work has value.

Topic and Scope: Mendelssohn, especially Mendelssohn's reputation after his death.

Purpose: To argue that Mendelssohn's reputation has been unfairly disparaged by critics and to rebut the critics by offering examples of Mendelssohn's talent

22. B

This is an Inference question asking you to describe the author's tone or point of view on a subject mentioned in the passage, in this case, Mendelssohn's critics. In the first sentence of the last paragraph, the author says Mendelssohn's critics have "moved far too illiberally"; that is, they have gone too far in their criticism of Mendelssohn. That makes (**B**), "ungenerous," the best fit.

If you did not know the definition of "illiberally," you could eliminate the other choices using the tone and context of the passage. The author likes Mendelssohn, so it follows

that he will dislike Mendelssohn's critics. That eliminates (C). (A) and (D) refer to critics as *ill-bred* and *cowardly*. These judgments are entirely too strong for the tone of the passage (and for the GRE in general). Finally, (E) makes claims about the critics that the author never mentions. The author may not agree with their judgments, but he never questions their sincerity or motives.

23. D

This is a Logic question asking *why* is the author mentions the later composers' admirers. The first two paragraphs outline the reasons that those who praised Wagner and Schoenberg disliked Mendelssohn. The author holds that these admirers "moved far too illiberally to certain conclusions"; that is, they were too harsh and unforgiving in their disparagement of Mendelssohn. This matches choice (**D**).

(A) misrepresents the author's purpose. The passage is about Mendelssohn, and has nothing to do with comparing the tastes of Wagner's proponents with those of Schoenberg's admirers.

(B) actually goes against what the author says: he states in the first paragraph that some who found Mendelssohn too restrained were enamored with Wagner.

(C) goes too far. This contention is too general for a tightly focused passage such as this.

(E) is tricky, but although the author mentions the other composer's styles, he does not do so in order to contrast them directly with Mendelssohn.

24. B, C

For this all-that-apply Inference question, take the answers one at a time.

(A) reflects the views of Mendelssohn's detractors, not of the author, who likes Mendelssohn. Discard this answer.

The views the author expresses in the third paragraph make it likely that he would agree with (**B**). If Mendelssohn's music "shows the imprint of an original mind," it should be innovative. If it inspired Turner to paint, it was influential.

(**C**) is in line with the author's main idea; the author argues that the later critics of Mendelssohn have treated him too harshly.

25. B

Here is another Logic question. The author defends Mendelssohn in paragraph 3. He does this by offering a number of examples that illustrate how good Mendelssohn actually was. This equates most closely with **(B)**.

(A) is out—the post-Wagnerian anti-Romantic critics didn't like Mendelssohn (paragraph 2).

(C) is also incorrect; the author does not seem to regard any of the other composers mentioned as greater than Mendelssohn.

(D) is way off; the author does not take this line of attack anywhere in the passage.

(E) is also wrong; nowhere does the author does compare Mendelssohn to Wagner in order to argue for Mendelssohn's superiority.

Desert Plants Passage

Par 1: How desert plants have evolved traits that help them survive, with illustrations of these traits.

Par 2: More adaptations.

Topic and Scope: Desert plants, specifically the adaptations that help them survive.

Purpose: To list and describe desert plant adaptations.

26. A, B, C

Research paragraph 2—the section of the passage about spines and thorns—to evaluate the choices in this Detail question. Take the answers one at a time.

(A) is true. Spines and thorns, identified in paragraph 2 as modified leaves and branches, are among the adaptations that plants have developed to help them cope with a desert environment.

(B) is true. The passage's final sentence states that spines and thorns help minimize water loss.

(C) is true. The third sentence of the paragraph 2 says that most of a desert plant's food is produced in its stem, not in its leaves, so spines and thorns have little or nothing to do with food production.

27. A, B

This is another Detail question. Reread the section on the functioning of guard cells, mentioned at the end of paragraph 1. This sentence discusses two closely related plant features: the stomata and the guard cells. You first read that daytime closing of the stomata is an adaptation to minimize daytime water loss. The second half of the sentence implies that guard cells control this opening and closing of the stomata. Now, evaluate the answers one at a time.

(A) is true. The guard cells force the stomata to close during the day, to minimize water loss, and they later cause the stomata to open when conditions for gas exchange between the plant and its environment are more favorable. they must facilitate gas and water exchange.

(B) is suggested by the reference to guard cells forcing the stomata to close during the day.

(C) is unjustified. Nothing in the passage links the functioning of guard cells to sudden downpours.

28. C

In this Inference question, the stem asks you to identify weather-related conditions especially beneficial to plants with shallow root systems. Shallow root systems are mentioned in the second sentence, which says that these specially adapted roots allow desert plants to take advantage of heavy, irregular flows of water. The only choice that comes close to this is **(C)**, a flash flood.

(A) and (B) are impossible; drought is an absence of water, and windstorms don't necessarily involve water at all.

(D) won't work because a light rain doesn't match the idea of a large, sudden quantity of water.

(E) is out, since the passage doesn't mention snow, and this choice doesn't characterize winter snowfall as large or sudden.

29. B

This is an Inference question. The second paragraph contains several examples of structures that in desert plants perform different functions than those they normally perform in plants in other environments. Spines and thorns in desert plants are leaves and branches, modified to reduce water loss. And as a result of their lack of normal leaves, most desert plants produce their food in their green, fleshy stems. This fits well with **(B)**.

There's no information to support (A), (D), or (E) in the passage.

(C) is out. While the passage does indicate that a small leaf surface area is a critical factor for desert plants, nothing suggests that leaf surface area (large or small) is less important for plants in other environments.

Reasoning Explanations

1. B

The words "most undermines" in the question stem indicate that this is a Weaken question. Find the conclusion and evidence in the stimulus. Then, predict the correct answer: one that makes the adviser's conclusion less likely to follow from his evidence.

This is one optimistic adviser! The logic (conclusion) keyword "clearly" indicates the conclusion: investing in Tolespinia's stock market "will guarantee significant returns." If something sounds too good to be true, it probably is. Consider the adviser's evidence. The stimulus opens with some background information about the country's currency, but the adviser's key evidence is a magazine's annual report: "the total value of the [stock portfolio's of the nation's top companies] has increased from $97.5 million (US dollars) ten years ago to well over $200 million in this year's issue." That sounds promising, but remember that your task is to weaken the connection from the evidence to the conclusion. Consider the kinds of facts that would make this report weaker evidence for future returns on investment? The adviser acknowledges some people's concerns about the Tolespinian economy, but maintains his prediction, so it seems unlikely that the correct answer will simply imply that the market is about to tank (though such an answer is technically possible). It's more likely that the right answer will undermine the evidence's relevance or representativeness. Any fact that makes change in total

value of the portfolios suspect will weaken the adviser's argument. The passage says the report covers the "highest-grossing companies in the country," but are these the same companies? Has one company shown outsize growth while the others have declined? Is the same number of companies included in each year's report? An answer suggesting that any of these questions could be answered with a "yes" would cast doubt on the adviser's conclusion.

(B) is correct: if the report used to include only twenty companies and now includes fifty, it's unreasonable to conclude that a higher total indicates improved financial health. Fifty weak and declining companies may well have a greater combined portfolio than twenty healthy companies. In (A), "some economists" predict that the economy will improve in the coming year. If anything, this would strengthen the adviser's conclusion. (C), which discusses the financial situation in a neighboring country, is irrelevant. (D) focuses on an irrelevant detail, the exchange rate. (E) is too vague: you don't know if the country's parliament will pass the legislation in question nor its impact (positive or negative) on the market if they do.

2. D

This is a Strengthen question, as indicated by "most strengthens" in the question stem. Find the conclusion and evidence in the stimulus. The logic (conclusion) keyword phrase "for this reason" points to the author's conclusion: a translation is actually an original work. This conclusion paraphrases the first sentence of the stimulus: translators are more like authors or artists than transcriptionists. The evidence offers the author's support for such an unconventional claim: whether poetry or prose, translation takes "interpretation" and "adaptation." Additionally, if a translator translated a translation back into the language in which it was written, it "would little resemble" the primary work. That sentence is difficult to parse, so consider an example: if a translator took a translation of *The Odyssey* and translated it back into Ancient Greek, the result would not look like Homer's original. The right answer must strengthen the author's claim that translations should be considered original works in light of the evidence that translations require "interpretation" and "adaptation" and that a reverse-translation would not resemble the original text.

(D) is correct: if "many" words do not have exact equivalents in other languages, the translator's job requires deciding which word to use. This supports the author's claim that translators are not merely transcribing the text. (A) is incorrect because it describes what is needed for an original work but fails to mention translations. (B) is irrelevant to the author's conclusion because it discusses playwrights but makes no mention of translation. (C) discusses the time frame necessary for "most writers and translators" to build their skills and achieve success, but commercial success has no impact on the author's conclusion. (E) makes an irrelevant distinction between translations that are praised for accuracy and those that are praised for beauty.

3.   B

For a Highlighted Statement question, read the entire passage, taking care to note the role that each sentence plays in the larger context. For this passage, the first sentence makes a claim about the growing importance that determining traffic flow will have for civil engineers who plan cities. The next three sentences offer evidence to demonstrate why the study of traffic flow is so critical and why civil engineers need to be forward thinking in their traffic plans. The final sentence in paragraph one, which is also the first highlighted statement, restates the conclusion by incorporating the supporting evidence.

In paragraph 2, the author spends the first two sentences describing the sophisticated tools that civil engineers use to track traffic patterns. The third sentence recommends that civil engineers not lose sight of how low-tech solutions can solve traffic challenges. This statement acts as a second main conclusion, which is subsequently supported by the next two sentences. The fourth sentence offers a concrete example of a low-tech solution that is further explained by the fifth and final sentence. This last sentence, which is the second highlighted statement in the passage, describes a cause-and-effect relationship between the use of roundabouts and the reduction of traffic accidents.

The roles of the two statements are best described by (B), which accurately describes the first highlighted statement as a paraphrase of the author's first main conclusion and the second highlighted statement as a cause-and-effect relationship used to support the second main conclusion. Eliminate (A), as the author does not introduce any counterpoints into the discussion of the first conclusion

and the second paragraph offers a second main conclusion rather than a subsidiary conclusion that merely supports the first. (C) inaccurately characterizes the first statement as background information and fails to recognize that the author has two separate conclusions. (D) is half right in that the first statement does describe the author's first main conclusion, but it inaccurately describes the second statement as introducing an opposing viewpoint. (E) is also half correct in that the second statement supports the author's second main conclusion, but it wrongly describes the first statement as a premise rather than a restatement of the first main conclusion.

4.   B

In this Weaken question, the author's conclusion advocates for switching the bar's beer menu from predominantly corporate brands to solely artisanal microbrews. The evidence supporting this proposed switch is the fervor with which artisanal beer drinkers hold their preference. However, whether that fanatic loyalty to microbrews makes any difference in serving this bar's patrons depends on the relative proportion of microbrew fans among its client base. If the customers are predominantly microbrew drinkers, then the switch makes sense. If, on the other hand, this bar's customers are predominantly brand-name beer drinkers, the proposed switch would take away most patrons' favorite beers. Choice (B) is correct because, if it is true, then it is somewhat more likely that the bar's patrons prefer mass-produced brands. This choice does not disprove the author's conclusion, but it makes her conclusion less likely to follow from the evidence she offers. Choice (A) is incorrect because a small number of potential counterexamples does not weaken a general conclusion based on average or relative preference. Choice (C) neither weakens nor strengthens because it involves people who don't care which choice the bar makes. Choice (D) yields no identifiable inclination towards either option. Choice (E) is interesting, but be careful not to read too much into it. The fact that microbrews' popularity has plateaued suggests that the bar is unlikely to see a higher percentage of microbrew fans in the future, but tells you nothing about the percentage of current patrons who will prefer these independent brands.

5. C

The author concludes that the future health of the economy depends on more babies being born to grow up into productive young workers. The supporting premise is that the declining birth rate means fewer young workers will be required to support more retirees, thus straining the economy and the national budget. The second sentence compounds the problem. It states that more people are working later in life rather than retiring, and notes that this situation, along with increased mechanization of labor, makes it tougher for young and prime-age workers to find employment. Indeed, in a couple of decades, the author predicts that unemployment will necessitate a universal basic income.

The contrast phrase "on the other hand" signals that author recognizes a conflict between the two premises—we need more young workers but there may be fewer jobs for them. Nonetheless, the author sides with increasing the birth rate in his conclusion. The author must assume that the benefits of additional young workers outweigh the potential burdens of providing for a larger population. This is choice (**C**).

Choice (A) is incorrect because the author states that young adult employment *is* a problem that will require drastic measures in the form of a universal basic income. (The author assumes that this problem is outweighed by the even bigger problem of needing to care for retirees.)

(B) is extreme; the argument does not require that older workers holding on to their jobs longer is always or inherently bad for the economy. (D) and (E) both digress substantially from the focus of the conclusion, which a necessary assumption cannot do. In (D), "ecological sustainability" is irrelevant because the conclusion is limited to the health of the economy. Choice (E) offers a reasonable conjecture but one not related to the author's conclusion that more young workers are needed.

6. C

This Weaken question features a twist on causal arguments. The author concludes that the arrival of humans on the island caused the decline of a bird species, *but* attributes the decline to a causal mechanism *other than* the small mammals brought by the humans. This is unusual, says the author, because small mammals brought by humans are known to have decimated bird populations on other

islands. The evidence supports the author's conclusion by noting that the nesting habits of the birds in question protect them from predation by small mammals.

To weaken this argument, you need a fact suggesting either 1) the arrival of humans was altogether unrelated to the bird's decline in population, or 2) that the small mammals brought by humans are to blame for the bird's demise despite the fact that the small mammals *did not eat* the birds. The second type of answer is more likely. Here, choice (**C**) is correct because it indicates that the small mammals brought by the humans caused the plight of the bird, not through predation, but by bringing disease-carrying parasites to the island. (A) is consistent with the author's assertion that small mammals were not involved in the bird's demise, and thus, strengthens the argument. (B) tells you that the bird did not succumb to pressure from competing bird species; this strengthens the argument by eliminating a potential non-human cause of the bird's decline. (D) also strengthens the author's conclusion by identifying a way other than the translocation of small mammals—in this case, pesticide use—that human arrival on the island could have caused the bird's decline. (E) is yet another strengthener; it rules out a cause other than the arrival of humans on the island.

7. D

Your task in this Inference question is to select the conclusion that must be true given the evidence in the passage. Don't argue with the stated facts; merely sum them up and predict the answer. The first sentence points out that while few people can routinely make others laugh, everybody believes that he or she has a sense of humor. The conclusion will explain how these two seemingly contradictory facts can both be true, and since the author concedes that most people are not simply deluding themselves, it must be the case that people define having a sense of humor as something other than the ability to consistently make others laugh. (**D**) does and is therefore the correct answer.

(A) might be true but doesn't have to be. People can define "sense of humor" however they need to in order to earnestly believe that they possess it.

(B) is off topic. It doesn't matter whether most people believe, as the author of the passage does, that a sense of humor is a uniquely human characteristic. What matters is how people decide whether they and others have a sense of humor. (C) might be true but it does follow definitely from the evidence. Consider 100 people, two of whom are utterly humorless. The other 98 could all agree on one definition of "sense of humor" by which they have a sense of humor and the two humorless people do not, and the two humorless people could do likewise. In this case, "most people" do in fact agree on what a sense of humor is.

(E) is superficially appealing but is not necessarily true for the same reasons as choice (C). It is possible that everybody applies the same definition of "sense of humor" to others as to themselves, so long as that definition entails something other than making people laugh.

8. B

Because this is a Strengthen question, begin by identifying the conclusion and evidence. The conclusion is that fixing the problem of unappetizing and unhealthy lunches requires increasing the food budget and, in turn, taxes. The evidence is that the current chefs don't have enough money to make the meals they want to make, and that hiring better chefs would strain the budget even further. This argument has two glaring holes:

1) It assumes that the current chefs are competent. It's possible that even if they had all the money in the world, the current chefs still might not be able to deliver tasty, healthy lunches.

2) It assumes that better chefs would not be able to compensate for a smaller budget. It's possible that superior chefs could deliver better tasting, healthier meals for even less money.

The correct answer will strengthen the argument by plugging one of these holes, that is, by helping to rule out one of those possibilities. Choice (**B**) rules out the first possibility and is therefore the correct answer. By assuring us that the present chefs could indeed make better lunches if they had more money, choice (B) strengthens the argument.

(A) is off-topic. Knowing that taxpayers have been willing to vote for small tax increases in the past doesn't affect the author's conclusion that yet another tax increase—and you're not told whether this one will be small or large—is required to improve the quality of the school's lunches.

(C) weakens the argument instead of strengthening it. The argument rejects the solution of hiring better chefs, yet this choice makes that solution viable.

(D), like (C), implies that hiring better chefs is a viable approach to solving the lunch problem, contrary to what the argument asserts.

(E) also weakens the argument. If there aren't any good ingredients to be had, then having more money to buy better ingredients wouldn't actually do anything. In that case, the only way for the school to improve its lunches would be to hire better chefs.

9. E

This is a Weaken question, so begin by taking the argument apart. The first sentence states a premise: most entry-level positions available at major corporations require that applicants hold an undergraduate degree. The speaker then concludes that this requirement will make it difficult for those who do not have an undergraduate degree to find work after high school. The speaker must assume that a significant number of the entry-level positions available to secondary school graduates are those at major corporations, or conversely, that entry-level positions outside of major corporations are limited. To weaken this argument, you must find the answer choice that, if true, undermines this assumption's credibility.

The answer that weakens the argument is (**E**), which introduces the possibility that secondary school graduates would have many other entry-level job opportunities besides those offered at major corporations. While it is unclear if these other jobs would have the same requirements, it undermines the speaker's assumption that positions at major corporations are the primary option. Because it fails to address *entry-level* jobs, (A) is irrelevant; if anything, it appears to strengthen the argument by indicating that even an undergraduate degree might not be sufficient for many positions within major corporations. (B) states that many of those who do not complete an undergraduate degree train for skilled work, but it neither weakens nor strengthens the argument because it says nothing about these people's job prospects. (C) states corporations' preferred undergraduate majors, but that's irrelevant to a conclusion about the job prospects of those who lack undergraduate degrees altogether. (D) tells you that most of the skills people *use* in entry-level jobs are those they learned in high school; even if that's true, it doesn't change the fact that large corporations require a bachelor's degree to even consider an application, so (D) has no impact on the job prospects of those who lack a college degree.

10. B

This is a Highlighted Statement question. The most efficient approach here is to break down the argument, determine the role of one statement, and eliminate any answer choices that do not match. Then, determine the role of the other statement and repeat the process of elimination. This author's argument starts with fossils, which have yielded "most" of what you know about dinosaurs. The contrast keyword "but" introduces a problem: fossils provide an "incomplete understanding." That sounds like a limitation of studying fossils, and indeed, the author follows by explaining why fossils leave an incomplete record. Then, the author introduces a new discovery that changes everything ("revolutionized"); this is the author's conclusion. The logic (evidence) keyword "because" explains why the discovery is significant. The final two sentences of this stimulus further explain the implications of the new discovery and reiterate the author's conclusion.

A strong prediction for the correct answer's description of the first highlighted statement is "a limitation of studying fossils." Compare that to the answer choices and eliminate any that do not match: (A), "judgment made by the author about a given explanation," is awkward, but might match if the "given explanation" is that fossils yield a complete understanding of the past. Keep this choice to evaluate its second statement. (B), "describes a limitation of a certain mode of inquiry," matches, so keep it as well. (C), "sums up the final conclusion of the argument," is incorrect: the author's conclusion comes later in the argument. Eliminate (C). (D), "describes the reason for the author's objection to a given line of inquiry," could match if, as in (A), the "given line of inquiry" is that fossils yield a complete understanding. Keep (D). (E), "expresses a conclusion that runs counter to the author's conclusion," is incorrect: the author concludes that the new specimen changes everything, so the first highlighted claim is consistent with the author's conclusion.

After eliminating (C) and (E), predict for the second statement and eliminate any of the remaining choices that do not match. The second highlighted statement is evidence for the author's conclusion. (A), "offers evidence for that judgment," is incorrect because the second highlighted statement is distinct from the first. Eliminate (A). (B), "offers an explanation for the author's conclusion," matches. **(B)** is correct. (D), "states a contradictory conclusion," is incorrect because the second highlighted statement is not a conclusion, contradictory or otherwise.

Issue Essay Explanations

Issue Essay #1: Sample Response

The claim presented here is that all college students, regardless of their majors, should be obligated to take "several" courses in the sciences, as if science were a useful afterthought to other fields of study. This claim is predicated on the belief that such courses would be more useful than "additional" courses in the students' own majors. Such a well-intentioned line of reasoning does not go far enough, since courses in science (defined strictly to include the hard sciences such as biology, chemistry, and physics) should not merely serve as supplements to the social sciences and humanities. Rather, such courses should help form the pedagogical bedrock from which any college program is built.

Consider that one of the core goals of a college education is to challenge and refine students' understanding of the world, and that the baseline of science is a ravenous commitment to the truth. A claim in astrophysics can only be taken seriously if it is falsifiable—that is, if further observation or experimentation could prove it wrong. Thus, an astrophysicist making a claim about the formation of a nebula must always be ready to have her work challenged or overturned during the peer review process, and should even appreciate that being wrong is a necessary and honorable part of science. In the same way, a college student, tasked with expanding her worldview and becoming a fuller and better-informed member of society, must consider her views subject to challenge before she can take advantage of the benefits of a college education. This makes a grounding in the sciences invaluable and necessary.

Moreover, science courses can easily be inserted into a college curriculum without entailing the sacrifice of in-major classes. Columbia University in New York City, for instance, already has a science requirement as part of its "Core Curriculum," a group of courses all Columbia undergraduates must take. Many students take "Core" courses before they even decide on a major, so it would be inaccurate to claim that the science requirement robs them of in-major opportunities. Further, any school that requires science courses is not necessarily limiting access to in-major courses, since students may instead forego electives or simply complete more credits overall.

Despite the guidance of schools such as Columbia, some students pursuing fields unrelated to science might consider taking science courses at the post-secondary level an unnecessary and impractical burden; after all, college courses can be expensive and time-consuming. This line of analysis might be more persuasive if "fields unrelated to science" existed. For example, consider the scope of a phenomenon such as climate change. On its face, climate change is a purely scientific issue, since our understanding of it is driven by scientific consensus. Further, fossil fuel technology has helped cause the current crisis, and alternative energy technology may yet help to mitigate it. However, the magnitude of this issue has implications that cut across disciplines. Historians, economists, and journalists all require a working understanding of how climate impacts public policy. Architects must learn to prepare for a future of extreme weather events. Even artists can better reflect the times they live in with a fuller appreciation of the relationship between humanity and its environment. Writer Cormac McCarthy, for instance, who penned the apocalyptic and ecologically-themed novel The Road, is also a fellow at the Santa Fe Institute, a scientific research center. To forego science in a college curriculum cannot be called practical, no matter one's prospective career, since the practical concerns of the world are based in science.

Ultimately, it is not unduly onerous to ask that individuals who aspire to complete a post-secondary degree should study how the universe functions and how to learn about that universe. Such requirements have already been successfully integrated into college curricula. Students who take science at the college level will be more honest, more open, and better prepared for the society that awaits them.

This essay takes a clear but nuanced position on the issue. While the writer agrees broadly with the claim and reason presented in the prompt, she also indicates how it fails to fully capture her stance: *"Such a well-intentioned line of reasoning does not go far enough, since courses in science [...] should not merely serve as supplements to the social sciences and humanities..."* She adds depth to the essay by arguing that science courses are foundational to a college education, rather than merely being generically good.

The essay also demonstrates the utility of including specific, relevant examples in your Issue essay. Paragraph 4 discusses Cormac McCarthy rather than simply referring to writers or artists in the abstract. Similarly, paragraph 3 brings up Columbia specifically, rather than only schools in general. The writer does not get bogged down providing unnecessary detail on these topics, however, and all of the information she provides is relevant to the points she makes.

The organization is easy to follow, with a clear thesis in the introduction and a single topic for each body paragraph. Transitional phrases help make it clear how one idea leads into the next, as in the start of paragraph 4 ("Despite the guidance of schools like Columbia, some students pursuing fields unrelated to science might feel taking science courses at the post-secondary level to be an unnecessary and impractical burden"). The conclusion, though relatively brief, manages to sum up the rest of the essay and reinforce the thesis.

The essay's language is purposeful, with a variety of sentence structures and lengths, as well as varied word choice. For all of the above reasons, the essay earns a score of **6**.

Issue Essay #2: Sample Response

There is no better way to learn about a society than to analyze and appreciate the great artwork it produces. In some cases, including ancient societies, art may be the only available means of understanding a people. When artists create, they not only reveal their personal beliefs and aspirations, but also provide an important lens through which to view the society they came from. Finally, art provides a unique means with which to compare populations living in different places or in different parts of the world.

From a historical perspective, the only way to learn about an ancient society may be through its art. This is because when a society changes or dies out, it is often the art that remains. The culture of the ancient Egyptians is long gone. However, we still have the Pyramids of Giza, one of the wonders of the ancient world. The way these massive burial tombs where built tells us that the Egyptians had a strong grasp of geometry and engineering, and that they used slave labor. Thus, through the study of art, we gain insight on many facets of a society (such as mathematical knowledge and social organization) that we couldn't know anything about otherwise. Extinct societies that failed to leave art behind, just like extinct species that failed to leave fossils behind, will remain mysterious forever.

Secondly, the purpose of art is to share our ideas and values, so great works of art tell us what societies care about the most. Returning to the pyramids example, the pyramids were enormous burial tombs built for pharaohs. This tells us that the pharaohs were obsessed with dying and maintained certain beliefs about the afterlife. Moreover, Egyptian society was organized around catering to this belief, to the point that laborers were forced to drag multi-ton rocks into place for the sake of giant monuments. This phenomenon of art reflecting societal desires and beliefs also holds true for more modern examples. For instance, zombie films such as George Romero's "Night of the Living Dead" depict average people reanimated as mindless walking corpses. When these films became popular in America, Americans were grappling with how to handle their own mortality, just like the ancient pharaohs did. This consideration of cross-cultural comparison demonstrates that art is the best way to comprehend societies, because art shows us what concerns societies share, not merely what separates them.

A counterargument to the claim that society is best understood through art would be that, compared to other means of learning about populations, art can be misleading. For example, if you took epic poems from ancient Greece like the Odyssey at face value, you would have to believe that the god Poseidon controlled the ocean and punished the unlucky sailors who angered him. However, this consideration ignores the fact that art it not interpreted in a vacuum. When we read the Odyssey, we do not interpret it as a historical record and conclude that Poseidon was a real figure who stopped Odysseus from getting home. We are able to appreciate that the Odyssey is a work of art, interpret it by those standards, and analyze why and how the Greeks would have told a fanciful story like this.

In conclusion, the finest way to learn about a people is to study their great works. Art reveals how societies are organized, what values they possess, and how they understand the world. Art also provides a point of comparison that shows what different societies share in common. There is no limit to what a connoisseur can learn about a society from great works of art.

This is a solid essay: it stays on topic, is organized clearly using the Kaplan template, and features a variety of sentence structures. Further, the writer grounds his major points in specific examples from history, myth, and popular culture. However, as the sample essay for the previous prompt deftly illustrates, the transitions from one paragraph to the next could be tighter. Further, the analysis of the issue here is shallower and less compelling. For instance, the fourth paragraph notes that "A counterargument to the claim that society is best understood through art would be that, compared to other means of learning about populations, art can be misleading…." The essay would be deeper if the writer actually indicated what these "other means" were, and compared art to them. Also, some of the essay's phrasing is inelegant or repetitive: "returning to **the pyramids** example, **the pyramids** were…" There are a few minor spelling and typographical errors present, but these do not detract from the essay's readability. The essay's word choice is reasonably varied. For these reasons, the essay earns a score of **5**.

Argument Essay Explanations

Essay 1: Sample Essay Response

In this argument, the marketing department for a railway company concludes that a new ecologically-themed advertising initiative will bring back passengers and bolster the company's bottom line. To support this conclusion, the writer cites a survey of commuters who indicated a high level of concern with the potential ecological costs of traveling by automobile. While it is conceivable that this recommendation could have the impact that the writer predicts, several critical questions must be answered before the argument can be evaluated.

First, are the survey results representative of all of the railway's passengers? The writer indicates that "over 90%" of those surveyed in "major cities where [the railway] operates" were concerned with the ecological impact of traveling by car. However, the memorandum fails to specify what proportion of the railway's passengers live in the cities in question. It is possible that the railway primarily services passengers in smaller towns and rural areas, and that those passengers were not considered in the survey. If those passengers are uninterested in the new green message, this would indicate that the recommendation may not have the marketer's intended effect.

Even if we grant that the survey cast an adequately wide net, this does not prove that the respondents actually feel the need to change their commuting practices. By linking consumer anxiety over automobile pollution to this initiative, the writer tacitly assumes that the commuters are worried about the environmental impact of their own travel. However, what if these commuters are already getting to work via relatively eco-friendly means, such as bicycle, carpool, or bus? In this case, greater awareness of the ecological benefits of rail travel would not inspire them to change their daily routines. If these consumers are in fact feeling guilty over their lengthy drives to work, however, we can view the argument more favorably.

Once we have determined whether consumers are concerned about their current commuting solutions, we must ask whether the advertising campaign in question would be adequately persuasive. Modern consumers are bombarded with advertisements and may interpret the campaign as a cheap gimmick rather than a legitimate effort to help the environment. Before evaluating the argument, we must ask a major question: how does the marketing department plan to overcome this natural cynicism?

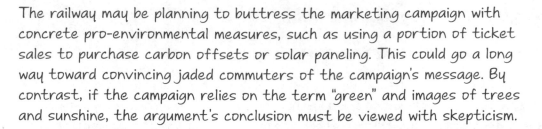

The railway may be planning to buttress the marketing campaign with concrete pro-environmental measures, such as using a portion of ticket sales to purchase carbon offsets or solar paneling. This could go a long way toward convincing jaded commuters of the campaign's message. By contrast, if the campaign relies on the term "green" and images of trees and sunshine, the argument's conclusion must be viewed with skepticism.

Lastly, we must step back from the specifics of the campaign to question the writer's larger strategy of increased profits through increased ridership. Worryingly, the writer cites decreased ridership in recent years. It may be the case that the railway has larger problems (such as poor customer service, transit delays, or safety concerns) that cannot be fixed with an advertising campaign. It may also be true that many commuters have destinations that are not currently serviced by the railway. In this case, the railway would need to expand operations before worrying about advertisements; even the best-designed marketing campaign cannot convince a commuter to board a train if it cannot take him where he wants to go. Perhaps increased ridership is not the best means to attain greater profits, either. What if taking on more passengers entails greater costs from running trains more frequently? Or, what if using the trains for freight would be more profitable than focusing on a shrinking commuter market? These possibilities must be ruled out before the argument that the railway should focus on attracting more passengers can be considered seriously.

The writer of this memorandum must answer larger questions before concluding that a marketing campaign is the optimal solution for the railway's woes. If the writer could provide another survey with assurances of greater demographical representativeness, as well as commuter feedback indicating a willingness to switch to rail-based travel, the argument would be considerably strengthened. Absent such evidence, however, we cannot yet accept that this campaign will best serve this company.

This author remains on topic throughout the essay, demonstrating attention to the specific direction to discuss "the questions that would need to be asked in order to evaluate the recommendation." Further, whenever posing a question, he explains why this question is important to the argument overall: "However, what if these commuters are already getting to work via relatively eco-friendly means, such as bicycle, carpool, or bus? In this case, greater awareness of the ecological benefits of rail travel would not inspire them to change their daily routines. If these consumers are in fact feeling guilty over their lengthy drives to work, however, we can view the argument more favorably." This ensures that the reader will always understand the significance of his points.

The essay's analysis focuses on important assumptions, citing the specifics of the argument to help demonstrate why it is incomplete: "The [argument] indicates that 'over 90%' of those surveyed in 'major cities where [the railway] operates' were concerned with the ecological impact of traveling by car. However, the memorandum fails to specify what proportion of the railway's passengers live in the cities in question." Further, the author gives the essay depth by analyzing the argument at different levels. Not only do they question whether the survey results indicate a population willing to commute by rail, but they also question whether a population willing to commute by rail would be convinced by the proposed advertising campaign.

The organization of the essay follows the Kaplan template: the introduction paraphrases the argument and provides a thesis statement, subsequent paragraphs focus on specific questions/assumptions, and the end of the essay briefly explains how additional evidence could strengthen the argument. Further, transitional phrases throughout the essay make it clear how one idea leads to the next: "Even if we grant that the survey cast an adequately wide net, this does not prove that the respondents actually feel the need to change their commuting practices."

The writer uses a variety of sentence lengths, and his word choice is appropriate and varied throughout the essay. For these reasons, the essay earns a score of **6**.

Essay 2: Sample Essay Response

An aquarium director writes that live shrimp are more nutritious for sparrowfish than "dry flakes." The evidence for this is that the aquarium gave dry flakes to one tank of fish and live shrimp to other fish. The fish that got shrimp lived longer and became bigger then the fish that got the flakes. Therefore they think the shrimp must be more nutritious.

There are other explanations that could rival the one in the argument. For example, it's more likely that fish get more exercize from chasing the brine shrimp around the tank then from eating flakes. This way, you can see that maybe the brine shrimp aren't more nutritious: they just help keep the fish healthy, because they're hard to catch. This is a good explanation for why the fish eating shrimp might have lived longer. Also, the fish in the tank that got shrimp could have been healthier than the other fish in the first place. In that case, the new diet might not have anything to do with the life span of the fish.

The fish that got the live shrimp grew larger than the fish that were fed flakes. The writer claims this is because shrimp are more nutritious. A good rival explanation for this fact is that maybe the shrimp have more calories but are not more nutritious than flakes. These fish might have just gotten more food then the fish getting flakes did. For example, humans can get larger and fatter, but this doesnt mean that their diet is nutritous. It might just mean they are eating a lot of fatty foods. In just that way, the fish eating shrimp might have gotten larger on a diet with poor nutrition. This shows how a different explanation can account for the facts in the argument.

All in all, it probably isn't true that live shrimp are more nutritious then flakes. The writer didn't consider other possible explanations when he made this argument. Maybe the fish got more exercize when they ate the shrimp, or maybe the shrimp was more fattetening but not better for the fish. If one of these explanations is true, then the shrimp are not better for the fish.

This is a classic "overlooked possibilities" prompt. The argument writer has taken a few pieces of evidence—namely, the shrimp-fed fish living longer and growing larger than the flake-fed fish—and concluded that "live brine shrimp meet the nutritional requirements of sparrowfish better than dry flakes do." The prompt requires you to describe "one or more explanations that could challenge the provided explanation." In other words, you must explain how the evidence provided could be used in a way that would not support the argument writer's conclusion.

The essay writer here has done a serviceable job of following the prompt directions. She references the evidence from the argument ("The fish that got the live shrimp grew larger than the shrimp that were fed flakes") and uses it to demonstrate that alternative conclusions are possible ("the fish eating shrimp might have gotten larger on a diet with poor nutrition"). Several other factors, however, hold the essay back. While the essay roughly follows the template, it lacks transitional phrases, and the progression of ideas in the supporting paragraphs is haphazard. In particular, paragraph 2 appears to discuss two separate ideas without explaining how they relate to each other. The second idea is critical but gets buried towards the end of the paragraph: ("the fish in the tank that got shrimp could have been healthier than the other fish in the first place..."). That's a strong alternative explanation for the results of the experiment and deserves deeper discussion. The argument's largest shortcoming is that the aquarium director assumes the fish in the different tanks to have been equally healthy in the first place. So, the essay writer should have given this possibility its own paragraph, fleshed out with examples to illustrate its implications: Perhaps the shrimp-fed tank had cleaner water, better filters, or a more consistent and appropriate temperature, and it was these factors—not the shrimp diet—that led to increased size and longevity for its occupants.

For the most part, this writer sticks to an objective tone, but occasionally, she inappropriately substitutes personal opinion for facts: "All in all, **it probably isn't true** that live shrimp are more nutritious than flakes." While it is reasonable and necessary to note that the argument is incomplete, and that it would need more evidence to be convincing, you should avoid language that seems to take sides against the argument like this.

This essay is generally clear, but it suffers from some repetitive language and a number of misspellings and grammatical errors, such as a persistent confusion of "then" and "than." At times, the prose is wordy, clumsy, or informal. For instance, a phrase like "This way, you can see that maybe…" could be streamlined to "Thus, perhaps…"

Despite its flaws, the essay successfully uncovers possibilities that the argument writer overlooked, earning a score of **4**.

GRE* FORMULA SHEET

Use this sheet to help you remember your math content. Be sure also to make use of the Kaplan Methods and Strategies on the reverse side.

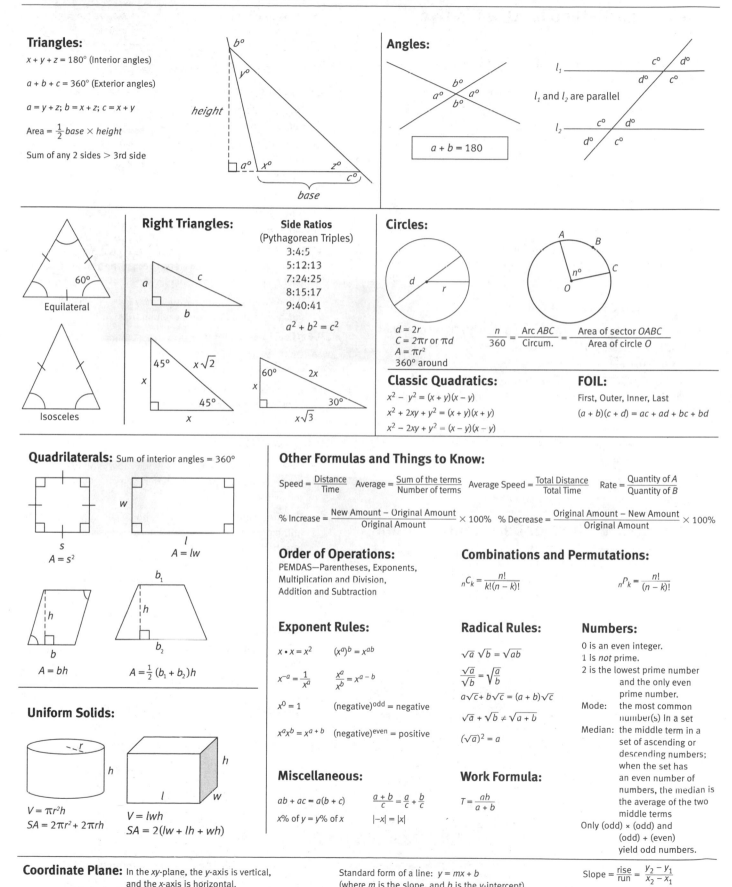

Triangles:

$x + y + z = 180°$ (Interior angles)

$a + b + c = 360°$ (Exterior angles)

$a = y + z; b = x + z; c = x + y$

Area $= \frac{1}{2}$ base $\times$ height

Sum of any 2 sides > 3rd side

Angles:

l_1 and l_2 are parallel

$$a + b = 180$$

Right Triangles:

Side Ratios
(Pythagorean Triples)
3:4:5
5:12:13
7:24:25
8:15:17
9:40:41

$a^2 + b^2 = c^2$

Equilateral

Isosceles

Circles:

$d = 2r$
$C = 2\pi r$ or πd
$A = \pi r^2$
$360°$ around

$$\frac{n}{360} = \frac{\text{Arc } ABC}{\text{Circum.}} = \frac{\text{Area of sector } OABC}{\text{Area of circle } O}$$

Classic Quadratics:

$x^2 - y^2 = (x + y)(x - y)$

$x^2 + 2xy + y^2 = (x + y)(x + y)$

$x^2 - 2xy + y^2 = (x - y)(x - y)$

FOIL:

First, Outer, Inner, Last

$(a + b)(c + d) = ac + ad + bc + bd$

Quadrilaterals: Sum of interior angles = 360°

$A = s^2$

$A = lw$

$A = bh$

$A = \frac{1}{2}(b_1 + b_2)h$

Uniform Solids:

$V = \pi r^2 h$
$SA = 2\pi r^2 + 2\pi rh$

$V = lwh$
$SA = 2(lw + lh + wh)$

Other Formulas and Things to Know:

$\text{Speed} = \frac{\text{Distance}}{\text{Time}}$ $\text{Average} = \frac{\text{Sum of the terms}}{\text{Number of terms}}$ $\text{Average Speed} = \frac{\text{Total Distance}}{\text{Total Time}}$ $\text{Rate} = \frac{\text{Quantity of } A}{\text{Quantity of } B}$

$\text{% Increase} = \frac{\text{New Amount} - \text{Original Amount}}{\text{Original Amount}} \times 100\%$ $\text{% Decrease} = \frac{\text{Original Amount} - \text{New Amount}}{\text{Original Amount}} \times 100\%$

Order of Operations:

PEMDAS—Parentheses, Exponents, Multiplication and Division, Addition and Subtraction

Combinations and Permutations:

$$_nC_k = \frac{n!}{k!(n-k)!}$$ $$_nP_k = \frac{n!}{(n-k)!}$$

Exponent Rules:

$x \cdot x = x^2$ $(x^a)^b = x^{ab}$

$x^{-a} = \frac{1}{x^a}$ $\frac{x^a}{x^b} = x^{a-b}$

$x^0 = 1$ (negative)^{odd} = negative

$x^a x^b = x^{a+b}$ (negative)^{even} = positive

Radical Rules:

$\sqrt{a}\,\sqrt{b} = \sqrt{ab}$

$\frac{\sqrt{a}}{\sqrt{b}} = \sqrt{\frac{a}{b}}$

$a\sqrt{c} + b\sqrt{c} = (a + b)\sqrt{c}$

$\sqrt{a} + \sqrt{b} \neq \sqrt{a + b}$

$(\sqrt{a})^2 = a$

Numbers:

0 is an even integer.

1 is *not* prime.

2 is the lowest prime number and the only even prime number.

Mode: the most common number(s) in a set

Median: the middle term in a set of ascending or descending numbers; when the set has an even number of numbers, the median is the average of the two middle terms

Only (odd) × (odd) and (odd) + (even) yield odd numbers.

Miscellaneous:

$ab + ac = a(b + c)$ $\frac{a + b}{c} = \frac{a}{c} + \frac{b}{c}$

$x\%$ of $y = y\%$ of x $|-x| = |x|$

Work Formula:

$T = \frac{ab}{a + b}$

Coordinate Plane:

In the *xy*-plane, the *y*-axis is vertical, and the *x*-axis is horizontal.

Standard form of a line: $y = mx + b$
(where *m* is the slope, and *b* is the *y*-intercept)

$\text{Slope} = \frac{\text{rise}}{\text{run}} = \frac{y_2 - y_1}{x_2 - x_1}$

GRE QUANTITATIVE STRATEGY SHEET

The Kaplan Method for Quantitative Comparison

STEP 1 Analyze the centered information and quantities.
STEP 2 Approach strategically.
Use one or more of the following approaches:
- Compare, don't calculate.
- Make the quantities look alike.
- Compare piece by piece.
- Do the same thing to both quantities.
- Use Picking Numbers.

The Kaplan Method for Problem Solving

STEP 1 Analyze the question.

Look at what the question is asking, the information given, and the area of math tested. Use the format of the answer choices (variables, numbers, expressions, fractions, etc.) to assess how to approach the question.

STEP 2 Identify the task.

Determine what the question asks — ask yourself, "What does the correct answer represent?"

STEP 3 Approach strategically.

Ask yourself, "How can I use the format of the question and the information it gives me to my advantage?" Use one or more of the following approaches:
- Use a strategy (Picking Numbers or Backsolving).
- Do the straightforward math.
- Guess strategically.

STEP 4 Confirm your answer.

Ask yourself, "Did I answer the question asked?"

The Kaplan Method for Data Interpretation

STEP 1 Analyze the tables and graphs.
- Pay attention to any titles, scales, notes, and keys.

STEP 2 Approach strategically.
- Determine which chart(s) or graph(s) is/are relevant to the question.
- Estimate where possible.
- Make sure you answered the question asked.

Quantitative Comparison Answer Choices

The answer choices on QCs never change, so memorize them to save valuable time on Test Day.

- (A) Quantity A is greater.
- (B) Quantity B is greater.
- (C) The two quantities are equal.
- (D) The relationship cannot be determined from the information given.

Picking Numbers

When Picking Numbers, be sure that the numbers are permissible and manageable:
- **Permissible** numbers follow the rules of the problem.
- **Manageable** numbers are those that are easy to work with in the problem—usually small, whole numbers.

When to Pick Numbers

Variables in the Question Stem
- Most people find it easier to perform calculations with numbers than to perform calculations with variables.
- Variables may be letters (n, x, t, etc.) or unspecified values (e.g., "a factory produces some number of units of a product each month").

Percents in the Answer Choices
- Since percent means "out of one hundred," pick 100 for the unknown value.

Variables in the Answer Choices
- After Picking Numbers, reread the question stem, substituting your number(s) for the variable(s).
- When Picking Numbers with variables in the answer choices, you always need to check each answer choice.

Must Be/Could Be/Cannot Be
- On these questions, you can pick numbers and plug them into every answer choice . . .
- . . . or you can pick different numbers for each answer, trying either to eliminate it or to confirm it.

Backsolving

- Like Picking Numbers, Backsolving allows you to plug numbers into the problem. In this case, the numbers are those in the answer choices.
- Plug in a value from an answer choice and solve the problem arithmetically. If your calculations are consistent with the question stem, then the answer is correct.
- The most efficient way to Backsolve is to plug in either (B) or (D) first. If you need a smaller or larger value to plug into the question, try another answer choice. Backsolving allows you to test, at most, two answer choices to find the correct answer to a standard multiple-choice question.
- For questions that have one or more correct answer, it is possible to use Backsolving if you're not sure how to set up the problem algebraically. Just know that for All-That-Apply questions, you must check *all* answer choices to determine which are correct.

"Which of the following" Questions

On "which of the following" questions with one correct answer, the answer is weighted disproportionately to be either (D) or (E). Work from the bottom up on these questions.

GRE Quantitative Pacing Chart

	Quantitative Comparison	Problem Solving	Data Interpretation
Number of Questions	approximately 7–8	approximately 9–10	approximately 3
Time per Question	1.5 minutes	1.5–2 minutes	2 minutes

GRE VERBAL STRATEGY SHEET

The Kaplan Method for Short Verbal

STEP 1 Read the sentence, looking for clues.
STEP 2 Predict the answer.
STEP 3 Select the best match(es) from among the choices.
STEP 4 Confirm your answer by reading it into the sentence.

Straight-Ahead Road Signs

And	Likewise
Since	Moreover
Also	Similarly
Thus	In addition
Because	Consequently
; (semicolon)	

Detour Road Signs

But	Although
Despite	While
Yet	On the other hand
However	Unfortunately
Unless	Nonetheless
Rather	Conversely

The Kaplan Method for Reading Comprehension

STEP 1 Read the passage strategically.
STEP 2 Analyze the question stem.
STEP 3 Research the relevant text.

- On Global questions, use the Topic, Scope, and Purpose to predict an answer.
- On Detail questions, review the particular part of the passage indicated in the question stem. For long passages, use your Passage Map to help locate the relevant text in the passage.
- On Inference questions, review the particular part of the passage, if one is indicated in the question stem. If the question is more open-ended, keep the Topic, Scope, and Purpose in mind.
- On Logic questions, review the particular part of the passage and use keywords to determine the author's intentions.
- On Reasoning questions, make sure you have identified the author's conclusion, evidence, and assumption(s).

STEP 4 Make a prediction.
STEP 5 Evaluate the answer choices.

GRE Verbal Pacing Chart

	Text Completion	Sentence Equivalence	Reading Comprehension
Number of Questions	approximately 6	approximately 4	approximately 10
Time per Question	1–1.5 minutes, depending on the number of blanks	1 minute	1–3 minutes, depending on length, to read the passage and 1 minute to answer each question

GRE ANALYTICAL WRITING STRATEGY SHEET

The Kaplan Method for the Issue Essay

STEP 1 Take the issue apart. (2 minutes)
- Consider both sides of the issue in your own words.

STEP 2 Select the points you will make. (4 minutes)
- Decide which side to support, coming up with two to four supporting points that address the specific instructions.

STEP 3 Organize, using Kaplan's Issue essay template. (2 minutes)
- **Paragraph 1:** Paraphrase the issue (the statement, claim, recommendation, or policy); state your position. Summarize the goal of your essay, according to the specific instructions.
- **Paragraph 2:** State and elaborate upon the strongest point in support of your position, within the scope of the specific instructions.
- **Paragraph 3:** State and elaborate upon another point in support of your position, within the scope of the specific instructions.
- **Additional paragraphs, as time permits:** State and elaborate upon other points in support of your position, within the scope of the specific instructions. (Time valve #1: skip if need be.)
- **Next-to-last paragraph:** Address any specific task in the directions. Some prompts will require you to address an opposing viewpoint and refute it. (Time valve #2: combine with conclusion if need be.)
- **Last paragraph:** Conclude by summarizing your position in a way that addresses the specific instructions.

STEP 4 Type your essay. (20 minutes)

STEP 5 Proofread your work. (2 minutes)

The Kaplan Method for the Argument Essay

STEP 1 Take the argument apart. (2 minutes)
- Determine the author's conclusion, evidence, and assumptions.
- Consider the circumstances under which the assumptions would be valid/invalid.
- Consider the kinds of facts that would strengthen or weaken the argument.

STEP 2 Select the points you will make. Which assumptions are most central? Which can you write the most about? (4 minutes)

STEP 3 Organize, using Kaplan's Argument essay template. (2 minutes)
- **Paragraph 1:** Paraphrase the conclusion and evidence. Summarize the goal of your essay, according to the specific instructions.
- **Paragraph 2:** State and evaluate the most important assumption the author makes, question to be answered, or possible alternative explanation (depending on the specific instructions).
- **Paragraph 3:** State and evaluate another assumption the author makes, question to be answered, or possible alternative explanation (depending on the specific instructions).
- **Additional paragraphs, as time permits:** State and evaluate additional assumptions the author makes, questions to be answered, or possible alternative explanations (depending on the specific instructions). Be sure you have responded to the task. For instance, some essay tasks require a discussion of how the argument might be strengthened. Another option is to address a specific task in each body paragraph, instead of devoting a paragraph to this. (Time valve: skip if need be.)
- **Last paragraph:** Conclude by summarizing your main points.

STEP 4 Type your essay. Use strong transitions to connect your paragraphs and ideas. (20 minutes)

STEP 5 Proofread your work. (2 minutes)

Arguments on the GRE

Knowing how the parts of arguments work is essential for the Argument essay and for some Reading Comprehension questions.

Evidence + Assumption(s) $\longrightarrow$ Conclusion

- **Conclusion:** the point the argument's author is trying to make
- **Evidence:** basis or proof offered to support the conclusion
- **Assumptions:** unspoken conditions or beliefs necessary for the conclusion to make sense in light of the evidence